PASSPORT READING

JOURNEYS™ II

Expanded Learning
Voyager®

ISBN 978-1-4168-0971-5

Printed in the United States of America   09 10 11 12 13 14 PAD 9 8 7 6 5 4 3

Table of Contents

EXPEDITION 11
Car Culture

How Cars Have Shaped Our World from Past to Present

EXPEDITION 12
Changes

Descriptions of Life's Challenging Moments

EXPEDITION 13
Literature and Life

Poems and Stories from Inside the Authors' Experiences

EXPEDITION 14
Imagine the Possibilities

How the Work You Do Makes a Difference in the World

EXPEDITION 15
Who Are We?

Self-Realization:
American Cultural
Perspectives

RETEACH BLACKLINE MASTERS

Reteach 21–30

WRITING BLACKLINE MASTERS

Writing 34–59

ADDITIONAL RESOURCES

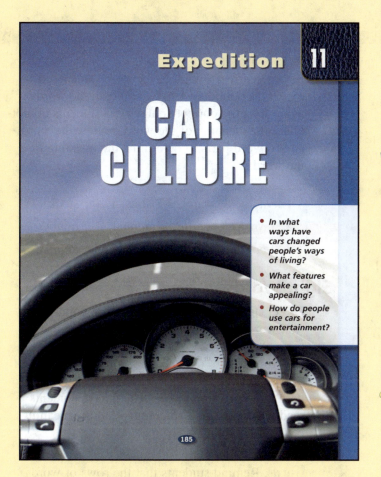

Expedition 11

CAR CULTURE

- *In what ways have cars changed people's ways of living?*
- *What features make a car appealing?*
- *How do people use cars for entertainment?*

DVD 11.1, 11.2

In this Expedition, the DVD segments help students explore the culture of cars. They explore the history of how cars came to shape our modern landscape and how various styles of cars reflect the people who drive them.

Strategic Online Learning Opportunities®

Students access the Web site http://solo.voyagerlearning.com for an interactive SOLO® session. In each session, students apply previously taught strategic skills to new readings on the student's appropriate Lexile® level. Consult the *Passport Reading Journeys*™ SOLO User Guide for a comprehensive overview of this component.

Passport Reading Journeys Library

Students may select reading materials from the *Passport Reading Journeys* Library. Partner and independent reading opportunities allow students to read authentic text on their Lexile level to build fluency. Teacher resources are provided in the *Passport Reading Journeys* Library Teacher's Guide.

In This Expedition

READINGS

Lessons 1 and 2
A Fast Argument

Lessons 3 and 4
Service to Go

Lessons 6 and 7
You *Need* This Car

Lesson 8
How to Sweeten Your Ride

Lesson 9 Assessment
Birth of the Car Culture

SKILLS

Text Structures Review
- Compare and Contrast
- Problem/Solution/Effect
- Sequential Order

Persuasion
- Emotional Appeals
- Logical Appeals

Advanced Word Study

Homographs

1. **Homographs are words that are spelled the same but have different meanings. Examining the sentence containing the homograph can help us determine which meaning to use.** Write *left* on the board. **This word is a homograph. In the sentence** *She left her wallet on the park bench.* **the word** *left* **means "did leave." In the sentence** *Turn left at the next stop sign.* **the word** *left* **means "a direction."**

2. Have students turn to page E11, Lesson 1, in the back of the Student Book. Direct them to line 1 in the first box. Point to the first homograph. **What is the word?** (vault) *Vault* **means "to jump or leap over" and "a secure room or compartment for valuables." Define the word** *vault* **in the sentence,** *The bank teller placed the day's deposits in the vault.* (secure room or compartment for valuables) **and** *The athlete could easily vault the hurdle.* (jump or leap over) Repeat with the remaining homographs. (The security guard *watches* the building's entrance. [observes carefully] I examined the *watches* on display. [clocks worn on the wrist]; That *squash* casserole is delicious. [a vegetable] He made clay models, then *squashed* them flat again. [flatten]; and The grocery store always has a *stock* of fresh bread. [a supply of goods] She bought *stock* in the successful company. [a financial investment]) Call on individuals to read the words in random order.

3. Direct students to line 2. Have students read the words, then determine which words are homographs. (crown, minor) Call on individuals to read the words in a different order. Ask students to tell the meanings of words. (crown—top of head/ornate headdress/symbol of victory; and minor—younger than an adult/something of lesser importance)

4. Direct students to line 3. Have them read the words. Call on individuals to read the words in a different order. Ask students to tell the meanings of the words.

▼ To Correct

Say the correct sound(s), then ask students to repeat the sound(s). Have them read the words again with the correct sound(s). If students do not know the meaning of the word, review the word and/or word parts to determine the meaning of the word.

1. vault	watches	squash	stock
2. crown	mettle	annual	minor
3. version	vehicles	champion	feverish

Sight Words

1. Direct students to line 1. Have them point to the first word. **This word is** *soups*. **Read the word.** (soups) **This is not a regular word. Let's read the word again.** (soups) **Let's spell the word.** (s-o-u-p-s) **What is the word?** (soups) Repeat with the remaining words. Then, have students read the words. Ask students to tell the meanings of the words.

2. Direct students to lines 2 and 3. **Let's read these words.** Remind students that the rows of words consist of regular and irregular words. Point to the first word. **What is the word?** (variety) Repeat with the remaining words. Call on individuals to read the words in a different order. Ask students to tell the meanings of the words.

▼ To Correct

For Regular Words: Say the sound(s) in the word, then ask students to repeat the sound(s). Have them read the word again with the correct sound(s). If students do not know the meaning of the word, review the word and/or word part to determine the meaning of the word.

For Irregular Words: Immediately say the correct word. Then have students read the word, spell it, and read it again. If students do not know the meaning of the word, review the word.

1. soups I	narrow I	similarity I	opposite I
2. variety I	especially I	envelope R	ordinary R
3. tough I	accidents I	accumulate I	outweigh I

Anthology Selection

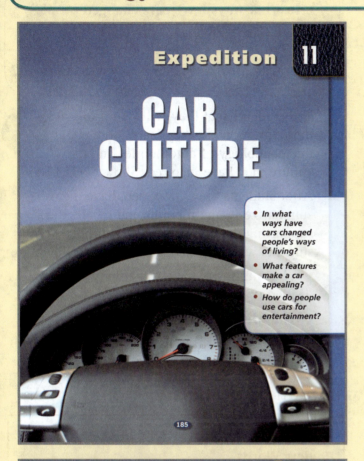

Expedition 11

CAR CULTURE

- In what ways have cars changed people's ways of living?
- What features make a car appealing?
- How do people use cars for entertainment?

185

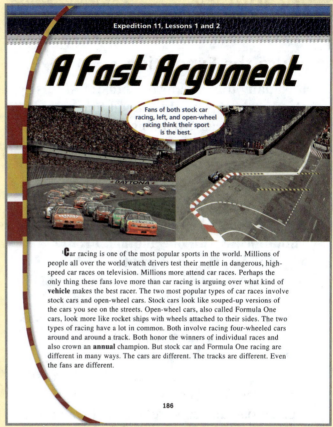

Expedition 11, Lessons 1 and 2

A Fast Argument

Fans of both stock car racing, left, and open-wheel racing think their sport is the best.

¹**C**ar racing is one of the most popular sports in the world. Millions of people all over the world watch drivers test their mettle in dangerous, high-speed car races on television. Millions more attend car races. Perhaps the only thing these fans love more than car racing is arguing over what kind of **vehicle** makes the best racer. The two most popular types of car races involve stock cars and open-wheel cars. Stock cars look like souped-up versions of the cars you see on the streets. Open-wheel cars, also called Formula One cars, look more like rocket ships with wheels attached to their sides. The two types of racing have a lot in common. Both involve racing four-wheeled cars around and around a track. Both honor the winners of individual races and also crown an **annual** champion. But stock car and Formula One racing are different in many ways. The cars are different. The tracks are different. Even the fans are different.

186

Expedition 11, Lessons 1 and 2

The Cars

²Races sponsored by the National Association for Stock Car Auto Racing (NASCAR) feature vehicles based on regular cars. In the first NASCAR race in 1949, the drivers bought cars straight off local car dealer lots. They were the standard cars that regular people drove to work and to the grocery store. That's why they are called stock cars. *Stock* means "standard." But those days are past. Over the years, NASCAR has allowed the drivers to make minor changes to the cars. These changes have made the cars safer and faster. Today's stock cars share little with standard cars other than the basic shape. Only the metal roof, hood, and trunk are made by the companies responsible for the **production** of regular cars. Stock car engines are similar to engines in regular cars, but they are much more powerful. These engines can push cars as fast as 200 miles per hour.

³Formula One racing, on the other hand, features cars that look completely different from regular vehicles. These low-slung cars have narrow bodies with tires sticking out of the side. On a Formula One car, you can see the entire wheel. By contrast, NASCAR wheels are hidden partly by fenders. Unlike stock cars, Formula One cars were never available from your local car dealer. From the first Formula One race in 1950, the cars were built for racing only. Today's Formula One cars can go about 30 miles per hour faster than NASCAR vehicles.

⁴NASCAR and Formula One cars are similar in some ways, however. Both are designed, built, and maintained by a team of experts. Both also use a variety of specially designed tires. The experts decide which set of tires will work best in a given race. Some tires work better on rough roads. Some work better on smooth roads. NASCAR and Formula One cars are similar in another way. Both are laden with safety features designed to protect drivers in case of accidents. That's especially important when you consider how fast they go!

The Tracks

⁵Another big difference between Formula One and NASCAR is the racetracks. The only similarity shared by the two types of tracks is that they are paved. Formula One racetracks have as many twists and turns as a butterfly's flight pattern. The drivers often have to slow down to make

187

Expedition 11, Lessons 1 and 2

sharp turns to the left or to the right. Sometimes the turns are so sharp that the drivers end up going in the opposite direction! Some Formula One races are even run on regular city streets.

⁶NASCAR races, however, take place on tracks built especially for car racing. These tracks are usually shaped like the letter *O*. Unlike Formula One drivers, NASCAR drivers have to make only two wide, gradual turns on each trip around the track. And those two turns are always to the left.

The Champions

⁷Drivers of both types of cars strive to win every race they enter. Similarly, both keep their eyes on a more important goal: the overall annual championship. In both types of racing, drivers are awarded points depending on where they finish in each race. The driver that accumulates the most points during the season is named champion. Because of the point system, both types of drivers can win the overall championship without winning a single race.

The Fans

⁸Most NASCAR fans live in the United States. By contrast, most Formula One fans live outside the United States. That's easy to understand if you consider where the races **occur**. All 39 NASCAR races take place in the United States. Formula One races, however, take place all over the world. Only one of the 18 Formula One races takes place in the United States.

⁹Wherever they live, NASCAR and Formula One fans love to **debate** which type of racing is more exciting. NASCAR fans like the fact that drivers race in cars similar to the ones they drive. They also like the fact that the tracks have more straight stretches. That makes it easier for the leader to be passed by other drivers. Formula One fans disagree. As **evidence**, they say their cars are faster, and the twisting tracks prove their drivers are more talented. In the end, which type of racing is best depends on who you ask. Only one thing is certain: Racing fans will never get tired of the argument.

188

Comprehension and Vocabulary   *Before Reading*

Introduce the Expedition

1. **How many things can you think of at this school or in this neighborhood that wouldn't exist without cars?** (parking lots, drive-through windows at restaurants, highways, gas stations, drive-in movie theaters) Write students' responses on the board.

2. **In the last Expedition, we learned about how technology has changed the way people communicate with one another. From the printing press to computer e-mail, communication technology fundamentally changed the world around us. In this Expedition, we will read how the automobile has not only changed our lives, but how it's changed our landscape too.**

   • **Do people really need cars? Why?** (Possible responses: Yes, because everything is so spread out, and cars are quicker than public transportation. No, because you can arrange your life so that you live close enough to walk or bike most places.)

   • **How do people use cars to have fun?** (Possible responses: They drive them to the mall or the movies; they alter the way they look and ride to suit their personalities; they watch them race.)

   • **If you could buy a car, what kind of car would you buy, and why?** (Responses will vary.) Point out the different motivations in students' responses, such as a need for transportation, a desire for status, or a love of speed.

3. **It's obvious that there's more to the automobile than simple transportation. In fact, we have created a culture that in many ways revolves around cars.** Have students turn to Anthology page 185. Read the title of the Expedition. Then call on individuals to read aloud each probing question.

   • **In what ways have cars changed people's ways of living?**
   • **What features make a car appealing?**
   • **How do people use cars for entertainment?**

4. Tell students that they will return to these questions as they learn more about the technology of automobiles and the culture they have inspired. Show DVD 11.1.

5. After students view the video, have them summarize its main points and recall supporting details. If necessary, prompt students with questions such as the following:

   • **What main message were the people in this video trying to communicate?**

   • **What did they have to say about _____?**

   • **What parts of the video helped illustrate or support this idea?**

Introduce Vocabulary

Vocabulary	
Review Words	
vehicle	*something that carries people or goods from one place to another*
annual	*happening every year*
production	*the act of making something*
occur	*happen; take place*
debate	*a discussion in which people take sides on an issue*
evidence	*proof; things studied for the purpose of learning something*
Challenge Words	
Word Meaning	
laden	*loaded*
	The apple tree is *laden* with ripe fruit.
strive	*to try very hard*
	At Hotel Posh, we *strive* to make your stay a pleasant one.

6. **Our article, "A Fast Argument," contains words with meanings we have already learned. We will review these words within the text we are reading.**

7. Write each Review Word on the board. Then ask students to locate the word in the article. Instruct them to read aloud the sentence containing the word, as well as any other sentences that provide context.
   - **What can you tell me about the word?**
   - Ask other questions that allow students to explore the word's meaning. (For example: **Is a train a *vehicle*? Name an *annual* holiday.**)

8. Ask students to respond to the following questions. Provide correction and feedback as necessary.
   - **What kinds of *vehicles* fly through the air?**
   - **If you had a job, would you prefer an *annual* raise or a raise once every five years? Why?**
   - **Why is the *production* of steel important to the car industry?**
   - **What could *occur* if you drove too fast through a quiet neighborhood?**
   - **Can you *debate* a subject with your fists? Why?**
   - **What *evidence* could you present to show that a car gets good gas mileage?**

9. Work with students to write a definition for each word on the board.

10. Include the Challenge Words to meet the needs of students who are advancing.

Review Text Structures

11. Write these article titles on the board: **SKILL** ✔
    - *Building a Car—from Start to Finish*
    - *Toll Roads: The Answer to Our Money Woes*
    - *How Automobiles Wreck the Environment*
    - *Cars vs. Trucks: Which Are Better?*
    - *Save the World: Take Public Transportation*

12. **In the last several Expeditions, we have learned about different kinds of expository writing.**
    - **What are some of the different kinds?** (sequential order, compare/contrast, cause/effect, problem/solution, and persuasion) Write these on the board next to the titles. Have students tell in their own words what each kind of writing does. (Sequential order tells events in the order in which they happened or should happen; compare/contrast tells how two or more things are alike and different; cause/effect tells how one event can lead to another; problem/solution identifies a problem and one or more ways of solving it; and persuasion tries to get the reader to do or to believe something.) Provide correction and feedback as needed.
    - **Look at the first article title on the board. What kind of expository article do you think it might be?** (sequential order) Draw a line connecting the title to the words *sequential order*. Repeat with each remaining title. (Toll Roads: The Answer to Our Money Woes—problem/solution; How Automobiles Wreck the Environment—cause/effect; Cars vs. Trucks: Which Are Better?—compare/contrast; Save the World: Take Public Transportation—persuasion)

13. **In this lesson, we will review one of these kinds of expository writing.** Have students return to Anthology page 186 and preview the article by looking at the images and reading the title.
    - **Which kind of expository writing do you think this article will be?** (compare/contrast)
    - **Why do you think so?** (The two photos show different types of racing or race cars. They show different types of tracks.)

14. On the board, draw a diagram like this:

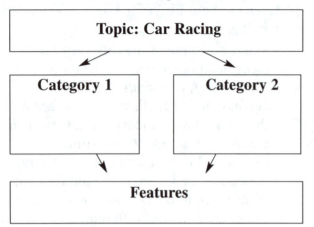

Topic: Car Racing

Category 1   **Category 2**

Features

The topic of this article is *car racing*. The article will compare and contrast two different kinds, or categories, of car racing. What are they? (Stock car [or NASCAR] racing and open-wheel [or Formula One] car racing) List them in the Category boxes.

15. To show how these types of racing are alike and different, the author will describe different *features* of each type of racing. For example, the author might tell us about the type of cars that are raced, the type of tracks they race on, and the type of people who like to watch the races. List these features in the bottom box. **As we read, let's watch for some different features that are compared and contrasted.**

16. Remember that compare-and-contrast texts usually include signal words and phrases that help show similarities and differences. Write *Compare* and *Contrast* on the board. Under *Compare*, write *like, just as, similar, both, also,* and *too*. Under *Contrast*, write *unlike, different, but, in contrast,* and *on the other hand*. **Be on the lookout for some of these signal words and phrases as we read.**

English Language Learners

Graphic Organizers for Brainstorming Background Knowledge

English language learners have an abundance of background knowledge on many subjects, but they often have difficulty putting these ideas together in grammatically correct sentences. In this activity, students' oral language is supported by a graphic organizer as they construct sentences to brainstorm background knowledge. Draw a graphic organizer like the following with the topic of the reading selection in the center oval. In the outside rectangles, place verbs or phrases that will elicit a variety of responses from students.

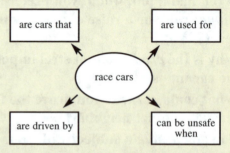

are cars that   are used for

race cars

are driven by   can be unsafe when

We can use this graphic organizer to help us make sentences about what we already know about race cars. For example, race cars are cars that are built to go *very* fast. Ask students to tell you what they already know about race cars by using the four quadrants of the graphic organizer as prompts. Encourage students to look at the images, title, and headings in the reading selection for additional ideas. Record students' responses next to each section of the graphic organizer. For more advanced students, model combining sentences to make more complex sentences: I can also connect two ideas to make a longer sentence. For example: *Race cars are built to go very fast, so they can be unsafe when the driver is not experienced.* After reading, have students use new versions of the same graphic organizer to discuss what they learned about stock cars and open-wheel cars.

ELL

Reading for Understanding

Reading

Names to Look For:
- Formula One
- National Association for Stock Car Auto Racing (NASCAR)

1. **As you read "A Fast Argument," you may come across some unfamiliar names.**
   - Write the words on the board.
   - Point to each word as you tell students the following: **In this article, you will read about two types of racing cars. Open-wheel cars look like rocket ships with wheels. They are used in *Formula One* races. Cars that are used by the *National Association for Stock Car Auto Racing*, also called *NASCAR*, look more like regular cars.**
   - Call on individuals to read the words.

2. **As we read this article, remember to look for the different features of Formula One car racing and NASCAR racing that are being compared and contrasted. Remember also to watch for the signal words and phrases listed on the board.**

3. Read aloud the first paragraph of the article. **In this paragraph, what signal words or phrases are used to show comparison?** (both) **What signal words or phrases are used to show a contrast?** (but, different) **Look for others as we keep reading.**

4. **Fluency** Have students read the remainder of the article in small groups, taking turns after paragraphs. Instruct students to pause after each section and identify any compare-and-contrast signal words or phrases that were used. Provide feedback and extended instruction as needed. If necessary, review the following fluency correction procedure with students to ensure accuracy: **Offer help when a group member comes to an unfamiliar word or makes a reading error. Pause, then say, "That word is _____. Let's read it again."** As students read, monitor for reading rate, accuracy, and expression.

5. When students have completed their reading, check for literal comprehension of the text by asking these questions: **KNOWLEDGE**
   - *Paragraph 2:* **What do stock cars have in common with regular cars?** (the basic shape) **How are stock cars different from regular cars?** (They are much more powerful.)
   - *Paragraph 3:* **What are Formula One cars like?** (They are completely different from regular cars. They have low, narrow bodies with tires sticking out the sides.) **Which are faster: NASCAR vehicles** (stock cars) **or Formula One cars?** (Formula One cars)
   - *Paragraphs 5 and 6:* **Which kind of car races on a track shaped like an *O*?** (NASCAR vehicles)
   - *Paragraph 8:* **Where do all NASCAR races take place?** (in the United States) **Where do Formula One races take place?** (all over the world)

Checking for Comprehension *After Reading*

1. Redirect students' attention to the diagram on the board. **What features, or different aspects, of stock car racing and open-wheel car racing does the article compare and contrast?** (the cars, the tracks, the champions, and the fans) Record these in the Features section in the box. Provide correction and feedback as necessary. **We will look more closely at each of these features in Lesson 2.**

2. **Challenge Questions If you were going to watch one type or race or the other, which would you watch? Why?** EVALUATION (Responses will vary.)

3. Have students work with partners to go on a "scavenger hunt" for the signal words and phrases listed on the board. Have students record the ones they find in a T-chart with *Compare* and *Contrast* as the heads. When students are finished, call on individuals to read a word or phrase from their chart. Circle each on the board as it is mentioned.

Extending Vocabulary

Homophones and Homographs

- **Remember that homographs are words that are pronounced and spelled the same but have different meanings.**

- Have students turn to the first paragraph on Anthology page 186. Read aloud the second sentence, *"Millions of people all over the world . . ."* **Notice the word *mettle*. Now turn to page 187.** In the section The Cars, read the tenth sentence, *"Only the metal roof . . ."* **Notice the word *metal*.** Write these words on the board.

- **These words are homophones. They sound the same, but they are spelled differently and have different meanings.** Point to the word *metal*. **The word *metal* means "a hard, shiny material."** Point to *mettle*. **The word *mettle* means "a person's ability to cope with difficulty."**

- Direct students' attention back to the section The Cars. Read the sixth sentence, *"But those days are past."* **Notice the word *past*.** Have students turn to Anthology page 188 and look at the section The Fans. Read the fourth sentence in paragraph 9, *"That makes it easier for the leader to be passed . . ."* **Notice the word *passed*.** Write these words on the board.

- **These words are also homophones. They sound the same, but they are spelled differently and have different meanings.** Point to the word *passed*. **In this sentence, the word *passed* means "to move by or beyond something."** Point to the word *past*. **In this sentence, *past* means "belong to a former time."**

- Have students turn back to the first paragraph. Read the fifth sentence, *"The two most popular types . . ."* **I see the word *types*. In this sentence, it means "kinds." What other meaning does the word *types* have?** (to use a typewriter; various font styles) **Words that sound alike and are spelled alike but have different meanings are called *homographs*. They are also called multiple-meaning words.**

- Have students work with partners or small groups to find other words in the article that have homophones or homographs. (Pairs of words do not have to appear together in the article.) Have students define both words in each pair, (for example, in the first paragraph: one/won, kind/kind, fan/fan). Then have students share their word pairs with the class. Write students' responses on the board.

Connect to Science

Use the following activity to help students investigate centripetal force.

Materials: small ball such as a tennis ball, with holes for string in each end; about 6 feet of string

- **You're in the passenger seat of a two-seated race car being driven at 175 miles an hour by Formula One driver Danica Patrick. Danica makes a tight left turn on the race track. What happens to you?**
- Write these choices on the board:
  1. You're thrown left.
  2. You're thrown right.
  3. You're not thrown in either direction.
  4. You're too scared to notice.
- Call on several individuals to select an answer. Then explain that answer 3 is correct. **You may** *feel* **as though your body is being thrown to the right, but it's going straight. On your straight path, you collide with the car door on its turning path.** Point out that if Danica were to drive in tight circles, students would *feel* as though they were being pushed into the door the whole time. Explain that this effect is caused by *centripetal force*—the force (in this case the car door) that pushes you toward the center of the turn circle, while your body tries to continue in a straight line. **Also, centripetal force supplied by the friction between the tires and pavement keeps Danica's car from going off the road when she's going around corners.**
- To demonstrate centripetal force, loop the string through the ball and have a student swing the ball overhead. Explain that to keep the ball from flying off in a straight line, the student must pull on the string, which supplies the centripetal force that pulls the ball toward the center of the circle.

To increase difficulty: Have students find and report on an online video segment that shows the forces that act on a race car in motion.

Science

Anthology Selection

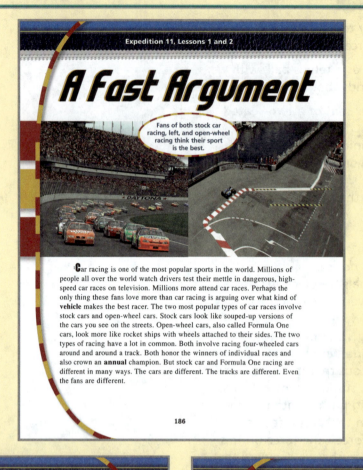

Expedition 11, Lessons 1 and 2

A Fast Argument

Fans of both stock car racing, left, and open-wheel racing think their sport is the best.

[1]Car racing is one of the most popular sports in the world. Millions of people all over the world watch drivers test their mettle in dangerous, high-speed car races on television. Millions more attend car races. Perhaps the only thing these fans love more than car racing is arguing over what kind of **vehicle** makes the best racer. The two most popular types of car races involve stock cars and open-wheel cars. Stock cars look like souped-up versions of the cars you see on the streets. Open-wheel cars, also called Formula One cars, look more like rocket ships with wheels attached to their sides. The two types of racing have a lot in common. Both involve racing four-wheeled cars around and around a track. Both honor the winners of individual races and also crown an **annual** champion. But stock car and Formula One racing are different in many ways. The cars are different. The tracks are different. Even the fans are different.

186

Expedition 11, Lessons 1 and 2

The Cars

[2]Races sponsored by the National Association for Stock Car Auto Racing (NASCAR) feature vehicles based on regular cars. In the first NASCAR race in 1949, the drivers bought cars straight off local car dealer lots. They were the standard cars that regular people drove to work and to the grocery store. That's why they are called stock cars. *Stock* means "standard." But those days are past. Over the years, NASCAR has allowed the drivers to make minor changes to the cars. These changes have made the cars safer and faster. Today's stock cars share little with standard cars other than the basic shape. Only the metal roof, hood, and trunk are made by the companies responsible for the **production** of regular cars. Stock car engines are similar to engines in regular cars, but they are much more powerful. These engines can push cars as fast as 200 miles per hour.

[3]Formula One racing, on the other hand, features cars that look completely different from regular vehicles. These low-slung cars have narrow bodies with tires sticking out of the side. On a Formula One car, you can see the entire wheel. By contrast, NASCAR wheels are hidden partly by fenders. Unlike stock cars, Formula One cars were never available from your local car dealer. From the first Formula One race in 1950, the cars were built for racing only. Today's Formula One cars can go about 30 miles per hour faster than NASCAR vehicles.

[4]NASCAR and Formula One cars are similar in some ways, however. Both are designed, built, and maintained by a team of experts. Both also use a variety of specially designed tires. The experts decide which set of tires will work best in a given race. Some tires work better on rough roads. Some work better on smooth roads. NASCAR and Formula One cars are similar in another way. Both are laden with safety features designed to protect drivers in case of accidents. That's especially important when you consider how fast they go!

The Tracks

[5]Another big difference between Formula One and NASCAR is the racetracks. The only similarity shared by the two types of tracks is that they are paved. Formula One racetracks have as many twists and turns as a butterfly's flight pattern. The drivers often have to slow down to make

187

Expedition 11, Lessons 1 and 2

sharp turns to the left or to the right. Sometimes the turns are so sharp that the drivers end up going in the opposite direction! Some Formula One races are even run on regular city streets.

[6]NASCAR races, however, take place on tracks built especially for car racing. These tracks are usually shaped like the letter *O*. Unlike Formula One drivers, NASCAR drivers have to make only two wide, gradual turns on each trip around the track. And those two turns are always to the left.

The Champions

[7]Drivers of both types of cars strive to win every race they enter. Similarly, both keep their eyes on a more important goal: the overall annual championship. In both types of racing, drivers are awarded points depending on where they finish in each race. The driver that accumulates the most points during the season is named champion. Because of the point system, both types of drivers can win the overall championship without winning a single race.

The Fans

[8]Most NASCAR fans live in the United States. By contrast, most Formula One fans live outside the United States. That's easy to understand if you consider where the races **occur**. All 39 NASCAR races take place in the United States. Formula One races, however, take place all over the world. Only one of the 18 Formula One races takes place in the United States.

[9]Wherever they live, NASCAR and Formula One fans love to **debate** which type of racing is more exciting. NASCAR fans like the fact that drivers race in cars similar to the ones the fans drive. They also like the fact that the tracks have more straight stretches. That makes it easier for the leader to be passed by other drivers. Formula One fans disagree. As **evidence**, they say their cars are faster, and the twisting tracks prove their drivers are more talented. In the end, which type of racing is best depends on who you ask. Only one thing is certain: Racing fans will never get tired of the argument.

188

Comprehension and Vocabulary *Before Reading*

1. In Lesson 1, we read "A Fast Argument."

- What kind of expository text did we decide it is? (compare/contrast)
- What was compared and contrasted? (stock car racing and open-wheel car racing)
- What were some of the features of stock car racing and open-wheel car racing that were compared? (cars, tracks, champions, fans)
- If you were going to watch one type of race or the other, which would you watch? Why? (Responses will vary.)

Vocabulary Review

2. Arrange students in pairs, and have them turn to Student Book page 139. Then call on individuals to read one of the vocabulary words listed in the box and tell what it means.

3. Read aloud the instructions for the Vocabulary Practice activity. Have students work in small groups to complete the chart.

4. When all groups are finished, call on students from each group to share their group's ideas for a new kind of racing. List each kind of racing and a few details about it on the board.

5. Call on individuals to tell which kind of race they would prefer to watch and why.

6. **Challenge Words** Write the following items on the board and have students complete them along with those on the Student Book page.

- *With what kinds of features will your vehicles be <u>laden</u>? Why?*
- *As race promoters, what main goal do you <u>strive</u> for? Why?*

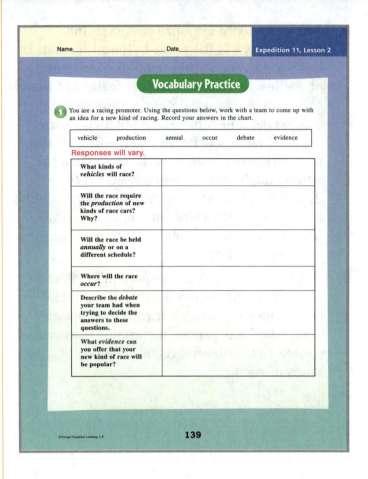

Introduce Text Structure: Compare and Contrast Point by Point

7. When authors compare and contrast two or more things, they can organize their writing in different ways. In Expedition 7, Lesson 8, we read an article comparing inexpensive jeans to expensive jeans. The author used the block format to describe the factors that affect the price of jeans, such as how much the workers who make them get paid and whether the jeans have a designer label.

8. Another way to organize compare-and-contrast texts is the point-by-point format. In this format, the author uses one paragraph or section to describe a single feature of both objects. For example, if an author were comparing and contrasting blueberries and oranges, he or she might use the first section to describe the taste of each fruit. Then the author might use the second section to describe the shape of each fruit. What might he or she use the third section to describe? (Possible responses: color, nutritional value, growing conditions)

9. The author of "A Fast Argument" uses the point-by-point format. Rather than tell all about stock car racing, then tell all about open-wheel car racing, the author uses each section to tell about a certain feature of *both* kinds of racing.

Reading for Understanding
Reading

1. Have students turn to Anthology page 186 and Student Book page 140. Read the Student Book instructions aloud. **What two kinds of racing does this article compare and contrast?** (stock car racing and open-wheel racing) Have students write these in the blanks at the top of the chart.

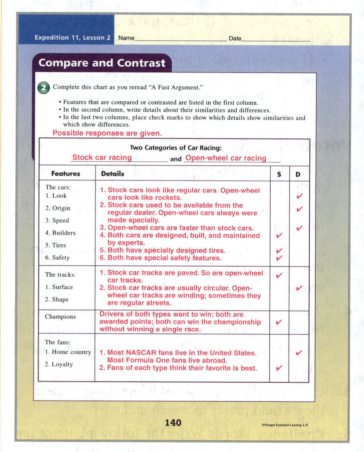

2. Read the first paragraph of the article aloud.

- **In the first paragraph, the author discusses how stock cars and open-wheel cars look. How does the article describe stock cars?** (They look like regular cars.) **Let's write that under** *Details*. **How do open-wheel cars look?** (They look like rockets with wheels.) **Let's add that under** *Details.*

- **From the description in the article, do stock cars look the same as open-wheel cars or are they different?** (different) **Let's put a check mark in column** *D* **for** *different.*

3. Read paragraph 2, under "The Cars." **Originally, where did stock cars come from?** (They were regular cars, bought straight off the dealer's lot.) **Read paragraph 3. How about open-wheel cars?** (They were built especially for racing.) **Let's write these details on the chart. From what we read, are the origins of these cars the same or are they different?** (different) **Let's put a check mark in the column for** *different.*

4. **Which of the two types of car is faster? If you don't remember what the author said, look back at the last sentence of paragraph 2 and the last sentence of paragraph 3.** (Open-wheel cars are faster than stock cars.) **Let's write that down under** *Details*. **Are they the same or different?** (different) **Let's put a check mark under** *D.*

5. Read paragraph 4 aloud. Guide students to identify and record the details about builders, tires, and safety, and to identify if they are the same or different.

6. Have students finish reading the article independently. Instruct them to pause and fill in other details as they encounter them. Remind students to place a check mark in the *S* column or *D* column for each detail they record. Encourage students to monitor their comprehension of the text by pausing occasionally to ask themselves *Am I understanding what I'm reading?* Tell students that when they do not understand what they are reading, they should reread that portion of the text.

Checking for Comprehension *After Reading*

After students have completed the Student Book page and the article, bring them together as a class. Call on students to identify the features and details they listed in the Student Book, and to tell whether each detail shows a similarity or difference. Provide correction and feedback as needed.

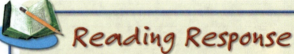

Reading Response

Have students turn to Student Book page 141. Read the instructions aloud. Then have students use the article and the paragraph frame to answer this question:

? **Which type of car racing is best?**

Students may work with partners or small groups. When students have completed their responses, discuss them as a class.

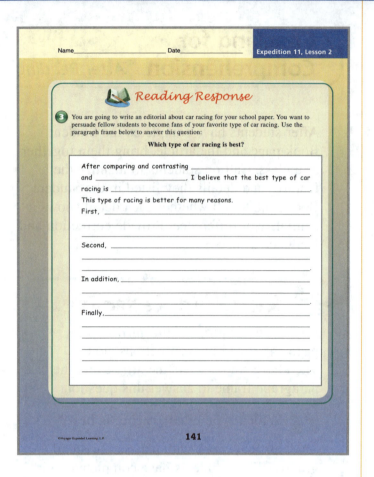

Name_____ Date_____ Expedition 11, Lesson 2

Reading Response

3 You are going to write an editorial about car racing for your school paper. You want to persuade fellow students to become fans of your favorite type of car racing. Use the paragraph frame below to answer this question:

Which type of car racing is best?

After comparing and contrasting _____
and _____, I believe that the best type of car
racing is _____.
This type of racing is better for many reasons.
First, _____
_____
_____
Second, _____
_____
_____
In addition, _____
_____
_____
Finally, _____
_____
_____
_____
_____
_____

©Voyager Expanded Learning, L.P.   141

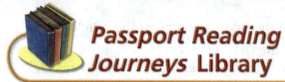

Passport Reading Journeys Library

Building Fluency

1. Place students in pairs according to reading level to build fluency. When pairing students, be sure that one student is a stronger reader (Student A) than the other student (Student B). However, do not reveal that stronger readers are paired with weaker readers. See *Passport Reading Journeys* Library Teacher's Guide for grouping guidelines.

2. Have students quickly choose reading material from the *Passport Reading Journeys* Library or another approved selection that is at the reading level of Student B. If students have not finished the previously chosen selection, they may continue reading from that selection. See *Passport Reading Journeys* Library Teacher's Guide for material selection guidelines.

3. Tell students that Student A will read one paragraph, and Student B will reread that same paragraph.

4. Have students follow this routine until the end of class.

5. If necessary, review the following practices to enhance fluency:
   • Rate and accuracy of reading
   • Expression during reading
   • Correction procedures

Library Highlights

Spotlight on an Author

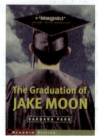

Level I

Barbara Park has written many novels for elementary and middle-school students. Her novels include *Skinnybones*, *My Mother Got Married*, and *The Kid in the Red Jacket*. *The Graduation of Jake Moon* is included in the *Passport Reading Journeys II* Library. Park has won more than 40 awards for her books.

Lesson 3

Advanced Word Study

Suffixes -ive and -tive

1. Write -ive on the board. **This word part is a suffix. Remember, a suffix is a word part that occurs at the end of a word and often helps us understand the meaning of the word. The sounds for this suffix are /iv/. Say the sounds for this suffix.** (/iv/) Write the word *impressive* on the board. Underline the suffix -ive. **What is this suffix?** (-ive) **Use the sounds you know to read the rest of the word.** (impress) **What is the word?** (impressive) **The suffix -ive means "tending to" or "having the qualities of." The word *impress* means "to amaze or influence." The word *impressive* means "tending to be impressed or influenced."**

   Have students turn to Student Book page E11, Lesson 3. Direct them to line 1 in the first box. **What is the underlined suffix in the first word?** (-ive) **Read the rest of the word.** (divis) **What is the word?** (divisive) Repeat with the remaining words. Call on individuals to read the words in random order. Ask students to tell the meanings of the words based on the meaning of the suffix.

2. Write -tive on the board. **The sounds for this suffix are /tiv/. Say the sounds for this suffix.** (/tiv/) Write the word *constructive* on the board. Underline the suffix -tive. **What is this suffix?** (-tive) **Use the sounds you know to read the rest of the word.** (construc[t]) **What is the word?** (constructive) **The suffix -tive means "tending to" or "having the qualities of." The word *construct* means "to build." The word *constructive* means "tending to build."** Direct students to line 2. **What is the underlined suffix in the first word?** (-tive) **Read the rest of the word.** (inven[t]) **What is the word?** (inventive) Repeat with the remaining words. Call on individuals to read the words in a different order. Ask students to tell the meanings of the words based on the meaning of the suffix.

3. Direct students to line 3. Have them read the words. Call on individuals to read the words in a different order. Ask students to tell the meanings of the words.

▼ To Correct

Say the correct sound(s) or prefix/suffix, then ask students to repeat the sound(s). Have students read the word again with the correct sound(s). If students do not know the meaning of the word, review the word and/or word parts to determine the meaning of the word.

1. divi<u>sive</u>	respon<u>sive</u>	reclu<u>sive</u>	mas<u>sive</u>
2. inven<u>tive</u>	atten<u>tive</u>	superla<u>tive</u>	inac<u>tive</u>
3. potential	permissive	intercom	furtive

Sight Words

1. Direct students to line 1. Have them point to the first word. **This word is *schedules*. Read the word.** (schedules) **This is not a regular word. Let's read the word again.** (schedules) **Let's spell the word.** (s-c-h-e-d-u-l-e-s) **What is the word?** (schedules) Repeat with the remaining words. Then, have students read the words. Ask students to tell the meanings of the words.

2. Direct students to lines 2 and 3. **Let's read these words.** Remind students that the rows of words consist of regular and irregular words. Point to the first word. **What is the word?** (narrow) Repeat with the remaining words. Call on individuals to read the words in a different order. Ask students to tell the meanings of the words.

▼ To Correct

For Regular Words: Say the sound(s) in the word, then ask students to repeat the sound(s). Have them read the word again with the correct sound(s). If students do not know the meaning of the word, review the word and/or word part to determine the meaning of the word.

For Irregular Words: Immediately say the correct word. Then have students read the word, spell it, and read it again. If students do not know the meaning of the word, review the word.

1. schedules I	soldiers I	errands I	restaurants I
2. narrow I	customers I	opposite I	similarity R
3. convenient I	soups I	espresso R	maximum R

Anthology Selection

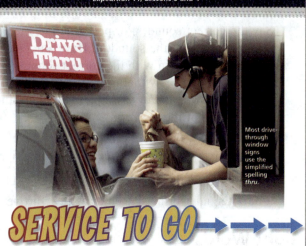

Most drive-through window signs use the simplified spelling *thru*.

SERVICE TO GO

¹Red Cheney had a problem. It was 1947, and Red was opening a new restaurant on a highway in Springfield, Missouri. The 2,000-mile-long highway was filled with potential customers on long car trips. But many of the customers were in a hurry. They didn't have time to stop, go inside a restaurant, and sit at a table for a meal. Red needed a strategy, or a lot of customers would speed right past his restaurant.

²For years, restaurants had offered curbside service to customers waiting in their cars. Customers would park at the curb outside the restaurant, where waiters would take orders and deliver food. This appealed to customers because they could get food fast and easily. But curbside service could not help Red. The curb outside his restaurant was a busy highway filled with speeding cars. People couldn't park there and wait for food to be delivered.

189

³Other restaurants offered drive-in service. At a drive-in restaurant, customers parked in a paved area off the road. A restaurant worker would come to their cars and take their orders. When the food was ready, the worker would take it out to the car. Then the customers could eat their food in their cars or take it home. But drive-in restaurants needed big parking lots and a lot of workers to serve customers. Red needed a better idea.

⁴Then it came to him. Red realized that he didn't need a drive-*in*. He needed a drive-*through*. So he knocked a hole in the wall of his restaurant and installed a window. Customers could drive up to the window, place an order, get their food, and get back on the road in a hurry. It was perfect. One worker could handle all the car customers. Since the customers would drive away with their food, Red did not need a big area for people to park while they ate. Because of this imaginative solution, Red's restaurant became a popular—and fast—stop for hungry travelers in a hurry.

Serving Soldiers

⁵Drive-through windows solved problems for more than just hungry travelers, however. For example, in 1975 a restaurant in Sierra Vista, Arizona, was losing business because of an army rule. Soldiers from the local army base were not allowed to wear their uniforms into non-military businesses. This meant soldiers couldn't stop at the restaurant for dinner on

190

the way home. They would have to drive home and change clothes first. A lot of soldiers decided just to eat at home. That was costing the restaurant valuable business. To solve this problem, the restaurant installed a drive-through window. As a result, soldiers could get food without having to enter the restaurant or go home to change clothes first. Even people who weren't soldiers found the drive-through more convenient than parking and walking into the restaurant to place a "to-go" order. Because people could pick up dinner with **ease**, the restaurant had more customers than ever.

The Need for Speed

⁶Drive-through windows quickly proved their worth to restaurants by increasing profits. But there were still problems to be worked out. One was speed. To make more money, restaurants needed to serve the maximum number of customers in the **minimum** amount of time possible. With just a window, a restaurant could help only one car customer at a time. The customer would drive up to the window, look at the menu, place an order, and wait for the food to be prepared. The next customer had to wait through this process before driving to the window and placing an order. Sometimes customers got **impatient** and drove away. That meant lost business.

⁷Restaurants solved this problem by setting up a menu board several car lengths away from the window. A menu board is a lighted sign with a list of the food served at the restaurant. The menu board also had an intercom. An intercom is a speaker and microphone that allows the customer to talk to the restaurant worker. With this new system, customers could place their order at the menu board, then drive up to the window to pay and pick up their food. While that customer was paying, the next customer could order. By setting the menu farther away from the window, restaurants could work on several orders at once. As a result, the restaurants reduced the amount of time customers had to wait in line.

⁸Restaurants thought of other ways to increase the speed of their service. One way was to have two windows. Customers would pay at the first window and pick up food at the second window. This system allowed different restaurant workers to concentrate on one part of the process. As a result, they could deliver food faster. This system also helped reduce the number of mistakes made when filling customer orders.

191

Stress Reliever

⁹Drive-through windows became so popular that they created an unexpected problem. Sometimes customers were not sure what they wanted to eat. They would sit at the menu board trying to decide if they would **prefer** a hamburger or a chicken sandwich. Hungry customers waiting to order would become frustrated. The customers at the menu board would start to feel a lot of pressure to hurry up and order. This slowed the process and caused a **decline** in customer satisfaction. Restaurants worried that they might start losing customers.

¹⁰Restaurants solved this problem by adding a preview menu to the drive-through line. Since the preview menu was a few car lengths ahead of the menu board and intercom, customers could decide what they wanted before it was their turn to order. The result was faster service and less stress on customers. Drive-through windows became more popular than ever.

They're Everywhere!

¹¹Today, drive-through windows are a huge success. The average American orders food from drive-through windows three and a half times a week. Restaurants with drive-through windows do about 60 percent of their business with customers who never leave their cars. Some restaurants serve 99 percent of their food through the drive-through window.

¹²Drive-through windows worked so well for restaurants that other businesses found ways to use them. Banks began offering drive-through windows so their customers could conduct business from their cars. People can pick up groceries, videos, laundry, drug prescriptions, library books, and even a cup of espresso without ever leaving their cars. There is even a drive-through window in Las Vegas where people can get married! Customers with active lifestyles depend on drive-through windows to help them take care of their errands and get on with their busy schedules. The faster they can take care of their errands, the sooner they can get home to relax and **decompress**.

192

532

Comprehension and Vocabulary
Before Reading

1. **What kinds of cars did we read about in the last two lessons?** (race cars or stock cars and open-wheel cars, or NASCAR vehicles and Formula One cars) **What was the author's purpose in writing the article?** (to compare and contrast the two kinds of racing)

2. **In Lessons 1 and 2, we reviewed compare/contrast texts. In Lesson 3, we'll review another kind of expository text. We'll also learn about another aspect of America's car culture.**

Building Background Knowledge

Extend students' knowledge of the topic of drive-through service by sharing the following:

- At the time drive-through windows were invented, World War II had recently ended, and Americans' way of life was changing dramatically. More people had cars and more people had money to spend. More people also had jobs, so they had less time to spend cooking or sitting in restaurants.
- The first drive-through window was installed in a café on U.S. Highway 66 in Springfield, Missouri. It had no microphone. Customers simply yelled their orders through the window.
- The café was called *Red's Giant Hamburgs*. It was supposed to be called *Red's Giant Hamburgers*, but Red measured the sign wrong.

Introduce Vocabulary

Vocabulary

Review Words

ease	*to make something less difficult or painful*
minimum	*as few or as small as can be*
impatient	*not patient; not willing to wait*
prefer	*to like one more than another*
decline	*to become weaker or fewer*
decompress	*to relax; to relieve pressure*

Challenge Words

Word Meaning

strategy   *plan*
What is our *strategy* for reaching the final round of the tournament?

Word Building

intercom   *intercommunication, communicate, communication, communicative, communicator*

3. **Lesson 3's article, "Service to Go," contains words with meanings we have already learned. We will review these words in the text we are reading.**

4. Write each Review Word on the board. Ask students to locate the word in the article. Instruct them to read aloud the sentence containing the word, and any other sentences that provide context.
   - **What can you tell me about the word?**
   - Ask other questions that allow students to explore the word's meaning. (For example: **What is the opposite of *minimum*? If you are *impatient*, are you calm? Why?**)

5. Ask students to respond to the following questions. Provide correction and feedback as necessary.
   - **Describe something you can do with *ease*.**
   - **What is the *minimum* amount of time you need to get ready for school?**
   - **When do you feel *impatient*? Explain.**
   - **Would you *prefer* a longer school day and a longer summer break or a shorter school day and a shorter summer break? Why?**
   - **What might cause the attendance at the local swimming pool to *decline*?**
   - **How do you *decompress* after a long day of school?**

6. Work with students to write a definition for each word on the board.

7. Include the Challenge Words to meet the needs of students who are advancing. For the Word Building Challenge Word, have students identify the base word (communicate), then guide them in determining how the base word can help them figure out the meaning of the larger words.

ELL To reinforce vocabulary word meaning for English language learners, create a matching activity with the words and conversational phrases.

Write each vocabulary word and a conversational phrase that illustrates the meaning of each word on the board in random order. For example:
prefer *I'll have ketchup instead of hot sauce.*
Model matching the first word with the appropriate sentence, then explain how the selection was made. Have students complete the matching activity with a partner. Then have students discuss the correct answers and how they selected each.

For a complete model of this strategy, see Expedition 9, Lesson 3.

Review Text Structures: Problem/Solution

8. Have students return to Anthology page 189 and preview the article by looking at the images and reading the title and headings. Then have them read the first paragraph of the article.

- **Which kind of expository text do you think this article will be?** (problem/solution)

- **Why do you think so?** (because the first sentence states that Red Cheney had a problem)

- **What was Red Cheney's problem?** (Potential customers didn't have time to stop at his restaurant.)

9. On the board, draw a diagram like this:

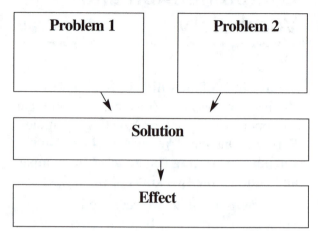

Write *Customers didn't have time to stop.* in the top left Problem box. **To a restaurant owner, the fact that customers didn't have time to stop at the restaurant was a problem. This article will describe how Red Cheney solved that problem. It will also describe how his solution solved another restaurant's problems too.**

10. **Remember that solutions to problems often create new effects. In other words, a solution can be the *cause* of a new effect. It can even be the cause of a new problem.**
SKILL ✓

- **For example, imagine you are really hungry, but there's no food in the house. You decide to buy a burger with the money your mom left you to pay for a class trip. This is your solution.**

- **What could be an effect of this solution?** (Possible responses: Your mom would be mad. You wouldn't have money to go on the class trip.)

The solution to your problem—using the trip money—would become the cause of a new effect, or a new problem. As we read "Service to Go," let's watch for the effects of each solution.

11. **Because problem/solution articles often describe causes and effects, they sometimes include cause-and-effect signal words. We learned some of these in Expedition 9.** Write *Cause* and *Effect* on the board. Under *Cause*, write *because, due to,* and *since.* Under *Effect*, write *therefore, so, as a result,* and *consequently.* **Look for some of these signal words and phrases as we read.**

Reading for Understanding   *Reading*

Places and Names to Look For:
- Red Cheney
- Springfield, Missouri
- Sierra Vista, Arizona
- Las Vegas, Nevada

1. **As you read this article, you may come across some unfamiliar places and names.**
   - Write the words on the board.
   - Point to each word as you tell students the following: *Red Cheney* owned a restaurant in *Springfield, Missouri*. But Cheney had a problem at his restaurant. Creative thinking helped him solve the problem. His solution came to be used by other restaurants, including one in *Sierra Vista, Arizona*. The solution even showed up in an unexpected business in *Las Vegas, Nevada*.
   - Call on individuals to read the words.
   - If possible, have students find each city and state on a U.S. map.

2. **As we read this article, remember to look for the solution to Red Cheney's problem and for the other problem it solved. Look for the effects of that solution, and also watch for the signal words and phrases on the board.**

3. **Fluency** Read aloud the first paragraph of the article. Then have students read the remainder of the article with a partner, taking turns after paragraphs. If necessary, review the following fluency goal with students to increase reading rate: **As you become more familiar with the text, try to increase the speed with which you read.**

4. When students have completed their reading, check for literal comprehension of the text by asking these questions: **KNOWLEDGE**
   - *Paragraph 2:* **What was Red Cheney's problem?** (Customers didn't have enough time to go into his restaurant to eat.) **Why couldn't he do what other restaurant owners had done: deliver food to the curb outside the restaurant?** (His curb was a busy highway. There wasn't enough room for people to park and wait for servers to deliver food.)
   - *Paragraph 4:* **What did Red Cheney do to solve his problem?** (He knocked a hole in the wall and invented the drive-through window.)
   - *Paragraph 5:* **What problem did the restaurant in Sierra Vista, Arizona have?** (Soldiers couldn't wear uniforms into the restaurant, so many soldiers just ate at home.) **How did the restaurant solve the problem?** (by installing a drive-through window)
   - *Paragraphs 7 and 8:* **How did restaurants solve the problem of impatient drive-through customers?** (They set up menu boards at a distance from the window. Some set up two windows: one for paying, and one for picking up food.)
   - *Paragraph 12:* **What other kinds of businesses have adapted the idea of drive-through windows to their needs?** (banks, groceries, video stores, dry cleaners, drug stores, libraries, coffee shops, wedding chapels)

Checking for Comprehension *After Reading*

1. Have students work with partners to scan the article for the signal words and phrases listed on the board. On a separate sheet of paper, have students record three sentences that include one of these signal words or phrases. Then call on individuals to read one of their sentences, identify the word or phrase, and explain how it shows either a cause or an effect. (Possible signal words and phrases: *because*, paragraphs 2, 4, and 5; *since*, paragraphs 4 and 10; *as a result*, paragraphs 5, 7, and 8; *so*, paragraph 4)

2. Encourage students to apply what they understood from the text by asking these questions:

    *   **How often would you say you visit a drive-through window each week? How does this compare to the national average of 3-1/2 times per week?** APPLICATION (Responses will vary.)

    *   **Drive-through windows have solved many problems, but they've also created some new problems in the way people eat. What are they?** SYNTHESIS (Possible responses: People eat more junk food. People eat alone more often, rather than with their families. Because of the convenience, people spend more money eating out than they might otherwise.)

3. **Challenge Question** **In your opinion, do drive-through windows help people get on with their busy lives, or do they actually add to the feeling of busyness that people have? Explain.** SYNTHESIS (Responses will vary.)

4. **Research** To close the lesson, ask students to brainstorm a list of ideas or topics about fast-food restaurants that they would like to know more about. List students' ideas on the board. Then discuss with students where or how they might locate information related to each subject.

For example, they might find a book in the library, check online resources, or interview someone who knows about the subject. Invite students to consult these resources for information and to bring what they find to the next class.

Extending Vocabulary

Suffixes *-tive, -ive*

*   Have students turn to paragraph 4 on Anthology page 190. Read the last sentence aloud. ("Because of this imaginative . . .") Write the word *imaginative* on the board. **What is the suffix at the end of this word?** (-tive) Underline this suffix.

*   Have students turn to the section They're Everywhere! on Anthology page 192. Read the next-to-last sentence aloud. ("Customers with active lifestyles . . .") Write the word *active* on the board. **What is the suffix at the end of this word?** (-ive) Underline this suffix.

*   **These suffixes mean "having the quality of" or "tending to." What does *imaginative* mean?** (having the quality of imagination) **What does *active* mean?** (tending to act)

*   Have students think of additional words with the suffixes *-ive* and *-tive*, and write their suggestions on the board. (Possible suggestions: competitive, impressive, combative, responsive, festive) Ask students what each word means. (Possible meanings: tending to compete, tending to impress, tending to combat, tending to respond, having the quality of a festival)

▶ Have students record these words, along with their meanings, in the Vocabulary Log.

Connect to Social Studies

Use the following activity to encourage students to think about the impact of fast food on family life.

- Point out that drive-through windows have made buying fast food even faster. **Many American families eat fast food for dinner several times each week, especially in households where both parents work full time.**

- Write these roles on the board:
  - *Owner of a fast-food restaurant in your town*
  - *Nutrition expert who thinks fast food is unhealthful*
  - *Busy parent who buys fast food several times a week*
  - *Author of a book about how eating fast food is weakening family ties*

- Arrange students in groups of four, and randomly assign one of the four roles to each group. Ask students to prepare a list of important points for a panel discussion among the four people described on the board.

- Have each group write at least five statements in support of their position.

- After students have prepared their statements, have them choose one student to be their spokesperson. Then have the spokespersons from the groups conduct a panel discussion for the class, using the written statements as "talking points."

To increase difficulty: Have students write summaries of the panel discussion, as if they were reporters who covered the discussion for their local newspaper.

Lesson 4

Anthology Selection

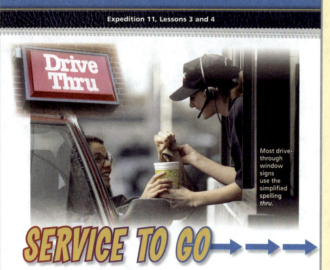

Most drive-through window signs use the simplified spelling *thru*.

SERVICE TO GO →→→

[1]Red Cheney had a problem. It was 1947, and Red was opening a new restaurant on a highway in Springfield, Missouri. The 2,000-mile-long highway was filled with potential customers on long car trips. But many of the customers were in a hurry. They didn't have time to stop, go inside a restaurant, and sit at a table for a meal. Red needed a strategy, or a lot of customers would speed right past his restaurant.

[2]For years, restaurants had offered curbside service to customers waiting in their cars. Customers would park at the curb outside the restaurant, where waiters would take orders and deliver food. This appealed to customers because they could get food fast and easily. But curbside service could not help Red. The curb outside his restaurant was a busy highway filled with speeding cars. People couldn't park there and wait for food to be delivered.

[3]Other restaurants offered drive-in service. At a drive-in restaurant, customers parked in a paved area off the road. A restaurant worker would come to their cars and take their orders. When the food was ready, the worker would take it out to the car. Then the customers could eat their food in their cars or take it home. But drive-in restaurants needed big parking lots and a lot of workers to serve customers. Red needed a better idea.

[4]Then it came to him. Red realized that he didn't need a drive-*in*. He needed a drive-*through*. So he knocked a hole in the wall of his restaurant and installed a window. Customers could drive up to the window, place an order, get their food, and get back on the road in a hurry. It was perfect. One worker could handle all the car customers. Since the customers would drive away with their food, Red did not need a big area for people to park while they ate. Because of this imaginative solution, Red's restaurant became a popular—and fast—stop for hungry travelers in a hurry.

Serving Soldiers

[5]Drive-through windows solved problems for more than just hungry travelers, however. For example, in 1975 a restaurant in Sierra Vista, Arizona, was losing business because of an army rule. Soldiers from the local army base were not allowed to wear their uniforms into non-military businesses. This meant soldiers couldn't stop at the restaurant for dinner on

the way home. They would have to drive home and change clothes first. A lot of soldiers decided just to eat at home. That was costing the restaurant valuable business. To solve this problem, the restaurant installed a drive-through window. As a result, soldiers could get food without having to enter the restaurant or go home to change clothes first. Even people who weren't soldiers found the drive-through more convenient than parking and walking into the restaurant to place a "to-go" order. Because people could pick up dinner with **ease**, the restaurant had more customers than ever.

The Need for Speed

[6]Drive-through windows quickly proved their worth to restaurants by increasing profits. But there were still problems to be worked out. One was speed. To make more money, restaurants needed to serve the maximum number of customers in the **minimum** amount of time possible. With just a window, a restaurant could help only one car customer at a time. The customer would drive up to the window, look at the menu, place an order, and wait for the food to be prepared. The next customer had to wait through this process before driving to the window and placing an order. Sometimes customers got **impatient** and drove away. That meant lost business.

[7]Restaurants solved this problem by setting up a menu board several car lengths away from the window. A menu board is a lighted sign with a list of the food served at the restaurant. The menu board also had an intercom. An intercom is a speaker and microphone that allows the customer to talk to the restaurant worker. With this new system, customers could place their order at the menu board, then drive up to the window to pay and pick up their food. While that customer was paying, the next customer could order. By setting the menu farther away from the window, restaurants could work on several orders at once. As a result, the restaurants reduced the amount of time customers had to wait in line.

[8]Restaurants thought of other ways to increase the speed of their service. One way was to have two windows. Customers would pay at the first window and pick up food at the second window. This system allowed different restaurant workers to concentrate on one part of the process. As a result, they could deliver food faster. This system also helped reduce the number of mistakes made when filling customer orders.

Stress Reliever

[9]Drive-through windows became so popular that they created an unexpected problem. Sometimes customers were not sure what they wanted to eat. They would sit at the menu board trying to decide if they would **prefer** a hamburger or a chicken sandwich. Hungry customers waiting to order would become frustrated. The customers at the menu board would start to feel a lot of pressure to hurry up and order. This slowed the process and caused a **decline** in customer satisfaction. Restaurants worried that they might start losing customers.

[10]Restaurants solved this problem by adding a preview menu to the drive-through line. Since the preview menu was a few car lengths ahead of the menu board and intercom, customers could decide what they wanted before it was their turn to order. The result was faster service and less stress on customers. Drive-through windows became more popular than ever.

They're Everywhere!

[11]Today, drive-through windows are a huge success. The average American orders food from drive-through windows three and a half times a week. Restaurants with drive-through windows do about 60 percent of their business with customers who never leave their cars. Some restaurants serve 99 percent of their food through the drive-through window.

[12]Drive-through windows worked so well for restaurants that other businesses found ways to use them. Banks began offering drive-through windows so their customers could conduct business from their cars. People can pick up groceries, videos, laundry, drug prescriptions, library books, and even a cup of espresso without ever leaving their cars. There is even a drive-through window in Las Vegas where people can get married! Customers with active lifestyles depend on drive-through windows to help them take care of their errands and get on with their busy schedules. The faster they can take care of their errands, the sooner they can get home to relax and **decompress**.

Comprehension and Vocabulary
Before Reading

1. **In Lesson 3, we read "Service to Go."**

- **What kind of expository text did we decide it is?** (problem/solution)
- **The article discussed the problem that Red Cheney had at his restaurant in Missouri. What was it?** (Customers didn't have enough time to go into his restaurant to eat.)
- **How did he solve it?** (He knocked a hole in his wall and invented the drive-through window.)
- **Drive-through windows solved the problem of another restaurant—one in Arizona. What was the problem at that restaurant?** (Soldiers were not allowed to go inside in their uniforms.)

2. Ask students who located additional information about fast-food restaurants to share the information with the class. Guide students to make connections between the new information and the other text they have read in this Expedition.

Vocabulary Review

3. Arrange students in pairs, and have them turn to Student Book page 142. Ask students to read the vocabulary words listed in the box. Call on students to tell what each word means.

4. Write the following word pairs on the board.
happy/sad
money/gravel
mad/angry
tree/lumber

Some words are related to each other. They might have the same meaning or the opposite meaning. Or they might go together in another way. Other words are not related to each other at all.

- **Which of the words on the board mean the same thing?** (mad/angry)

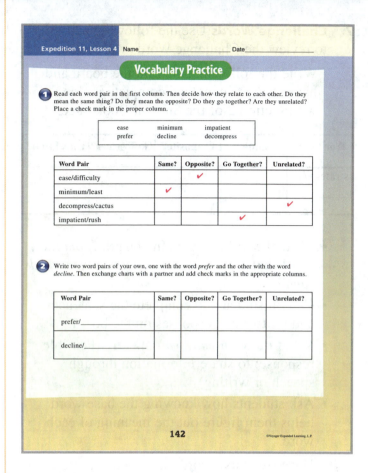

- **Which mean the opposite?** (happy/sad)
- **Which go together?** (tree/lumber)
- **Which are not related?** (money/gravel)

5. Read aloud the instructions for section 1 of the Vocabulary Practice activity. Then read the first word pair aloud. **These words are related in a particular way. They are opposites. Let's place a check mark under *Opposite*.** Have partners work together to complete the chart. When all partners are finished, review students' responses as a class, providing correction and feedback as needed.

6. Have students turn to section 2 of the Vocabulary Practice. Read the instructions aloud. Have students write word pairs and then trade Student Books with a partner to complete the chart. Monitor students as they work. When all partners are finished, invite students to share what is recorded in their charts.

7. Challenge Words Use the following activities to review the Challenge Words with students.

- Write the following chart on the board and have students copy and complete it along with section 2 of the Student Book page.

Word Pair	Same?	Opposite?	Go Together?	Unrelated?
strategy/ _____				

- Write the following on the board: *From the word communicate, we can make other words such as _____.*
- Call on students to complete the sentence, and write their responses on the board.
- **What does *communicate* mean?** (Possible response: to share information through speech or writing)
- Ask students how knowing the base word helps them figure out the meaning of each word.

▶ Have students record these words and their possible meanings in the Vocabulary Log.

Reading for Understanding   *Reading*

1. Have students turn to Anthology page 189 and Student Book page 143. Read the Student Book instructions aloud.

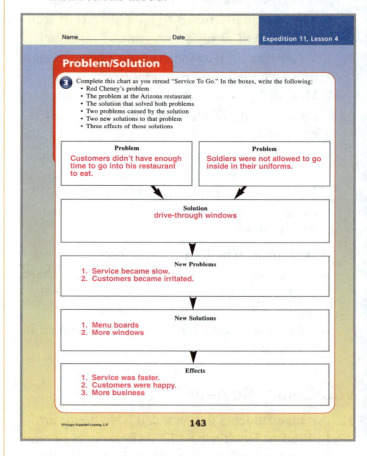

Name_____ Date_____   Expedition 11, Lesson 4

Problem/Solution

3 Complete this chart as you reread "Service To Go." In the boxes, write the following:
- Red Cheney's problem
- The problem at the Arizona restaurant
- The solution that solved both problems
- Two problems caused by the solution
- Two new solutions to that problem
- Three effects of those solutions

Problem
Customers didn't have enough time to go into his restaurant to eat.

Problem
Soldiers were not allowed to go inside in their uniforms.

Solution
drive-through windows

New Problems
1. Service became slow.
2. Customers became irritated.

New Solutions
1. Menu boards
2. More windows

Effects
1. Service was faster.
2. Customers were happy.
3. More business

©Voyager Expanded Learning, L.P.   143

2. Earlier we identified Red Cheney's main problem. What was it? (Customers didn't have enough time to go into his restaurant to eat.) **We also identified the problem of the restaurant in Arizona. What was it?** (Soldiers were not allowed to go inside in their uniforms.) Have student record these problems in the top two boxes.

3. Read paragraphs 1–4 aloud. **Paragraph 4 explains how Red solved his problem.** Have students read the fourth sentence. **Here we have the solution to Red's problem. What signal word does the author use to help us recognize this?** (so) **Let's write the solution, *drive-through windows*, on our chart.**

4. Have students finish reading the article independently. Direct students to pause and fill in the chart as they come across the answers. Tell them to leave the last Effects box blank for now.

Checking for Comprehension *After Reading*

1. After students have completed the Student Book page and the article, bring them together as a class. Call on students to identify the new problem, new solutions, and the effects they listed in the Student Book. Provide correction and feedback as needed.

2. **There is still one blank box in the diagram. We know restaurant owners used menu boards and added new windows.**
  - **What was the effect of these additions on the service?** (Service was faster.)
  - **What was the effect on customers when service speeded up?** (Customers were happy.)
  - **What was the effect of happy customers?** (more business) **Let's write these in the Effects box.**

3. To close the lesson, revisit the following probing question: **In what ways have cars changed people's ways of living?**

Have students use information from "Service to Go" to revise and expand their earlier responses to this question.

Reading Response

Have students turn to Student Book page 144. Read the instructions aloud. Then have students use both the article and the graphic organizer on Student Book page 143 to find the answers to these questions:

 **Early restaurants with drive-through service were sometimes slow and lost business.
What solutions did restaurant owners come up with?
What effects did these solutions lead to?**

Have partners work together to complete the paragraph. When all students are finished, call on individuals to read aloud their completed paragraphs.

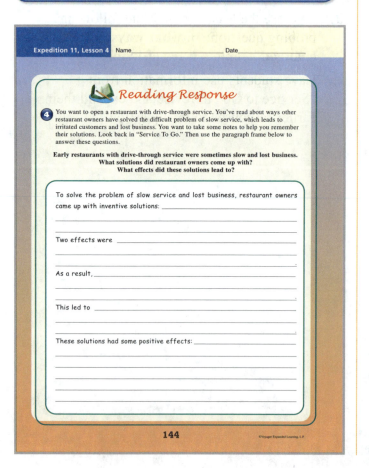

Expedition 11, Lesson 4 Name_____ Date_____

Reading Response

4 You want to open a restaurant with drive-through service. You've read about ways other restaurant owners have solved the difficult problem of slow service, which leads to irritated customers and lost business. You want to take some notes to help you remember their solutions. Look back in "Service To Go." Then use the paragraph frame below to answer these questions.

**Early restaurants with drive-through service were sometimes slow and lost business.
What solutions did restaurant owners come up with?
What effects did these solutions lead to?**

To solve the problem of slow service and lost business, restaurant owners came up with inventive solutions: _____

Two effects were _____

As a result,_____

This led to _____

These solutions had some positive effects: _____

144
©Voyager Expanded Learning, L.P.

Passport Reading Journeys Library

Building Fluency

1. Place students in pairs according to reading level to build fluency. When pairing students, be sure that one student is a stronger reader (Student A) than the other student (Student B). However, do not reveal that stronger readers are paired with weaker readers. See *Passport Reading Journeys* Library Teacher's Guide for grouping guidelines.

2. Have students quickly choose reading material from the *Passport Reading Journeys* Library or another approved selection that is at the reading level of Student B. If students have not finished the previously chosen selection, they may continue reading from that selection. See *Passport Reading Journeys* Library Teacher's Guide for material selection guidelines.

3. Tell students that Student A will read one paragraph, and Student B will reread that same paragraph.

4. Have students follow this routine until the end of class.

5. If necessary, review the following practices to enhance fluency:
   • Rate and accuracy of reading
   • Expression during reading
   • Correction procedures

Library Highlights

Spotlight on an Author

Level I

Surviving the Applewhites received numerous awards such as the ALA Best Book for Young Adults and the Newbery Honor Book award. Author Stephanie S. Tolan has written other young adult novels that include *The Face in the Mirror*, *Plague Year*, and *Listen*.

Lesson 5

Strategic Online Learning Opportunities®

Students read a passage about the popularity of automobile trips and camping out of cars during the early 1900s. Each Expedition 11–15 reading passage has two Lexile levels instead of three. This modification supports the instructional scaffold as students transition to higher levels of reading independence.

Content Connection

Social Studies

Autocamping to Motels
by Autumn L. Fenton

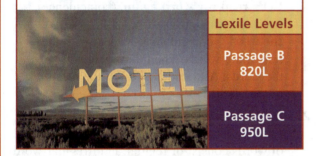

Lexile Levels
Passage B 820L
Passage C 950L

Assessment
- Metacognition
- Content
- Vocabulary
- Main Idea
- Summary

SKILL ✓

Based on their assessment scores, students automatically are assigned either the Skills Practice for reinforcement or the Independent Practice and Extension Opportunities.

SKILLS PRACTICE

Vocabulary Strategies
- Context
- Word Parts: Prefixes and Suffixes
- Word Parts: Compound Words

Dictionary Skills

Main Idea Strategy: W–I–N
- Identifying the Most Important *Who* or *What*
- Identifying the Most Important *Information*
- Stating the Main Idea in a Small *Number* of Words

Questioning

Writing
- Writing a Summary Statement

INDEPENDENT PRACTICE

Vocabulary Strategies

Writing
- Writing a Summary Statement

EXTENSION OPPORTUNITIES
- Online Books
- Book Cart
- Review of Previous Passages

Advanced Word Study

Multisyllabic Words

1. **Remember, we can use what we know about word parts such as open and closed syllables, prefixes, and suffixes to read longer words.** Write the word *usefulness* on the board. Underline *use*. **What is this word part?** (use) Underline *-ful*. **What is this suffix?** (-ful) Underline *-ness*. **What is this final suffix?** (-ness) **I can read these word parts and use the sounds I know to read the word. The word is** *usefulness*. **The word** *usefulness* **means "the state of being useful or helpful."**

   Have students turn to Student Book page E11, Lesson 6. Direct students to line 1. **What is the first word part?** (e) **What is the next part?** (co) **What kind of syllable is this?** (open) **How do we know?** (It has a long vowel sound without any consonants following it, or closing it in.) **What is the next part?** (nom) **What kind of syllable is this?** (closed) **How do we know?** (It has a short vowel sound followed by one or more consonants.) **What is the next part?** (ic) **What is the suffix?** (-al) **What is the word?** (economical) Repeat with the remaining words. Call on individuals to read the words in random order. Ask students to tell the meanings of the words.

2. Direct students to lines 2 and 3. Have them read the words. Then, call on individuals to read the words in a different order. Ask students to tell the meanings of the words.

   #### ▼ To Correct
   For Multisyllabic Words: **What is the first word part? What is the next part? What is the word?** If students do not know the meaning of the word, review the word and/or word parts to determine the meaning of the word.

   For Sounds in Words: Say the correct sound(s), then ask students to repeat the sound(s). Have students read the word again with the correct sound(s). If students do not know the meaning of the word, review the word and/or word parts to determine the meaning of the word.

1. economical	powerful	collision	quality
2. hesitation	substantive	positive	transportation
3. understandable	honcho	personally	mustard

Sight Words

1. Direct students to line 1. Have them point to the first word. **This word is** *coincidence*. **Read the word.** (coincidence) **This is not a regular word. Let's read the word again.** (coincidence) **Let's spell the word.** (c-o-i-n-c-i-d-e-n-c-e) **What is the word?** (coincidence) Repeat with the remaining words. Then, have students read the words. Ask students to tell the meanings of the words.

2. Direct students to lines 2 and 3. **Let's read these words.** Remind students that the rows of words consist of regular and irregular words. Point to the first word. **What is the word?** (schedules) Repeat with the remaining words. Call on individuals to read the words in a different order. Ask students to tell the meanings of the words.

   #### ▼ To Correct
   For Regular Words: Say the sound(s) in the word, then ask students to repeat the sound(s). Have them read the word again with the correct sound(s). If students do not know the meaning of the word, review the word and/or word part to determine the meaning of the word.

   For Irregular Words: Immediately say the correct word. Then have students read the word, spell it, and read it again. If students do not know the meaning of the word, review the word.

1. coincidence I	bruised I	jealous I	swollen I
2. schedules I	errands I	minor R	convertible R
3. soldiers I	restaurants I	magazine I	earlier I

Anthology Selection

You Need This Car

Would I steer you wrong?

¹Good afternoon, and welcome to Crazy Carl's Car Corner! No, I'm not Crazy Carl. He's the owner, the big cheese, the head honcho. He's on vacation. My name's Al. What's your name? Felix, eh? My grandfather's name was Felix. I'm pleased to meet you, Felix. I can see by the mustard stain on your shirt that you've already taken advantage of our free hot dog offer. Do you mind if I ask you a couple of questions so I can better understand which cars to show you? First of all, what kind of car do you drive right now? A sports car, eh? What do you like most about your sports car? The powerful engine, you say? I like to drive fast too. But not too fast, right? Always obey the speed limit, I say, but it's nice to be able to get up to the speed limit as quickly as possible. Know what I mean? Let me give you my honest

193

---

opinion, Felix. I think that what you need is a brand new Panther LX. It's the perfect car for you for four reasons: power, style, safety, and economy.

Power

²You say you like your current car's powerful engine, Felix? Well, power is what makes the Panther the perfect car for you. The Panther is the most powerful car of its type. It goes from 0 to 60 miles per hour in 5 seconds flat! The only thing faster is a jet! The Panther is 30 percent more powerful than the car you drove in here. Just imagine how all that power is going to feel when you are cruising down the highway leaving all the other drivers in your dust. Now, our competition sells a similar car called the Tiger 200X. It's not a bad car, but it's no Panther LX. *Car Buyer* magazine tested the Panther and the Tiger, and the tests showed that the Panther was 19 percent more powerful than the Tiger. You'll feel that extra 19 percent of power every time you step on the gas of your new Panther.

Style

³But the Panther is not just powerful, it's also the most beautiful car on the highway. You don't just want to go fast, you want to go fast and look good while you're doing it. Style is the second reason the Panther is the perfect car for you. Just look at the Panther's sleek lines! And if this isn't stylish enough for you, the Panther is also **available** as a convertible. Just imagine cruising down the highway on a lovely spring day with the top down and the wind blowing through your hair. Some people might argue about the usefulness of style, but you and I know better. Style is what makes everyone stop and look at you and your sleek new Panther. Style is what will make your neighbors jealous.

Safety

⁴Another reason this car is perfect for you is safety. The Panther has airbags that inflate if you are in a head-on collision, but it also has side airbags in case someone runs into the side of your car. Are you a married

194

---

man, Felix? What's your wife's name? Victoria! What a coincidence! My sister is named Victoria! Now, you could save a little money by buying a Tiger 200X, but it doesn't have side airbags. Imagine that Victoria is driving down the street one day when some jerk runs a red light and—bam!—rams into the side of this cheap, flimsy Tiger. Think about how you would feel seeing your lovely wife at the hospital, her face all swollen and bruised from the accident. What are you going to tell her, Felix? "Well, honey, at least we saved a little bit of money." But that's not going to happen, because you're not the kind of guy who's going to risk your wife's safety just to save a few bucks, are you, Felix?

Economy

⁵I think I know you pretty well by now, Felix. You will not hesitate to spend a little extra money on a product that is of the highest quality, like the Panther, but you're not the type of guy who's going to throw money away. That's another reason why this car is perfect for you. The Panther gets an **estimated** 28 miles per gallon on the highway and about 15 miles per gallon in the city. The fuel tank has a **capacity** of 18 gallons, so with a full tank, you can drive more than 500 miles! Can you do that in your car now? I don't think so. To tell you the truth, Felix, I'm not sure that car of yours can go another 500 miles, no matter how much gas you put in it. I'm just kidding around with you, pal.

⁶Are you a football fan, Felix? Well, so am I, and we both know that one football fan would never steer another football fan wrong. I'll let you in on a little secret, Felix. Crazy Carl is the biggest football fan in the world. You might even say he's crazy about football—get it? So, as a football fan who works for a football fan, I'm telling you that this car is perfect for you.

Think About This . . .

⁷I know what you're thinking, Felix. You're thinking, "I don't need a fancy car. I'm just looking for basic transportation. I prefer a cheaper car, maybe something with a little less power and a little less style and a few more miles per gallon." Let me tell you something, Felix. Buying a new car isn't about what you think you need, it's about what you *know you want*.

195

Sure, you can buy a cheaper car, but you'll regret it every time you step on the gas and remember how the power of the Panther LX felt. You'll regret it every time you drive by your neighbor's house and see his shiny new Panther LX gleaming in the driveway. You'll regret it every sunny, spring day when you think about how nice the wind feels blowing through your hair.

⁸You don't want to live with all that regret, do you Felix? The Panther LX is the perfect car for you because it's powerful, stylish, safe, and economical. I'm not exaggerating when I say that the Panther is the greatest car ever made. Now, I don't want you to feel like there's any **pressure** on you, but there was another gentleman in here earlier today looking at this very car. It's the last Panther LX that we have on the lot, so you need to make a decision as soon as possible. If you take advantage of this **opportunity**, I guarantee that you will never regret it. If the Panther LX doesn't live up to everything I told you, you can return it to us, and Crazy Carl will personally refund every penny you paid. Now, what do you think, Felix?

196

Comprehension and Vocabulary *Before Reading*

1. Review the topic of car culture by using the questions from Anthology page 185 and DVD 11.1 to generate prior knowledge. After showing DVD 11.1, call on individuals to read the questions. Have students discuss their responses using information from the DVD and the Lessons 1–4 articles.

2. **In this Expedition, we've been talking about automobile technology and the way cars have transformed our culture. What is one way people use cars for entertainment that we've read about?** (They watch cars race.) **What is one way that business owners try to lure busy customers who don't have time to get out of their cars?** (drive-through windows)

3. **The article in Lesson 6 deals with buying a new car. In it, we'll hear a high-pressure sales pitch from Al down at Crazy Carl's Car Corner. And to hear him tell it, Al is absolutely sure that you *need* this car.**

Introduce Vocabulary

Vocabulary

Review Words

available	*ready to be used*
estimate	*to roughly calculate*
capacity	*the maximum amount something can hold*
pressure	*the force of weight against something; application of influence or intimidation*
opportunity	*a good time or chance to do something*

Challenge Words

Multiple Meaning

economy   *spending as little as possible*
The first rule of *economy* is to buy only what you need, not what you want.
the making, buying, and selling of goods and services in a community
Our state's *economy* is based on farming, ranching, and mining.

Word Building

convertible   *convert, converter, conversion*

4. **Our next article, "You *Need* This Car," contains words with meanings we have already learned. We will review these words within the text we are reading.**

5. Write each Review Word on the board. Then ask students to locate the word in the article. Instruct them to read aloud the sentence containing the word, as well as any other sentences that provide context.
   - **What can you tell me about the word?**
   - Ask other questions that allow students to explore the word's meaning. (For example: **Is *available* the same as *missing*? If you have filled a cup to *capacity*, can it hold any more?**)

6. Ask students to respond to the following questions. Provide correction and feedback as necessary.
   - **Just because a product is *available*, does that mean you should buy it? Why or why not?**
   - **Why would it be important to know the *estimated* number of miles that a car can travel on a gallon of gas?**
   - **What is your *capacity* for listening to a long sales pitch? Do you get irritated if someone tries to sell you something?**
   - **When do you feel more *pressure*: when someone says you *have* to do something or when someone *suggests* that you do something?**
   - **Would you trust a salesman who called buying a car an *opportunity*? Why or why not?**

7. Work with students to write a definition for each word on the board.

8. Include the Challenge Words to meet the needs of students who are advancing. For the Word Building Challenge Word, have students identify the base word (convert), then guide them in determining how the base word can help them figure out the meaning of the larger words.

Review Text Structure: Persuasion

9. **In this Expedition, we've been reviewing different kinds of expository texts.** Write *Expository Texts* on the board and underline it.

- **What kind of text was the article about stock cars and open-wheel cars?** (compare/contrast) Write this on the board and place a check mark next to it.

- **What kind of text was the article about drive-through windows?** (problem/solution) Write this on the board and place a check mark next to it.

- Add *Sequential Order* and *Persuasion* to the list. **These are two kinds of expository text we have not yet reviewed.**

10. Have students return to Anthology 193 and preview the article by looking at the image and reading the title and headings.

- **Which kind of expository text do you think this article will be—sequential order or persuasion?** (persuasion) Place a check mark next to *Persuasion* on the board.

- **What do you think the author of this article will try to persuade someone to do?** (to buy a car)

11. **Remember that persuasive writing has four main parts.** Under *Persuasion* on the board write and bullet *Opinion Statement, Supporting Reasons and Details, Counterarguments,* and *Conclusion.* Have students tell what they remember about each part. **We'll talk more about these parts in the next lesson. For now, just keep in mind that the author of a persuasive text usually states his or her opinion, then gives reasons that support it.** Place check marks next to *Opinion Statement* and *Supporting Reasons and Details.*

12. **In an earlier Expedition, we talked about credibility.** Write *credibility* on the board and underline *credibil-.* **What does it mean if a person is credible?** (It means that he or she is believable or trustworthy.) **Speakers in persuasive texts have to show that they are trustworthy. They must use an appropriate tone, or attitude, and they must show that**
they are knowledgeable about the topic.
- **Which tone is more likely to persuade someone: an angry tone or a calm one?** (calm)

- **Who would you be more likely to listen to on the topic of cars: someone who sells cars for a living or someone who test drives them for a living?** (the test-driver)

13. **To judge a person's credibility, you also have to consider his or her motivation. Does the person have other people's best interests in mind? Or is he or she only looking out for his or her best interests? Let's think about these questions as we read today's article.**

Introduce Elements of Persuasion: Emotional Appeals and Logical Appeals

14. **Authors of persuasive texts know that readers respond with both their minds and their hearts. Readers can be persuaded by strong logic, or reasoning. But they can also be persuaded by strong emotions.**

SKILL ✓

15. On the board write: *You really should buy Cat's Meow jeans because:*
- *they are an excellent value for the price, and*
- *you'll be the envy of the entire school.*

Which of these reasons appeals to the logical mind? (the first) **Which appeals to the emotional heart?** (the second)

16. **Authors often use emotional appeals because they can be very strong. Sometimes emotional appeals are valid. They might have some truth in them. Often, though, they are not based on truth. Readers must think carefully about each emotional appeal. Is it supported by facts? Is it just a trick to persuade me to do something?**

Reading for Understanding

Reading

Places and Names to Look For:
- Crazy Carl's Car Corner
- Felix
- Victoria
- Panther LX
- Tiger 200X

1. **As you read this article, you will come across some unfamiliar places and names.**
- Write the words on the board.
- Point to each word as you tell students the following: **Al is a car salesman who works at *Crazy Carl's Car Corner*. He is trying to persuade *Felix* to buy the new *Panther LX* rather than the *Tiger 200X*. Funny, but it turns out *Victoria* is the name of both Felix's wife *and* Al's sister. Imagine that.**
- Call on individuals to read the words.

2. **As we read this article, let's think about Al's credibility. Does he have a calm tone? Does he have knowledge about the topic? Let's also think about the kinds of reasons he gives. Do they appeal to the mind or to the emotions?**

3. **Fluency** Read the first paragraph aloud. Then have students read the remainder of the article in pairs, taking turns after paragraphs. If necessary, review the following fluency correction procedure with students to ensure accuracy: **Offer help when your partner comes to an unfamiliar word or makes a reading error. Pause, then say, "That word is _____. Let's read it again."** As students read, monitor for reading rate, accuracy, and expression.

4. When students have completed their reading, check for literal comprehension of the text by asking these questions: **KNOWLEDGE**
- *Paragraph 1:* **What does Al want Felix to do?** (buy the Panther LX, a sports car Al sells)
- *Paragraph 2:* **How does the Panther compare to the Tiger, in terms of power?** (According to *Car Buyer* magazine, the Panther is 19 percent more powerful.)
- *Paragraph 3:* **How does Al define "style"?** (Style is what makes your neighbors jealous.)
- *Paragraph 5:* **According to Al, how many miles can the Panther go on a full tank?** (500 miles)
- *Paragraph 8:* **According to Al, why does Felix need to make a decision as soon as possible?** (There was another man looking at the same car earlier today.)

Checking for Comprehension *After Reading*

1. Have students apply what they understood from the text by asking the following questions:

   • **What is one fact about the Panther's power that Al uses to try to persuade Felix? Remember that a fact can be proven true.** ANALYSIS (Possible responses: It goes from 0 to 60 in 5 seconds. It is 30 percent more powerful than Felix's current car. It is 19 percent more powerful than the Tiger.)

   • **Al says the Panther is so stylish it will make Felix's neighbors jealous. Is this a logical appeal or an emotional appeal?** SYNTHESIS (emotional) **In your opinion, is this a fair tactic for Al to use?** EVALUATION (Responses will vary.)

   • **How would you describe Al's tone?** ANALYSIS (It is falsely friendly.)

2. **Challenge Questions** Let's think about whether Al is credible, or believable.

   • **First, how much knowledge does Al have about the car he is selling?** COMPREHENSION (a lot)

   • **Why do you think Al really wants Felix to buy the car? What is his motivation?** COMPREHENSION (Al will probably make money on the deal.)

   • **In your opinion, how credible is Al?** EVALUATION (Possible response: not very, because although he knows a lot about the car, his motive is selfish)

Extending Vocabulary

Word Part Review

• Write *re-*, *-tion*, and *-ness* on the board. Ask students to tell the meaning of each word part. If necessary, provide the meaning for them. (*Re-* means "to do again"; *-tion* means "act of doing"; and *-ness* means "state of being.")

• Have students work in pairs to scan paragraphs 3, 7, and 8 for the words that contain the prefix *re-* and the suffixes *-tion* and *-ness*.

• When students are finished, call on individuals to name the words they located. (*refund* in paragraph 8, *transportation* in paragraph 7, and *usefulness* in paragraph 3) Write these on the board.

• Point to *refund*. **What prefix or suffix is used in this word?** (the prefix *re-*) **How does this prefix help you figure out the meaning of the word?** (*Re-* means "to do again," so *refund* must mean "to fund again.")

▶ Have students write this word and its meaning in the Vocabulary Log.

• Repeat the previous step with the remaining words on the board. (*-Tion* means the "act of doing," so *transportation* must be "the act of transporting"; *-ness* means a "state of being," so *usefulness* must mean the "state of being useful.")

• Have students name other words they know containing the word parts *re-*, *-tion*, and *-ness* and to use the meanings of the word parts to determine the meanings of the words.

▶ Have students record an additional word containing each word part, along with each word's meaning, in the Vocabulary Log.

Lesson 7

Anthology Selection

You Need This Car

Would I steer you wrong?

¹Good afternoon, and welcome to Crazy Carl's Car Corner! No, I'm not Crazy Carl. He's the owner, the big cheese, the head honcho. He's on vacation. My name's Al. What's your name? Felix, eh? My grandfather's name was Felix. I'm pleased to meet you, Felix. I can see by the mustard stain on your shirt that you've already taken advantage of our free hot dog offer. Do you mind if I ask you a couple of questions so I can better understand which cars to show you? First of all, what kind of car do you drive right now? A sports car, eh? What do you like most about your sports car? The powerful engine, you say? I like to drive fast too. But not too fast, right? Always obey the speed limit, I say, but it's nice to be able to get up to the speed limit as quickly as possible. Know what I mean? Let me give you my honest

193

opinion, Felix. I think that what you need is a brand new Panther LX. It's the perfect car for you for four reasons: power, style, safety, and economy.

Power

²You say you like your current car's powerful engine, Felix? Well, power is what makes the Panther the perfect car for you. The Panther is the most powerful car of its type. It goes from 0 to 60 miles per hour in 5 seconds flat! The only thing faster is a jet! The Panther is 30 percent more powerful than the car you drove in here. Just imagine how all that power is going to feel when you are cruising down the highway leaving all the other drivers in your dust. Now, our competition sells a similar car called the Tiger 200X. It's not a bad car, but it's no Panther LX. *Car Buyer* magazine tested the Panther and the Tiger, and the tests showed that the Panther was 19 percent more powerful than the Tiger. You'll feel that extra 19 percent of power every time you step on the gas of your new Panther.

Style

³But the Panther is not just powerful, it's also the most beautiful car on the highway. You don't just want to go fast, you want to go fast and look good while you're doing it. Style is the second reason the Panther is the perfect car for you. Just look at the Panther's sleek lines! And if this isn't stylish enough for you, the Panther is also **available** as a convertible. Just imagine cruising down the highway on a lovely spring day with the top down and the wind blowing through your hair. Some people might argue about the usefulness of style, but you and I know better. Style is what makes everyone stop and look at you and your sleek new Panther. Style is what will make your neighbors jealous.

Safety

⁴Another reason this car is perfect for you is safety. The Panther has airbags that inflate if you are in a head-on collision, but it also has side airbags in case someone runs into the side of your car. Are you a married

194

man, Felix? What's your wife's name? Victoria! What a coincidence! My sister is named Victoria! Now, you could save a little money by buying a Tiger 200X, but it doesn't have side airbags. Imagine that Victoria is driving down the street one day when some jerk runs a red light and—rams into the side of this cheap, flimsy Tiger. Think about how you would feel seeing your lovely wife at the hospital, her face all swollen and bruised from the accident. What are you going to tell her, Felix? "Well, honey, at least we saved a little bit of money." But that's not going to happen, because you're not the kind of guy who's going to risk your wife's safety just to save a few bucks, are you, Felix?

Economy

⁵I think I know you pretty well by now, Felix. You will not hesitate to spend a little extra money on a product that is of the highest quality, like the Panther, but you're not the type of guy who's going to throw money away. That's another reason why this car is perfect for you. The Panther gets an **estimated** 28 miles per gallon on the highway and about 15 miles per gallon in the city. The fuel tank has a **capacity** of 18 gallons, so with a full tank, you can drive more than 500 miles! Can you do that in your car now? I don't think so. To tell you the truth, Felix, I'm not sure that car of yours can go another 500 miles, no matter how much gas you put in it. I'm just kidding around with you, pal.

⁶Are you a football fan, Felix? Well, so am I, and we both know that one football fan would never steer another football fan wrong. I'll let you in on a little secret, Felix. Crazy Carl is the biggest football fan in the world. You might even say he's crazy about football—get it? So, as a football fan who works for a football fan, I'm telling you that this car is perfect for you.

Think About This . . .

⁷I know what you're thinking, Felix. You're thinking, "I don't need a fancy car. I'm just looking for basic transportation. I prefer a cheaper car, maybe something with a little less power and a little less style and a few more miles per gallon." Let me tell you something, Felix. Buying a new car isn't about what you think you need, it's about what you *know you want*.

195

Sure, you can buy a cheaper car, but you'll regret it every time you step on the gas and remember how the power of the Panther LX felt. You'll regret it every time you drive by your neighbor's house and see his shiny new Panther LX gleaming in the driveway. You'll regret it every sunny, spring day when you think about how nice the wind feels blowing through your hair.

⁸You don't want to live with all that regret, do you Felix? The Panther LX is the perfect car for you because it's powerful, stylish, safe, and economical. I'm not exaggerating when I say that the Panther is the greatest car ever made. Now, I don't want you to feel like there's any **pressure** on you, but there was another gentleman in here earlier today looking at this very car. It's the last Panther LX that we have on the lot, so you need to make a decision as soon as possible. If you take advantage of this **opportunity**, I guarantee that you will never regret it. If the Panther LX doesn't live up to everything I told you, you can return it to us, and Crazy Carl will personally refund every penny you paid. Now, what do you think, Felix?

196

Comprehension and Vocabulary
Before Reading

1. **In Lesson 6, we read "You *Need* This Car."**
   - **What kind of expository text did we decide this selection is?** (persuasive)
   - **Who is Al?** (a car salesman at Crazy Carl's Car Corner)
   - **What does Al want to persuade Felix to do?** (to buy a particular car—the Panther LX, which Al is selling)
   - **Did you find him credible or not credible? Why?** (Possible responses: No, he's just trying to make some money. Yes, he knows a lot about the vehicle.)

Vocabulary Review

2. **Remember that authors of persuasive texts choose their words carefully. They choose words that have certain connotations, or shades of meaning, that move the reader to see the issue from their point of view. For example, the title of this article is "You *Need* This Car."** Write *Need* on the board. Under it, write *Should Consider*. **What if the title were "You Should Consider This Car"?** (The title would be weaker.) **Why?** (The word *need* implies that you *have* to have it. It implies that the car is essential. "Should consider" is much weaker. *Consider* means you should think carefully about it. The author does not want you to think carefully.)

3. Arrange students with partners and have them turn to Student Book page 145. Read the instructions aloud.

4. **Let's look at the first pair of sentences. Read them aloud. The boldfaced vocabulary word is *estimated*. *Estimated* means "an approximate calculation." *Roughly* means the same thing. But *estimated* sounds more scientific; *roughly* sounds rugged or harsh. That's not an association you want Felix to make with the Panther.** Have students write this explanation, or one of their own, on the lines under the first sentence pair.

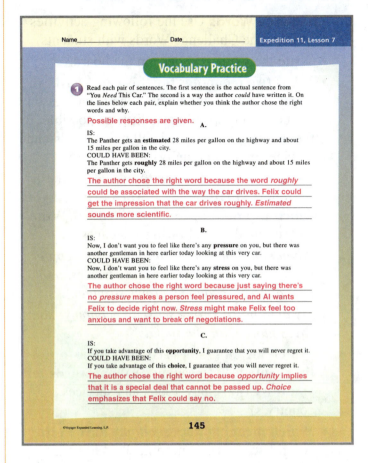

5. Read the next pair of sentences aloud. Call on individuals to tell whether they think the author used the right word, and why. List several students' thoughts on the board. Invite students to record in their Student Book the one with which they most agree.

6. Have partners complete the final item. When all students are finished, call on partners to report their reasoning.

7. Have students scan the article for other strong words or phrases, ones that were chosen to elicit a certain feeling. (Possible responses: perfect, cruising, in your dust, jerk, bam!, rams into, cheap, flimsy) Ask students to suggest replacement words. Tell them to choose words that are more neutral. (Possible responses: appropriate, driving, behind you, person, smack, hits, poorly constructed) Record the pairs on the board as students find them and suggest alternatives.

8. Challenge Words Use the following activities to review the Challenge Words with students.

- Write the word *economy* on the board.
- **What two meanings for this word have we learned?** Write and number the meanings on the board. (1. spending as little as possible; 2. the making, buying, and selling of goods and services in a community)
- **Usually, the context, or the words and sentences surrounding a word, will tell you which meaning the author intended.** Write on the board the following sentences:

  When more jobs are available, more people have money to buy goods and services, and the country's economy grows stronger.

  My aunt has a strong sense of economy: she saves more than she spends.

- **Which meaning does *economy* have in the first sentence?** (meaning 2) **What words tell you this?** (jobs, buy goods and services, country's)
- **Which meaning does *economy* have in the second sentence?** (meaning 1) **What words tell you this?** (saves more than she spends)

▶ Have students record the word and its meanings in the Vocabulary Log.

- Next, write the following on the board: *From the word convert, we can make other words such as _____.*
- Call on students to complete the sentence, and write their responses on the board.
- **What does *convert* mean?** (Possible response: to change)
- Ask students how knowing the base word helps them figure out the meaning of each word.

▶ Have students record the word and its possible meanings in the Vocabulary Log.

Review Text Structure: Persuasion

9. In the last lesson, we discussed our impression of Al. We considered his tone and credibility. Now we will look more closely at the logic of his arguments.

SKILL ✓

Write *Persuasion* on the board. Under it, write and bullet *Opinion Statement, Supporting Reasons, Counterarguments,* and *Conclusion.* **Let's review the purpose of each of these parts of persuasive writing.** Elicit the following purposes from students:

- An opinion statement gives the author's opinion. It tells what the author believes the reader should do or believe.
- A supporting reason is a *because*. It tells why the reader should do or believe something.
- A counterargument is an argument against other opinions or alternatives. It helps an author discredit the other options available to the reader or listener.
- The conclusion wraps up the argument. It might summarize what the author has said, or it might give new reasons or information.

We will look for each of these elements as we reread "You *Need* This Car."

ELL English language learners find prepositions confusing and often use them incorrectly. Instruct students briefly on the meaning of the grammatical term *preposition*: **A preposition often tells when or where something is in relation to something else. In the phrase on the rooftop, the word on is a preposition.** Write other common prepositions on the board. Write several sentences from "You *Need* This Car" on the board with blank lines in place of all of the prepositions. Model finding the correct preposition for the blank: **Let's do the first one together: *Well, power is what makes the Panther the perfect car _____ you.* What word makes sense in the first blank? We would say the Panther is the perfect car *for* someone, so the correct phrase is *the perfect car for you*.** Pause after each question to provide wait time. Have students independently fill in the remaining blanks in the sentences on the board.

For a complete model of this strategy, see Expedition 10, Lesson 2.

Reading for Understanding — *Reading*

1. Have students turn to Anthology page 193 and Student Book page 146. Read the Student Book instructions aloud.

Expedition 11, Lesson 7   Name_____ Date_____

Persuasive Writing

2 Complete this chart as you reread "You *Need* This Car." Write the author's opinion statement in the top box. Then list the supporting reasons he gives. Consider each reason. If it is a fact—if it can be proven—place a check mark under *F*. If it is an opinion, or an unproven belief, place a check mark under *O*.

Opinion Statement:
I think that what you need is a brand new Panther LX. It's the perfect car for you for four reasons: power, style, safety, and economy.

Supporting Reasons	F	O
Power:		
1. It is the most powerful car of its type.	✔	
2. The Panther goes from 0 to 60 in 5 seconds.	✔	
3. The only thing faster is a jet.	✔	
4. It is 30 percent more powerful than Felix's current car.	✔	
5. The Panther is 19 percent more powerful than the Tiger.	✔	
Style:		
1. It is the most beautiful car on the highway.		✔
2. It is available in a convertible.	✔	
3. Everyone will look at you.		✔
4. It will make your neighbors jealous.		✔
Safety:		
1. It has front airbags.	✔	
2. It has side airbags.	✔	
3. The competing car does not have side airbags.	✔	
4. Victoria will be badly hurt if Felix doesn't buy the Panther.		✔
Economy:		
1. Felix isn't the type to waste money.		✔
2. The Panther gets about 28 mpg highway and 15 mpg city.	✔	
3. The fuel tank can hold 18 gallons.	✔	
4. The car will travel more than 500 miles on a tank of gas.	✔	
5. Football fans don't steer each other wrong.		✔
6. Crazy Carl is the biggest football fan in the world.		✔

Which argument that Felix gives is illogical? In other words, which argument is unrelated to the opinion statement or lacks sound reasoning?

3 Football fans don't steer each other wrong. Crazy Carl is the biggest football fan in the world.

146

---

2. As we begin rereading the sales pitch, let's look closely for a statement of the author's opinion. Read the first paragraph of the article aloud. **Is there an opinion statement anywhere in this paragraph? What is it? Remember, the opinion statement can be more than one sentence.** (Yes: I think that what you need is a brand new Panther LX. It's the perfect car for you for four reasons: power, style, safety, and economy.) **Let's write this in the Opinion Statement box on the chart.**

3. The opinion statement includes Al's four main supporting reasons. What are they? (The Panther LX provides power, style, safety, and economy.) **Al describes each of these main reasons in detail. Let's follow his argument.**

4. Direct students' attention to the section titled "Power." Read aloud the first three sentences of paragraph 2. **What does Al say about the power of the Panther?** (It is the most powerful car of its type.) **Let's write this under *Power* in the first box on the chart. Is this reason a fact or an opinion? Can it be tested and proven or disproven?** (Yes, it can be tested and proven or disproven. It is a fact.) **Let's place a check mark under *F*.**

5. Read aloud the next two sentences. **These two sentences offer two more details that support Al's argument about the power of the Panther. What are they?** (The Panther goes from 0 to 60 in 5 seconds, and the only thing faster is a jet.) **Let's write these two under *Power* on the chart. Are they facts or opinions?** (facts) **Let's put check marks in the *F* column.**

6. Read the next sentence.
- **Al says that the Panther is 30 percent more powerful than Felix's current car. Is this a fact?** (Yes; one could test to determine whether the Panther is 30 percent more powerful than Felix's current car.) **Let's put it in our chart and put a check mark in the *F* column. This sentence discredits one of Felix's options: keeping his current car. Al includes it to persuade Felix that his old car is slow. If Felix wants a fast car, he should choose the Panther.**
- **Al says the Panther is 19 percent more powerful than the Tiger. This is another supporting reason. Let's write it in our chart. Is it a fact?** (yes) **Let's put a check mark under *F*.**

7. Have partners finish reading the article independently. Instruct them to pause after each section (Style, Safety, and Economy) to finish filling in their charts. Remind them to place check marks under *F* or *O* when they determine whether each reason is a fact or an opinion. Instruct them to leave section 3 for later.

8. Encourage students to monitor their comprehension of the text by pausing occasionally to ask themselves *Am I understanding what I'm reading?* Tell students that when they do not understand what they are reading, they should reread that portion of the text.

Checking for Comprehension *After Reading*

1. After partners have completed the Student Book page and the article, bring students together as a class. Call on students to identify the reasons they listed in the Student Book and to tell whether each is a fact or an opinion. List each reason on the board, along with an *F* or an *O*.

   - **Which reasons do you find most convincing? Why?** (Responses will vary.)
   - **Does the reason you chose appeal to your emotions or to your logic?** (Responses will vary depending on the reasons students chose.)
   - **How does Al conclude his persuasive appeal?** (First, he offers a counterargument that anticipates Felix's worry about the cost of the vehicle. Next, he appeals to Felix's emotions and reminds him of his main arguments [power, style, safety, and economy]. Then he puts pressure on Felix by saying someone else is interested in the car. Finally, he offers Felix a safety net by saying that Carl will refund the money if Felix doesn't like the car.)

2. Review that some reasons are logical and others are illogical. **Logical reasons directly support the author's opinion. Illogical reasons, even if they are facts, do not support the author's opinion.** On the board, write *Crazy Carl's sells more cars than any other dealer in the state.* **Imagine that Al had offered this as an argument to buy the car. It may be a fact, but does this statement support the argument that the Panther LX is powerful, stylish, safe, or economical?** (no)

3. Direct students' attention to section 3 of the Student Book page. Have students discuss and answer the question in small groups. Then have groups report their answers to the class. Discuss any discrepancies in students' responses.

4. Ask students to scan the article for any other illogical arguments. **What are some statements that Al makes that seem intended to gain Felix's trust but that do not support the four main arguments?** (Possible responses: My grandfather's name was Felix. My sister's name is Victoria.)

5. Conclude the lesson by taking a tally to see whether more students were persuaded or not persuaded by the pitch. **If you were Felix, do you think you'd buy the Panther LX based on Al's sales pitch? Why or why not?** (Responses will vary. Some students may point out that they wouldn't rely on Al's information alone. They would do research in the library and online before they went to the dealership.)

Reading Response

Tell students they will now write an extended response about the Panther LX. Have them turn to Student Book page 147. Read the instructions aloud. Then have students review Student Book page 146. **You have already planned for the Reading Response by completing this graphic organizer. Use the information you recorded here to help you write your answer.** Encourage students to include details and additional information from the article, as well. Then, have them work individually to write a response to this question:

 Why should YOU buy the Panther LX?

When students are finished, call on individuals to read their responses aloud.

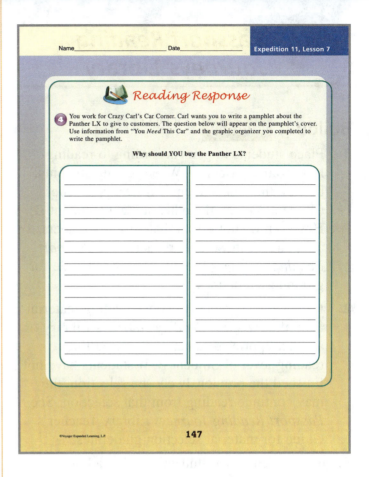

Passport Reading Journeys Library

Building Fluency

1. Place students in pairs according to reading level to build fluency. When pairing students, be sure that one student is a stronger reader (Student A) than the other student (Student B). However, do not reveal that stronger readers are paired with weaker readers. See *Passport Reading Journeys* Library Teacher's Guide for grouping guidelines.

2. Have students quickly choose reading material from the *Passport Reading Journeys* Library or another approved selection that is at the reading level of Student B. If students have not finished the previously chosen selection, they may continue reading from that selection. See *Passport Reading Journeys* Library Teacher's Guide for material selection guidelines.

3. Tell students that Student A will read one paragraph, and Student B will reread that same paragraph.

4. Have students follow this routine until the end of class.

5. If necessary, review the following practices to enhance fluency:
   - Rate and accuracy of reading
   - Expression during reading
   - Correction procedures

Library Highlights

Content Connection—Social Studies

Level III

Footsteps: The Great Migration provides information about the movement of African Americans in the United States from the southern states to the northern states. The magazine also provides a bibliography of additional books.

Content Connection—Science

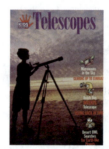

Level III

Kids Discover: Telescopes provides information about the structure of a telescope, how to use a telescope, and types of telescopes. The magazine also has photos taken in space with telescopes.

Lesson 8

Advanced Word Study

Spelling

1. Direct students to Student Book page E11, Lesson 8. **We use the sounds we know and hear in a word to spell the word. The word parts *-ive* and *-tive* are suffixes. Remember, a suffix is a word part that occurs at the end of a word and often helps us understand the meaning of the word. Let's spell words with these suffixes. The first word is *plaintive*. Say the word parts in the word *plaintive*.** (plain, tive) **What is the first syllable?** (plain) **What are the sounds in *plain*?** (/p/ /l/ /ā/ /n/) **Write these sounds. What is the suffix?** (-tive) **What are the sounds in the suffix *-tive*?** (/t/ /i/ /v/) **Write those sounds.** Repeat with *captive, negative, repressive, passive,* and *conclusive*.

2. Write the words on the board as students check and correct their words. Have them read the list of words.

1.	plaintive	4.	repressive
2.	captive	5.	passive
3.	negative	6.	conclusive

Sight Words

1. Direct students to line 1. Have them point to the first word. **This word is *geometric*. Read the word.** (geometric) **This is not a regular word. Let's spell the word.** (g-e-o-m-e-t-r-i-c) **What is the word?** (geometric) Repeat with the remaining words. Then, have students read the words. Ask students to tell the meanings of the words.

2. Direct students to lines 2 and 3. **Let's read these words.** Remind students that the rows of words consist of regular and irregular words. Point to the first word. **What is the word?** (swollen) Repeat with the remaining words. Call on individuals to read the words in a different order. Ask students to tell the meanings of the words.

▼ To Correct

For Regular Words: Say the sound(s) in the word, then ask students to repeat the sound(s). Have them read the word again with the correct sound(s). If students do not know the meaning of the word, review the word and/or word part to determine the meaning of the word.

For Irregular Words: Immediately say the correct word. Then have students read the word, spell it, and read it again. If students do not know the meaning of the word, review the word.

1. geometric I   hydraulics I   insignias I   interior I
2. swollen I   modified R   metallic R   coincidence I
3. compartment R   jealous I   bruised I   material I

Building to Fluency

1. Direct students to the phrases in the Student Book. Have them read through each phrase for accuracy. Then, have students reread the phrases to increase their accuracy and fluency so that the phrases sound like natural speech.

2. Direct students to the Anthology article to locate the sentences containing the phrases. Have them read the sentences in the article accurately and fluently. Remind students to read in a way that sounds like natural speech.

▼ To Correct

Immediately say the correct word. Have students reread the word, then read the phrase or sentence again.

1. . . . exactly what I'm going to do in this article . . . *paragraph 2*
2. . . . check out some low-rider magazines or books . . . *paragraph 3*
3. . . . ditched the seats and bought some really cool . . . *paragraph 5*

557

Anthology Selection

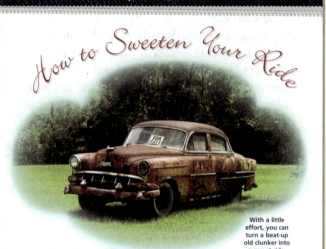

How to Sweeten Your Ride

With a little effort, you can turn a beat-up old clunker into a sweet ride.

¹My favorite thing in the world is jumping in my car, cranking up some tunes, and driving slowly with nowhere to go. In that way, I'm like a lot of kids my age. But there's a big difference. Most kids cruise around in cars that look pretty much like they did when they first rolled off the car lot. I just can't roll like that. My ride needs to be unique. It needs to reflect who I am. It needs to stand out in the crowd of cookie-cutter cars rolling down the street. That's why I drive a low-rider. Specifically, I drive a tricked out, modified 1968 Chevy Impala. It's painted a dark metallic blue with light blue geometric designs down each side. The **entire** hood is covered with a coiled up cobra.

197

²The first thing people ask me about my low-rider is, "Dude, where did you get that sweet ride?" They're shocked when I say, "I bought it at Dirt Dog's Junkyard for 500 bucks." But it's true. A year ago, my low-rider was a rusty pile of junk. The gas tank had a hole in it, and the engine was completely rusted together. I had to have it towed back to my house. Then I worked on it every spare moment for six months to turn it into the sweet ride you see before you today. The second thing everyone asks me about my car is, "Dude, will you show me how to make a low-rider?" That's exactly what I'm going to do in this article—tell you how I built my low-rider, from the first step to the last.

Find a Car

³The first step, of course, is to find a car. A lot of people buy used cars to turn into low-riders. Some people even buy new cars. But I didn't have that kind of money in the bank. Besides, I was going to change everything anyway. If a car is already running, what's the sense in fixing it? So I started hanging out at junkyards. Buying from a junkyard saved me tons of money. I also **recycled** something that would otherwise just rust away. Before you start visiting junkyards, check out some low-rider magazines or books and decide what kind of car you want.

⁴While you're looking, pay close attention to the condition of each car's body. The main thing you're looking for is a car without many dents. The engine and seats and stuff don't really matter. You'll probably want to replace them anyway. Finally, have your car towed to a place where you can work on it. It's best to have a place with a roof overhead to keep your work from being rained on. If you don't have a roof, cover your car with tarps when you're not working on it.

Tear It Apart

⁵Next, disassemble your car. First, tear apart the interior. Remove the seats and rip out the carpets. If the seats are in good shape, hang on to them. Some seats can be cleaned, and others can be covered with new material. In my case, I ditched the seats and bought some really cool replacements. Next, work on the

198

exterior. Remove the bumpers. Then take off all the insignias, like the hood ornament and the car company's name. After that, take off the trunk lid and the hood and set them aside. Then rip out the carpeting from the trunk, and check out the gas tank. If it's rusted out like mine was, remove it and install a new one. Next, remove the engine and all the parts under the hood. As you remove each part, look at it closely. If it's in pretty good shape, hang on to it. If it's not, get rid of it. Finally, haul all your trashed parts back to the junkyard.

Clean It

⁶The next step is cleaning all the parts you kept. Start with a trip to your local car parts store. There are several products that will degrease different parts of your car. Use one of these products to clean all the grease out of the engine compartment. Then use an electric sander to remove every last **layer** of paint from your car's body, including the hood and trunk. Cars have several coats of paint, so this might take a while. Once the entire car body is clean and free of paint, carefully spray everything with primer. This special type of paint will protect your car from rusting.

Paint It

⁷The next step is to paint the body of the car. In the factory, the car body is dipped in giant vats of paint so the paint is distributed **throughout** the entire vehicle. You probably don't have giant vats of paint, so your car will have to be spray painted. If you have the skills and want to do it yourself, go for it. Otherwise, I recommend hiring a professional painter. They have all the gear, and they know all the different painting **methods**. Your paint job is the most visible thing about your car, so you want it to be perfect. Hiring a professional will increase your chances of having a perfect paint job.

199

Put It Back Together

⁸While your car is being painted, get everything ready to put your low-rider together. Clean and repair all the parts you took off and saved. Buy all the new parts you will need. Since you're building a low-rider, you'll need a hydraulics kit. The hydraulics are the parts that make the front or back of your low-rider bounce up and down. You will also need a new suspension system that will let your car ride lower to the ground. After all, that's why it's called a low-rider.

⁹Organize everything neatly in your work area. After the paint on your car body is completely dry, start putting your low-rider together. Begin with the interior. First, put new carpeting in, then reinstall your seats. This is the point in my project when I installed my special steering wheel made out of chrome chain. When the interior's finished, install your hydraulics and your low-rider suspension. This will be easier without the weight of the engine. Then put all your engine parts back together and replace the trunk and hood. Next, replace the bumpers and insignias. Finally, mount some shiny new chrome wheels, and you're good to go. Now you can start saving money for that new stereo system.

¹⁰I hope this article has inspired you to get to work on your own low-rider. It won't be easy. In fact, it might be the hardest thing you've done in your entire life. You'll feel like giving up again and again. But if you stick to it, one day people will stop you on the street and ask, "Dude, where did you get that sweet ride?"

200

Comprehension and Vocabulary *Before Reading*

1. **We've been reading about different segments of the American car culture. What have we read about in this Expedition?** (car racing, drive-through windows, a car salesman and his pitch) **In Lesson 8, we'll read about how one person changed his car so that it would reflect his personality. And we'll learn the steps he took to get it looking just the way he wanted.**

Building Background Knowledge

Extend students' knowledge of the topic by sharing the following:

Social Studies

- A low-rider is a car or a truck with a suspension system that has been modified so that the body of the vehicle rides as closely as possible to the ground.
- Low-riders that use hydraulic suspension can be made to bounce up and down. This is called "hitting switches."
- Low-riders often are created from classic cars—vehicles that were made in the 1940s, 1950s, or 1960s.

Introduce Vocabulary

Vocabulary

Review Words

entire	*whole; complete*
recycle	*to use again*
layer	*a single thickness of something that lies over or under something else*
throughout	*in, to, or during every part of*
method	*a way of doing something*

Challenge Words

Word Building

metallic *metal, metallurgy, metalwork, metalworking*

Word Meaning

geometric *using straight lines and simple shapes* *If your bedspread has a geometric pattern, you should probably choose a solid-colored rug.*

2. **Our next article, "How to Sweeten Your Ride," contains words with meanings we have already learned. We will review these words within the text we are reading.**

3. Write each Review Word on the board. Ask students to locate the word in the article. Instruct them to read aloud the sentence containing the word, and any other sentences that provide context.

- **What can you tell me about the word?**
- Ask other questions that allow students to explore the word's meaning. (For example: **Is an *entire* pie the same as a slice of pie? Is *throughout* the same as *everywhere*?**)

4. Ask students to respond to the following questions. Provide correction and feedback as necessary.

- **Would you like to eat an *entire* turkey? Why?**
- **Name a material that you can *recycle*.**
- **In winter, what is usually your outer *layer* of clothing?**
- **Can you think of anything about humans that has remained constant *throughout* time?**
- **What is a healthy *method* for reducing stress?**

5. Work with students to write a definition for each word on the board.

6. Include the Challenge Words to meet the needs of students who are advancing. For the Word Building Challenge Word, have students identify the base word (metal), then guide them in determining how the base word can help them figure out the meaning of the larger words.

Review Text Structure: Sequential Order

7. **We've been reviewing kinds of expository text in this Expedition.** Write *Expository Text* on the board and underline it. Underneath it, write *Compare/Contrast*, *Problem/Solution*, *Cause/Effect*, and *Persuasion*.

- **First, in Lessons 1 and 2, we read an article that compared and contrasted two different types of racing.** Place a check mark next to *Compare/Contrast*.

- **Next, in Lessons 3 and 4, we read about a restaurant in Missouri and one in Arizona. Both wanted to serve customers without the customers having to leave their cars. What was their solution to this problem?** (drive-through windows) Place a check mark next to *Problem/Solution*.

- **Most recently, in Lessons 6 and 7, we read a pitch from a guy named Al. What was Al trying to do?** (to persuade a customer to buy a car) Put a check mark next to *Persuasion*.

8. **We've just reviewed the earlier lessons of this Expedition. We talked about what we did first, next, and last. If we were writing about this process in an expository text, what kind of order would we be using?** (sequential order) Add *Sequential Order* to the list on the board. **What is sequential order?** (the order in which events happen in time)

9. Have students turn to Anthology page 197 and preview the article by looking at the images and reading the title and headings.

- **What do you predict this article will be about?** (a person who customizes his car)

- **What clues tell you that the article will present information in sequential order?** (the before and after pictures, the "How to" in the title, and the headings, which are in sequential order)

10. **When presenting information in sequential order, authors use words to help you keep track. If there are three steps in a process, what would the signal words be?** (first, next, last; or first, second, third) Write these words on the board. **What are some other words that can be used to show the order in which something happens?** (before, after, then, finally, next, soon, when, at last, now, last week, today, next month, during) Write these words on the board, along with any others that students name.

11. **As we read, "How to Sweeten Your Ride," let's watch for some of these signal words. Let's also think about the order in which the author changed his car from a rotting hulk to a fine set of wheels.**

SKILL ✓

Reading for Understanding

Reading

Places and Names to Look For:
• Chevy Impala   • Dirt Dog's Junkyard

1. As you read this article, you may come across some unfamiliar places and names.

• Write the words on the board.

• Point to each word as you tell students the following:

A 1968 *Chevy Impala* is a classic car. Although Chevy still makes an Impala, the 1968 version looks much different from the model they sell today. The 1968 model is big and long and has a dashboard made of metal. The author of this article bought his 1968 Impala at *Dirt Dog's Junkyard* for $500.

• Call on individuals to read the words.

2. **Fluency** Read the first two paragraphs of "How to Sweeten Your Ride" aloud. Then have students read the remainder of the selection with partners, taking turns reading each paragraph. If necessary, review fluency goals with students and monitor for reading rate, accuracy, and expression.

3. When students have completed their reading, check for literal comprehension of the text by asking these questions: **KNOWLEDGE**

• *Paragraph 3:* **Why did the author buy his car at a junkyard?** (He didn't have money to buy one in better condition. Besides, he was going to change it all anyway.)

• *Paragraph 4:* **Why does the author recommend paying special attention to the condition of the car's body?** (You want to make sure it doesn't have many dents.)

• *Paragraph 8:* **What do the hydraulics do?** (Make the car bounce.)

• *Paragraph 9:* **What kind of steering wheel did the author choose?** (a chrome chain)

4. Have students reread "How to Sweeten Your Ride" independently. Remind them to pay special attention to the order of events.

ELL To help English language learners gain proficiency in comprehension and oral language, have students retell a reading selection. Depending on each student's level of language proficiency, he or she will require different levels of support when retelling. Provide support by gradually giving the student more responsibility for the retell. The following four levels of support may be used:

• Teacher models a retelling.
• Teacher and student retell together.
• Student retells independently.
• Student retells again.

For a complete model of this strategy, see Expedition 8, Lesson 1.

Checking for Comprehension *After Reading*

1. When all students are finished reading, have them turn to Student Book page 148. Read the instructions aloud. Then have students work with a partner to complete the activity. After students complete the activity, call on individuals to give a number for each step in the sequence. Provide correction and feedback as necessary.

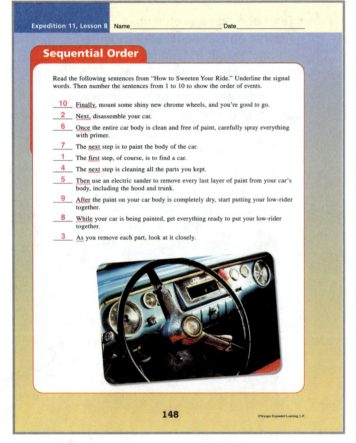

Expedition 11, Lesson 8   Name_____ Date_____

Sequential Order

Read the following sentences from "How to Sweeten Your Ride." Underline the signal words. Then number the sentences from 1 to 10 to show the order of events.

10 <u>Finally</u>, mount some shiny new chrome wheels, and you're good to go.

2 <u>Next</u>, disassemble your car.

6 <u>Once</u> the entire car body is clean and free of paint, carefully spray everything with primer.

7 The <u>next</u> step is to paint the body of the car.

1 The <u>first</u> step, of course, is to find a car.

4 The <u>next</u> step is cleaning all the parts you kept.

5 <u>Then</u> use an electric sander to remove every last layer of paint from your car's body, including the hood and trunk.

9 <u>After</u> the paint on your car body is completely dry, start putting your low-rider together.

8 <u>While</u> your car is being painted, get everything ready to put your low-rider together.

3 <u>As</u> you remove each part, look at it closely.

148   ©Voyager Expanded Learning, L.P.

2. **Challenge Questions** Did your opinion of the author change from the beginning of the article to the end? How and why? EVALUATION (Possible response: yes, because at first I thought he was crazy for wanting to drive such an old car, but then I became impressed with his knowledge of cars and the dedication and energy he put into remodeling his.) Would you want to go for a ride in the author's low-rider? Why or why not? APPLICATION (Responses will vary.)

Connect to the Author

Have students discuss the following questions in small groups.

- **Why did the author present the information in "How to Sweeten Your Ride" in sequential order?** (so the reader would understand the order of the process)

- **The author incorporates slang throughout, rather than using only standard English. Why?** (Possible responses: He writes like he speaks. He wants to use language to connect with his audience.)

- **What questions would you like to ask the author?** (Responses will vary.)

Listening and Speaking Have group members present their ideas to the class. Before they begin, encourage them to use body language that will help them express their ideas. Remind students that body language includes facial expressions, posture, and gestures. After each presentation, call on audience members to evaluate the effectiveness of each speaker's nonverbal messages.

Extending Vocabulary

- Write *de-* and *dis-* on the board. Ask students to tell the meaning of each word part, providing the meaning if necessary. (Both *de-* and *dis-* mean "opposite of.")

- Have students work with partners to scan paragraphs 5 and 6 for words that contain the prefixes *de-* and *dis-*.

- When students are finished, call on individuals to name the words they located. (*disassemble* in paragraph 5 and *degrease* in paragraph 6) Write these words on the board.

- Point to *disassemble*. **What prefix is in this word?** (dis-) **How does this prefix help you figure out the meaning of the word?** (*Dis-* means "the opposite of," so *disassemble* must mean "the opposite of assemble," or "to take apart.")

▶ Have students write this word and its meaning in the Vocabulary Log.

- Repeat the previous step with *degrease*. (*De-* also means "the opposite of," so *degrease* must mean "the opposite of grease," or "to take the grease off of.")

- Have students name other words they know containing the prefixes *de-* or *dis-* and use the meanings of the word parts to determine the meanings of the words.

▶ Have students record an additional word containing each word part, along with its meaning, in the Vocabulary Log.

Connect to Careers

Use the following activity to acquaint students with a college program for professional car restorers.

- Ask students to guess the connection between "The Tonight Show" host Jay Leno and students who are learning to restore old cars. Explain that Leno is a collector of antique cars.

- **Leno helps fund and promote a degree program in auto restoration at McPherson College in Kansas—the only college in the United States that offers a 4-year degree in automotive restoration. As of 2006, 110 students were enrolled in the program, four of whom were women.**

- Point out that auto restorers are highly skilled technicians with knowledge about all of a car's systems, from its body to its brakes. Share this quote from Leno: "I consider automotive restoration the same as restoring paintings by the Old Masters. . . . It takes a deft touch to do it properly. I want to help give respect to this skill and people learning it."

- Write this additional quote from Jay Leno on the board: *"We live in a country where working with our hands has become less important than working at a computer."*

- Have students write a paragraph in which they state whether they agree or disagree with Leno's statement, giving supporting reasons for their opinions.

- When students have finished their paragraphs, call on individuals willing to read them to the class.

To increase difficulty: Have students research requirements for admission to the auto restoration program at McPherson College and report their findings to the class.

Careers

Lesson 9

Anthology Selection

Social Studies

Expedition 11, Lesson 9 Assessment

BIRTH OF THE CAR CULTURE

Cars were an important part of American life in the 1930s, but by 1950, they had become a necessity.

[1]America's love affair with the car started a hundred years ago. And like any love affair, it has gone through stages. In the early years, people considered cars to be important, but not essential. Many people didn't even own cars. Instead, they used public transportation or their feet to get where they were going. Some even rode horses to school or to work. But after America and its allies won World War II, everything was different. Americans still loved their cars, just as they did before the war. But before the war, it was as if Americans were "dating" their cars. After the war, Americans "married" their cars. Before the war, few families owned more than one car. After the war, by contrast, two-car families were common. Unlike pre-war

201

Expedition 11, Lesson 9 Assessment

times, it became more common for teenagers to own their own cars. Before the war, many people considered cars a luxury. After the war, however, most people thought of a car as a necessity, as important as a home or clothes. America's love for cars was similar before and after the war. What had changed was the ability of the average family to afford not just one, but two and sometimes more cars.

America Falls in Love

[2]A hundred years ago, automobiles were expensive playthings for the wealthy. Cars were made by hand in a process so difficult that only a few thousand were built each year. Then Henry Ford figured out how to make cars cheaper, so more people could afford them. By 1916, Ford had cut the cost of a car to about $360, and American car production topped 1 million for the first time. America was in love with the automobile. Over the next 13 years, the American economy boomed, and so did car sales. People were making more money, and more people were spending some of that money on cars. In 1929, the number of cars produced annually topped 4 million.

[3]Then it all came crashing down. In 1929, the American economy began to collapse. Millions of people lost their jobs. Banks ran out of money, and people lost their life savings. Americans still loved cars, but fewer and fewer people could afford one. Car production plummeted for the next few years and fell below 1 million by 1932. Things improved slowly over the next few years, but people soon had more important things to think about than cars. War was raging across Europe. America's allies called for help. When America joined the war, car production came to a complete halt. Companies stopped making cars and started making tanks, airplanes, bombs, and other

202

Expedition 11, Lesson 9 Assessment

war supplies. People were asked to use less gasoline to save fuel for the war effort. America's love affair with the car was put on hold.

[4]In 1945, after America and its allies won the war, American confidence soared. So did the economy. America was now the richest country in the world. People were making more money, and after scrimping during the war, Americans were ready to go shopping. Companies started making cars again, cranking out a record 5 million cars in 1949. The next year, production shot up to 6.5 million. Making cars became America's biggest business. The car became a central feature of American culture.

America Moves to the Suburbs

[5]Before cars, Americans had to live close enough to their jobs to walk or take public transportation. That started to change in the 1920s as car ownership became more common. With a car, a family could live farther from work and school. Some moved to new neighborhoods called "suburbs" that were built just outside the crowded cities. Suburbs were relatively rare before the war.

[6]By comparison, suburbs grew so fast after the war that every major American city was completely surrounded by these new neighborhoods. After the war, home construction surged. During the 1950s, 13 million new homes were built, and 85 percent of them were built in suburbs. Without the huge increase in car ownership that occurred after the war, this would not have been possible. Early suburbs consisted mainly of houses. There were few places for people who lived in the suburbs to work or shop. Most jobs and shopping areas were still in the city, so people needed cars to get there.

203

Expedition 11, Lesson 9 Assessment

America Buys an Extra Car

[7]Before the war, few families owned more than one car. However, that began to change after the war. One reason was that so many families moved into the new suburbs. The parent who worked in the city, usually the father, needed a car to get to work. The parent who stayed home, usually the mother, needed a car to go buy groceries and run errands. Since people were making more money in the post-war boom, it was easier for families to afford more than one car.

[8]The war changed America's car needs in another way. During the war, almost all of the soldiers were men. Many women contributed to the war effort by working in factories that built war supplies. Some of these women found that they enjoyed working outside the home. When their husbands returned, many of these women kept their jobs. With both parents working, families needed two cars. They also had more money, so they could afford an additional car. When their children got old enough to drive, many parents added a third car to the family driveway. The abundance of jobs in the post-war boom also meant more teenagers could afford to buy their own cars. As a result, the number of cars on American roads jumped from 40 million to 60 million during the 1950s.

[9]Today, there are more than 200 million cars on American roads. There are more cars than there are people with driver's licenses. In fact, the state of California has more cars than it does people, with or without licenses. More than 90 percent of American households have at least one car, and the average household has two cars. Americans take about 90 percent of their long-distance trips in cars, and they drive more than 1.5 trillion miles a year. America remains married to the automobile, and there's no end in sight.

204

Expedition Review

1. Use the following activity to review text structures, the topics of the selections in this Expedition, and vocabulary reviewed in this Expedition.

   • Arrange students in four groups. Assign each group one of the articles ("A Fast Argument," "Service to Go," "You *Need* This Car," or "How to Sweeten Your Ride").

   • List the different kinds of expository text on the board (compare/contrast, problem/solution, cause/effect, sequential order, and persuasion).

   • Have each group review the content of its article, recall which kind of text it is, and work together to come up with a short paragraph that summarizes the article.

   • Have students incorporate signal words into their summaries to reflect the text structure. Instruct students to include at least one vocabulary word from that selection in their summary statements. (For example: In "How to Sweeten Your Ride," the author describes the process of turning a junkyard reject into a tricked out low-rider. He recommends the following steps: First, find the car. Next, tear it apart. Then, clean it by removing all the grease and every *layer* of paint. After that, paint the body. Finally, put it back together.)

   • **Challenge Words** If students have learned the Challenge Words, instruct them to include at least one of them in their summary.

   • When students are finished, have them present their summaries to the class. Call on individuals to identify signal words used in each summary. Write the words on the board.

   • **Listening and Speaking** Encourage students to stay alert and to remain focused on what they are hearing. Explain that sitting up straight and keeping their eyes on the speaker is considered active listening and will help them comprehend what is being said. During each presentation, monitor audience members for active listening. Encourage students who are demonstrating good listening skills, and provide correction to others as needed.

2. To review homophones, homographs, and word parts, write the following words on the board: *mettle/metal, past/passed, types/types, imaginative, refund, usefulness, disassemble.*

   • Ask students what the first two pairs of words are. (homophones) **What are homophones?** (words that sound the same—and are usually spelled differently—but have different meanings) **What does each homophone in the first pair mean?** (The word *metal* means "a hard, shiny material that conducts heat and electricity." The word *mettle* means "a person's ability to cope with difficulty.") **What do the words in the second pair of homophones mean?** (over, went by)

   • Ask students what the words *types/types* are. (homographs) **What are homographs?** (words that sound alike and are spelled alike—but have different meanings) **What are two meanings for the homographs in the third pair?** (to use a typewriter, a kind of something)

   • Underline the following word parts in the remaining words: *-tive, re-, -ness, dis-.* Call on individuals to tell the meaning of each word part, then the meaning of the word. (*-Tive* means "tending to," so *imaginative* means "tending to imagine"; *re-* means "again or back," so *refund* means "to fund again"; *-ness* means "state of being" so *usefulness* means "state of being useful"; *dis-* means "to do the opposite of," so *disassemble* means "to do the opposite of assemble," or "take apart.")

Assessment

1. Have students turn to Student Book page 149. Then have them turn to Anthology page 201. Explain that students will read the article "Birth of the Car Culture" before they answer the questions on the Student Book page.

2. Read aloud the Tips for Success and assessment instructions. Then have students complete the assessment independently.

Reteaching Guidelines

Comprehension

If students incorrectly answer more than 2 out of 11 questions on the Comprehension Assessment, refer to the Reteach lesson on page 569a. Using the Comprehension section, reteach the skills, guide students in completing the practice activity, and reassess comprehension.

Vocabulary

If more than 20 percent of the students miss certain vocabulary items, reteach and practice those words using the Vocabulary section of the Reteach lesson on page 569c.

Name_____ Date_____ Expedition 11, Lesson 9

Comprehension Assessment

Tips for Success! **Use Clues to Figure Out the Answer:** Sometimes answers are not in plain view. You might look back to the text to find an answer but come up empty-handed. If this happens, look for clues in the text. Look for information that is related, but not exactly what you need. Then add these ideas to what you already know to determine the correct answer.

Multiple Choice 3 points each
Read "Birth of the Car Culture" to answer questions 1–5. Look back in the article. Fill in the bubble next to the best answer.

1. Why did only rich people own cars 100 years ago?
   Ⓐ Cars were a central feature of the American landscape.
   Ⓑ Allies called for American help during World War II.
   Ⓒ Women contributed to the war effort.
   Ⓓ Cars were made by hand in a difficult process.

2. When did the number of cars produced first top 4 million per year?
   Ⓐ 1945
   Ⓑ 1932
   Ⓒ 1929
   Ⓓ 1949

3. In the 1950s, why was it necessary for people in the suburbs to own a car?
   Ⓐ Most jobs and shopping areas were in the city.
   Ⓑ Many families had two or more cars.
   Ⓒ Most people could not afford cars.
   Ⓓ Many companies made bombs and tanks.

4. How did the role of many women change after World War II?
   Ⓐ They made dinner.
   Ⓑ They had children.
   Ⓒ They stayed home.
   Ⓓ They had jobs.

5. In what state are there now more cars than people?
   Ⓐ New York
   Ⓑ Texas
   Ⓒ California
   Ⓓ Florida

©Voyager Expanded Learning, L.P.   **149**

Expedition 11, Lesson 9   Name_____ Date_____

Short Response 4 points each
Read "Birth of the Car Culture" to answer questions 6–10. Look back in the article. Then write your answer on the line(s).

6. How did the post-war boom cause more teenagers to own cars?
   There were more jobs after World War II. Because both parents often were working, they could afford to buy a car for their teenagers. Because more teenagers had jobs, they could often afford to buy their own cars.

7. How did the collapse of the American economy in 1929 eventually affect car production?
   Millions of people could no longer afford to buy cars, so car production plummeted.

8. Place the following events in sequential order. Number them 1–6.
   _5_ During the 1950s, millions of new homes were built in suburbs.
   _1_ Henry Ford figured out how to build cheaper cars.
   _6_ Today, there are more than 200 million cars on American roads.
   _4_ In 1945, after America and its allies won the war, American confidence soared.
   _3_ America entered World War II, and car production came to a complete halt.
   _2_ Ordinary people, not just the wealthy, could then afford to buy a car.

9. What problem did Henry Ford solve? How did he solve it? What effect did this have?
   Problem: Cars were expensive because they were made by hand.
   Solution: Ford figured out how to make cars cheaper.
   Effect: Possible response: American car production topped 1 million for the first time.

10. Find a signal word in the article. Write a sentence using the word. Underline it. Write whether the word signals sequential order, compare/contrast, or cause/effect.
    Sentence: Responses will vary.
    _____

    What the word signals: _____

150   ©Voyager Expanded Learning, L.P.

566

Extended Response 20 points

Read "Birth of the Car Culture" to answer question 11. Look back in the article. Use the information you find to complete the chart below.

11. "Birth of the Car Culture" is an expository text that describes American car culture during two periods of time. Answer the questions in the chart below to show how these periods were alike and different.

The Birth of American Car Culture		
	Before World War II	**After World War II**
What transportation did most people use?	public transportation, bicycles, horses, their feet	cars
How many cars were produced?	relatively few; more than 4 million in 1929, but production fell below 1 million by 1932	By 1949, production was up to 5 million. Today, there are more than 200 million.
Who owned cars?	the rich	almost everyone
Were cars considered essential or a luxury?	luxury	essential
How affordable were cars?	Ford made them relatively affordable, but the economy crashed in 1929, so only a few people could afford them.	Post-war prosperity and abundant jobs helped people earn enough money to buy a car, or even more than one.

Vocabulary Assessment 3 points each

For questions 12–26, read each sentence. Fill in the bubble next to the correct meaning for the underlined word.

12. What <u>evidence</u> do you have that this is the fastest car?
    What does the word *evidence* mean?
    - Ⓐ hopes and dreams
    - Ⓑ gasoline and oil
    - **Ⓒ facts and information**
    - Ⓓ music and dancing

13. I'm offering you the <u>opportunity</u> to own a sleek new car.
    What does the word *opportunity* mean?
    - Ⓐ place to put something
    - Ⓑ idea to make something
    - Ⓒ way to sell something
    - **Ⓓ chance to do something**

14. I also <u>recycled</u> something that would otherwise just rust away.
    What does the word *recycle* mean?
    - **Ⓐ to use again**
    - Ⓑ to throw away
    - Ⓒ to go around
    - Ⓓ to climb inside

15. This race is an <u>annual</u> event.
    What does the word *annual* mean?
    - Ⓐ exciting
    - Ⓑ traditional
    - Ⓒ funny
    - **Ⓓ yearly**

16. More than 15 <u>vehicles</u> entered the race.
    What does the word *vehicle* mean?
    - **Ⓐ an object used for transportation**
    - Ⓑ a piece of furniture used at school
    - Ⓒ an item worn to cover the body
    - Ⓓ a person who can drive a car

17. I'm not trying to <u>pressure</u> you to buy this car.
    What does the word *pressure* mean?
    - Ⓐ instruct or advise
    - Ⓑ own or use
    - **Ⓒ influence or intimidate**
    - Ⓓ lift or set

18. When do you expect the awards ceremony to <u>occur</u>?
    What does the word *occur* mean?
    - **Ⓐ happen**
    - Ⓑ end
    - Ⓒ display
    - Ⓓ frighten

19. Did you eat the <u>entire</u> pie?
    What does the word *entire* mean?
    - Ⓐ apple
    - **Ⓑ whole**
    - Ⓒ common
    - Ⓓ free

---

20. Customers can order their food with <u>ease</u>.
    What does the word *ease* mean?
    - Ⓐ a feeling of hunger
    - Ⓑ a kind of mustard
    - Ⓒ a teenage employee
    - **Ⓓ a lack of difficulty**

21. What are the proper <u>methods</u> for creating a low-rider?
    What does the word *methods* mean?
    - Ⓐ auto parts
    - Ⓑ ways to pay for something; financing
    - Ⓒ steering wheels
    - **Ⓓ ways to do something; procedures**

22. Would you <u>prefer</u> a low-rider or a new car?
    What does the word *prefer* mean?
    - **Ⓐ like better**
    - Ⓑ drive faster
    - Ⓒ pay more
    - Ⓓ buy cheaper

23. They made this window with <u>recycled</u> glass.
    What does the word *recycled* mean?
    - **Ⓐ used again**
    - Ⓑ extra hard
    - Ⓒ slightly tinted
    - Ⓓ put together

24. The car's <u>capacity</u> is five people.
    What does the word *capacity* mean?
    - Ⓐ natural tendency to act
    - **Ⓑ maximum amount something can hold**
    - Ⓒ condition of being protected
    - Ⓓ strong feeling of wanting something

25. The <u>production</u> of steel is important to the car industry.
    What does the word *production* mean?
    - Ⓐ cost of designing
    - Ⓑ difficulty of selling
    - **Ⓒ act of making**
    - Ⓓ joy of buying

26. Do you get <u>impatient</u> if you have to wait in line?
    What does the word *impatient* mean?
    - Ⓐ service
    - Ⓑ relieved
    - **Ⓒ irritated**
    - Ⓓ amused

Expedition Wrap-Up

1. After students have completed the assessment, bring them together to discuss the probing questions as a way to provide closure for Expedition 11. Briefly discuss each of the Expedition articles. Then watch DVD 11.2 together as a class. Have students turn to Anthology page 185. Ask students to summarize the response to each probing question that was given on the DVD.

2. Conclude the Expedition by asking students to name something they learned about automobile technology and the American car culture that they did not know before. Then ask them to name topics or issues related to cars that they would like to know more about. Discuss with students where they could find out more about these topics. Have students record and save these topics and keep them for possible future research topics.

Strategic Online Learning Opportunities®

Session 2 — http://solo.voyagerlearning.com

Students read a passage about Alice Ramsey, who became the first woman to drive across the United States in 1909 when she drove 4,000 miles from New York to San Francisco.

Content Connection
Social Studies

Coast to Coast
by Louise Boyd James

Lexile Levels
Passage B 830L
Passage C 920L

Assessment
- Metacognition
- Content
- Vocabulary
- Main Idea
- Summary

Based on their assessment scores, students automatically are assigned either the Skills Practice for reinforcement or the Independent Practice and Extension Opportunities.

SKILLS PRACTICE

Vocabulary Strategies
- Context
- Word Parts: Prefixes and Suffixes
- Word Parts: Compound Words

Dictionary Skills

Main Idea Strategy: W–I–N
- Identifying the Most Important *Who* or *What*
- Identifying the Most Important *Information*
- Stating the Main Idea in a Small *Number* of Words

Questioning

Writing
- Responding to Texts
- Writing a Summary Statement

INDEPENDENT PRACTICE

Vocabulary Strategies

Writing
- Writing a Summary Statement
- Responding to Texts

EXTENSION OPPORTUNITIES
- Online Books
- Book Cart
- Review of Previous Passages

■ Comprehension

Reteach Skills
Text Structure Review

✔ Sequential Order	Expedition 6
✔ Compare and Contrast	Expedition 7
✔ Persuasion	Expedition 8
✔ Cause and Effect	Expedition 9
✔ Problem/Solution	Expedition 10

Before Reading

Text Structures

1. On the board, write *Expository Texts* and underline it. Under this, write and bullet: *Sequential Order*, *Compare and Contrast*, *Persuasion*, *Cause and Effect*, and *Problem/Solution*.

2. **What is an expository text?** (a text that gives information about a subject) **Expository texts can come in a variety of forms, and are written for a variety of purposes.**

   - **Expository texts might give the order of events or tell steps in a process. This text would be written in *sequential order*.**

   - **Others might tell how two things are alike and different. What kind of text would this be?** (compare-and-contrast)

   - Point to the remaining three text structures on the board. **What would a persuasive expository text do?** (try to convince the reader to do or believe something) **What would a cause-and-effect text do?** (explain how one event leads to another) **What would a problem/solution text do?** (identify a problem and one or more ways of solving it)

3. **Let's say we wanted to write a text that gave information about buying a car. If our text was titled "How to Buy Your Dream Car in Three Easy Steps," what kind of text would it most likely be?** (sequential order)

4. Have students provide possible titles for each of the remaining text structures. Provide correction and feedback as needed. Write these titles on the board.

Reading for Understanding

1. Have students turn to Anthology page 201. **Some expository texts include elements of more than one kind of text structure. As we read this text, let's try to decide what kind of text structure—or structures—the author uses.**

2. Read aloud the first paragraph of the article, then have students read the remainder of the article aloud with you.

After Reading

Text Structures: Sequential Order and Compare-and-Contrast

1. Distribute copies of Reteach page 21. Read the instructions and the question aloud.

   - When students identify the text as compare-and-contrast, have them locate common compare-and-contrast signal words in the text. (paragraph 1—*different*, *by contrast*, *unlike*; paragraph 6—*by comparison*)

   - Guide students to conclude that the article compares and contrasts "car culture" before and after World War II, and that it describes events from these time periods in sequential order.

2. Have students fill in the chart. Then have them complete section 2. Call on students to share their sentences.

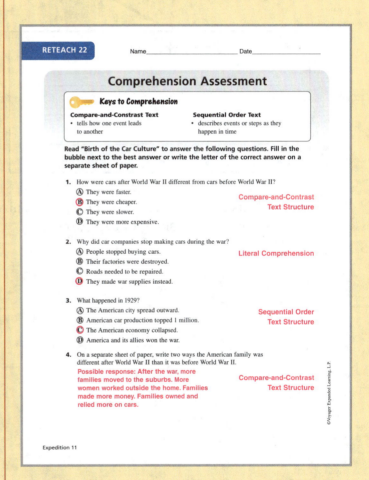

Checking for Comprehension

1. Distribute copies of Reteach page 22. Then have students turn to "Birth of the Car Culture" on Anthology page 201. Explain to students that they will read this text before answering the questions on Reteach page 22.

2. Read aloud the Keys to Comprehension section and the assessment instructions. Then have students complete the assessment independently.

3. Review the correct answers and discuss any questions that students answered incorrectly.

Extra Support

Text Structures

If students need additional support, write the following titles on strips of paper: *How to Build Your Own Car; A Brief History of Things with Wheels; What Causes Tires to Squeal When You "Burn Rubber"?; Why We Should Have Drive-Through School; If You Need a Date, Buy This Car;* and *The Pedal-Car vs. the Paddle Boat: Which Is Faster?* On another set of strips, write the text structures students have learned. Then have students work to match each title with the appropriate text structure. When students have made all their matches, ask them to explain their thinking aloud.

■ Vocabulary

1. Write on the board the specific words students have missed. Guide students in writing an example and a non-example of each of the words by placing a graphic organizer such as the following on the board.

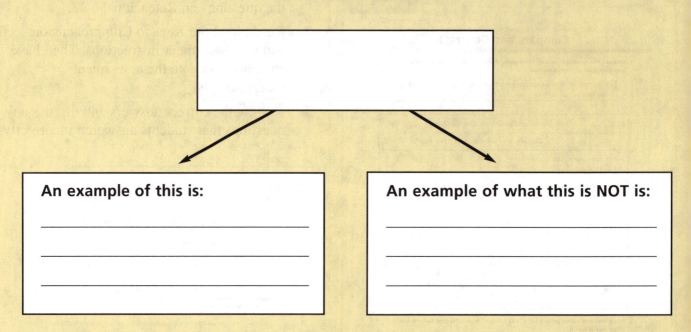

An example of this is:

_____

_____

_____

An example of what this is NOT is:

_____

_____

_____

2. When students have completed the graphic organizer, check comprehension by having them write in their own words the meaning of each word.

■ Multiparagraph Writing

Teach and Model

1. **You have learned to write many kinds of expository paragraphs: paragraphs that describe, paragraphs that compare and contrast, and paragraphs that persuade. Each of these paragraphs is an essay. An** *essay* **is a written work that expresses a writer's personal view or opinion. Some essays are longer than a single paragraph. Longer essays are called** *multiparagraph essays*. **Multiparagraph essays are not simply paragraphs stacked on top of each other like blocks. The paragraphs in these essays all relate to the idea expressed in the topic sentence or opinion statement. This idea is like a nail that connects the blocks. In this lesson, you'll learn to write a multiparagraph essay that is persuasive. Your essay will have five paragraphs. The nail that connects the paragraphs of your essay will be your opinion statement.**

2. Write *Persuasive Paragraph* as a heading on the board. **Let's review what we know about persuasive writing. What is the purpose of a persuasive paragraph?** (to convince the reader to think a certain way or to do something in particular) **Remember the four elements in a persuasive paragraph: the opinion statement, the supporting reasons, the counterargument, and the conclusion.**

Anthology Connection

Review the topic of "car culture" by revisiting the reading selections from Expedition 11. Pay special attention to the following passages:

"A Fast Argument"

"Service to Go"

"You *Need* This Car"

"How to Sweeten Your Ride"

Next, list the following text structures on the board: sequential order, compare and contrast, cause and effect, problem/solution, and persuasion. Ask students to list three or four aspects of car culture they have read about. Then have them take turns reading one of the items aloud to a partner, along with one of the text structures. The partner should then provide a sentence about that aspect of car culture that reflects the text structure. For example, if the first student says *race-car driving*, *cause and effect*, the second student might say *Not wearing the proper safety gear can lead to serious injuries*. Tell students that their sentences can be as comical or creative as they wish.

Writing Samples

1. Distribute Writing page 34 to students. **This persuasive paragraph argues to lower the driving age to 14.** Read Passage 1 aloud to students. **What is the opinion statement in the paragraph?** (I believe that the driving age should be lowered to 14.)

2. **What reasons does the writer give to support the opinion statement?** (Kids are more mature these days. Lowering the driving age would save grownups money. Letting 14-year-olds drive would make the streets safer.)

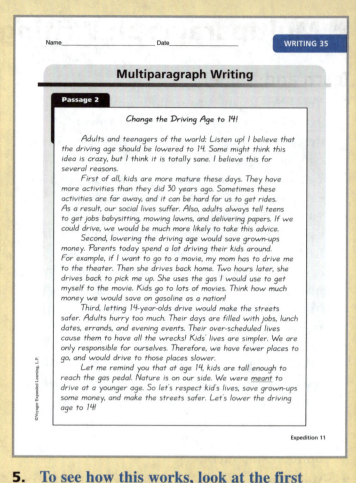

WRITING 34

Name_____ Date_____

Multiparagraph Writing

Passage 1

Change the Driving Age to 14!

I believe that the driving age should be lowered to 14. I believe this for several reasons. First of all, kids are more mature these days than they used to be. They have more activities to go to than they did 30 years ago. Second, this would save grown-ups money, because parents spend a lot of extra money driving their kids around. Third, this would make the streets safer. Adults are in too much of a hurry. They're the ones having all the wrecks! In conclusion, I'd like to remind you that at age 14, kids are tall enough to reach the gas pedal. Nature is on our side. Lower the driving age to 14!

Expedition 11

©Voyager Expanded Learning, L.P.

3. **What is the writer's conclusion?** (Since kids can reach the gas pedal at 14, nature is on their side. We should raise the driving age to 14.)

4. Distribute Writing page 35 to students, and read Passage 2 aloud. **This multiparagraph essay makes the same persuasive argument about lowering the driving age that you read in Passage 1. It also contains the same opinion statement and reasons that are in Passage 1. In Passage 2, the writer added elaboration to each reason by using specific details and personal observations to give the reader more information. In Passage 2, each reason from Passage 1 is expanded into its own paragraph.**

Name_____ Date_____

WRITING 35

Multiparagraph Writing

Passage 2

Change the Driving Age to 14!

Adults and teenagers of the world: Listen up! I believe that the driving age should be lowered to 14. Some might think this idea is crazy, but I think it is totally sane. I believe this for several reasons.

First of all, kids are more mature these days. They have more activities than they did 30 years ago. Sometimes these activities are far away, and it can be hard for us to get rides. As a result, our social lives suffer. Also, adults always tell teens to get jobs babysitting, mowing lawns, and delivering papers. If we could drive, we would be much more likely to take this advice.

Second, lowering the driving age would save grown-ups money. Parents today spend a lot driving their kids around. For example, if I want to go to a movie, my mom has to drive me to the theater. Then she drives back home. Two hours later, she drives back to pick me up. She uses the gas I would use to get myself to the movie. Kids go to lots of movies. Think how much money we would save on gasoline as a nation!

Third, letting 14-year-olds drive would make the streets safer. Adults hurry too much. Their days are filled with jobs, lunch dates, errands, and evening events. Their over-scheduled lives cause them to have all the wrecks! Kids' lives are simpler. We are only responsible for ourselves. Therefore, we have fewer places to go, and would drive to those places slower.

Let me remind you that at age 14, kids are tall enough to reach the gas pedal. Nature is on our side. We were _meant_ to drive at a younger age. So let's respect kid's lives, save grown-ups some money, and make the streets safer. Let's lower the driving age to 14!

Expedition 11

©Voyager Expanded Learning, L.P.

5. **To see how this works, look at the first sentence in Passage 1. Which element of persuasive writing is this?** (the opinion statement) **Where in Passage 2 do you see this sentence?** (the second sentence) **Passages 1 and 2 are based on the same opinion statement. But in Passage 2, the writer begins the essay with a call to adults and kids alike. These starting sentences get the reader's attention. Then, the writer gives the opinion statement. Next, the writer acknowledges that this idea might sound crazy but says that there are three reasons why it makes sense. All these pieces together make up the introduction to the essay.**

6. Read the third sentence in Passage 1 aloud. **This is the first reason that supports the opinion statement in this paragraph.** Have students find a similar sentence in Passage 2. Read the first sentence of the second paragraph aloud. **This is also the first reason that supports the opinion statement, but here it is the main idea of the second paragraph. The writer added elaboration to this reason to make a full paragraph.** Read the remaining sentences in the paragraph. **What details or personal observations did the writer add about the idea that kids are more mature these days?** (Sometimes these activities are far away, and it can be hard for us to get rides. As a result, our social lives suffer. Also, adults are always telling teens to get jobs babysitting, mowing lawns, and delivering papers. If we could drive, we would be much more likely to take this advice.)

7. Read the fifth sentence in Passage 1 aloud. **This sentence tells the writer's second reason. Where do you see this sentence in Passage 2?** (beginning of paragraph 3) **What details and personal observations are used in Passage 2 to add elaboration to the idea that dancing is a great form of exercise?** (For example, if I want to go to a movie, my mom has to drive me to the theater. Then she drives back home. Two hours later, she drives back to the theater to pick me up. She is using twice the gas I would use to get myself to the movie. Kids go to lots of movies. Think how much money we would save on gasoline as a nation!)

8. Read the sixth sentence in Passage 1 aloud. Point out that this is the writer's third reason, then have students identify the same reason and its elaboration in paragraph 4 of Passage 2. (Their days are filled with jobs, lunch dates, errands, and evening events. Because of their over-scheduled lives, they're the ones having all the wrecks! Kids' lives are simpler. We are only responsible for ourselves. Therefore, we have fewer places to go, and would drive to those places slower.)

9. **What is the conclusion of Passage 1?** (In conclusion, I'd like to remind you that at age 14, kids are tall enough to reach the gas pedal. Nature is on our side. Lower the driving age to 14!) **Now let's read the conclusion in Passage 2.** Read the conclusion aloud. **Here, the writer doesn't have to say "in conclusion." The fact that this is the last paragraph of the essay tells the reader that this is the conclusion. How else is this conclusion different from the conclusion in Passage 1?** (It elaborates on the nature idea. It briefly restates the first three reasons. Finally, it restates the opinion statement, but in a different way.)

Guided Practice

1. Distribute Writing page 36 to students. **Now we'll work together to start writing a multiparagraph persuasive essay. First, we'll plan the essay.** Write *PLAN* on the board vertically, leaving space between the letters. **To plan the essay, we will use the four PLAN steps that we learned earlier. The first step is** *Pay attention to the prompt*. Write it on the board next to the *P*. **The second step is** *List ideas*. Write this on the board next to the *L*. **The third step is** *Add elaboration.*, **and the fourth step is** *Number your ideas*. Add these to the board.

2. **To pay attention to a prompt, you need to read it.** Invite a student to read the prompt aloud. **Next, underline once what you are being asked to write about. What does this prompt ask you to write about?** (raising money) Have students draw one line under *how students can raise money* on their prompts. **Finally, underline twice the kind of writing you are asked to do. What kind of writing does this prompt ask for?** (a persuasive letter) Have students draw two lines under *persuasive letter*.

WRITING 36

Name_____ Date_____

Multiparagraph Writing

Read the prompt below. Write an opinion statement that responds to the prompt. Use the graphic organizer to start planning your writing. List three reasons that support your opinion statement. Add elaboration to support each reason.

Prompt: The student council is trying to decide how students can raise money for the school. They are considering a car wash or a bake sale. Write a persuasive letter to the school paper taking a side and giving your opinion on this issue.

Supporting Reason:
_____
_____

Elaboration:
• _____
• _____

Supporting Reason:
_____
_____

Elaboration:
• _____
• _____

Supporting Reason:
_____
_____

Elaboration:
• _____
• _____

©Voyager Expanded Learning, L.P.

Expedition 11

3. **Now let's talk about the next step in planning an essay: listing ideas. A good way to get started with this step is to brainstorm as many responses to the prompt as you can think of. Then choose the one you like best.** Discuss with students possible responses to the prompt. Ask questions to spur discussion: **Would you rather wash cars or sell baked goods? Why? Which activity would raise more money? Why do you think so?**

4. **Let's choose one of these ideas as our opinion statement. You remember that an opinion statement may start with *I believe* or *In my opinion*.** Help students formulate an opinion statement and write it on the board. (Possible response: I believe that students should hold a car wash to raise money for the school.) Read the instructions at the top of page Writing page 36. Have students copy the opinion statement from the board onto their graphic organizers.

5. **We have our opinion statement. Let's think of three reasons that would convince the reader to agree with it. As we brainstorm our ideas, think about which reasons make strong arguments.** Guide students as they think of three reasons to support the opinion statement. Help them choose the three most convincing reasons. Write the reasons they choose on the board in boxes labeled *Supporting Reason*. Have students copy the sentences on their graphic organizers. (Possible responses: A car wash would appeal to more people. More students know how to wash cars. Car washing can be a form of exercise.)

6. Have partners work together. Direct their attention to the *A* in *PLAN*. **The next step of planning an essay is to add elaboration. How could you add elaboration to the two reasons we listed?** (by adding details and/or personal observations that support the ideas) **List two supporting details or observations for each reason listed on the graphic organizer.** Have students add supporting details and observations to their graphic organizers. Monitor students as they work, and provide correction and feedback as needed.

7. Direct students' attention to the *N* in *PLAN*. **The last step of planning an essay is to number your reasons. To complete this step, decide which of the two reasons is most important to your argument. Put a *1* by this reason. Then decide which is second most important, and which is third most important. Number these reasons *2* and *3*. When you write your essay, you will write the reasons in that order.**

8. Have students come together as a class. Read aloud the first reason on the board and the graphic organizer. Have students share the details and observations they listed to elaborate the reason. Write their responses on the board. Repeat for the second and third reasons. Discuss which reason students decided was most important and why they chose their order. Make sure students understand that no one way is better to order the reasons.

9. Review students' graphic organizers to ensure that they understood the lesson and completed the graphic organizer.

Independent Practice

1. Distribute Writing pages 37 and 38 to students. **This is a frame for writing a multiparagraph persuasive essay. You will use this frame for writing your essays about the school fund-raiser. The frame has words that will help you connect the sentences and paragraphs in your essay.**

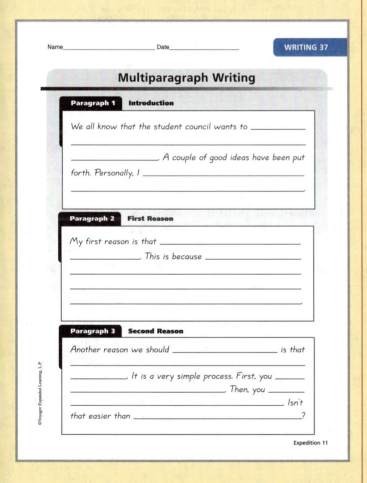

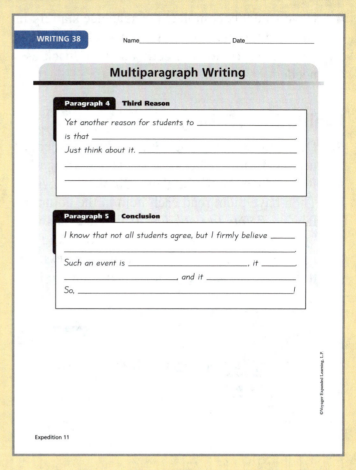

2. Direct students' attention to the graphic organizer on Writing page 36. **As you work, remember to use the information you wrote on your graphic organizer. For example, your opinion statement from the graphic organizer will appear in your first paragraph.** Read the sentence starters for paragraph 1. **In which blank will it appear?** (the last one) **Where will your first reason and elaboration appear?** (the second paragraph) **Where will your second and third reasons and elaboration appear?** (the third and fourth paragraphs)

3. Read aloud the sentence starters in the concluding paragraph frame. **What will go in the first blank?** (the opinion statement) **What will go in the second blank?** (the three reasons, briefly restated) **What could go in the last blank?** (a statement that tells students what they should do)

569h

4. Have students complete the sentence starters in each paragraph frame. Monitor students as they write, and provide correction and feedback as needed.

Evaluating Writing

1. Distribute Writing page 39, and have students use the Writing Checklist to evaluate their work. Have them read their complete essays. Then have them read each item in the column labeled *Points to Look For*. If they can answer "yes" to a point, they should put a check in the first column. Have students revise their essays to improve at least one of the items on the list.

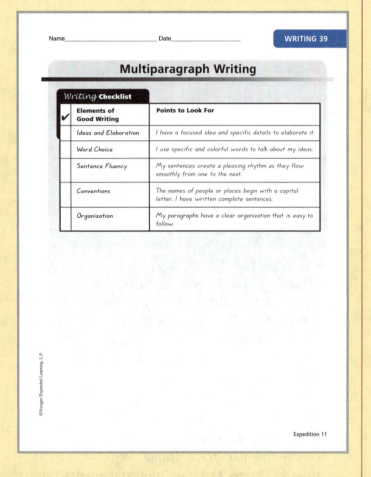

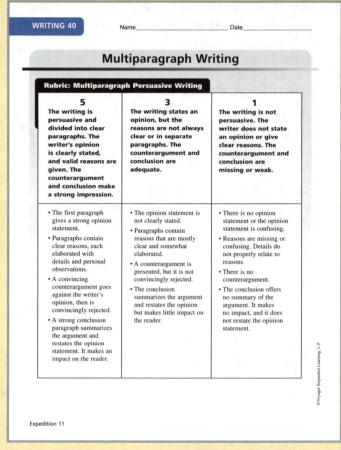

2. Distribute Writing page 40. **This rubric focuses on writing a multiparagraph persuasive essay.** Read the rubric aloud. Then have students get into pairs for peer editing. Instruct them to exchange papers, then read each other's work aloud. Students should first tell one thing the writer did well. Then students should choose a score for the paper based on the rubric on page 40. Finally, students should offer one idea for improving the paper. Remind students that they should treat each other with respect as they work together.

3. Close the lesson by reminding students that this multiparagraph essay is the foundation for many types of writing, such as writing to explain the steps in a process or writing to compare and contrast two or more things. Each of these text structures has its own unique format, but a multiparagraph essay will have the same basic elements every time: an introduction, several middle paragraphs, and a conclusion. For a how-to essay, the introduction will tell the reader what is being explained, the middle paragraphs will list and elaborate on the steps, and the conclusion will summarize the process. For a compare-and-contrast essay, the introduction will tell the reader what is being compared, the middle paragraphs will tell and elaborate on ways the things are alike and different, and the conclusion will wrap up the writer's ideas. The topics for writing change, but the structure and process remain basically the same for every topic.

Extended Writing

Using Different Text Structures to Write Multiparagraph Essays

To give students practice in writing multiparagraph essays for different purposes, use the following prompts.

- *Sequential Order:* **What is your idea of the perfect road trip? Tell what you would do first, next, and last.**

- *Compare and Contrast:* **Would you rather drive a car or a motorcycle? Why?**

- *Cause and Effect:* **You drive your little brother to school every day, but you don't wear your seat belt. What are some possible effects of this action?**

- *Problem/Solution/Effect:* **You have a car, but your friends don't. You drive them everywhere. You decide to start charging them. What are some effects of this solution?**

To help students plan their essays, use a graphic organizer like the one found on Writing page 36. Change *Supporting Reason* to *First*, *Next*, and *Last* for sequential order; *Point 1*, *Point 2*, and *Point 3* for compare and contrast; *Effect 1*, *Effect 2*, and *Effect 3* for cause and effect; and *Solution*, *Effect 1*, and *Effect 2* for problem/solution/effect. Have students follow the steps of the *PLAN* process, then use the information on the graphic organizer to write a five-paragraph essay on their own paper.

Expedition 12

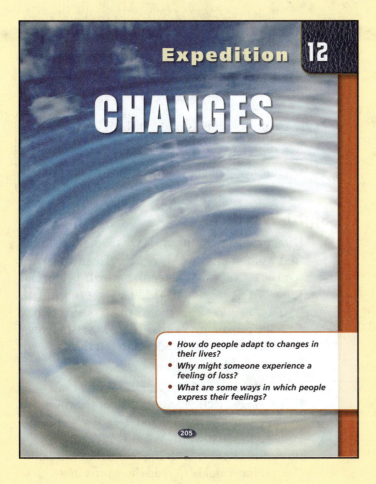

Expedition 12

CHANGES

- *How do people adapt to changes in their lives?*
- *Why might someone experience a feeling of loss?*
- *What are some ways in which people express their feelings?*

205

DVD 12.1, 12.2
In this Expedition, the DVD segments help students explore the ways in which we are all affected by changes in our lives. Students will investigate different kinds of changes that could occur and the real-life effects that could stem from them.

Strategic Online Learning Opportunities®

Students access the Web site http://solo.voyagerlearning.com for an interactive SOLO® session. In each session, students apply previously taught strategic skills to new readings on the student's appropriate Lexile® level. Consult the *Passport Reading Journeys*™ SOLO User Guide for a comprehensive overview of this component.

Passport Reading Journeys Library

Students may select reading materials from the *Passport Reading Journeys* Library. Partner and independent reading opportunities allow students to read authentic text on their Lexile level to build fluency. Teacher resources are provided in the *Passport Reading Journeys* Library Teacher's Guide.

In This Expedition

SKILLS

Elements of Description
- **Concrete Details**
- **Sensory Details**
- **Figurative Language**
- **Regional Language**

Lesson 1

Advanced Word Study

Suffixes *-ic* and *-ish*

1. Write *-ic* on the board. **This word part is a suffix. Remember, a suffix is a word part that occurs at the end of a word and often helps us understand the meaning of the word. The sounds for this suffix are /ik/. Say the sounds for this suffix.** (/ik/) Write the word *athletic* on the board. Underline the suffix *-ic*. **What is this suffix?** (-ic) **Use the sounds you know to read the rest of the word.** (athlet[e]) **What is the word?** (athletic) **The suffix *-ic* means "relating to." The word *athletic* means "relating to athletes."** Have students turn to page E12, Lesson 1, in the back of the Student Book. Direct them to line 1 in the first box. **What is the underlined suffix in the first word?** (-ic) **Read the rest of the word.** (magnet) **What is the word?** (magnetic) Repeat with the remaining words. Call on individuals to read the words in random order. Ask students to tell the meanings of the words based on the meaning of the suffix.

2. Write *-ish* on the board. **The sounds for this suffix are /ish/. Say the sounds for this suffix.** (/ish/) Write the word *bookish* on the board. Underline the suffix *-ish*. **What is this suffix?** (-ish) **Use the sounds you know to read the rest of the word.** (book) **What is the word?** (bookish) **The suffix *-ish* means "relating to." The word *bookish* means "relating to books."** Direct students to line 2. **What is the underlined suffix in the first word?** (-ish) **Read the rest of the word.** (fool) **What is the word?** (foolish) Repeat with the remaining words. Call on individuals to read the words in a different order. Ask students to tell the meanings of the words based on the meaning of the suffix.

3. Direct students to line 3. Have them read the words. Call on individuals to read the words in a different order. Ask students to tell the meanings of the words.

▼ **To Correct**
Say the correct sound(s) or prefix/suffix, then ask students to repeat the sound(s). Have them read the words again with the correct sound(s).

If students do not know the meaning of the word, review the word and/or word parts to determine the meaning of the word.

1. magne*tic*	prehistor*ic*	pathe*tic*	metal*lic*
2. fool*ish*	snobb*ish*	replen*ish*	ban*ish*
3. grouchy	picnics	rattled	selfishness

Sight Words

1. Direct students to line 1. Have them point to the first word. **This word is *cousin*. Read the word.** (cousin) **This is not a regular word. Let's read the word again.** (cousin) **Let's spell the word.** (c-o-u-s-i-n) **What is the word?** (cousin) Repeat with the remaining words. Then, have students read the words. Ask students to tell the meanings of the words.

2. Direct students to lines 2 and 3. **Let's read these words.** Remind students that the rows of words consist of regular and irregular words. Point to the first word. **What is the word?** (insignias) Repeat with the remaining words. Call on individuals to read the words in a different order. Ask students to tell the meanings of the words.

▼ **To Correct**
For Regular Words: Say the sound(s) in the word, then ask students to repeat the sound(s). Have them read the word again with the correct sound(s). If students do not know the meaning of the word, review the word and/or word part to determine the meaning of the word.

For Irregular Words: Immediately say the correct word. Then have students read the word, spell it, and read it again. If students do not know the meaning of the word, review the word.

1. cousin I	quiet I	stomach I	videos I
2. insignias I	geometric I	irritated R	tough I
3. hydraulic I	memorized R	interior I	favorite I

Anthology Selection

Expedition 12

CHANGES

- How do people adapt to changes in their lives?
- Why might someone experience a feeling of loss?
- What are some ways in which people express their feelings?

205

Expedition 12, Lessons 1 and 2

Long Distance Love

206

Expedition 12, Lessons 1 and 2

Dear Gaby,

¹I can't believe you've only been gone for two weeks. Time has been dragging by since you left. So how's the big city? Full of interesting people and cool things to do, right? If I had super powers, I would **transform** this dull town into a place like that. Then maybe I wouldn't die of boredom.

²Speaking of boredom, I'm in study hall now. Coach Barnes is reading the paper, Jamal is sitting next to me snoring, and the clock is ticking so loud it's driving me nuts. Of course, since you left, everything about this place seems to bug me. It bugs me how the same old gang hangs out at the Frostee Freeze waiting for somebody to drive down Main, honking their car horn. Then everyone hollers and struts and puts on the same old show. It bugs me to flip through the lame collection of CDs at Frank's so-called music store. How about a little salsa or some hip-hop? And if I really want to get irritated, there's always our famous video store. I've memorized the *Die Hard* movies, and the rest of their selection stinks. I'm not going back there until they get some videos from this century.

³You can probably tell that missing you makes me pretty grouchy. Like yesterday when Uncle Carlos was helping me put new wheels on my skateboard, the drill slipped and he dinged the finish. I yelled and got really mad. You should've seen the look on my uncle's face. It was like I had punched him in the stomach. I felt like the lowest worm on Earth, so I got on my board and went riding down where the pavement is really rough. It rattled my whole body, but I couldn't shake the bad feelings. I rode out of town to Boot Hill and hiked up to that grassy spot under the trees that we like. That was a foolish move because the place was too quiet and lonely without you. I got depressed looking down at the town. I started thinking, "This is my prison, and I'm stuck here where nothing interesting will ever happen."

⁴I know it's a long way off, but my only way out is to get my driver's license and then get **access** to some wheels. I'm going to buy my cousin's truck, paint it black, and then put bright chrome wheels and really fat tires on it. I'll put in a sound system that will send the beat right through you too. When it's all fixed up, I'll come get you. So don't find anyone else before then. Promise?

Love, Mario

207

Expedition 12, Lessons 1 and 2

Dear Mario,

⁵I can't believe I haven't seen you for two whole weeks. It seems strange to think I really live here now. I keep thinking I'll wake up and be back in my old room with my friends and my old life and YOU! You can't imagine how much I miss everyone at Valley High. My new school is about five times bigger than Valley. There are so many kids that I don't see any of the same people twice in one day. Each class is a whole different group. I don't think I'll ever make friends. Back home I had a lot of **confidence**, but here I feel like such an outsider. I just act shy and keep to myself.

⁶Thinking of home makes a big lump swell up in my throat, then the tears just come spilling out. I never realized how lucky I was to have a whole **network** of friends and relatives around. It made me feel like I belonged— you know, like I mattered. I really miss that. Sometimes I just lie on my bed and daydream about being back home, doing familiar things and seeing familiar people. I picture myself riding through town with my cousins in the afternoons, and I can just hear the gang at the Frostee Freeze calling out and trying to get us to stop. Everybody on the street honks and waves at us like we're somebody. Here, when I walk down the street, I might as well be invisible.

⁷I love to imagine going downtown with you to all our favorite places— the park, the Frostee Freeze, the video store, and of course Frank's. It was so much fun joking with Frank about his ancient rock-and-roll CDs, the ones you called prehistoric. Is he still promising to order some salsa for you? Let me know if there's a **specific** CD you want, and I'll send it to you. There's a monster music store near here with the biggest **variety** of music in the city. It's two stories high and has glass booths where you can listen to CDs before buying them. I feel kind of lost in there, but they're sure to have any CD you want.

⁸It's getting late so I'd better stop and do my homework. I'd give anything to be at our spot on the hill watching the lights come on in town and enjoying the quiet. Please wait for me, and don't take anyone else to our special place. I'm trying to convince my parents to let me come back and live with relatives.

Love, Gaby

208

573

Comprehension and Vocabulary *Before Reading*

Introduce the Expedition

1. Have students imagine they are making a video tour of your town or community. Ask them to close their eyes and picture one or two places they would film. Have them think carefully about the sights and sounds the video camera would record there. Explain that even the smallest detail is important. Then have students open their eyes and take several minutes to write down everything they remember from their "mental video."

2. Call on three or four individuals to read aloud what they have written. As they read, write on the board each student's name and some of the details they report.

3. **In this Expedition you will explore descriptions of places and people. The way people feel when things happen to them can bring out rich images also. Think of a time when something happened to you that brought about big changes. How could you explain the way you felt when this happened?** (Accept reasonable responses.)

4. Have students turn to Anthology page 205. Read the title of the Expedition. Then call on individuals to read aloud each probing question.

   - **How do people adapt to changes in their lives?**
   - **Why might someone experience a feeling of loss?**
   - **What are some ways in which people express their feelings?**

5. Tell students that they will return to these questions as they learn more about life changes. Show DVD 12.1.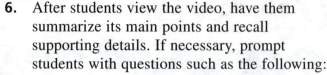

6. After students view the video, have them summarize its main points and recall supporting details. If necessary, prompt students with questions such as the following:
   - **What main message were the people in this video trying to communicate?**
   - **What did they have to say about ____?**
   - **What parts of the video helped illustrate or support this idea?**

Introduce Vocabulary

Vocabulary

Review Words

transform	*to change completely*
access	*the ability or right to enter a place or use something*
confidence	*feeling sure of yourself*
network	*a group of people or things that are connected in some way*
specific	*clearly described or explained*
variety	*a collection of different kinds*

Challenge Words

Word Meaning

irritate	*to annoy someone*
	Terrance's favorite thing to do is to irritate me with his whistling.

Word Building

prehistoric	*history, prehistory, historical, historically, historian*

7. **Lesson 1's reading, "Long Distance Love," contains words with meanings we have already learned. We will review these words within the text we are reading.**

8. Write each Review Word on the board. Then ask students to locate the word in the letters. Instruct them to read aloud the sentence containing the word, as well as any other sentences that provide context.
   - **What can you tell me about the word?**
   - Ask other questions that allow students to explore the word's meaning. (For example: **How can you relate the way *network* is used in the passage to a television network? What is the opposite of *confidence*?**)

574

9. Ask students to respond to the following questions. Provide correction and feedback as necessary.
   - **What are some things people do to *transform* their appearance?**
   - **What would someone need in order to get *access* to your locker?**
   - **Which takes more *confidence*—performing on stage or performing in front of a mirror? Why?**
   - **Would you like to have a large *network* of friends? Why?**
   - **Which names a *specific* dessert—sweets or sundae?**
   - **Which offers more *variety*—a supermarket or a convenience store? Why?**

10. Work with students to write a definition for each word on the board.

11. Include the Challenge Words to meet the needs of students who are advancing.

Introduce Elements of Description: Concrete Details

12. **When we took our "mental tour" of local places, you might have had a hard time thinking of specific sights or sounds. You were trying to pinpoint details about things and people that you see every day—and it can be difficult to see very familiar things with new eyes. This is what authors must do when they are writing descriptive texts.**

13. Write and underline *Descriptive Text* on the board. **Descriptive text is writing that describes, or tells how something looked, sounded, moved, or felt.** Under *Descriptive Text*, write *1. Details*. **Details are the main ingredients of descriptive writing. They are the many small pieces of information that help readers picture a scene in their mind. If you think about descriptive writing as a jigsaw puzzle, you could say that each detail is one of the unique little pieces that helps create a clear and interesting picture.**

14. Return students' attention to one of the details listed on the board, and follow the steps below using that detail. Alternatively, write the following detail on the board, and use it: *Sometimes there are people hanging out at the park.*
   - **This detail gives me some information about a place in our community. But the detail isn't very specific. It wouldn't give a reader enough information to picture the place.**
   - Underline *Sometimes*. **For example, this word is very vague. In descriptive writing, an author might make this part of the detail more concrete, or specific. He or she might say *On sunny weekends* instead of *Sometimes*.** Write *On sunny weekends* above *Sometimes*.
   - Underline *people*. **This word isn't very specific.** *People* **could mean 2-year-olds or 65-year-olds. Think about one particular group of people you see at the park. If we were writing a description, we might say *elderly people*, *young children*, or *groups of teenagers* to help the reader picture them.** Write *young children* above *people*. **I can add a little more description to help the reader picture these children. I might describe them as *loud* or *rowdy*. Which word is more specific and lively—*loud* or *rowdy*?** (rowdy) Insert *rowdy* before *young children*.
   - Underline *hanging out*. **I think that young children do much more at the park than "hang out." For example, I might say that they're *playing* or *swarming on the jungle gym*. Which word creates a more vivid picture in your mind—*playing* or *swarming*?** (swarming) Write *On sunny weekends, there are rowdy young children swarming on the jungle gym at the park.*
   - **This detailed description is much more concrete, or specific, than the original one. It is also more vivid, or clear and distinct. If it were in a story I was reading, I would be able to picture what was going on. I would be able to hear and see the scene just as it was in the author's mind.**

15. Write and bullet *Concrete* on the board under *Details*. **As we read the texts, try to see through the authors' eyes. Look for details that are concrete, or specific, and vivid— details that bring each scene to life.**

(ELL) To support English language learners as they brainstorm their background knowledge on a topic, use a graphic organizer such as this one.

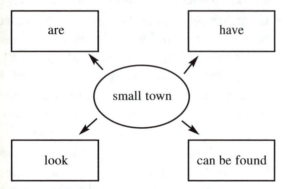

Ask students to tell you what they already know about the topic by using the four quadrants of the graphic organizer as prompts. Record students' oral responses next to each section of the graphic organizer.

For a complete model of this strategy, see Expedition 11, Lesson 1.

Reading for Understanding   *Reading*

Places and Names to Look For:
- Gaby
- Mario
- Frostee Freeze
- Boot Hill
- Valley High

1. **As you read these texts, you may come across some unfamiliar places and names.**
- Write the words on the board.
- Point to each word as you read the following:

You will read the words of two teenagers in love. The girl, *Gaby*, has recently moved to a big city, while her boyfriend, *Mario*, remains behind in their small hometown. In their letters, the two share memories about familiar places like the local burger joint called the *Frostee Freeze* and a hill outside of town called *Boot Hill*. Gaby tells how her new school is different from *Valley High*, the hometown school that Mario still attends.
- Call on individuals to read the words.

2. **As we read this text, remember to watch for concrete, vivid details.**

3. Read the first paragraph of the article aloud with students. **What kind of text is this?** (a letter) **How can you tell?** (It starts with *Dear Gaby*. It directly addresses Gaby.)

4. [Fluency] Have students read the remainder of the article with a partner, taking turns after paragraphs. If necessary, review the following fluency correction procedure with students to ensure accuracy: **Offer help when your partner comes to an unfamiliar word or makes a reading error. Pause, then say, "That word is _____. Let's read it again."** As students read, monitor for reading rate, accuracy, and expression.

5. When students have completed their reading, check for literal comprehension of the text by asking these questions: **KNOWLEDGE**

- *Paragraphs 1 and 2:* **Why are Gaby and Mario separated?** (Gaby has just moved to the big city from her small hometown.) **How long has she been gone?** (2 weeks)

- *Paragraphs 2 and 3:* **How does Mario feel about their hometown? Why?** (Possible response: He doesn't like it, and everything seems boring. Things seem dull because Gabby's not there, and he imagines that things in the big city must be more exciting for her.)

- *Paragraph 3:* **What made Mario so mad that he went out to Boot Hill?** (His uncle accidentally put a ding in the finish of Mario's skateboard.)

- *Paragraph 5:* **How is Gaby's new school different from Valley High?** (It is much bigger. There are different kids in every class.)

- *Paragraphs 6 and 7:* **How does Gaby feel about their hometown? Why?** (Possible response: She likes it and feels homesick. She feels like an outsider in the big city, so she misses the familiar people and places in her hometown. She only remembers the good things.)

Checking for Comprehension *After Reading*

1. Have students apply what they understood from the text by asking the following questions:

- **Do you think writing letters to each other makes Mario and Gaby feel better, or worse? Why?** **ANALYSIS** (Responses will vary.)

- **Why do you think Mario refers to the special spot on Boot Hill as "a prison"?** **ANALYSIS** (because it makes him feel trapped in his loneliness)

- **What do you predict will happen to Gaby over the next few months? Why?** **SYNTHESIS** (Possible response: She will make new friends because there are many kids at her new school and there are bound to be some that she likes. She will stop missing Mario so much.)

2. **Challenge Questions** **Have you ever moved to a new city or school, or have you ever been forced to have a "long-distance friendship"? If so, how did you feel? Based on this experience, what advice would you give to Gaby?** **EVALUATION** (Responses will vary.)

Extending Vocabulary

Synonyms

- **Remember that synonyms are words that have similar—but not exactly the same— meanings.**

- **When writers are trying to make details vivid and concrete, they think carefully about synonyms.** Direct students' attention to the fifth sentence of paragraph 1 (*I would transform . . . place like that.*). Write the word *dull* on the board, and ask students to think of some synonyms for this word. (Possible responses: uninteresting, boring, monotonous, tedious, dreary) Write these on the board. **In your opinion, did Mario choose the best word in this case? Or do you think one of the other synonyms creates a stronger statement about how Mario sees the town?** (Responses will vary.)

- Direct students' attention to the fifth sentence of paragraph 2 in the first letter (*Then everyone hollers and struts and puts on the same old show.*). Read the sentence aloud. Write *struts* on the board. **The word *struts* has several synonyms. One of them is *walks*.** Write *walks* under *struts*. **What are some other synonyms for the word *struts*?** (Possible responses: swagger, prance, march, move) **Mario might have used any of these synonyms.** Reread the sentence. **Why do you think he chose *struts*?** (Possible response: because it helps the reader imagine his friends moving with a cocky attitude to get attention) ***Struts* is a strong word. It is a word that you really notice when you come across it. It helps the reader see exactly what was going on. It brings the scene to life.**

- Guide students to identify and evaluate synonyms for some or all of the following words from the selection: *bug* (paragraph 2), *grouchy* (paragraph 3), *mad* (paragraph 3), *quiet* (paragraph 3), *strange* (paragraph 5), *shy* (paragraph 5), *calling out* (paragraph 6), and *convince* (paragraph 8).

- Have students share some of their synonyms with the class. Write students' responses on the board.

Lesson 2

Anthology Selection

Expedition 12, Lessons 1 and 2

Long Distance Love

Dear Gaby,

¹I can't believe you've only been gone for two weeks. Time has been dragging by since you left. So how's the big city? Full of interesting people and cool things to do, right? If I had super powers, I would **transform** this dull town into a place like that. Then maybe I wouldn't die of boredom.

²Speaking of boredom, I'm in study hall now. Coach Barnes is reading the paper, Jamal is sitting next to me snoring, and the clock is ticking so loud it's driving me nuts. Of course, since you left, everything about this place seems to bug me. It bugs me how the same old gang hangs out at the Frostee Freeze waiting for somebody to drive down Main, honking their car horn. Then everyone hollers and struts and puts on the same old show. It bugs me to flip through the lame collection of CDs at Frank's so-called music store. How about a little salsa or some hip-hop? And if I really want to get irritated, there's always our famous video store. I've memorized the *Die Hard* movies, and the rest of their selection stinks. I'm not going back there until they get some videos from this century.

³You can probably tell that missing you makes me pretty grouchy. Like yesterday when Uncle Carlos was helping me put new wheels on my skateboard, the drill slipped and he dinged the finish. I yelled and got really mad. You should've seen the look on my uncle's face. It was like I had punched him in the stomach. I felt like the lowest worm on Earth, so I got on my board and went riding down where the pavement is really rough. It rattled my whole body, but I couldn't shake the bad feelings. I rode out of town to Boot Hill and hiked up to that grassy spot under the trees that we like. That was a foolish move because the place was too quiet and lonely without you. I got depressed looking down at the town. I started thinking, "This is my prison, and I'm stuck here where nothing interesting will ever happen."

⁴I know it's a long way off, but my only way out is to get my driver's license and then get **access** to some wheels. I'm going to buy my cousin's truck, paint it black, and then put bright chrome wheels and really fat tires on it. I'll put in a sound system that will send the beat right through you too. When it's all fixed up, I'll come get you. So don't find anyone else before then. Promise?

Love, Mario

207

Expedition 12, Lessons 1 and 2

Dear Mario,

⁵I can't believe I haven't seen you for two whole weeks. It seems strange to think I really live here now. I keep thinking I'll wake up and be back in my old room with my friends and my old life and YOU! You can't imagine how much I miss everyone at Valley High. My new school is about five times bigger than Valley. There are so many kids that I don't see any of the same people twice in one day. Each class is a whole different group. I don't think I'll ever make friends. Back home I had a lot of **confidence**, but here I feel like such an outsider. I just act shy and keep to myself.

⁶Thinking of home makes a big lump swell up in my throat, then the tears just come spilling out. I never realized how lucky I was to have a whole **network** of friends and relatives around. It made me feel like I belonged—you know, like I mattered. I really miss that. Sometimes I just lie on my bed and daydream about being back home, doing familiar things and seeing familiar people. I picture myself riding through town with my cousins in the afternoons, and I can just hear the gang at the Frostee Freeze calling out and trying to get us to stop. Everybody on the street honks and waves at us like we're somebody. Here, when I walk down the street, I might as well be invisible.

⁷I love to imagine going downtown with you to all our favorite places—the park, the Frostee Freeze, the video store, and of course Frank's. It was so much fun joking with Frank about his ancient rock-and-roll CDs, the ones you called prehistoric. Is he still promising to order some salsa for you? Let me know if there's a **specific** CD you want, and I'll send it to you. There's a monster music store near here with the biggest **variety** of music in the city. It's two stories high and has glass booths where you can listen to CDs before buying them. I feel kind of lost in there, but they're sure to have any CD you want.

⁸It's getting late so I'd better stop and do my homework. I'd give anything to be at our spot on the hill watching the lights come on in town and enjoying the quiet. Please wait for me, and don't take anyone else to our special place. I'm trying to convince my parents to let me come back and live with relatives.

Love, Gaby

208

579

Comprehension and Vocabulary   *Before Reading*

1. **In Lesson 1, we read about two teenagers named Gaby and Mario.**

   • **What kind of place had Gaby recently left?** (her hometown, a small town) **What was Mario's connection to that place?** (It was his hometown, too, and he stayed behind when Gaby moved.) Write *hometown* on the board. Under it, write the two column heads: *Mario* and *Gaby*.

   • **Imagine that you are Mario. What words might you use to describe your hometown?** (Possible responses: boring, predictable, lame, dull, awful, old-fashioned, behind-the-times) Write some of these descriptive words on the board.

   • **Now imagine that you are Gaby reminiscing about her hometown. What words might you use to describe your hometown?** (Possible responses: fun, familiar, friendly, wonderful, close-knit, caring) Write some of these words on the board.

   • **How is it possible that two people can use such different words to describe the same town?** (Each experiences the town differently. They each see things differently.)

2. **In this lesson, we will reread Mario's and Gaby's letters. We'll take a closer look at how each teenager describes his or her hometown.**

Vocabulary Review

3. Arrange students with partners, and have them turn to Student Book page 154. Ask students to read the vocabulary words listed in the box. Call on individuals to tell what each word means.

4. Read aloud the instructions for section 1 of the Vocabulary Practice activity. **Strong words are words that you notice when you are reading. They are unusual or startling. They bring a scene or a detail to life. Weak words, on the other hand, are words you might not notice**

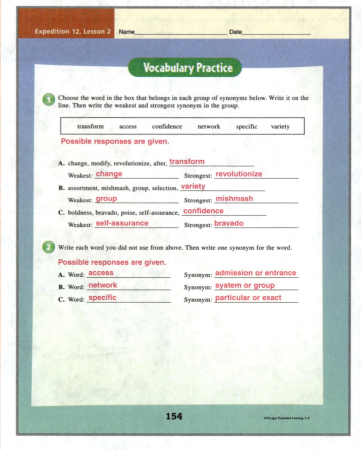

at all. Weak words are used more commonly. They are not very original or specific.**

5. Model the first item for students.

   • Read the group of words aloud. **I'll look back at the words in the box to find a word with a similar meaning. *Change* is not a synonym for *access* because *access* means "permission to use or view something." *Change* isn't a synonym for *confidence* or *network*, either, because *confidence* is "a feeling of being unafraid" and *network* means "people or things that are connected." *Change* doesn't match the meaning of *specific*, which is "relating to a particular one." But *transform* means "to change." This definitely matches the meanings of *change, modify, revolutionize*, and *alter*. *Transform* is the word that belongs here. Let's write it on the line.**

   • **Even though these words all mean about the same, some are stronger than others. Some are more vivid and lively. In my mind, *revolutionize* is the liveliest. It means** to change so drastically that it's like a revolution. I would notice this word if I came across it in my reading. Let's write it down as the strongest word.

- The other synonyms are weaker. A person might not even notice some of them when reading. The word *change* is pretty common. It gets used all the time. It's not very lively. I think it's the weakest. Let's write it down.

6. Have students work with partners to complete items B and C. Then review students' responses as a class.

7. Have students turn to section 2 of the Vocabulary Practice. Read the instructions aloud. Then have partners complete the activity. Call on individuals to share the synonyms they wrote. Write some of the synonym pairs on the board, and call on other students to tell which is stronger and which is weaker.

8. **Challenge Words** Use the following activities to review the Challenge Words with students.

- Write *irritate* on the board and have students provide several synonyms for it. (Possible responses: *bother, annoy, bug, aggravate, infuriate, exasperate*) Write these on the board. Then have students scale the words from weakest to strongest.

- Write the following on the board: *From the word history, we can make other words such as _____ .*

   – Call on students to complete the sentence, and write their responses on the board.

   – **What does *history* mean?** (past events, or a written record of past events)

   – Ask students how knowing the base word helps them figure out the meaning of each word.

▶ Have students record these words and their possible meanings in the Vocabulary Log.

Review Elements of Description: Concrete Details

9. Write *Descriptive Writing* on the board. Under it, write *1. Details*. We learned in the last lesson that when authors write descriptions, they use details. Write and bullet *Concrete* under *Details*. We learned that authors try to be as clear and concrete as possible when they give a detail. They try to tell *exactly* what something looked, felt, or sounded like.

10. Along with concrete details, authors also use strong words in their descriptions. Write *2. Strong Words* on the board. We just looked at some strong words in the vocabulary activity. We learned that strong words are words that are unusual, noticeable, and very specific. As we reread the letters, we'll be looking for more strong words.

Reading for Understanding   *Reading*

1. Have students turn to Anthology page 206 and Student Book page 155. Read the Student Book instructions aloud.

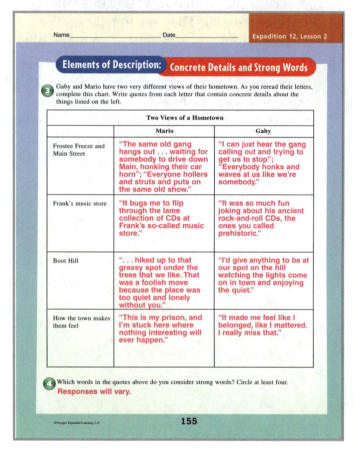

2. Read the first three paragraphs of the first letter aloud. **Mario describes the gang at the Frostee Freeze in the second paragraph.** *Frostee Freeze and Main Street* **is one of the items listed in the chart. Let's look back to see exactly how Mario describes them.** Read the fourth and fifth sentences of paragraph 2 aloud. **He describes the way the "same old gang" waits around for someone to drive by and then "hollers and struts and puts on the same old show." Let's write these details in the chart.** Pause to let students record the details. **When we get to Gaby's letter, we'll look for her description of the gang at the Frostee Freeze.**

3. Have students finish reading the letters independently. Remind them to pause to fill in other details about the gang at the Frostee Freeze, Frank's music store, Boot Hill, and the way the town makes them feel as they encounter them. Instruct students not to complete section 4 of the Student Book page at this time.

4. Encourage students to monitor their own comprehension of the text by pausing occasionally to ask themselves *Am I understanding what I'm reading?* Tell students that when they do not understand what they are reading, they should reread that portion of the text.

582

Checking for Comprehension *After Reading*

1. When all students are finished, review their responses as a class. For each set of details, ask students to tell which they think is more concrete, or specific, and vivid. Discuss how Mario's and Gaby's feelings impact their descriptions. (For example, Mario says the gang "struts and puts on the same old show" because everything seems boring without Gaby. Gaby feels invisible in the city so she describes the same gang as making her feel like she's "somebody.")

2. Have partners complete section 4 of the Student Book page. Then call on individuals to identify some of the strong words they circled. List several of them on the board, and challenge students to come up with some weaker and stronger synonyms for each.

Reading Response

Have students turn to Student Book page 156. Read the instructions aloud. Then have students use the selection and the letter frame to answer these questions:

? What is Mario's view of his hometown? What is Gaby's?

Students may work with partners or small groups. Encourage students to complete the letter with some of the more concrete, vivid details from Mario's and Gaby's letters. When students have completed their responses, call on individuals to read their letters aloud. Have students identify strong words in their writing.

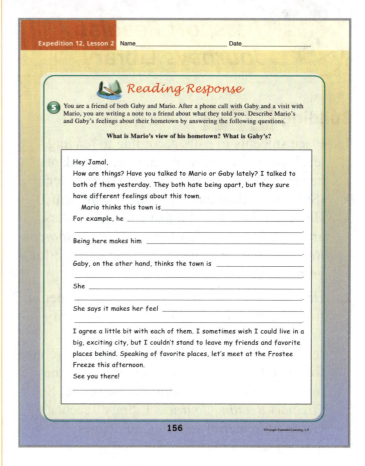

583

Passport Reading Journeys Library

Building Fluency

1. Place students in pairs according to reading level to build fluency. When pairing students, be sure that one student is a stronger reader (Student A) than the other student (Student B). However, do not reveal that stronger readers are paired with weaker readers. See *Passport Reading Journeys* Library Teacher's Guide for grouping guidelines.

2. Have students quickly choose reading material from the *Passport Reading Journeys* Library or another approved selection that is at the reading level of Student B. If students have not finished the previously chosen selection, they may continue reading from that selection. See *Passport Reading Journeys* Library Teacher's Guide for material selection guidelines.

3. Tell students that Student A will read one paragraph, and Student B will reread that same paragraph.

4. Have students follow this routine until the end of class.

5. If necessary, review the following practices to enhance fluency:
   - Rate and accuracy of reading
   - Expression during reading
   - Correction procedures

Library Highlights

Spotlight on Magazines

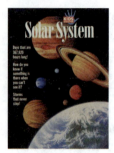

Level I

Kids Discover: Solar System contains informative articles, charts, and images about the solar system and its planets. The magazine also describes asteroids and comets that frequent Earth's solar system.

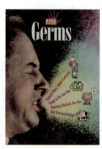

Level III

Kids Discover: Germs is a unique compilation of information about germs, infectious diseases, and viruses. What is a germ? Where do they come from? Using captivating images and illustrative diagrams, this magazine answers these questions and more. It also provides a historical timeline about the history of germs such as malaria, smallpox, and the flu.

Advanced Word Study

Prefix ex-

1. Write *ex-* on the board. **This word part is a prefix. Remember, a prefix is a word part that occurs at the beginning of a word and often helps us understand the meaning of the word. The sounds for this prefix are /eks/. Say the sounds for this prefix.** (/eks/) Write the word *expert* on the board. Underline the prefix *ex-*. **What is this prefix?** (ex-) **Use the sounds you know to read the rest of the word.** (pert) **What is the word?** (expert) **The prefix *ex-* means "out" or "outward." The word *expert* means "to demonstrate skill or authority."**

   Have students turn to Student Book page E12, Lesson 3. Direct them to line 1 in the first box. **What is the underlined prefix in the first word?** (ex-) **Read the rest of the word.** (pression) **What is the word?** (expression) Repeat with the remaining words. Call on individuals to read the words in random order. Ask students to tell the meanings of the words based on the meaning of the prefix.

2. Direct students to lines 2 and 3. Have them read the words. Call on individuals to read the words in a different order. Ask students to tell the meanings of the words.

   #### ▼ To Correct
   Say the correct sound(s) or prefix/suffix, then ask students to repeat the sound(s). Have them read the word again with the correct sound(s). If students do not know the meaning of the word, review the word and/or word parts to determine the meaning of the word.

   1. expression   expectant   exertion   explosive
   2. deployed   explained   creature   extremely
   3. unimportant   mumbled   outlandish   photographers

Sight Words

1. Direct students to line 1. Have them point to the first word. **This word is *cadets*. Read the word.** (cadets) **This is not a regular word. Let's read the word again.** (cadets) **Let's spell the word.** (c-a-d-e-t-s) **What is the word?** (cadets) Repeat with the remaining words. Then, have students read the words. Ask students to tell the meanings of the words.

2. Direct students to lines 2 and 3. **Let's read these words.** Remind students that the rows of words consist of regular and irregular words. Point to the first word. **What is the word?** (bandana) Repeat with the remaining words. Call on individuals to read the words in a different order. Ask students to tell the meanings of the words.

   #### ▼ To Correct
   For Regular Words: Say the sound(s) in the word, then ask students to repeat the sound(s). Have them read the word again with the correct sound(s). If students do not know the meaning of the word, review the word and/or word part to determine the meaning of the word.

   For Irregular Words: Immediately say the correct word. Then have students read the word, spell it, and read it again. If students do not know the meaning of the word, review the word.

   1. cadets I   enthusiastic I   swallowed I   defiantly I
   2. bandana I   soldiers I   stomach I   quiet I
   3. videos I   envelope R   cousin I   wounded I

Anthology Selection

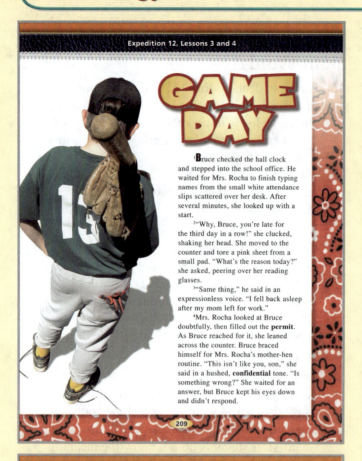

GAME DAY

¹Bruce checked the hall clock and stepped into the school office. He waited for Mrs. Rocha to finish typing names from the small white attendance slips scattered over her desk. After several minutes, she looked up with a start.

²"Why, Bruce, you're late for the third day in a row!" she clucked, shaking her head. She moved to the counter and tore a pink sheet from a small pad. "What's the reason today?" she asked, peering over her reading glasses.

³"Same thing," he said in an expressionless voice. "I fell back asleep after my mom left for work."

⁴Mrs. Rocha looked at Bruce doubtfully, then filled out the **permit**. As Bruce reached for it, she leaned across the counter. Bruce braced himself for Mrs. Rocha's mother-hen routine. "This isn't like you, son," she said in a hushed, **confidential** tone. "Is something wrong?" She waited for an answer, but Bruce kept his eyes down and didn't respond.

209

⁵"Well!" she huffed, insulted by his refusal to speak. "I'm sure I don't know what's gotten into you."

⁶Bruce took the permit and left. He was surprised at how little Mrs. Rocha's disapproval bothered him. His life seemed like a TV show he was watching without much interest. Being tardy wasn't the only thing he had done differently this week, and he was getting used to people being upset with him. He had fallen asleep in class twice. Instead of eating in the cafeteria with friends, he had spent lunch period alone in the courtyard. He had pitched so badly in practice that the coach suggested he get his eyes examined. The weird thing was that Bruce didn't seem to care what people said. It was as if the kid he used to be had been swallowed up by a beast that was now in charge.

⁷The beast had moved in the day his father was deployed to Iraq. Since then, every day felt endless, boring, unimportant. Nighttime was a different story, though. At night, Bruce felt as if he were being buried alive, crushed under the weight of that strange, dark creature that was always with him now. He lay awake while TV news pictures flashed through his mind—pictures of explosions and rolling tanks, of soldiers taking cover behind crumbled walls, of wounded people with bloodstained clothes.

⁸As Bruce made his way through the crowded halls to his locker, his best friend Tyrone caught up with him. "Hey, Jackson!" he said enthusiastically. "Are you ready for the big game tonight?"

⁹"Not really," Bruce mumbled. He'd been trying not to think about the game because he didn't **anticipate** a win after the way he'd pitched in practice all week. Anyway, it was impossible to imagine pitching for the championship without his dad there. For a moment, he pictured his dad sitting in the front row cheering and twirling his lucky red bandana above his head. Bruce fumbled with his lock and blinked hard to stop the tears.

¹⁰Tyrone looked around uncomfortably then said, "Hey, I'm sorry your dad was deployed, but he's going to be OK. Before you know it he'll be back here watching you pitch your senior season."

¹¹"Oh, yeah? How do you know?" snarled Bruce. Bruce could see the **impact** of his cold response in the hurt look on Tyrone's face, but the

210

avalanche of angry words continued. "You don't know anything about it, so just keep your mouth shut!" He slammed his locker and stormed off toward his math class.

¹²The rest of the day dragged by. When the final bell rang, Bruce took the back way out of the building, hoping he wouldn't see Tyrone. He walked along the athletic field where the JROTC was practicing for a drill competition. The cadets were in full dress uniform, and one was carrying a United States flag. The sight of the military uniforms and the flag led Bruce's thoughts far away. Then, suddenly, he realized he wasn't alone. Several guys had gathered nearby and were taunting the cadets.

¹³"Hey, G.I. Joe," yelled one. "Does playing dress-up make you feel like a big man?"

¹⁴"Oooh, look out," called another. "The enemy's right behind you. Too late—you're dead!" Then he grabbed his heart and made a face of mock pain.

¹⁵At that, the whole group burst out laughing. Bruce's blood boiled. Without a thought, he whirled and tackled the kid who was still hamming it up. Bruce pinned him down, but before he could land a punch, others in the group grabbed his arms and pulled him off.

¹⁶Coach Summers saw the scuffle from the coaching office and came rushing across the field like a shot from a gun. "What in the world **prompted** you to pull a stunt like that, Jackson?" he demanded.

¹⁷Coach Summers was an ex-Marine who took discipline very seriously. The other boys were obviously shaken by the coach's tone, but Bruce was defiantly silent. He kept clenching and unclenching his fists as he glared at his escaped victim.

¹⁸"You'd better go home and get your act together," warned the coach. "You have the **potential** to pitch a winner tonight, but not with this attitude. If you show up with this chip on your shoulder, don't expect to pitch the game."

¹⁹Bruce spent the rest of the afternoon in his room with his music turned up loud. He stared at the photographs on his walls. His dad was in a lot of them—catching for Bruce, standing outside the stadium with Bruce, holding up a trophy with Bruce. His dad had been his best coach over the years. He spent all his free evenings and weekends helping his

211

son become a great pitcher. Now Bruce felt that his reason for playing ball was gone.

²⁰"Bruce!" called his mother as she came in from work. "Are you ready? It's nearly time to leave." She came into her son's room and turned down the music. One look at Bruce's face told her he was nowhere near ready to face a championship game.

²¹"Rough day?" she asked.

²²"You might say that," said Bruce, avoiding eye contact.

²³"Wait here," she said.

²⁴A few minutes later she returned with a brown envelope. "Your dad wanted me to give you this before the game tonight," she explained.

²⁵Bruce's heart pounded as he took the envelope. He reached inside and pulled out his dad's red bandana. For the first time in days, Bruce smiled.

²⁶An hour later, he stood near the dugout scanning the packed stands. He spotted his mom sitting in the front row with Tyrone and Tyrone's dad like always. Bruce waved his hat at them and they waved back.

²⁷When it was time to take the field, Bruce pulled out the red bandana, studied it for a moment, then tucked it back in his pocket. As he walked toward the mound, the weight in his heart lifted. For the moment, the beast was under control.

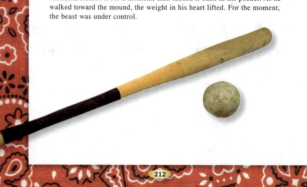

212

Comprehension and Vocabulary *Before Reading*

1. Have students take out a sheet of paper. **Think of a person you love because of their fun, lively personality. Picture them standing serious and still as if for a driver's license photograph. Now, on the paper, write a description of the person—*just* a factual statement of what the person looks like, not what makes the person fun or how the person acts. For example, instead of writing** *funny Aunt Mimi who uses goofy voices and makes faces when she tells jokes,* **just write** *short middle-aged woman with gray hair.*

2. Have students exchange papers with a neighbor. Tell students to read what their partner has written and to imagine meeting this person. **What would you think about the person? What would you expect the person to act like? What kind of personality would you expect the person to have? Why?** Then have students take turns explaining what the people they wrote about are actually like.

3. When all students are finished, bring the class together for a discussion.
   - **Was it challenging to describe *just* the appearance of a person? Why?** (Possible response: Yes, because it is difficult to see just the physical traits of a person whom you love for his or her personality.)
   - **Think of an object or a place that has a lot of meaning for you. Do you think others could look at it and see it as you do?** (Possible response: No, because it wouldn't have the same memories or meaning for them.)
   - **Why do people see different people, places, and objects in very different ways?** (Possible responses: because they have special meaning or importance to some people but not to others; because they remind us of past events and experiences that are unique to us)

4. **In Lessons 1 and 2, we read letters that showed how differently two teenagers viewed their hometown. In this lesson, we'll read another text that helps us see through another person's eyes.**

Introduce Vocabulary

Vocabulary

Review Words

permit	*a document or paper that gives official permission to do something* (noun); *to allow* (verb)
confidential	*meant to be kept private or secret*
anticipate	*to wait for or expect*
impact	*a strong effect or influence*
prompt	*to move to action*
potential	*possibility; talent not yet used*

Challenge Words

Word Building
expressionless   *express, expressive, expressively, expression, unexpressive*

Word Meaning
deploy   *to send troops or weapons to a certain place to prepare for military action* The U.S. Army will soon *deploy* more troops to the Middle East.

5. **Lesson 3's story, "Game Day," contains words with meanings we have already learned. We will review these words within the text we are reading.**

6. Write each Review Word on the board. Then ask students to locate the word in the article. Instruct them to read aloud the sentence containing the word, as well as any other sentences that provide context.
   - **What can you tell me about the word?**
   - Ask other questions that allow students to explore the word's meaning. (For example: **Does *anticipate* mean the same as *imagine*? What is a synonym for *confidential*?**)

7. Ask students to respond to the following questions. Provide correction and feedback as necessary.
   - **What is the purpose of a parking *permit*?**
   - **Which should be kept *confidential*—a friend's personal problems or the date of a parade? Why?**
   - **What is something people do if they *anticipate* rain?**
   - **Which has more *impact*—a hurricane or a spring shower? Why?**
   - **Which is more likely to *prompt* an argument—an accusation or a compliment? Why?**
   - **Who has more *potential*—a rookie or a well-known pitcher who has retired? Why?**

8. Work with students to write a definition for each word on the board.

9. Include the Challenge Words to meet the needs of students who are advancing. For the Word Building Challenge Word, have students identify the base word (express), then guide them in determining how the base word can help them figure out the meaning of the larger words.

Literal and Figurative Language

10. Have students turn to Anthology page 209 and preview the story by looking at the images and reading the title. Then have them read the first paragraph of the story.
    - **What kind of text do you think this will be?** (a story; a narrative)
    - **Why do you think so?** (because the picture and the first sentence introduce a character named Bruce)

11. **In this reading, we will see people, places, and events through the eyes of someone named Bruce. Some of the things we see will be described in a literal way.** Write *Literal* on the board. Next to it, write *tall mountains*. **A literal description tells just what something is. When you wrote down a description of a lively person—just the person's appearance and nothing else—that was a literal description.** Point to *tall mountains*. **This is a literal description of some mountains. It simply states that they are tall. When looking at the mountains, most people would agree with this description.**

SKILL ✔

12. Remind students that concrete details and strong words help bring a description to life. **How could we make the literal description *tall mountains* more vivid?** (Possible responses: peaks that pierce the sky; steep, rugged, snow-covered mountains) Write students' responses on the board.

13. **Other descriptions in this reading will be *figurative*.** Write *Figurative* on the board. Next to it, write *mountains that ruled the landscape like kings*. **A figurative description tells what something seems like to a certain person. Figurative descriptions often compare one thing to another.** Point to the figurative description on the board. **This description compares mountains to kings. In a descriptive text, this comparison would help the reader picture more clearly how impressive or powerful the mountains were. It would help the reader understand how the author or a character *perceived* the mountains.**

14. **As we read this text, let's look for literal descriptions that tell what things actually are. Let's also look for figurative descriptions that tell how things *seem* to Bruce.**

Reading for Understanding

Reading

Places and Names to Look For:
- Bruce Jackson
- JROTC
- Coach Summers
- Iraq
- G.I. Joe
- Tyrone

1. **As you read this text, you may come across some unfamiliar places and names.**
   - Write the words on the board.
   - Point to each word as you read the following:

   In "Game Day," you will read about a tough day for a boy named *Bruce Jackson*, whose father has been sent to fight in *Iraq*. Bruce loses interest in baseball and other things he cares about. He even pulls away from his friend *Tyrone*. Watching students in the *JROTC*, or Junior Reserve Officers' Training Corps, reminds Bruce of his dad in Iraq. When bullies make fun of the JROTC cadets and call them *G.I. Joe*, Bruce snaps. *Coach Summers* warns him to straighten up or he'll miss the biggest game of his life.
   - Call on individuals to read the words.

2. **As we read this text, remember to look for literal and figurative descriptions.**

3. **Fluency** Read the first paragraph aloud with students. Then have students read the remainder of the story in small groups, taking turns after paragraphs. If necessary, review the following fluency correction procedure with students to ensure accuracy: **Offer help when a group member comes to an unfamiliar word or makes a reading error. Pause, then say, "That word is _____. Let's read it again."** As students read, monitor for reading rate, accuracy, and expression.

4. When students have completed their reading, check for literal comprehension of the text by asking these questions: **KNOWLEDGE**
   - *Paragraphs 2 and 3:* **What has Bruce done three days in a row?** (come to school late) **What reason does Bruce give for this?** (He says he fell back asleep after his mom left.)
   - *Paragraph 7:* **What does Bruce feel as if he has been swallowed by a beast?** (His father has been deployed to Iraq.)
   - *Paragraph 9:* **What does Bruce have to do tonight?** (pitch in the championship baseball game after a week of bad practices—and without his dad being there)
   - *Paragraph 15:* **What makes Bruce so mad that he tries to start a fight?** (a group of teasing members of the JROTC)
   - *Paragraph 18:* **What does Coach tell Bruce to do?** (go home and cool off so he'll be able to pitch a winning game)
   - *Paragraphs 24 and 25:* **What does Bruce's mom do to help him feel better?** (gives him his dad's red bandana)

English Language Learners

Using Descriptive Language

When English language learners read aloud, they may concentrate more on pronouncing words correctly than on building mental images and retaining meaning. Use the following activity to help them visualize and internalize what they read.

List these paragraph numbers on the board: *1, 9, 12, 19.* **As you reread "Game Day" with your partner, stop after each of these paragraphs and work together to create a mental image of what you read. Let's try one together.** Read paragraph 1 aloud with students, then model the following process:

- **First, let's list concrete details or sensory details in this paragraph. I see the concrete detail that Mrs. Rocha is typing.** Write this on the board while students write it on a sheet of paper. Repeat with other details in the paragraph.

- **Now, let's quickly draw a picture of this scene as we imagine it in our minds. Include as many of the concrete and sensory details from the story as you can.** Draw a picture on the board while students draw on their papers. Use colored chalk, if possible.

- **Next, below the picture, let's write a description of the scene.** Write this sentence frame on the board: *In this scene, _____.* **In this scene, Bruce is standing by Mrs. Rocha's desk, which is covered with small white slips of paper.** Complete the sentence with this information.

- **Take turns describing the scene aloud with your partner. Try not to look at what you've drawn or written.** Listen to students' descriptions, providing correction as needed.

- **Finally, let's reread the paragraph with our picture and our description in mind.** Reread the paragraph aloud with students. Have students repeat these steps for each of the three remaining paragraphs.

ELL

Checking for Comprehension *After Reading*

1. **Before reading, what kind of text did we predict this would be?** (a story or narrative) **Was this prediction correct?** (yes) **What elements, or parts, of the text told you that this was a story?** (It has a main character, a setting, and a plot with a beginning, a middle, and an end.) Write *Character*, *Setting*, and *Plot* on the board. Under *Plot*, write *Beginning*, *Middle*, and *End*. Then have students give details that tell about each element of this story. (*Character*—Bruce; *Setting*—Bruce's home and school; *Beginning*—Character and part of setting are introduced. We learn that Bruce's behavior has recently changed for the worse. *Middle*—Bruce is rude to his friend and starts a fight over a small incident. *End*—As Bruce prepares to pitch the big game, he finds encouragement in a gift from his father.)

2. Write the following phrases on the board: *TV news pictures, American flag, JROTC cadets, family photographs, front row at the stadium, red bandana.* **If you saw these people, places, and objects from Bruce's life for the first time, you might just think of them as routine parts of a high school student's day. On this particular day, Bruce sees them very differently.** Call on individuals to describe how Bruce sees the people, places, and objects. Prompt students, as necessary, by asking these questions:

   SKILL ✓

   - **Why is a TV newscast that is routine to most people different for Bruce?** (Pictures of the war stick in his mind and make him worry about his father's safety.)

   - **What do the flag and JROTC uniforms remind Bruce of?** (his father)

   - **What does Bruce think of when he looks at the front row of the stadium?** (His father sitting in his regular seat and cheering him on.)

590

- **What do the family photographs make Bruce think of?** (his father coaching him; that without his dad he has no reason to play)
- **What does the red bandana mean to Bruce?** (His father is thinking of him and supporting him even though he's in Iraq.)

3. **Challenge Questions** **Think of an object you own that in your mind connects you to another person. What would an alien from outer space see when it looked at the object? What do you see? What explains the difference?** APPLICATION (Responses will vary.)

Connect to the Author

Have student discuss the following questions in small groups.

- **What was the author's purpose for writing this story?** (Possible responses: to entertain; to help readers understand the complex feelings of loss; to make readers think about the reasons behind someone's actions)
- **Imagine that a local newspaper ran a story about Bruce's father leaving to serve his country, and the family he must leave behind. How would that text be different from this one?** (Possible responses: It would give mainly the facts. It might mention that the family would miss the father and hope for his safe return, but it wouldn't describe the day-to-day feelings of loss. It would not describe Bruce's feelings from his point of view.)

Listening and Speaking Have a representative from each group present their group's ideas to the class. Encourage students to listen carefully to each speaker. To verify student understanding, have individuals restate in their own words the other group's ideas.

Extending Vocabulary

Prefix ex-
- Have students turn to paragraph 17 on Anthology page 211. Read the first sentence of the paragraph aloud. Write the word *ex-Marine* on the board. **What is the prefix at the beginning of this hyphenated word?** (ex-) Underline this prefix.
- **This prefix means "former." What does *ex-Marine* mean?** (former Marine) **The coach was a former Marine, or used to be in the Marines.**
- Write the following words on the board: *ex-boyfriend*, *ex-mayor*, and *ex-convict*. Ask students how the prefix *ex-* helps them know the meaning of each word. (Possible responses: It adds "former" or "used to be" to the word's meaning. A girl's ex-boyfriend is her former boyfriend. An ex-mayor used to be the mayor. An ex-convict is a former convict who has finished serving his or her time in prison.)
- ▶ Have students record these words with their meanings in the Vocabulary Log.

Connect to Careers

Use the following activity to help students experience one aspect of United States Marine Corps training.

- Explain that in the story "Game Day," it's possible that Bruce's father is one of more than 20,000 Marines serving in Iraq. **The U.S. Marine Corp has land, air, and naval forces. Marines are usually the first to arrive at places where U.S. military forces are needed.**

- Call on individuals to tell what they know about the Marines. Ask students if they know the Marine motto (*semper fidelis* or *semper fi*, for short, which means "always faithful") and the traditional description of marines as "the few, the proud." **What do the motto and description say about the Marines?**

- Point out that for new Marine recruits, the 12 weeks of basic training are rigid and intense. During this time, recruits are trained to be mentally and physically tough. Explain that one of the first things trainees undergo is an Initial Strength Test (IST). On the board, write the following requirements to pass the IST:
  - Males: 2 dead-hang pull-ups, 44 crunches in 2 minutes, and a 1.5-mile run in 13.5 minutes
  - Females: a flex-arm hang for 12 seconds, 44 crunches in 2 minutes, and 1.5 miles in 15 minutes

- Call on willing individuals to take any one or more parts of the test.

To increase difficulty: Have students conduct research to learn more about marine training through a local recruiting office, library resources, or online at http://www.usmc.mil.

Careers

Lesson 4

Anthology Selection

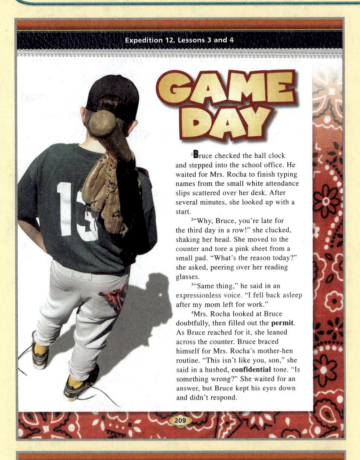

GAME DAY

[1]Bruce checked the hall clock and stepped into the school office. He waited for Mrs. Rocha to finish typing names from the small white attendance slips scattered over her desk. After several minutes, she looked up with a start.

[2]"Why, Bruce, you're late for the third day in a row!" she clucked, shaking her head. She moved to the counter and tore a pink sheet from a small pad. "What's the reason today?" she asked, peering over her reading glasses.

[3]"Same thing," he said in an expressionless voice. "I fell back asleep after my mom left for work."

[4]Mrs. Rocha looked at Bruce doubtfully, then filled out the **permit**. As Bruce reached for it, she leaned across the counter. Bruce braced himself for Mrs. Rocha's mother-hen routine. "This isn't like you, son," she said in a hushed, **confidential** tone. "Is something wrong?" She waited for an answer, but Bruce kept his eyes down and didn't respond.

209

[5]"Well!" she huffed, insulted by his refusal to speak. "I'm sure I don't know what's gotten into you."

[6]Bruce took the permit and left. He was surprised at how little Mrs. Rocha's disapproval bothered him. His life seemed like a TV show he was watching without much interest. Being tardy wasn't the only thing he had done differently this week, and he was getting used to people being upset with him. He had fallen asleep in class twice. Instead of eating in the cafeteria with friends, he had spent lunch period alone in the courtyard. He had pitched so badly in practice that the coach suggested he get his eyes examined. The weird thing was that Bruce didn't seem to care what people said. It was as if the kid he used to be had been swallowed up by a beast that was now in charge.

[7]The beast had moved in the day his father was deployed to Iraq. Since then, every day felt endless, boring, unimportant. Nighttime was a different story, though. At night, Bruce felt as if he were being buried alive, crushed under the weight of that strange, dark creature that was always with him now. He lay awake while TV news pictures flashed through his mind—pictures of explosions and rolling tanks, of soldiers taking cover behind crumbled walls, of wounded people with bloodstained clothes.

[8]As Bruce made his way through the crowded halls to his locker, his best friend Tyrone caught up with him. "Hey, Jackson!" he said enthusiastically. "Are you ready for the big game tonight?"

[9]"Not really," Bruce mumbled. He'd been trying not to think about the game because he didn't **anticipate** a win after the way he'd pitched in practice all week. Anyway, it was impossible to imagine pitching for the championship without his dad there. For a moment, he pictured his dad sitting in the front row cheering and twirling his lucky red bandana above his head. Bruce fumbled with his lock and blinked hard to stop the tears.

[10]Tyrone looked around uncomfortably then said, "Hey, I'm sorry your dad was deployed, but he's going to be OK. Before you know it he'll be back here watching you pitch your senior season."

[11]"Oh, yeah? How do you know?" snarled Bruce. Bruce could see the **impact** of his cold response in the hurt look on Tyrone's face, but the

210

avalanche of angry words continued. "You don't know anything about it, so just keep your mouth shut!" He slammed his locker and stormed off toward his math class.

[12]The rest of the day dragged by. When the final bell rang, Bruce took the back way out of the building, hoping he wouldn't see Tyrone. He walked along the athletic field where the JROTC was practicing for a drill competition. The cadets were in full dress uniform, and one was carrying a United States flag. The sight of the military uniforms and the flag led Bruce's thoughts far away. Then, suddenly, he realized he wasn't alone. Several guys had gathered nearby and were taunting the cadets.

[13]"Hey, G.I. Joe," yelled one. "Does playing dress-up make you feel like a big man?"

[14]"Oooh, look out," called another. "The enemy's right behind you. Too late—you're dead!" Then he grabbed his heart and made a face of mock pain.

[15]At that, the whole group burst out laughing. Bruce's blood boiled. Without a thought, he whirled and tackled the kid who was still hamming it up. Bruce pinned him down, but before he could land a punch, others in the group grabbed his arms and pulled him off.

[16]Coach Summers saw the scuffle from the coaching office and came rushing across the field like a shot from a gun. "What in the world **prompted** you to pull a stunt like that, Jackson?" he demanded.

[17]Coach Summers was an ex-Marine who took discipline very seriously. The other boys were obviously shaken by the coach's tone, but Bruce was defiantly silent. He kept clenching and unclenching his fists as he glared at his escaped victim.

[18]"You'd better go home and get your act together," warned the coach. "You have the **potential** to pitch a winner tonight, but not with this attitude. If you show up with this chip on your shoulder, don't expect to pitch the game."

[19]Bruce spent the rest of the afternoon in his room with his music turned up loud. He stared at the photographs on his walls. His dad was in a lot of them—catching for Bruce, standing outside the stadium with Bruce, holding up a trophy with Bruce. His dad had been his best coach over the years. He spent all his free evenings and weekends helping his

211

son become a great pitcher. Now Bruce felt that his reason for playing ball was gone.

[20]"Bruce!" called his mother as she came in from work. "Are you ready? It's nearly time to leave." She came into her son's room and turned down the music. One look at Bruce's face told her he was nowhere near ready to face a championship game.

[21]"Rough day?" she asked.

[22]"You might say that," said Bruce, avoiding eye contact.

[23]"Wait here," she said.

[24]A few minutes later she returned with a brown envelope. "Your dad wanted me to give you this before the game tonight," she explained.

[25]Bruce's heart pounded as he took the envelope. He reached inside and pulled out his dad's red bandana. For the first time in days, Bruce smiled.

[26]An hour later, he stood near the dugout scanning the packed stands. He spotted his mom sitting in the front row with Tyrone and Tyrone's dad like always. Bruce waved his hat at them and they waved back.

[27]When it was time to take the field, Bruce pulled out the red bandana, studied it for a moment, then tucked it back in his pocket. As he walked toward the mound, the weight in his heart lifted. For the moment, the beast was under control.

212

593

Comprehension and Vocabulary
Before Reading

1. **In Lesson 3, we read "Game Day."**
   - **What kind of text did we decide that it was?** (narrative or story)
   - **Who was the main character in the story, and what problem did he face?** (Bruce, who was dealing with his father's deployment to Iraq)
   - **What were some of the things we learned about Bruce as we followed him through his day at home and school?** (We learned how he has changed since his father was deployed to Iraq, that he feels like a "beast" has taken over inside him and he now has trouble sleeping; that he has pulled away from his best friend; that his dad had spent a lot of time coaching and encouraging him over the years; that Bruce doesn't believe he can pitch a winning championship game without his dad.)
   - **We also learned that different objects and events can have different meanings for different people or characters. For example, at the end of the story, what did the red bandana mean to Bruce?** (Possible response: It meant that he knew his dad cared about him no matter how far away he was.)

Vocabulary Review

2. Have students turn to Student Book page 157, and arrange them in pairs. Have students read the vocabulary words in the box, then call on individuals to provide meanings and sample sentences for the words.

3. Read aloud the instructions for section 1. On the board, draw a chart like the one in the Student Book.
   - **We have just given meanings for these words that match the way they are used in the story. Some of these words, though, have other meanings.**

- **Write the word *permit* in the Word box. In the story, the word *permit* means "a document or paper that gives official permission to do something."** Write this definition in the first Meaning box. **Mrs. Rocha fills out a *permit* that will allow Bruce to enter class late.** Call on a student to supply a sentence using this word, and write it in the Sample Sentence box.

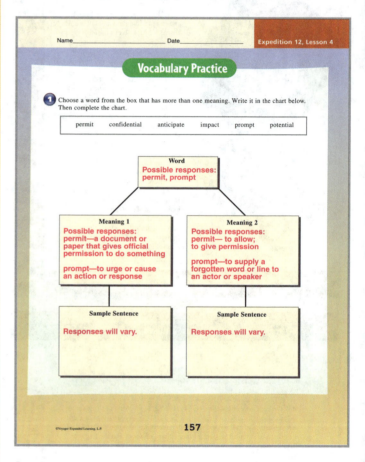

- **The word *permit* has another meaning. It can also mean "to allow to give permission or consent."** Write this definition in the second Meaning box. **Your parents probably do not *permit* you to drive the car or stay up all night.** Call on another student to supply a sentence using *permit*, and write it in the second Sample Sentence box.

4. Have students work with their partners to identify a second word with multiple meanings and to use it to complete the chart in the Student Book. Encourage students to use a dictionary, if needed, to determine which words have multiple meanings and what those meanings are.

5. When all students are finished, review their responses as a class.

6. **Challenge Words** Use the following activities to review the Challenge Words with students.

   • Ask students to give a meaning for the word *deploy* and to provide sentences that contain the word.

     – Next, draw the following graphic organizer on the board:

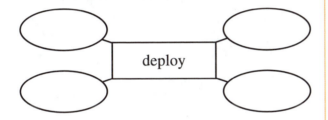

     – Read the words in the inner ovals aloud. Explain that these words are synonyms for *deploy* but that synonyms never have exactly the same meanings or uses.

     – Ask students what kinds of people or objects are typically *deployed*. (soldiers or weapons) Then point to the oval containing *position*, and ask what kinds of things can be *positioned*. (Possible response: headphones, furniture, computer monitors) Write some of students' responses near the word position. Repeat with the other three verbs.

     – Have students provide sentences using each of the verbs on the board. Guide them to decide which verbs are interchangeable, and which are not.

   • Write the following on the board: *From the word <u>expression</u>, we can make other words such as ____ .*

     – Call on students to complete the sentence, and write their responses on the board.

   – **What does *express* mean?** (to state an idea or a feeling in words)

   – Ask students how knowing the base word helps them figure out the meaning of each word.

   ▶ Have students record these words and their possible meanings in the Vocabulary Log.

Review Elements of Description: Literal and Figurative Language

7. On the board, write *literal language* and *figurative language*. **In the last lesson we learned about literal and figurative language. What is literal language?** (language that tells just what something is) Write *what something is* under *literal language*. **What is figurative language?** (Possible responses: language that tells what something *seems* to be; language that compares something with something else) Write *seems to be; compares* under *figurative language*. Next, write *The furious woman yelled.* and *Mrs. Peabody bellowed like a bull.* on the board. **Which is a literal description?** (the first) **Which is figurative?** (the second) **In the second, what two things are being compared?** (Mrs. Peabody's bellowing and a bull's bellowing)

8. **Comparisons are one kind of figurative language authors use to help the reader "see" something in a new way or from a certain character's perspective. Another kind of figurative language authors use is *symbols*.** Write *symbol* on the board. **A symbol is something that stands for or represents something else. For example, a skull is often used as a symbol for danger. A horseshoe is used as a symbol for good luck. What are some other symbols you can think of?** (Responses will vary.)

9. **In stories, authors sometimes use an important object, place, or event as a symbol for something else. As we reread "Game Day," think about the "beast" Bruce imagines inside him. Ask yourself what the beast represents.**

Reading for Understanding *Reading*

1. Have students turn to Anthology page 209 and Student Book page 158. Read the Student Book instructions aloud.

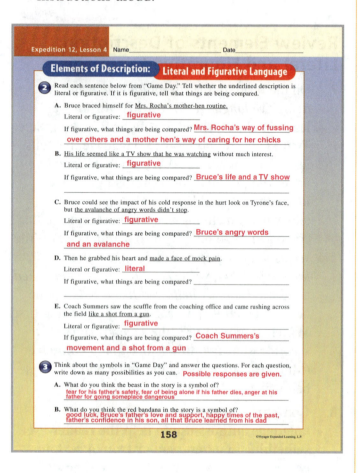

2. Read the first four paragraphs of the story aloud with students. **The first description listed in the Student Book appears in paragraph 4.** Read the first sentence in the Student Book aloud. **This description is figurative. It tells what Mrs. Rocha's behavior *seems* like to Bruce. What two things are compared in this description?** (Mrs. Rocha's way of fussing over others and a mother hen's way of caring for her chicks) Have students write these responses in the Student Book.

3. Have students finish reading the story independently. Instruct them to pause each time they encounter one of the descriptions in the Student Book to discuss and complete that item. Instruct students not to complete section 3 of the Student Book at this point.

Checking for Comprehension *After Reading*

1. After students have finished reading and completing the Student Book activity, review students' responses as a class. Provide correction and feedback as needed.

2. Have students turn to section 3 of Student Book page 158. Read the instructions and item A aloud.

   - **In this story, the author uses a beast that Bruce imagines as a symbol of something.**

   - **What does the beast mean to Bruce? To another person, a beast might represent hatred or evil or power. In this story, the beast stands for something that Bruce may not even be able to name. Though Bruce may not know the answer for sure, we may be able to use the author's clues to figure out what the beast stands for.**

   - **To figure out what the beast represents, look back at the story for clues.** Have students turn back to paragraphs 6 and 7, and read them aloud. **Notice the words** *as if* **near the end of paragraph 6. They tell us that the language is figurative. Paragraph 7 gives us several clues about what the beast means. The text says that the beast came when Bruce's father left and that it bothers him mostly at night, the same time that he thinks about TV pictures of the war. Bruce says he feels crushed or buried alive by the beast. These clues can help us decide what this particular beast inside Bruce might stand for.**

3. Ask students to write what they believe the beast stands for. Have each student share his or her response with the class. Write and tally students' responses on the board. Point out that a symbol can stand for many different things, but that one main meaning—such as "fear"— can usually be identified for a central symbol in a story.

4. Have students read aloud paragraphs 9, 25, and 27. Read item B aloud. Then have students write an answer. Repeat the steps of having students share, tally, and compare their answers.

Reading Response

Have students turn to Student Book page 159. Read the instructions aloud. Instruct students to look back in the story to help them find answers to these questions:

 What do you see?
What does each place, object, or person (or group of people) mean to Bruce?

Students may work independently or with a partner to complete the paragraphs. When all students are finished, call on individuals to read aloud what they have written.

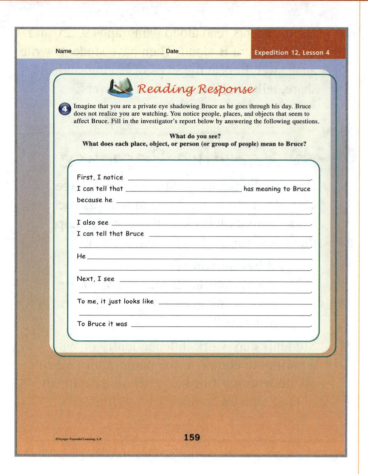

Name_____ Date_____ Expedition 12, Lesson 4

Reading Response

4 Imagine that you are a private eye shadowing Bruce as he goes through his day. Bruce does not realize you are watching. You notice people, places, and objects that seem to affect Bruce. Fill in the investigator's report below by answering the following questions.

What do you see?
What does each place, object, or person (or group of people) mean to Bruce?

First, I notice _____.

I can tell that _____ has meaning to Bruce

because he _____

_____.

I also see _____.

I can tell that Bruce _____

He _____

_____

Next, I see _____

_____.

To me, it just looks like _____

_____.

To Bruce it was _____

_____.

©Voyager Expanded Learning, L.P.   **159**

Passport Reading Journeys Library

Building Fluency

1. Place students in pairs according to reading level to build fluency. When pairing students, be sure that one student is a stronger reader (Student A) than the other student (Student B). However, do not reveal that stronger readers are paired with weaker readers. See *Passport Reading Journeys* Library Teacher's Guide for grouping guidelines.

2. Have students quickly choose reading material from the *Passport Reading Journeys* Library or another approved selection that is at the reading level of Student B. If students have not finished the previously chosen selection, they may continue reading from that selection. See *Passport Reading Journeys* Library Teacher's Guide for material selection guidelines.

3. Tell students that Student A will read one paragraph, and Student B will reread that same paragraph.

4. Have students follow this routine until the end of class.

5. If necessary, review the following practices to enhance fluency:
   - Rate and accuracy of reading
   - Expression during reading
   - Correction procedures

Library Highlights

Spotlight on a Book

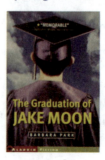

Level I

Written by Barbara Park, *The Graduation of Jake Moon* is the story of Jake, an eighth-grade student who lives with his mother and grandfather. When Jake's grandfather begins to suffer from the effects of Alzheimer's disease, it is as if Jake has become the adult and his grandfather the child.

SOLO Strategic Online Learning Opportunities®

Session 1   http://solo.voyagerlearning.com

Students read a passage about a group of artists who painted the truth about what they saw in New York City during the early 1900s.

Content Connection
Social Studies

"Apostles of Ugliness:" The Ashcan Artists *by Joelle Ziemian*

Lexile Levels
Passage B 830L
Passage C 900L

Assessment
- Metacognition
- Content
- Vocabulary
- Main Idea
- Summary

SKILL ✔

Based on their assessment scores, students automatically are assigned either the Skills Practice for reinforcement or the Independent Practice and Extension Opportunities.

SKILLS PRACTICE

Vocabulary Strategies
- Context
- Word Parts: Prefixes and Suffixes
- Word Parts: Compound Words

Dictionary Skills

Main Idea Strategy: W–I–N
- Identifying the Most Important *Who* or *What*
- Identifying the Most Important *Information*
- Stating the Main Idea in a Small *Number* of Words

Questioning

Writing
- Writing a Summary Statement

INDEPENDENT PRACTICE

Vocabulary Strategies

Writing
- Writing a Summary Statement

EXTENSION OPPORTUNITIES
- Online Books
- Book Cart
- Review of Previous Passages

Lesson 6

Advanced Word Study

Multisyllabic Words

1. **Remember, we can use what we know about open and closed syllables, prefixes, and suffixes to read longer words.** Write the word *collection* on the board. Underline the word part *col*. **What is this first word part?** (col) **What kind of syllable is this first word part?** (closed) **How do we know?** (It has one short vowel sound with one or more consonants following it.) **What short sound does the vowel make?** (/o/) Underline *lec*. **What is the next word part?** (lec) Underline the suffix *-tion*. **What is this suffix?** (-tion) **What is the word?** (collection) **The word *collection* means "the act of collecting or assembling."**

2. Have students turn to Student Book page E12, Lesson 6. Direct students to line 1. **What is the first word part?** (col) **Read the rest of the word.** (lapsed) **What is the word?** (collapsed) Repeat with the remaining words. Call on individuals to read the words in random order. Ask students to tell the meanings of the words.

3. Direct students to lines 2 and 3. Have them read the words. Then, call on individuals to read the words in a different order. Ask students to tell the meanings of the words.

   ▼ **To Correct**

   For Multisyllabic Words: **What is the first word part? What is the next part? What is the word?** If students do not know the meaning of the word, review the word and/or word parts to determine the meaning of the word.

   For Sounds in Words: Say the correct sound(s), then ask them to repeat the sound(s). Have students read the word again with the correct sound(s). If students do not know the meaning of the word, review the word and/or word parts to determine the meaning of the word.

1.	collapsed	enjoyable	volunteers	hurricane
2.	umbrellas	completely	exterminate	surrounded
3.	toothbrushes	crumpled	hospital	reporters

Sight Words

1. Direct students to line 1. Have them point to the first word. **This word is *disguise*. Read the word.** (disguise) **This is not a regular word. Let's read the word again.** (disguise) **Let's spell the word.** (d-i-s-g-u-i-s-e) **What is the word?** (disguise) Repeat with the remaining words. Then, have students read the words. Ask students to tell the meanings of the words.

2. Direct students to lines 2 and 3. **Let's read these words.** Remind students that the rows of words consist of regular and irregular words. Point to the first word. **What is the word?** (evacuate) Repeat with the remaining words. Call on individuals to read the words in a different order. Ask students to tell the meanings of the words.

   ▼ **To Correct**

   For Regular Words: Say the sound(s) in the word, then ask students to repeat the sound(s). Have them read the word again with the correct sound(s). If students do not know the meaning of the word, review the word and/or word part to determine the meaning of the word.

   For Irregular Words: Immediately say the correct word. Then have students read the word, spell it, and read it again. If students do not know the meaning of the word, review the word.

1.	disguise I	figured I	damage I	judgment I
2.	evacuate I	misfortune I	cadets I	defiantly I
3.	pieces I	levee R	enthusiastic I	swallows I

Anthology Selection

Social Studies

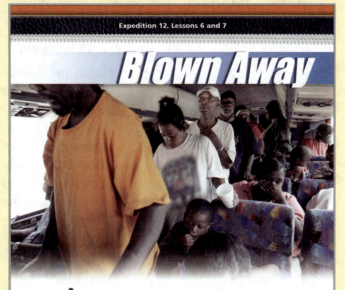

Expedition 12, Lessons 6 and 7

Blown Away

[1]**September 1, 2005** It's Thursday afternoon—the fourth day of my bad dream. I want to write down everything that's happened so I can get it on paper and out of my head. On Monday, Hurricane Katrina hit New Orleans. Lots of people left town before then, but we stayed. Our neighborhood is on high ground, and my dad thought it would be safe from flooding. I trust my dad's judgment, so I wasn't worried, at least not at first. But the more I listened to the news, the more I worried that staying in our home might have terrible **consequences**. My dad, brother, and I all stayed glued to the TV news as the storm got bigger. The reporters could hardly keep from blowing away, and the wind turned their umbrellas inside out. Officials **classified** Katrina as a category 5 hurricane—one of the biggest storms in United States history!

213

Expedition 12, Lessons 6 and 7

[2]By the time the storm hit land, it was down to a category 4, but it was so strong that I wished we hadn't stayed behind. The sky turned kind of greenish, and the rain poured down. The wind whipped around our house and howled so loud that we had a hard time hearing each other talk. We heard loud clunks and crashes when the wind blew things against our house. Each time a big gust would come along, the house swayed back and forth, and I screamed. I kept picturing our roof turning inside out like one of the reporters' umbrellas. It was the worst morning of my life.

[3]The next day, we checked out the damage. It was unbelievable! The wind had pulled several huge trees right out of the ground, and one had fallen on our truck and crushed it! We all felt bad, but I was especially sorry for Deshaun. He just got his driver's license, and now there's nothing to drive. Two houses near us were completely flattened, and every **structure** in the neighborhood was damaged. The porch was missing from Mr. Rendon's store, and the roof of Willie's gas station had collapsed. The whole place looked like there had been an explosion. The streets and yards were littered with all kinds of things—a crumpled grocery basket, a car fender, pieces of houses, part of a billboard, a baby stroller. It made me feel kind of sick to see the neighborhood so destroyed and trashed out.

[4]All the streets lower than ours were filled with water. We thought the water would start going down right away, but instead it started rising. By the next morning, our street was gone! We were surrounded by water, and we couldn't figure out why. The power had been out since the storm, so we couldn't get any news. Dad got worried and told us to pack a bag so we could get to safety. We waded toward a nursing home that was a few blocks away. At times, the dark, smelly water was up to my shoulders. Yuk! When we finally got to the nursing home, the director told us the levee had broken and New Orleans was in big trouble. A bus was coming to evacuate the nursing home patients. We decided we'd better get on it, too.

[5]So that's why I'm on this bus that is half-driving, half-floating across New Orleans. It doesn't look like New Orleans anymore, though. It looks like a nightmare.

[6]**September 3, 2005** It's too noisy to nap so I guess I'll write. I'm on a cot in the Astrodome in Houston, Texas, with thousands of other people who wish they were home. It's like a beehive here, with Red Cross workers passing out snacks and clothes, babies crying, people calling out names as

214

Expedition 12, Lessons 6 and 7

they search for lost family members, children squealing and running around, and lots of folks watching the giant TV to figure out what's going on back home. As crowded as this place is, I was glad to get here. We pulled in late last night, and volunteers came out to help us off the bus and get us settled in. A volunteer named Betty Jo took us under her wing right from the start. She gave me a big, warm hug and a paper cup of sweet lemonade. She made me feel better even though I was really tired and unhappy. The funny way she talks and calls everyone "honey" reminds me of Meemaw. When I asked her if I could get a toothbrush, she told me I was going to get the whole shootin' match. I wondered if she was saying I ought to be shot for asking. I figured out what she really meant when she came back with bags of supplies. Clothes, blankets, shampoo, soap, toothbrushes, and even dental floss—it was all there.

[7]We spent the next half hour wandering around with our things trying to find empty cots to sleep on. There were thousands of cots! When we finally found three together, Dad, Deshaun, and I took turns going to the showers while one of us kept an eye on our things. That was the most wonderful shower I have ever taken. The steam and hot water eased my tired muscles, and the sweet smell of soap replaced the stench of Katrina. I threw away my filthy, flood-soaked clothes and put on the new ones that Betty Jo had given me. It felt like heaven to lie down on soft, clean sheets and sleep.

[8]It was weird waking up in this huge place with people all around me today. It was like being onstage for anyone to look at. I want to be back home with my friends. What if they never come back to New Orleans? It feels like Katrina blew my whole life into pieces. Betty Jo tells me to keep my chin up. She keeps saying that with a good attitude, starting over will be just like falling off a log—whatever that means! Half the time I don't understand what Betty Jo is saying, but she does cheer me up.

[9]Right now, Dad's in line to talk to a social worker. He wants to find out if we're **eligible** for a government loan. On the news, they said that the hospital where Dad works is completely destroyed. He wants to find a job here now, so Betty Jo got him an **application** to fill out. A lot of companies are going to hold job **interviews** right here at the Astrodome. Betty Jo told Dad that misfortune can be a blessing in disguise and that he might just find a job even better than the one he had before. Dad says he'll settle for anything that keeps him from sitting around this place worrying all day. I know just how he feels.

215

Comprehension and Vocabulary   *Before Reading*

1. Review the topic of changes by using the questions from Anthology page 205 and DVD 12.1 to generate prior knowledge. After showing DVD 12.1, call on individuals to read the questions. Have students discuss their responses using information from the DVD and the Lessons 1–4 articles.

2. **In this Expedition, we've been talking about how change can affect the way we see the world around us.**
   - **In Lessons 1 and 2, what were Mario and Gaby writing about?** (their hometown)
   - **What change affected the way each teenager saw the people and places in their town?** (Gaby had moved away and missed her hometown. Mario stayed behind and felt lonely and bored.)
   - **How were their views of the town different?** (Mario thought everybody did the same old things, and the places in town were boring and old-fashioned. Gaby remembered how friendly and warm everyone was to her and how fun it was to do all their favorite things and go to all their favorite places.)
   - **In Lessons 3 and 4, what change did Bruce experience?** (His father had left to fight in Iraq.) **How did Bruce's feelings affect the way he saw things around him?** (Feeling depressed made him see his routine activities as unimportant. Missing his father made him see the cadets as symbols of what his father was doing. Fear for his dad's safety made him see the bully's taunting as an insult to his father's service.)

3. **In this lesson's reading, we'll get yet another view of the world through someone else's eyes.**

Building Background Knowledge

Extend students' knowledge about the topic of Hurricane Katrina's effect on New Orleans and its citizens.

- Hurricane Katrina was one of the largest hurricanes, and probably the costliest, ever to hit the United States. It made landfall near New Orleans on August 29, 2005, with gusts around 140 miles an hour. Following the storm, levees around New Orleans gave way, allowing water to flood the city. The hurricane and the flooding it caused did staggering damage to the Gulf Coast, killed hundreds of people, and left many more homeless.

- Thousands of people evacuated before Hurricane Katrina made landfall. After the city flooded, thousands more who had not evacuated were stranded at shelters such as the Superdome, hospitals, nursing homes, private homes, and apartments. It took days to evacuate them. Many had to be rescued by boat or helicopter. Buses and planes took evacuees to shelters all over the country. One of the largest shelters was the Astrodome in Houston, Texas, which hosted nearly 15,000 evacuees. In the weeks that followed, people in the big shelters slowly found housing in apartments, motels, and smaller shelters where the government assisted in paying their expenses.

Introduce Vocabulary

Vocabulary

Review Words

consequence	*result or effect of certain actions*
classify	*to put in groups*
structure	*something built with many parts*
eligible	*having the needed skills or requirements*
application	*a written request for a job*
interview	*a meeting in which an employer asks a job seeker questions to see if he or she is right for the job*

Challenge Words

Word Meaning

category	*a group of things that are similar in some way*
	The story "Beauty and the Beast" falls into the fairy tale *category*.
stench	*a very disgusting smell*
	The *stench* coming from the garbage pail was caused by rotting vegetable matter.

4. **The Lesson 6 text, "Blown Away," contains words with meanings we have already learned. We will review these words within the text we are reading.**

5. Write each Review Word on the board. Then ask students to locate the word in the article. Instruct them to read aloud the sentence containing the word, as well as any other sentences that provide context.

   • **What can you tell me about the word?**

   • Ask other questions that allow students to explore the word's meaning. (For example: **Are *consequences* the same as causes? How is the meaning of *application* related to the meaning of apply?**)

6. Ask students to respond to the following questions. Provide correction and feedback as necessary.

   • **What are possible *consequences* of not wearing a seatbelt?**

   • **Which are *classified* as insects—sparrows or beetles?**

   • **Did you ever want to build a fun *structure* when you were young? Describe it.**

   • **When will you be *eligible* to vote?**

   • **Which requires an *application*—getting into college or getting into an amusement park? Explain.**

   • **What are some reasons a person might go to an *interview*?**

7. Work with students to write a definition for each word on the board.

8. Include the Challenge Words to meet the needs of students who are advancing.

To reinforce vocabulary word meaning for English language learners, create a matching activity with the words and conversational phrases.

Write each vocabulary word and a conversational phrase or sentence that illustrates the meaning of each word on the board in random order. For example:
consequence *That's what happens when you tell lies: Someone gets hurt.*
Model matching the first word with the appropriate sentence. Have students complete the other matches with a partner. Then have them discuss the correct matches and how they selected each.
For a complete model of this strategy, see Expedition 9, Lesson 3.

Review Elements of Description

9. **In this Expedition, we've been reading different kinds of descriptive texts.** Write the following on the board:

   Descriptive Writing

   1. Details
   • *Concrete*
   •

   2. Figurative language
   3. Strong words

   These are some of the elements of description that we've learned about.

- **As we read Mario's and Gaby's letters about their hometown, we looked for concrete, vivid details that the writers used to describe the town.** Place a check mark next to *Concrete*.

- **We also looked for "strong words"—words that are lively and unusual and that get the reader's attention.** Place a check mark next to *Strong words*.

- **When we read the story about Bruce, we looked for figurative language—language that tells what something *seems* like to someone, often by comparing the object or person to something else.** Place a check mark next to *Figurative language*.

10. Next to the list on the board, write the following:

    - *The shimmering drops of dew on the spider web looked like diamonds set in the daintiest kind of lace.*

    - *The angry flood waters roared through the narrow canyon and created a watery grave for startled animals that had no chance to escape.*

    - *A pudgy toddler in a starched white sailor suit stepped into a mud puddle and giggled as the muck oozed up between his toes.*

    Read the sentences aloud. Then have students locate examples of concrete details, strong words, and figurative language in the sentences. Underline and label correct examples that students identify. (Possible responses: concrete details—sparkling drops of dew, flood waters roared through the narrow canyon, startled wildlife, pudgy toddler, starched white sailor suit, muck oozed up between his toes; figurative language—drops of dew on the spider web looked like diamonds set in the daintiest kind of lace, angry flood waters created a watery grave; strong words—shimmering, daintiest, roared, watery, startled, pudgy, starched, oozed)

Introduce Elements of Description: Sensory Details

11. Add this sentence to those on the board: *The crisp, white strips of potato began to sizzle and fry the moment they dropped into the bubbling oil.*

12. **We've been talking about how people "see" and describe the world. However, we don't experience the world just with our eyes. We use all our senses—hearing, tasting, touching, smelling, and seeing—to experience the things around us.** Write these five senses on the board. Then write *Sensory* next to the empty bullet under *Concrete*. **When writers want to bring something to life in the mind of the reader, they try to use details that appeal to all five of the senses.**

    SKILL ✓

13. Point to the new sentence on the board and read it aloud. **Details in this sentence appeal to at least three different senses.**

    - Underline the first six words. **What does this information do to my senses? First, it makes me picture a potato cut into white strips. The strips are crisp and white, so they must be raw. I know that crisp, raw potatoes are crunchy and moist. These details appeal to my sense of touch as well as my sense of sight.**

    - Next, underline *sizzle and fry*. **This detail helps me imagine the sound of the potato strips cooking. I can also imagine them turning golden as they fry. For those reasons, this detail appeals to my sense of hearing as well as my sense of sight.**

    - Underline *bubbling oil*. **Which of your senses does this detail appeal to? Does it make you imagine that you are seeing, tasting, smelling, feeling, or hearing something?** (hearing and seeing something) **This detail probably appeals to your senses of hearing and sight. Since you know that bubbling oil is very hot, it may also appeal to your sense of touch.**

14. **As we read this lesson's text, let's look for sensory details—details that help us to see, hear, taste, touch, or smell something in our minds. Let's also look for the other elements of descriptive writing we've learned about: concrete, vivid details; strong words; and figurative language.**

Reading for Understanding

Reading

Places and Names to Look For:
- Deshaun
- New Orleans
- Hurricane Katrina
- Houston, Texas
- Red Cross
- Astrodome

1. Have students turn to Anthology page 213. **As you read "Blown Away," you may come across some unfamiliar places and names.**
   - Write the words on the board.
   - Point to each word as you read the following:

   In this reading, a girl, her father, and her brother *Deshaun* **survive a terrible hurricane in the city of** *New Orleans*. **The storm is called** *Hurricane Katrina*. **When flooding from the hurricane threatens their home, the family evacuates to** *Houston, Texas*. **Unable to return to their home, they are forced to stay in a** *Red Cross* **shelter in the** *Astrodome*.
   - Call on individuals to read the words.

2. **As we read, remember to look for sensory details and other kinds of descriptive language.**

3. Read paragraph 1 aloud. **What kind of text are we reading?** (a journal or a diary of some kind) **How can you tell that this is a journal?** (Each entry has a date; the girl explains that she wants to write down what has been happening for the past four days.) **Where does the girl live?** (New Orleans) **As you read, you will find that this journal becomes a travel journal. A travel journal contains descriptions of different sights and events that the writer experiences on a trip. Most travel journals describe pleasure trips, but the girl writing this journal is taking a trip of a different kind. It is an unwelcome trip that begins soon after Hurricane Katrina hits New Orleans.**

4. Read the second paragraph aloud. **This paragraph contains a couple of sensory details. The girl uses the words** *whipped* **and** *howled* **to describe the wind around her house. What senses do these words appeal to?** (touch and hearing) **What other words in this paragraph appeal to your sense of hearing?** (clunks, crashes) **In one sentence, the girl says, "Each time a big gust would come along, the house swayed back and forth, and I screamed." What senses does this description appeal to?** (sight, touch, hearing) **Why?** (sight because you can picture a house moving back and forth; touch because you can imagine feeling the house move under your feet; hearing because you can imagine the sound of the girl's scream)

5. **Fluency** Have students read the remainder of the article with partners, taking turns reading paragraphs. Encourage them to note other examples of sensory language as they read. If necessary, review the following fluency goal with students to increase reading rate: **As you become more familiar with the text, try to increase the speed with which you read.**

6. When students have completed their reading, check for literal comprehension of the text by asking these questions: **KNOWLEDGE**
   - *Paragraph 1:* **What kind of storm hit New Orleans?** (a hurricane)
   - *Paragraph 4:* **What surprising thing happens the day after the storm?** (The water rises rather than goes down.)
   - *Paragraphs 4 and 5:* **Where do the girl and her family go?** (Houston, Texas) **How do they get there?** (They ride on a bus with nursing home patients.)
   - *Paragraph 6:* **When Betty Jo says "the whole shootin' match," what does she mean?** (everything, "the works") **What does the girl** *think* **it means?** (that she would be shot for asking for a toothbrush)
   - *Paragraph 9:* **What new plans does the girl's father have for getting a new life started?** (He is going to try to get a government loan and also apply for a job in Houston.)

Checking for Comprehension *After Reading*

1. Display Transparency 13, and give each student a copy of it. Write the title of the selection in the top row; write *Sense* at the top of the first column; and write *Detail* at the top of the second column. Have students do the same.

   • *Sight* **is one of the five senses. Let's write it on the chart. What are the other senses?** (hearing, smell, taste, and touch) Write these in the chart as students name them, and instruct them to do the same.

   • Next, list paragraphs 2, 3, 4, 6, and 7 on the board. Arrange students in groups, and instruct group members to work together to find one sensory detail in each paragraph and to list it in the chart. When all groups are finished, review their responses as a class. (Possible responses: **sight**—paragraph 2: *sky turned kind of greenish, rain poured down*; paragraph 3: *wind had pulled several huge trees right out of the ground, one (tree) had fallen on our truck and crushed it, two houses . . . were completely flattened, streets and yards were littered with all kinds of things*; paragraph 4: *streets . . . filled with water*

   hearing—paragraph 2: *wind . . . howled, loud clunks and crashes, I screamed*; paragraph 6: *babies crying, people calling out names, children squealing*

   smell—paragraph 4: *dark, smelly water*; paragraph 7: *sweet smell of soap; stench of Katrina*

   taste—paragraph 6: *sweet lemonade*

   touch—paragraph 2: *wind . . , whipped, house swayed back and forth*; paragraph 4: *dark, smelly water was up to my shoulders*; paragraph 6: *big, warm hug*; paragraph 7: *filthy, flood-soaked clothes; soft, clean sheets*)

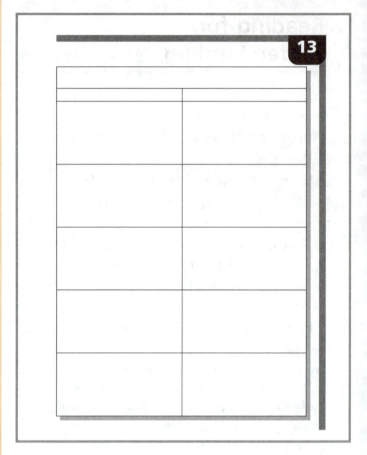

2. Have students apply what they understood from the text by asking the following questions:

   • **Why does the girl call this experience a "bad dream"?** COMPREHENSION (Possible response: Her house has been destroyed, and it seems like her life has been destroyed. She is far from home, stranded with thousands of strangers. She is tired and afraid.)

   • **What does the girl learn about simple things such as toothbrushes and clean sheets?** ANALYSIS (Possible response: She learns that they are luxuries for people who have to go without them.)

3. **Challenge Questions** **Have you or anyone you know ever lost your home? If so, what did you miss most? If not, what do you imagine you would miss most?** APPLICATION (Responses will vary.)

Extending Vocabulary

Affix Review

- Write *un-*, *mis-*, and *-ment* on the board. Ask students to tell the meaning of each word part. Provide the meaning if necessary. (*un-*: not or the opposite of; *mis-*: wrong, wrongly, bad, or badly; *-ment*: the act, state, or process of)

- Have students work with partners to scan paragraphs 1, 3, 6, and 9 for words that contain the prefixes *un-* and *mis-* and the suffix *-ment*.

- When students are finished, call on individuals to name the words they located. (*judgment* [paragraph 1], *unbelievable* [paragraph 3], *unhappy* [paragraph 6], and *misfortune* [paragraph 9]) Write these on the board.

- Point to *judgment*. **What word part is in this word?** (the suffix *-ment*) **How does this suffix help you figure out the meaning of the word?** (*-Ment* means "the act, state, or process of," so *judgment* must mean "the process of judging.")

▶ Have students write this word and its meaning in the Vocabulary Log.

- Repeat the previous step with each of the three remaining words on the board. (*Un-* means "not" or "the opposite of," so *unbelievable* must mean "not believable" and *unhappy* must mean "not happy"; *mis-* means "wrong," "wrongly," "bad," or "badly," so *misfortune* must mean "bad fortune.")

- Have students name other words they know containing the word parts *mis-*, *un-*, and *-ment* and to use the meanings of the word parts to determine the word meanings.

▶ Have students write an additional word containing each word part in the Vocabulary Log.

Connect to Social Studies

Use the following activity to help students connect with the experience of being a volunteer during the aftermath of Hurricane Katrina.

- Explain that thousands of people such as Betty Jo in the story "Blown Away" volunteered their time and energy to help those in need after Hurricane Katrina.

- On the board write the heading *Why People Volunteer*. Then write these categories below the heading:
  – *for a sense of achievement*
  – *for personal growth*
  – *to give something back*
  – *to bring about social change*
  – *for recognition*

- Write the heading *Volunteer Opportunities* on the board. Have students brainstorm situations and organizations that call for volunteer help. (Possible responses: natural disasters, wars, community projects, libraries, hospitals, schools) Write these on the board.

- Have students choose one item from each list and write a paragraph in which they explain why they would be willing to volunteer their time and effort in a particular situation or for a particular organization.

- When students have finished writing their paragraphs, call on individuals to read them aloud.

To increase difficulty: Have students investigate volunteer opportunities in their community and work together as a group to create a brochure in which they describe the opportunities and provide contact information. Ask them to make copies of the information and distribute it in the classroom or throughout the school.

Social Studies

Lesson 7

Anthology Selection

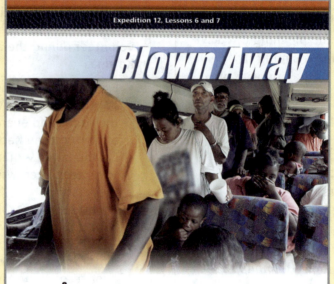

Blown Away

[1]**September 1, 2005** It's Thursday afternoon—the fourth day of my bad dream. I want to write down everything that's happened so I can get it on paper and out of my head. On Monday, Hurricane Katrina hit New Orleans. Lots of people left town before then, but we stayed. Our neighborhood is on high ground, and my dad thought it would be safe from flooding. I trust my dad's judgment, so I wasn't worried, at least not at first. But the more I listened to the news, the more I worried that staying in our home might have terrible **consequences**. My dad, brother, and I all stayed glued to the TV news as the storm got bigger. The reporters could hardly keep from blowing away, and the wind turned their umbrellas inside out. Officials **classified** Katrina as a category 5 hurricane—one of the biggest storms in United States history!

213

[2]By the time the storm hit land, it was down to a category 4, but it was so strong that I wished we hadn't stayed behind. The sky turned kind of greenish, and the rain poured down. The wind whipped around our house and howled so loud that we had a hard time hearing each other talk. We heard loud clunks and crashes when the wind blew things against our house. Each time a big gust would come along, the house swayed back and forth, and I screamed. I kept picturing our roof turning inside out like one of the reporters' umbrellas. It was the worst morning of my life.

[3]The next day, we checked out the damage. It was unbelievable! The wind had pulled several huge trees right out of the ground, and one had fallen on our truck and crushed it! We all felt bad, but I was especially sorry for Deshaun. He just got his driver's license, and now there's nothing to drive. Two houses near us were completely flattened, and every **structure** in the neighborhood was damaged. The porch was missing from Mr. Rendon's store, and the roof of Willie's gas station had collapsed. The whole place looked like there had been an explosion. The streets and yards were littered with all kinds of things—a crumpled grocery basket, a car fender, pieces of houses, part of a billboard, a baby stroller. It made me feel kind of sick to see the neighborhood so destroyed and trashed out.

[4]All the streets lower than ours were filled with water. We thought the water would start going down right away, but instead it started rising. By the next morning, our street was gone! We were surrounded by water, and we couldn't figure out why. The power had been out since the storm, so we couldn't get any news. Dad got worried and told us to pack a bag so we could get to safety. We waded toward a nursing home that was a few blocks away. At times, the dark, smelly water was up to my shoulders. Yuk! When we finally got to the nursing home, the director told us the levee had broken and New Orleans was in big trouble. A bus was coming to evacuate the nursing home patients. We decided we'd better get on it, too.

[5]So that's why I'm on this bus that is half-driving, half-floating across New Orleans. It doesn't look like New Orleans anymore, though. It looks like a nightmare.

[6]**September 3, 2005** It's too noisy to nap so I guess I'll write. I'm on a cot in the Astrodome in Houston, Texas, with thousands of other people who wish they were home. It's like a beehive here, with Red Cross workers passing out snacks and clothes, babies crying, people calling out names as

214

they search for lost family members, children squealing and running around, and lots of folks watching the giant TV to figure out what's going on back home. As crowded as this place is, I was glad to get here. We pulled in late last night, and volunteers came out to help us off the bus and get us settled in. A volunteer named Betty Jo took us under her wing right from the start. She gave me a big, warm hug and a paper cup of sweet lemonade. She made me feel better even though I was really tired and unhappy. The funny way she talks and calls everyone "honey" reminds me of Meemaw. When I asked her if I could get a toothbrush, she told me I was going to get the whole shootin' match. I wondered if she was saying I ought to be shot for asking. I figured out what she really meant when she came back with bags of supplies. Clothes, blankets, shampoo, soap, toothbrushes, and even dental floss—it was all there.

[7]We spent the next half hour wandering around with our things trying to find empty cots to sleep on. There were thousands of cots! When we finally found three together, Dad, Deshaun, and I took turns going to the showers while one of us kept an eye on our things. That was the most wonderful shower I have ever taken. The steam and hot water eased my tired muscles, and the sweet smell of soap replaced the stench of Katrina. I threw away my filthy, flood-soaked clothes and put on the new ones that Betty Jo had given me. It felt like heaven to lie down on soft, clean sheets and sleep.

[8]It was weird waking up in this huge place with people all around me today. It was like being onstage for anyone to look at. I want to be back home with my friends. What if they never come back to New Orleans? It feels like Katrina blew my whole life into pieces. Betty Jo tells me to keep my chin up. She keeps saying that with a good attitude, starting over will be just like falling off a log—whatever that means! Half the time I don't understand what Betty Jo is saying, but she does cheer me up.

[9]Right now, Dad's in line to talk to a social worker. He wants to find out if we're **eligible** for a government loan. On the news, they said that the hospital where Dad works is completely destroyed. He wants to find a job here now, so Betty Jo got him an **application** to fill out. A lot of companies are going to hold job **interviews** right here at the Astrodome. Betty Jo told Dad that misfortune can be a blessing in disguise and that he might just find a job even better than the one he had before. Dad says he'll settle for anything that keeps him from sitting around this place worrying all day. I know just how he feels.

215

Comprehension and Vocabulary
Before Reading

1. **In Lesson 6, we read "Blown Away."**
   - **What kind of descriptive text did we decide this was?** (a travel journal)
   - **What was the author's purpose in writing the journal entries?** (to describe what she saw and experienced during Hurricane Katrina, after the storm, and in the Red Cross shelter in Houston)
   - **What were some things the author saw in New Orleans after the storm?** (Possible responses: flattened homes and damaged businesses, uprooted trees, trash and debris strewn over her neighborhood, streets filled with water)
   - **What were some things the author saw in the Astrodome?** (Possible responses: thousands of cots, Red Cross workers passing out snacks and clothes, some people searching for lost family members and others watching the news on a giant TV, children running around)

Vocabulary Review

2. Arrange students with partners, and have them turn to Student Book page 160. Read the vocabulary words in the box aloud. Call on individuals to tell what each word means. Then read the instructions aloud.

3. **Let's look at the first item. The snippet of the conversation we hear is: "Is a hornet considered a bee or a wasp?" Now let's look at the first word in the box. It is *consequences*. *Consequences* means "results or effects of certain actions." Maybe a hornet is about to sting one of the people in the conversation. This seems like a stretch. Let's look at the next word. It's *classified*. *Classified* means "assigned to a group or category." The speaker is asking whether a hornet is assigned to the same group as bees**

or hornets. That is the same as asking whether a hornet is classified as a bee or a wasp. *Classified* must be the right answer. Let's write it on the line.**

4. Have partners complete the remaining items. When all students are finished, call on them to report their responses and to explain their thinking.

5. **Challenge Words** Write the following items on the board, along with the words *category* and *stench*. Have students complete the items along with those in the Student Book.

   "Arrange these snacks in two groups: healthful, and unhealthful." (category)

   "This moldy sandwich truly stinks." (stench)

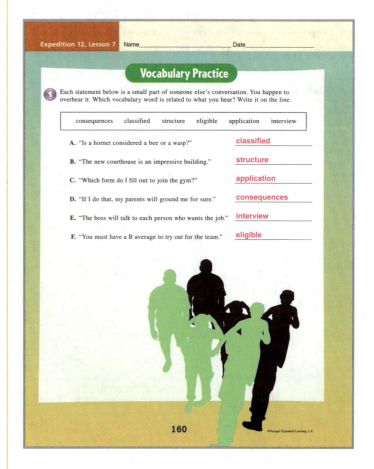

Introduce Elements of Description: Regional Language

6. **When writers are trying to describe a place, they often include the** 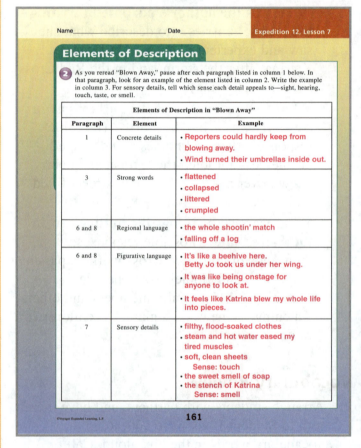 **language and expressions of people who live in that place. This is because people talk differently in different parts of the country. For example, many people in the southern United States refer to other people as *y'all*, while many people in the northern United States refer to other people as *you guys*. In some states, people refer to sweet, fizzy drinks as *soda*, while in others they call it *pop*.** Supply additional examples of words or phrases that are unique to your region, and then ask students to do the same.

7. **In Houston, the young journal writer has trouble understanding some of the local expressions that the Red Cross worker, Betty Jo, uses. Let's watch for these expressions, too, as we reread "Blown Away."**

Reading for Understanding   *Reading*

1. Arrange students in pairs and have them turn to Anthology page 213 and Student Book page 161. Read the Student Book instructions aloud.

Name_____ Date_____   Expedition 12, Lesson 7

Elements of Description

2 As you reread "Blown Away," pause after each paragraph listed in column 1 below. In that paragraph, look for an example of the element listed in column 2. Write the example in column 3. For sensory details, tell which sense each detail appeals to—sight, hearing, touch, taste, or smell.

Elements of Description in "Blown Away"

Paragraph	Element	Example
1	Concrete details	• Reporters could hardly keep from blowing away. • Wind turned their umbrellas inside out.
3	Strong words	• flattened • collapsed • littered • crumpled
6 and 8	Regional language	• the whole shootin' match • falling off a log
6 and 8	Figurative language	• It's like a beehive here. Betty Jo took us under her wing. • It was like being onstage for anyone to look at. • It feels like Katrina blew my whole life into pieces.

7	Sensory details	• filthy, flood-soaked clothes
		• steam and hot water eased my tired muscles
		• soft, clean sheets
		  Sense: touch
		• the sweet smell of soap
		• the stench of Katrina
		  Sense: smell

©Voyager Expanded Learning, L.P.   **161**

2. The first paragraph listed in the chart is paragraph 1. In column 2, the element listed is concrete details. **As I read the first paragraph aloud, follow along in your book. Then we'll look for concrete details.**

3. Read paragraph 1, then pause. **The writer describes what she sees on the news. She writes, "The reporters could hardly keep from blowing away." This is a concrete detail. It helps me imagine seeing the reporters in the strong winds. Let's write this as our first example.**

4. **What is another concrete detail in this paragraph?** (The wind turned their umbrellas inside out.) Have students record this detail in the chart.

5. Instruct students to read the remainder of the selection independently, pausing to locate and record examples after each paragraph listed in column 1. Point out that when they record the sensory details they find in paragraph 7, they should also record the sense to which the details appeal.

6. Encourage students to monitor their own comprehension of the text by pausing occasionally to ask themselves *Am I understanding what I'm reading?* Tell students that when they do not understand what they are reading, they should reread that portion of the text.

Checking for Comprehension   *After Reading*

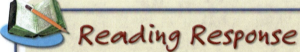

1. When all students are finished, have them review their responses with a partner and make adjustments if needed. Remind students that some paragraphs contain more than one example of the element listed. Then review all students' responses as a class. Provide guidance and feedback as needed.

2. Challenge students to look back through the selection to find and list additional examples of each element. Then call on one individual to name an element and a paragraph number (for example, "Sensory detail, paragraph 2"), and call on another to locate the example.

Reading Response

Tell students that they will now write an extended response about traveling as a hurricane evacuee. Have them turn to Student Book page 162. Read the instructions aloud. Then have students turn back to Student Book page 161. **You have already planned for the Reading Response question by completing this graphic organizer. Use the information you recorded here to help you write your answer.** Encourage students to include details and additional information from the text, as well. Then, have students work individually to write a response to this question:

 What have I done, seen, heard, and felt since Hurricane Katrina hit?

When students are finished, call on individuals to read their responses aloud.

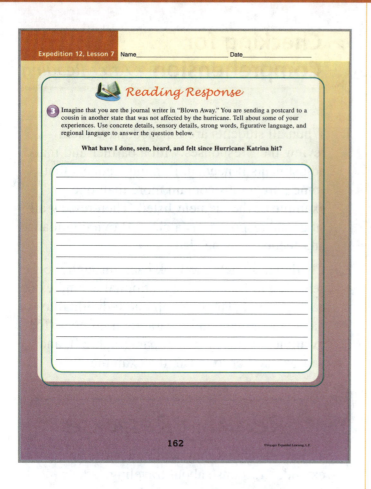

Expedition 12, Lesson 7   Name_____ Date_____

Reading Response

3 Imagine that you are the journal writer in "Blown Away." You are sending a postcard to a cousin in another state that was not affected by the hurricane. Tell about some of your experiences. Use concrete details, sensory details, strong words, figurative language, and regional language to answer the question below.

What have I done, seen, heard, and felt since Hurricane Katrina hit?

162

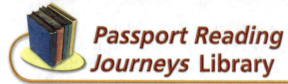

Passport Reading Journeys Library

Building Fluency

1. Place students in pairs according to reading level to build fluency. When pairing students, be sure that one student is a stronger reader (Student A) than the other student (Student B). However, do not reveal that stronger readers are paired with weaker readers. See *Passport Reading Journeys* Library Teacher's Guide for grouping guidelines.

2. Have students quickly choose reading material from the *Passport Reading Journeys* Library or another approved selection that is at the reading level of Student B. If students have not finished the previously chosen selection, they may continue reading from that selection. See *Passport Reading Journeys* Library Teacher's Guide for material selection guidelines.

3. Tell students that Student A will read one paragraph, and Student B will reread that same paragraph.

4. Have students follow this routine until the end of class.

5. If necessary, review the following practices to enhance fluency:
   - Rate and accuracy of reading
   - Expression during reading
   - Correction procedures

Library Highlights

Student Assessment

Level I

The assessments for some of the books and magazines are multiple choice questions with extended response questions. The assessment may be given to students to complete while they read or after they have completed the book or magazine.

Advanced Word Study

Spelling

1. Direct students to Student Book page E12, Lesson 8. **We use the sounds we know and hear in a word to spell the word. *-Ic* and *-ish* are suffixes. Remember, a suffix is a word part that occurs at the end of a word and often helps us understand the meaning of the word. Let's spell words with these suffixes. The first word is *athletic*. Say the word parts in the word *athletic*.** (ath, let, ic) **What is the first syllable?** (ath) **What are the sounds in *ath*?** (/a/ /th/) **Write those sounds. What is the next syllable?** (let) **What are the sounds in *let*?** (/l/ /e/ /t/) **Write those sounds. What is the suffix?** (-ic) **What are the sounds in the suffix *-ic*?** (/i/ /k/) **Write those sounds.** Repeat with *caustic, plastic, sluggish, lavish,* and *bookish.*

2. Write the words on the board as students check and correct their words. Have them read the list of words.

1.	athletic	4.	sluggish
2.	caustic	5.	lavish
3.	plastic	6.	bookish

Sight Words

1. Direct students to line 1. Have them point to the first word. **This word is *pierce*. Read the word.** (pierce) **This is not a regular word. Let's read the word again.** (pierce) **Let's spell the word.** (p-i-e-r-c-e) **What is the word?** (pierce) Repeat with the remaining words. Then, have students read the words. Ask students to tell the meanings of the words.

2. Direct students to lines 2 and 3. **Let's read these words.** Remind students that the rows of words consist of regular and irregular words. Point to the first word. **What is the word?** (influential) Repeat with the remaining words. Call on individuals to read the words in a different order. Ask students to tell the meanings of the words.

▼ To Correct

For Regular Words: Say the sound(s) in the word, then ask students to repeat the sound(s). Have them read the word again with the correct sound(s). If students do not know the meaning of the word, review the word and/or word part to determine the meaning of the word.

For Irregular Words: Immediately say the correct word. Then have students read the word, spell it, and read it again. If students do not know the meaning of the word, review the word.

1. pierce **I**	legendary **I**	bough **I**	worse **I**
2. influential **I**	damage **I**	atmosphere **I**	figured **I**
3. disguise **I**	profoundly **R**	judgment **I**	reverend **R**

Building to Fluency

1. Direct students to the phrases in the Student Book. Have them read through each phrase for accuracy. Then, have students reread the phrases to increase their accuracy and fluency so that the phrases sound like natural speech.

2. Direct students to the Anthology article to locate the sentences containing the phrases. Have them read the sentences in the article accurately and fluently. Remind students to read in a way that sounds like natural speech.

▼ To Correct

Immediately say the correct word. Have students reread the word, then read the phrase or sentence again.

1. . . . orchards groan and sag with fruit; *stanza 4*
2. . . . loss of love is a terrible thing; *stanza 6*
3. . . . wrote a novel, plays, and stories for children. *Connect to the Author*

Anthology Selection

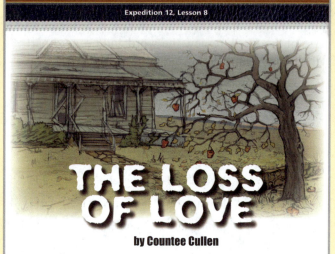

THE LOSS OF LOVE

by Countee Cullen

In this poem, Cullen uses rich images, such as a crumbling house and decaying fruit, to describe the emotional pain he feels. The poem's traditional structure reflects Cullen's respect for romantic European poetry.

¹All through an empty place I go,
And find her not in any room;
The candles and the lamps I light
Go down before a wind of gloom.

²Thick-spraddled lies the dust about,
A fit, sad place to write her name
Or draw her face the way she looked
That legendary night she came.

spraddled: spread in an ugly way

216

³The old house crumbles bit by bit;
Each day I hear the ominous thud
That says another rent is there
For winds to pierce and storms to flood.

⁴My orchards groan and sag with fruit;
Where, Indian-wise, the bees go round;
I let it rot upon the bough;
I eat what falls upon the ground.

⁵The heavy cows go laboring
In agony with clotted teats;
My hands are slack; my blood is cold;
I marvel that my heart still beats.

⁶I have no will to weep or sing,
No least desire to pray or curse;
The loss of love is a terrible thing;
They lie who say that death is worse.

ominous: warning that something bad is going to happen

rent: an opening made by a tear

slack: hanging loosely

Connect to the Author

In the 1920s, Countee Cullen was the most famous African American writer in the United States. Some biographers think that Cullen was born in Louisville, Kentucky, in 1903. But his birthplace is uncertain. When he was 15, Countee moved in with the influential Rev. Frederick A. Cullen, from whom he got his name. The Reverend lived in Harlem, New York, at a time when African American art and writing were beginning to flower into what became known as the Harlem Renaissance. The atmosphere in Harlem influenced Cullen profoundly. So did the poems he read in school. Cullen began winning awards for his poetry while he was still in high school. By the age of 25, Cullen was celebrated as one of the leaders of the Harlem Renaissance. In addition to poems, Cullen wrote a novel, plays, and stories for children. He also taught high school English, French, and creative writing. Cullen died in 1946.

Countee Cullen

217

Comprehension and Vocabulary *Before Reading*

1. **What life changes have we read about in this Expedition?** (moving away from a hometown, adjusting to separation from a parent in the military, evacuation after a hurricane) **We've gotten to take a look at each of these situations through the eyes of another person. The author or writer of each text— whether it was a letter, a story, or a travel journal—helped us see people, places, and situations from his or her perspective.**

2. **In this lesson we will read about how change can affect daily activities. Have you ever had trouble doing your chores or schoolwork because you were feeling sad or angry about something? Why was it hard to concentrate on routine things that needed to be done? What was your perspective about those things at that time?**

3. Have students turn to Anthology page 216 and preview the text. **This reading is a poem. The narrator and main character of this poem will describe his life after losing someone he loves. His descriptions will help us see his home and his surroundings. They will help us experience what he is feeling without his loved one.**

Vocabulary Strategy Review

4. Display Transparency 2, and give a copy to each student. Write the words *gloom* and *marvel* in the *Word* rows. Have students do the same. Then read the words aloud, and have students repeat them.

5. **As we read "The Loss of Love," we will encounter these words. One or both of them may be unfamiliar. You may also find other words that are unfamiliar. Remember that when you come across an unfamiliar word, you can use the CPR strategy to figure out its meaning.**

SKILL ✔

Vocabulary Strategies			2
Word:			
Context	Parts of a Word	Resource: dictionary	
Word:			
Context	Parts of a Word	Resource: dictionary	
Word:			
Context	Parts of a Word	Resource: dictionary	

- **What does *C* stand for?** (context) **How can you use context to figure out a word's meaning?** (You can look for clues in the words and sentences surrounding the unfamiliar word.)
- **What does *P* stand for?** (word parts) **How can you use word parts to figure out a word's meaning?** (You can look for prefixes, suffixes, or roots that you know, and use those meanings to help you come up with the meaning.)
- **What does *R* stand for?** (resources, such as a dictionary) **When should you use a dictionary or other resource to find a word's meaning?** (when context or word parts don't help)
- Point out that in this poem, the meanings of some difficult words are provided in the margin near the word's appearance.

6. Read aloud the first four lines of the poem.

7. **The word *gloom* appears in the fourth line of the poem. Let's think about this word's meaning.**

   • **Does *gloom* have word parts that can give us a clue to its meaning?** (no)

   • **Let's look at the lines before the word and see if we can find clues in the poem to help us understand what *gloom* means.**

   • Reread lines 3 and 4. Explain that the lamps and candles "go down," or are blown out, by a "wind of gloom." Write this under *Context* on the transparency, and have students do the same on their copy.

   • **How might a room look if the lamps and candles lighting it were blown out?** (dark, shadowy) **So a "wind of gloom" is a wind that brings darkness and shadows. *Gloom* must mean "dark and shadowy."** Write this meaning on the transparency and have students write it on their copy.

8. **As we read the text, we'll look for the word *marvel*. When we come to it, we'll pause to use the CPR strategy to figure out its meaning.**

Review Elements of Description

9. **In this Expedition, we've been discussing some different elements of descriptive writing. What are some of these elements?** (regional language, concrete details, sensory details, strong words, figurative language) Write these on the board, adding those that students omit.

10. Underline *regional language*. **What is regional language?** (the unique words, phrases, or pronunciations used by people in different regions or areas of the country) **The poem we will read is written in the author's own literary voice, so it does not include regional language, but it does include the other four elements.**

11. Underline *concrete details* on the board. **What are concrete details?** (vivid, literal details that help the reader picture what the author sees) **In this poem, the poet uses concrete details to help us picture the place where he lives and the things around him.**

12. Underline *sensory details* on the board. **What are sensory details?** (details that appeal to our sense of sight, hearing, taste, smell, or touch) **In "The Loss of Love," the poet uses sensory details to help us experience what he sees, hears, and feels after losing his loved one.**

13. Underline *strong words* on the board. **What are strong words?** (lively, uncommon words that make the reader take notice of them) **Strong words make the details in this poem more powerful.**

14. Underline *figurative language* on the board. **What is figurative language?** (language that tells what something seems like, often by comparing the object or person with something else) **Why does an author use figurative language?** (to help the reader understand how the author or a character perceived something)

15. **As we read "The Loss of Love," we'll watch for these four elements of descriptive writing.**

Reading for Understanding

Reading

1. Have students turn to Anthology page 216. **In "The Loss of Love," you'll read about the day-to-day life of a man who is grieving for a lost loved one. He describes his empty house, his neglected farm, and how he feels inside after the loss.**

2. Explain that "The Loss of Love" is both the title and the topic of this poem. **The author wrote this poem to say something about the loss of love. As we read and study the poem, try to decide what is the author's main idea, or message, about losing love.**

3. Point out that a poem is not written in paragraphs, as an article or story is.
   - **This poem, like many poems, is divided into stanzas. There is a blank space following each stanza.**
   - **In this poem, most of the stanzas contain one long sentence that is divided into lines. How many lines are in each stanza?** (four)
   - **Each stanza in this poem expresses a complete idea or image. All of these ideas and images help put across the author's main message about the loss of love.**

4. Read aloud the poem for students. **As I read, don't worry about any words or lines you find difficult to understand. Just try to understand the main message of the poem. Listen for things the narrator—the person talking in the poem—sees, hears, feels, and does. Listen also for things that the narrator does not see, hear, feel, or do.** Read the poem aloud, pausing briefly after each stanza to let students think about the words they have just heard.

5. **Now let's reread the poem and talk about what each part means.** As you read the poem again, pause after every other line to help students paraphrase those two lines of the stanza. If a line contains a word that has been defined in the margin, have students read and discuss the definition before paraphrasing the line. You also may use the CPR chart to build meaning for these and other words.

6. As you help students paraphrase the poem, use the following questions and strategies as needed to build background or clarify meaning.
   - Stanza 1: **In the first two lines, the narrator says he goes through an empty place and can't find "her." The reader never finds out if the lost love was his mother, wife, daughter, or some other female in his life. The reader doesn't know if the lost love died, moved away, or simply decided to leave the relationship. How might these uncertainties make the poem have a different meaning for different readers?** (Possible responses: People will create their own picture of the person he lost and the way in which he lost her. They can relate the poem to losing a female who is important in their own life.) **In the last line, the author says that the candles and lamps "Go down before a wind of gloom." How does this description help us understand the way the poet feels?** (Possible response: His grief makes him experience the wind as a dark and hopeless thing.)
   - Stanza 2: **The author describes the layer of dust in the house and then imagines how it might be used. What does the author want you to picture when he asks, "A fit, sad place to write her name?"** (using a finger to write her name in the dust) **In the last two lines, what does the author think about drawing in the dust?** (a picture of her face) **What strong word tells you how important it was to the narrator that this person came into his life?** (legendary)
   - Stanza 3: **What is happening to the narrator's house?** (It is crumbling and getting holes in it.) **Why do you think he isn't fixing the house?** (He is too depressed to take care of it.)
   - Stanza 4: **What action words does the narrator use to describe what is happening**

to his orchard? (groan, sag) **The trees in the orchard are groaning because they are carrying too heavy a load. Can an orchard really groan?** (no) **Who might groan when carrying a heavy load?** (a person) **Why is this an example of figurative language?** (The trees and their fruit are being compared with people who would groan if they had too heavy a load.)

- Stanza 5: **In the first two lines, the poet describes the cows as "heavy" and "laboring in agony" because they have "clotted teats." Farmers must milk their cows every day or the cows' udders, or teats, become too full. If the milk stays in the udders for too long, it hardens, or clots. What would cause the narrator's cows to be in this painful condition?** (He has not milked them.) **Which words in this description seem like uncommon, vivid words to you?** (Possible responses: laboring, agony, clotted)

- **The word *marvel* appears in the last line of this stanza. Let's go back to our CPR chart. Does the word *marvel* contain a word part that we know?** (no) **What other strategy can we try?** (context) Reread the sentence in which *marvel* appears. **What clues does this sentence give us about the meaning of *marvel*?** (It says the narrator's hands are slack, or hanging loosely, and his blood is cold. Then it says that he marvels that his heart still beats.) Write these clues under *Context* on the transparency, and have students do the same. **What do you think of when you picture someone with cold blood and hands that hang loosely?** (They are lifeless.) **How can you use these ideas to help you understand the meaning of *marvel*?** (They tell that the narrator feels amazed that his heart is beating, since he feels lifeless. So *marvel* must mean "to feel amazed.") **Let's write the definition in our chart.**

- Stanza 6: **In the first two lines, the narrator says that he doesn't want to cry or sing and that he doesn't have the slightest desire to pray or curse. People cry when they are sad, sing when they are happy, pray to seek help or hope, and curse to show anger. What words could you use to describe someone who has no desire to show any of these feelings?** (Possible responses: numb, hopeless, lifeless)

7. **Challenge Questions What is the main idea of this poem?** (Possible response: Losing love makes life empty and painful.) **If you had to use one sentence from the poem to summarize the author's message, which lines would you choose? Why?** (Possible response: the last two lines [last sentence] because they tell what all the other lines in the poem show—that the loss of love is worse than death)

SKILL ✓

618

Checking for Comprehension *After Reading*

1. Ask students to turn to Student Book page 163. Read the instructions for section 1 aloud. Review the elements and provide examples as needed.

2. Have groups of students work together to read the verses listed in the activity and record the examples of the descriptive elements that they find. Call on members from each group to read aloud their responses. Write the responses on the board. Provide correction and feedback as necessary.

3. Read aloud the instructions for section 2. Then have students work independently to complete the section.

4. Invite students to share with a group or partner their description and picture from section 2.

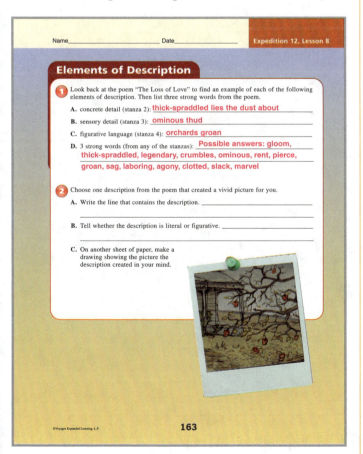

ELL English language learners find prepositions confusing and often use them incorrectly. Instruct students briefly on the meaning of the grammatical term *preposition*:

A *preposition* often tells when or where something is in relation to something else. In the phrase *the book in my bag*, the word *in* is a preposition. Write other common prepositions on the board.

Write several sentences from "Blown Away" on the board with blank lines in place of some of the prepositions. Model finding the correct preposition for the blank: ***My dad, brother, and I all stayed glued _____ the TV news . . . .*** **What word makes the most sense in the blank?** (to) Pause to provide wait time. Then have students independently fill in the remaining blanks in the sentences.

For a complete model of this strategy, see Expedition 10, Lesson 2.

Connect to the Author

Arrange students in groups. Then have students read the author biography on Anthology page 217 before discussing the following questions:

- **Experts are not sure, but some believe that Cullen spent his younger years in rural Kentucky. What details in this poem show that the poet might have lived in a rural place?**

- **In "The Loss of Love," the narrator's heavy heart is reflected in descriptions of things around him. What are some descriptive words that Countee Cullen uses to show this heavy feeling?**

- **Countee Cullen wrote many other poems. Would you like to read more works by this poet? Why or why not?**

Connect to Social Studies

Use the following activity to help students learn more about key figures in the Harlem Renaissance.

- Explain that Countee Cullen was one of many African Americans associated with the Harlem Renaissance. **During this time, writers, philosophers, political activists, artists, dancers, and musicians influenced and inspired one another's creativity.**

- Point out that during this important moment in history, African American artists and writers used culture—rather than direct political methods—to further their goals of equality at a time when they were being denied basic civil rights in the United States.

- On the board, write these names associated with the Harlem Renaissance and any others you may want to include:
  – *Romare Bearden*
  – *W.E.B. DuBois*
  – *Duke Ellington*
  – *Ella Fitzgerald*
  – *Langston Hughes*
  – *Zora Neale Hurston*
  – *Adam Clayton Powell, Sr.*
  – *Bessie Smith*

- Assign one of the names to partners or small groups of students. Have students use classroom, library, or online resources to gather information for a brief biography of the person assigned to them. Ask students to write a biographical paragraph on the person. Encourage them to include a quote, poem, or other example of the person's work.

- When students have finished the activity, call on individuals to share their information.

To increase difficulty: Have students organize a classroom celebration of the Harlem Renaissance, using the information gathered in the activity and any other resources such as jazz recordings and photographs of key figures and artworks from this time.

Social Studies

Lesson 9

Anthology Selection

INVASION

¹One year ago, I lived in a different world. My life was going along just fine except for the occasional screaming match between my parents. They always seemed back to normal the next day, so I didn't worry about it much. Then one day, I found out those fights were a bigger deal than I thought. My mom's exact words are burned into my memory: "Carlos, your father and I have tried to work things out, but we can't, so we're getting a divorce. I want you to know that this has nothing to do with you."

218

²Nothing to do with me—yeah, right! It was only an end to life as I knew it. From then on, I lived in two places and moved my stuff back and forth every week. I felt like a yo-yo! At least they both promised to stay in Dallas so I wouldn't have to take an airplane back and forth. Unfortunately, they didn't promise to stay single. My parents both started dating, and that was totally weird. After a few months, my dad introduced me to Sara, the woman he was dating, and before I knew it, they were getting married.

³That's when my life got really complicated. Sara and her two little kids moved in, and Dad expected me to act all big brother and everything. Suddenly our house was overflowing with noise and toys and people I didn't even know.

⁴The noise always reminds me that invaders have taken over. For one thing, there is lots of lame music. You see, my stepmom sings golden oldies while she cooks, while she gets ready for work, even while she's driving. It never stops! Her daughter, Marisa, is even noisier. She is hooked on cartoons, and she has them blaring all afternoon. I hear her loud, goofy laugh the whole time the TV is on. As if that's not bad enough, each cartoon is followed by what I consider to be a kind of torture. Marisa corners me and makes me listen while she repeats every detail. ". . . and then the rabbit, he was hiding because he wanted to trick the duck, so he was hiding, hiding behind the tree. And then the duck tried to find the rabbit, but he couldn't because the rabbit was hiding behind the tree, and then . . ." It goes on forever!

⁵Only Luis, my new stepbrother, is quiet. Problem is that he's like a little shadow watching everything I do. I'm in my room repairing my radio-controlled plane when I get the feeling I'm not alone. I look up, and there's Luis, standing in the hallway watching me. I'm outside practicing end-overs on my skateboard, and there he is at the window—just staring at me. I'm tuning up my dirt bike in the garage, and suddenly I catch a glimpse of Luis in my rearview mirror. I nearly jump out of my skin! I'm starting to feel like I'm being haunted.

⁶The worst part is that Sara thinks Luis and I should be best buddies. "Why don't you see if Luis wants to go skateboarding with you?" she says to me, or "I'll bet you boys would have fun at the arcade together." It's like she can't see how different we are. Luis is a whole 5 years younger than I am,

219

and we don't like to do the same stuff. Heck, he still collects action figures!

⁷Last Saturday, I finally got to spend some time alone with my dad. His car had been running rough, and he was putting in a new carburetor. He always lets me help, because I love to work on engines. Anyway, we'd been working out on the driveway for about an hour when I notice Luis. He's just sitting on the front steps watching us.

⁸That's when Dad says, "Hey, Luis, come hand me that wrench, and I'll show you what we're doing." Well, the kid was on that wrench like a duck on a June bug. Dad started showing Luis stuff and telling him the name of everything under the hood, just like he did with me when I was younger. I got a little bent out of shape because I figured Luis was just acting interested to get my dad's attention.

⁹I was kind of mad at the world after that, so I went to my room to play video games. I'd been holed up there for a couple of hours when I thought I heard one of my friends coming up the driveway on a skateboard. When I looked outside, I realized it was Luis. He was on a cheesy little skateboard trying to do end-overs like he'd seen me doing. He was letting the nose go up too high so the turns weren't really working, but he wasn't giving up. He just kept on trying. I started to get the idea that maybe it wasn't Dad's attention he wanted after all.

¹⁰I was tired of playing video games, so I grabbed my board and an old one I don't use anymore. My old board is way better than the one Luis was riding. I went outside and handed Luis the old board and started doing end-overs up and down the driveway. At first he just stood by watching me, but I gave him some pointers and told him to try a couple. He started getting the hang of it right away.

¹¹Luis is turning out to be an OK kid. I think he's got real potential as a skateboarder, but he's going to need a lot of lessons. I let him help me finish the repairs on my radio-controlled plane and told him he could come with Dad and me to fly it this weekend. Of course, Marisa is bugging me to come along, and Sara said she'd like to see it fly, too. I guess if Sara promises not to sing, that would be OK. Might as well let the whole . . . well, family . . . get in on the fun. As long as they don't expect me to hang out with them ALL the time!

220

Expedition Review

1. Arrange students in five groups. Assign each group one of the characters from the texts (Mario and Gaby from "Long Distance Love," Bruce from "Game Day," the girl who keeps the travel journal in "Blown Away," and the narrator in the poem "The Loss of Love").

2. **In this Expedition, we've taken looks at the world through the eyes of different characters. A character's descriptions of the world give readers important information about settings, places, and experiences. These descriptions also give us important information about the character who reports them.**

3. Have students review the content of the letters, story, travel journal, or poem that features their character. Then have them work together to create a profile of the character. The profile should contain answers to these questions:

   • **What is your character's life like? Has it changed? If so, how?**

   • **What do you know about his or her family or loved ones? Use figurative language to describe how the character feels about one person in his or her life. For example,** *The woman's memory haunts him like a ghost.*

   • **What is one specific thing that arouses a strong feeling in your character? It could be something that the character finds interesting, special, enjoyable, or beautiful; or something the character finds unpleasant, frightening, or irritating. For example,** *This character loves the feeling of soft, clean sheets.*

   • **Based on the text, what important change has occurred in this character's life? Use figurative language to describe how the change affected your character. For example:** *This character's hometown is like a prison to him after his girlfriend moves away.*

   • **What words best describe your character? Write some sentences about your character that include those words.** Explain to students that their character profile should contain as many strong words as possible and at least one vocabulary word from the selection they are working with.

4. **Challenge Words** If students have learned the Challenge Words, instruct them to include at least one of those words in their character profile.

5. **Listening and Speaking** Ask a representative from each group to share the character profile with the class. Remind students to use standard English rather than slang in their presentations. Encourage them to speak slowly, taking the time needed to choose words that will best communicate their message.

6. When all groups have presented their profiles, review synonyms by calling on students to supply words with meanings similar to those listed on the board. List these on the board as well. Ask if each synonym given is stronger or weaker than the original word.

Assessment

1. Have students turn to Student Book page 164. Then have them turn to Anthology page 218. Explain to students that they will read the article "Invasion" before they answer the questions on the Student Book page.

2. Read aloud the Tips for Success and the assessment instructions. Then have students complete the assessment independently.

Reteaching Guidelines

Comprehension

If students incorrectly answer more than 2 out of 11 questions on the Comprehension Assessment, refer to the Reteach lesson on page 626a. Using the Comprehension section, reteach the skills, guide students in completing the practice activity, and reassess comprehension.

Vocabulary

If more than 20 percent of the students miss certain vocabulary items, reteach and practice those words using the Vocabulary section of the Reteach lesson on page 626c.

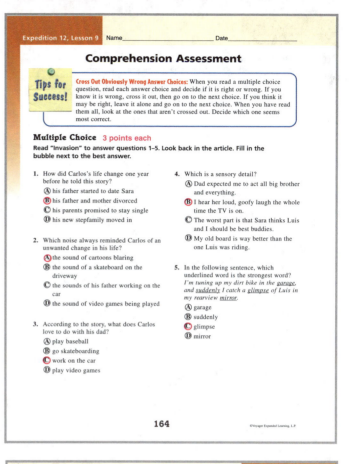

Expedition 12, Lesson 9   Name_____ Date_____

Comprehension Assessment

Tips for Success! **Cross Out Obviously Wrong Answer Choices:** When you read a multiple choice question, read each answer choice and decide if it is right or wrong. If you know it is wrong, cross it out, then go on to the next choice. If you think it may be right, leave it alone and go on to the next choice. When you have read them all, look at the ones that aren't crossed out. Decide which one seems most correct.

Multiple Choice   3 points each
Read "Invasion" to answer questions 1–5. Look back in the article. Fill in the bubble next to the best answer.

1. How did Carlos's life change one year before he told this story?
   - Ⓐ his father started to date Sara
   - Ⓑ his father and mother divorced
   - Ⓒ his parents promised to stay single
   - Ⓓ his new stepfamily moved in

2. Which noise always reminded Carlos of an unwanted change in his life?
   - Ⓐ the sound of cartoons blaring
   - Ⓑ the sound of a skateboard on the driveway
   - Ⓒ the sounds of his father working on the car
   - Ⓓ the sound of video games being played

3. According to the story, what does Carlos love to do with his dad?
   - Ⓐ play baseball
   - Ⓑ go skateboarding
   - Ⓒ work on the car
   - Ⓓ play video games

4. Which is a sensory detail?
   - Ⓐ Dad expected me to act all big brother and everything.
   - Ⓑ I hear her loud, goofy laugh the whole time the TV is on.
   - Ⓒ The worst part is that Sara thinks Luis and I should be best buddies.
   - Ⓓ My old board is way better than the one Luis was riding.

5. In the following sentence, which underlined word is the strongest word? *I'm tuning up my dirt bike in the garage, and suddenly I catch a glimpse of Luis in my rearview mirror.*
   - Ⓐ garage
   - Ⓑ suddenly
   - Ⓒ glimpse
   - Ⓓ mirror

164   ©Voyager Expanded Learning, L.P.

Name_____ Date_____   Expedition 12, Lesson 9

Short Response   4 points each
Read "Invasion" to answer questions 6–10. Look back in the text. Then write your answer on the line(s).

6. A literal detail tells how something really is. A figurative detail tells how something seems. Give an example of one literal detail and one figurative detail Carlos uses to describe people or experiences in his life. **Possible responses are given.**
   literal: . . . my stepmom sings golden oldies while she cooks, while she gets ready for work, even while she's driving; Only Luis, my new stepbrother, is quiet; He's just sitting on the front steps watching us; He was letting the nose go up too high so the turns weren't really working . . .

   figurative: I felt like a yo-yo; Problem is, he's like a little shadow watching everything I do; I nearly jump out of my skin; I'm starting to feel like I'm being haunted; Well, the kid was on that wrench like a duck on a June bug; I got a little bent out of shape.

7. List four ways that Carlos's life changed after Sara, Marisa, and Luis moved into the house.
   a. He hears Sara singing golden oldies all the time.
   b. Cartoons are blaring every afternoon.
   c. Luis is always watching him.
   d. He doesn't get to spend as much time alone with his dad.

8. Carlos uses a regional expression when he says, "Well, the kid was on that wrench like a duck on a June bug." Based on the context in the story, what do you think the underlined expression means?
   Possible responses: to do something quickly; to be eager to do something

9. What made Carlos think Luis was trying to get his dad's attention?
   Luis stared at them while they worked on the car and ran right over as soon as Carlos's dad invited him to help.

   Later, Carlos says *I started to get the idea that maybe it wasn't Dad's attention he wanted after all.* What does Carlos figure out that made him say that?
   When he sees Luis trying to imitate his moves on the skateboard, Carlos realizes that Luis is trying to get *his* attention, not his father's.

10. The last paragraph shows a change in Carlos's perspective. Tell what he sees differently. Give at least two details from the text that support your answer.
    He sees his stepfamily differently. I can tell because he says Luis is OK and that he's going to give him skateboard lessons. He also is going to include Luis, Sara, and Marisa in flying his radio-control plane when he could have the time alone with his dad. At the end, he calls them his family instead of invaders.

©Voyager Expanded Learning, L.P.   165

623

Extended Response 20 points

Read "Invasion" to answer question 11 by completing the graphic organizer.

11. What details most help the reader imagine what Carlos didn't like about his life after his parents' divorce? Write one detail in each oval below. Give the most lively, colorful, vivid, and concrete details you can find. **Possible responses are given.**

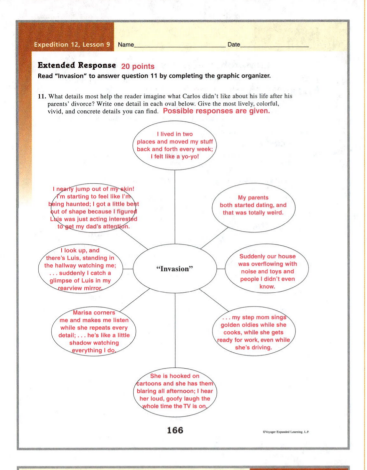

166   ©Voyager Expanded Learning, L.P.

---

20. Bruce had the potential to become a great pitcher.
What does the word *potential* mean?
- Ⓐ luck
- Ⓑ possibility
- Ⓒ plan
- Ⓓ training

21. If you break the rules, you'll suffer the consequences.
What does the word *consequences* mean?
- Ⓐ reasons for doing something
- Ⓑ systems for keeping order
- Ⓒ results of certain actions
- Ⓓ regrets for causing trouble

22. Storms are classified according to the speed of their winds.
What does the word *classified* mean?
- Ⓐ assigned to a particular group or category
- Ⓑ tracked or followed on a map
- Ⓒ controlled or slowed down
- Ⓓ predicted and prepared for

23. I anticipate a win because our team has been doing great at practice.
What does the word *anticipate* mean?
- Ⓐ dread
- Ⓑ expect
- Ⓒ promise
- Ⓓ doubt

24. Gaby had confidence at home, but became shy and quiet in the city.
What does the word *confidence* mean?
- Ⓐ a fear of crowds
- Ⓑ common sense
- Ⓒ faith in oneself
- Ⓓ nervousness

25. The black clouds cast a sense of gloom over the picnic.
What does the word *gloom* mean?
- Ⓐ fear
- Ⓑ darkness
- Ⓒ excitement
- Ⓓ hunger

26. I plan to leave town as soon as I can get access to a truck.
What does the word *access* mean?
- Ⓐ permission or ability to use something
- Ⓑ a loan from a bank
- Ⓒ a passing score on a test
- Ⓓ instruction in how to use something

168   ©Voyager Expanded Learning, L.P.

Vocabulary Assessment 3 points each

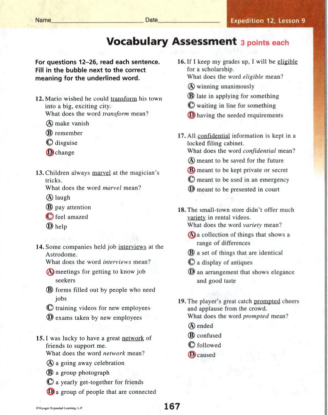

For questions 12–26, read each sentence. Fill in the bubble next to the correct meaning for the underlined word.

12. Mario wished he could transform his town into a big, exciting city.
What does the word *transform* mean?
- Ⓐ make vanish
- Ⓑ remember
- Ⓒ disguise
- Ⓓ change

13. Children always marvel at the magician's tricks.
What does the word *marvel* mean?
- Ⓐ laugh
- Ⓑ pay attention
- Ⓒ feel amazed
- Ⓓ help

14. Some companies held job interviews at the Astrodome.
What does the word *interviews* mean?
- Ⓐ meetings for getting to know job seekers
- Ⓑ forms filled out by people who need jobs
- Ⓒ training videos for new employees
- Ⓓ exams taken by new employees

15. I was lucky to have a great network of friends to support me.
What does the word *network* mean?
- Ⓐ a going away celebration
- Ⓑ a group photograph
- Ⓒ a yearly get-together for friends
- Ⓓ a group of people that are connected

16. If I keep my grades up, I will be eligible for a scholarship.
What does the word *eligible* mean?
- Ⓐ winning unanimously
- Ⓑ late in applying for something
- Ⓒ waiting in line for something
- Ⓓ having the needed requirements

17. All confidential information is kept in a locked filing cabinet.
What does the word *confidential* mean?
- Ⓐ meant to be saved for the future
- Ⓑ meant to be kept private or secret
- Ⓒ meant to be used in an emergency
- Ⓓ meant to be presented in court

18. The small-town store didn't offer much variety in rental videos.
What does the word *variety* mean?
- Ⓐ a collection of things that shows a range of differences
- Ⓑ a set of things that are identical
- Ⓒ a display of antiques
- Ⓓ an arrangement that shows elegance and good taste

19. The player's great catch prompted cheers and applause from the crowd.
What does the word *prompted* mean?
- Ⓐ ended
- Ⓑ confused
- Ⓒ followed
- Ⓓ caused

©Voyager Expanded Learning, L.P.   **167**

Expedition Wrap-Up

1. After students have completed the assessment, bring them together to discuss the probing questions as a way to provide closure for Expedition 12. Briefly discuss each of the Expedition articles. Then watch DVD 12.2 together as a class. Have students turn to Anthology page 205. Ask students to summarize the response to each probing question that was given on the DVD.

2. Conclude the Expedition by asking students to summarize the life changes they read about in each lesson. Ask students how each character's perspective was affected by the change in his or her life. Then ask students to name real events from the news or from history that must have caused life changes for the people who experienced them. Discuss what accounts might have been written about these events and from whose perspective the accounts might be written. (Possible responses: settling the West from the perspective of a teenager who kept a journal, the fall of the World Trade Center Towers on 9/11 from the perspective of someone who lost a loved one that day, fighting the Nazis from the perspective of a young soldier) Discuss with students where they might locate primary documents, interviews, and eyewitness accounts of such events. Then have students record and save these ideas as possible future research topics.

 ## Strategic Online Learning Opportunities®

Students read a passage about photographer Lewis Hine who took pictures of immigrant children as they came to the United States.

Content Connection
Social Studies

Lewis Hine and the Children of Ellis Island *by Mary Lou Burket*

Lexile Levels

Passage B
830L

Passage C
900L

Assessment
- Metacognition
- Content
- Vocabulary
- Main Idea
- Summary

 SKILL ✓

Based on their assessment scores, students automatically are assigned either the Skills Practice for reinforcement or the Independent Practice and Extension Opportunities.

SKILLS PRACTICE

Vocabulary Strategies
- Context
- Word Parts: Prefixes and Suffixes
- Word Parts: Compound Words

Dictionary Skills

Main Idea Strategy: W–I–N
- Identifying the Most Important *Who* or *What*
- Identifying the Most Important *Information*
- Stating the Main Idea in a Small *Number* of Words

Questioning

Writing
- Responding to Texts
- Writing a Summary Statement

INDEPENDENT PRACTICE

Vocabulary Strategies

Writing
- Writing a Summary Statement
- Responding to Texts

EXTENSION OPPORTUNITIES

- Online Books
- Book Cart
- Review of Previous Passages

■ Comprehension

Before Reading

Elements of Description: Concrete and Sensory Details

1. On the board, write *Descriptive Writing*. **Descriptive writing describes, or tells how something looks, moves, or feels. It is used in expository *and* in narrative texts. A magazine article might describe a deadly storm. A short story might describe how a character looks.**

2. Write *1. Concrete Details* under the heading.

   • **Descriptive writing includes lively, interesting details. Some of these details are *concrete details*.**

   • Write *hat* on the board. **This detail is vague. It is hard to picture.**

   • Write *blue baseball cap* on the board. **This, on the other hand, is a concrete detail. It gives specific information. It is easy to imagine.**

   • Write *shoes*, *game system*, *person*, and *car* on the board, and have students provide concrete details to describe each item.

3. Write *2. Sensory Details* on the board.

   • **Descriptive writing also includes *sensory details*.** Underline *sens*. **Sensory details appeal to seeing, hearing, smelling, feeling, and tasting.**

   • Write *We had a cookout.* on the board. **This detail doesn't bring the event to life.**

   • Write *We roasted plump, juicy hotdogs over a bright, crackling fire*. **This detail, on the other hand, appeals to feeling, tasting, seeing, and hearing.**

   • Write *sun*, *waterfall*, and *football game* on the board. Have students provide sentences with sensory details related to each.

Reading for Understanding

1. Have students turn to Anthology page 218. **As we read this text, let's watch for both concrete and sensory details.**

2. Read the first paragraph of the article aloud, then have students read the rest of the article with you.

After Reading

Elements of Description: Concrete and Sensory Details

1. Distribute copies of Reteach page 23, and read the instructions aloud.

2. Read paragraph 4 of "Invasion" aloud, and model finding the concrete detail *golden oldies*. Have students record this detail in a box on the graphic organizer.

3. Write *toy (paragraph 5)* and *skateboard (paragraph 9)* on the board and have students find and record a concrete detail for each. (radio-controlled airplane; cheesy little skateboard)

4. Model finding in paragraph 4 the sensory detail *loud, goofy laugh*, which appeals to the sense of hearing. Have students record this detail in the graphic organizer.

5. Have students locate sensory details in the story, identify the sense(s) to which each detail appeals, and record them in the ovals on the graphic organizer.

6. If students have difficulty identifying concrete and sensory details, model how to do so using the instructional frameworks in Lessons 1 and 6.

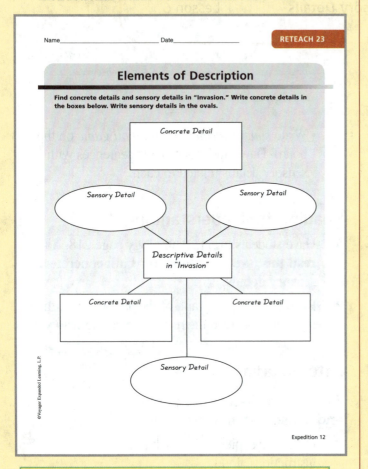

Extra Support

Elements of Description

If students need additional support, write the following nouns on strips of paper: *drink, bag, soup,* and *shop.* On another set of strips, write these concrete details: *Jumpin Jerry's Energy Juice; tattered nylon backpack, potato corn chowder,* and *Marli's Uptown Boutique.* On a third set, write each of the five senses, one per strip. Have students first work to match each noun with the appropriate concrete detail. Next, have students draw a sense and provide a detail that appeals to that sense for one of the nouns.

Checking for Comprehension

1. Distribute copies of Reteach page 24. Then have students turn to "Invasion" on Anthology page 218. Explain to students that they will read this text before answering the questions on Reteach page 24.

2. Read aloud the Keys to Comprehension section and the assessment instructions. Then have students complete the assessment independently.

3. Review the correct answers and discuss any questions that students answered incorrectly.

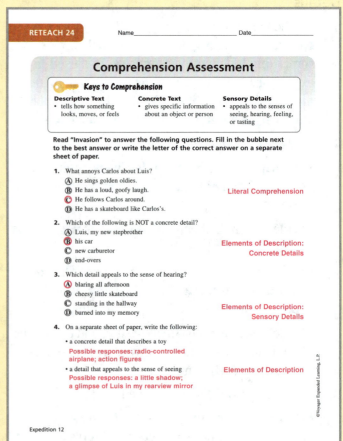

■ Vocabulary

1. Write on the board the specific words that students have missed, along with a concept map such as the one below. Then guide students in completing the graphic organizer for each of the words.

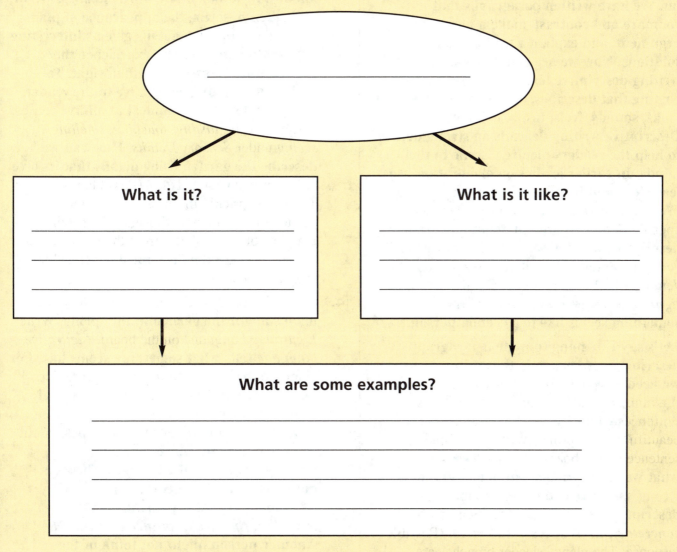

2. When students have completed the concept maps, check comprehension by having them write in their own words the meaning of each word.

■ Description

Teach and Model

1. **We have studied a variety of writing styles so far. We have written paragraphs that compare and contrast, make a persuasive argument, and explain a problem and solutions. Now we are going to learn about writing descriptive text.** *Descriptive text* **is writing that describes, or tells how something looks, sounds, feels, tastes, or moves. Descriptive writing depends on strong details to help the readers picture a scene in their minds. In earlier lessons on elaboration, we learned about being specific in our writing. We practiced elaboration when we used specific details to expand on an idea. In our descriptive writing, we will use specific, or** *concrete,* **details. We will also use** *sensory details,* **which appeal to the five senses, and** *figurative language,* **which tells what something seems like to a certain person.**

2. **Let's say I'm going to write a paragraph describing my garden in the spring. As usual, we need to write a topic sentence that states the main idea of the paragraph. What topic sentences could I write?** (My garden is beautiful in the spring.) Write your topic sentence on the board. **Now that we know what we are writing about, let's think of a strong, concrete detail to start our description of the garden. Remember, a** *concrete detail* **is specific and vivid.** (Possible response: The plants' slender branches are covered in bright, green leaves.) **That starts to paint a picture in the reader's mind and is much more specific and vivid than something like** *The leaves are green.* **Now let's think about sensory details that can add information to our descriptive paragraph.**

3. Write *Sensory Details* on the board. **Most of the time, we describe something by talking about how it looks. The words** *slender, bright,* **and** *green* **describe the appearance of plants in the garden. Such details give us interesting information, but we can experience the garden using senses other than sight. To make your writing come alive to the reader, try using details that appeal to all five senses.** Write *hearing, tasting, touching, smelling, seeing* under *Sensory Details.* **How can we describe the garden using details that involve senses other than seeing?** (Possible responses: The roses' prickly thorns are sharp, and perfume from the new flowers fills the air. Droplets of dew splatter from the leaves.) **What senses do these details appeal to?** (touching, smelling, hearing)

4. **I can also use figurative language to write details about the garden in the spring.** Write *Figurative Language* on the board. *Figurative language* **tells what something seems like. For example, the description** *orange butterflies* **does not use figurative language. It merely states what color the butterflies are: orange. Most people looking at the butterflies would call them orange. However,** *figurative language* **can describe the butterflies in a more detailed way according to how they seem to a particular person:** *I see many butterflies that are as orange as a sunset.* **Another person might not think of the butterflies in exactly that way. Figurative language often uses comparisons to create vivid descriptions.**

5. **Now I can write a descriptive paragraph using concrete details, sensory details, and figurative language. Remember that a paragraph needs a conclusion that contains a summary of the ideas.** Write these sentences on the board and have a student read them aloud: *My garden is beautiful in the spring. The roses' prickly thorns are sharp, and perfume from the new flowers fills the air. Droplets of dew splatter from the leaves. I see many butterflies that are as orange as a sunset. I love the way my garden looks, feels, smells, and sounds in the spring.* Draw a box around the topic sentence and the conclusion. Underline a concrete detail once, a sensory detail twice, and an example of figurative language three times.

Writing Samples

1. Have students turn to Writing page 41, and read the passage aloud. **This paragraph describes an unusual Valentine card. Let's look at how the writer presents descriptive details.**

2. **The topic sentence tells us what the paragraph will be about. What is the main idea in this paragraph?** (an unusual Valentine card)

3. **The writer describes the card using specific, concrete details. What concrete detail tells specific information?** (It is made of folded paper, like those open-and-close fortune telling games.)

4. **The writer uses sensory details to tell more about the valentine. What details tell how the paper looks and feels?** (The paper is crisp and pink.) **What other details appeal to one or more of the senses?** (*soft, silky rose petal* appeals to the sense of feeling; *mild, sweet scent of roses*)

5. **The writer also uses figurative language. How is figurative language used to describe holding the card?** (Holding the card is like holding a small bouquet.)

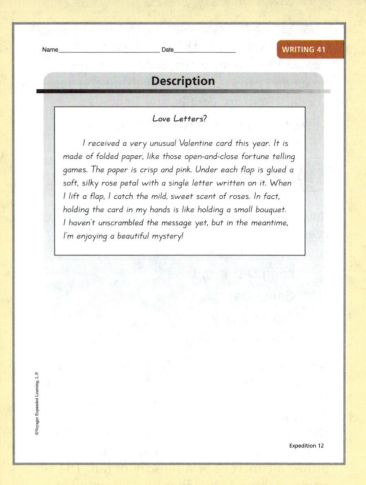

Name_____ Date_____   WRITING 41

Description

Love Letters?

I received a very unusual Valentine card this year. It is made of folded paper, like those open-and-close fortune telling games. The paper is crisp and pink. Under each flap is glued a soft, silky rose petal with a single letter written on it. When I lift a flap, I catch the mild, sweet scent of roses. In fact, holding the card in my hands is like holding a small bouquet. I haven't unscrambled the message yet, but in the meantime, I'm enjoying a beautiful mystery!

©Voyager Expanded Learning, L.P.

Expedition 12

6. **Which sentence sums up the writer's ideas about the card?** (I haven't unscrambled the message yet, but in the meantime, I'm enjoying a beautiful mystery!)

Evaluating Writing

1. Have students turn to Writing page 42. Read the rubric. **This rubric focuses on descriptive writing: writing that uses concrete details, sensory details, and figurative language.**

2. Call on an individual to reread the paragraph on Writing page 41. Have students use the criteria on the rubric to evaluate the paragraph, identifying the following:

- a concrete detail
- a sensory detail that appeals to one of the five senses
- an example of figurative language that tells how something seems
- a topic sentence and a conclusion

3. Using the rubric, what score would you give this paragraph? (5) **Why?** (because it contains a topic sentence that states the main idea and offers descriptions using concrete details, sensory details, and figurative language; a conclusion sums up the description)

Anthology Connection

Review the topic of changes by revisiting the reading selections from Expedition 12. Pay special attention to the following passages:

"Long Distance Love"

"Game Day"

"Blown Away"

"The Loss of Love"

Next, have students list three or four of the specific changes they have read about. Then have them take turns reading one of the items aloud to a partner. The partner should then provide a descriptive sentence about that event. The sentence should contain either a concrete or a sensory detail. The first student should then identify the detail as concrete or sensory.

Guided Practice

1. Now we'll work together to write a descriptive paragraph about a part of our community. Distribute Writing page 43, and draw the contents of the page on the board. Read the instructions above the graphic organizer. **First let's read the prompt. Remember that we can use our PLAN to help us think about what we are writing. What part of the PLAN can help us with the prompt?** (the P) Write *Pay attention to the prompt.* on the board. **What kind of paragraph are you being asked to write?** (a descriptive one) **What are you being asked to write about?** (a place in our community) **How does the prompt suggest you organize your paragraph?** (by using at least one concrete detail, one sensory detail, and one example of figurative language)

Name_____ Date_____   WRITING 43

Description

1. **Read the writing prompt. Use the graphic organizer to brainstorm at least two concrete details, two sensory details, and two examples of figurative language.**

There are many new residents in your community. They joined your community when a huge hurricane destroyed their homes. Your class is writing a guide to your community for these new neighbors. Descriptions of all parts of your community will be included in the guide.

Write a descriptive paragraph in which you use details to describe a place in your community. You can write about a particular neighborhood, a building, a business or restaurant, or an outdoor location. Include at least one concrete detail, one sensory detail, and one example of figurative language in your paragraph.

Location you are writing about: _____

Descriptive Details	
Concrete Details	
Sensory Details	
Figurative Language	

2. **Write your descriptive paragraph on your own paper using the information in your graphic organizer. In addition to specific details, make sure you have a clear topic sentence and a conclusion that summarizes your ideas.**

Expedition 12

©Voyager Expanded Learning, L.P.

2. Next you need to decide which location you will write about. Think about a place you can describe in detail. Write that place on your graphic organizer. If I were writing for the community guide, I would write about my favorite restaurant. Write *favorite restaurant* on the board. **Remember that you will write the place you choose on your chart. That place will become the focus of your topic sentence when you write your paragraph.**

3. Now let's think about details that describe these places. What is one example of a concrete detail that describes the place you chose? Here's a concrete detail that describes the restaurant: *a small hamburger stand near the post office.* **Write this detail on the board in the first box on the chart. Make sure you write a specific detail that describes the place *you* chose. A good way to start might be to tell *what* your place is and *where* your place is.**

4. **Now we will write a sensory detail about our places. Remember that a sensory detail appeals to one of the five senses: seeing, hearing, smelling, tasting, touching. Here's a sensory detail that describes the hamburger stand:** *The smell of those hamburgers cooking makes my mouth water.* **Write this detail in the second box. What sense is being appealed to here?** (smelling)

5. **Finally, use an example of figurative language to describe your place. Figurative language tells how things seem to be and often describes one thing in comparison to another. Here's my example of figurative language:** *I love the hamburger stand because it's as cozy and comfortable as a hug.*

6. Have students work in small groups or in pairs to brainstorm a concrete detail, a sensory detail, and an example of figurative language that describe the place they are writing about. Have them write their ideas in the graphic organizer on Writing page 43. Guide students by asking these questions:

   • **Where, exactly, is your place located?**

   • **Which of your senses is most affected when you are in this place?**

   • **What could you compare your place to?**

7. Have students share their details with the class. Write students' responses on the board. Be sure all students have listed one appropriate detail in each box on the graphic organizer before moving on.

Writing and Technology

When computers are available, encourage students to use the *Thesaurus* feature in a word processing program to identify additional strong word choices. Instruct students on the variations in meaning for word choices they find.

Independent Practice

1. Have students turn back to the rubric they used on Writing page 42. Review the criteria for descriptive writing that scores a 5 on the rubric.

2. **Continue planning your paragraph on your own by writing more descriptive details in each category. Write at least one more detail in each box.**

3. Read aloud the second set of instructions on Writing page 43. **Now you're ready to write a descriptive paragraph. On your own paper, write a topic sentence that states the main thing you want to say about the place you chose.**

4. Have students use the descriptive details from their graphic organizers as they write their descriptive paragraphs. Monitor students as they write, and provide correction and feedback as needed.

5. After students have completed their paragraphs, have them share their work with the class. Discuss which paragraphs present the clearest, most vivid details about a place.

6. Have students return to their paragraphs and strengthen their details to make them more specific. Point out to students that this step, which they have been doing all along, is called revision. **When you** *revise,* **you go back over your writing and make changes to improve it. Focusing on word choice is a good way to revise. You should use the most colorful, specific words you can think of.** Have students read their paragraphs again and replace any vague words with strong words—words that catch the reader's attention and are very specific.

7. Distribute Writing page 44 and have students use the checklist to evaluate their work. Have them read their paragraphs. Then have them read each item in the column labeled *Points to Look For*. If they can answer "yes" to a point, they should put a check in the first column. Have students revise their paragraphs to improve at least one of the items on the list.

WRITING 44   Name_____ Date_____

Description

Writing **Checklist**

✔	Elements of Good Writing	Points to Look For
	Ideas and Elaboration	*I have a focused idea and specific details to elaborate it.*
	Word Choice	*I use specific and colorful words to talk about my ideas.*
	Sentence Fluency	*My sentences create a pleasing rhythm as they flow smoothly from one to the next.*
	Conventions	*I use apostrophes correctly to show possession, as in Jimmy's book. I use commas correctly, as in I am hungry, so I will have a snack. I see red, green, and yellow apples.*
	Organization	*My paragraphs have a clear organization that is easy to follow.*

©Voyager Expanded Learning, L.P.

Expedition 12

---

8. Close the lesson by reminding students that descriptive writing is based on details. Tell students to make details specific, just as they did when they learned about elaborating an idea. To write lively, interesting descriptions, they must pay attention to word choice and paint a picture in the reader's mind.

Extended Writing

Elaborating Details in Descriptive Writing

Use this activity to help students elaborate the details they include in their writing.

- **On Writing page 43, we listed some concrete and sensory details about a place in our community. Let's elaborate these details.** Write the following questions on the board, one next to another.

  – *Does this place have a specific name? Is it located in a specific part of town?*

  – *What is the function, or purpose, of this place? Can I describe what happens in this place more specifically? Can I use figurative language to compare the place to something else?*

  – *Can I more fully describe what the place looks like? Can I add details that appeal to all five of the senses?*

Read each question aloud and discuss possible responses with students, using the topic *hamburger stand*. Record your responses on the board.

- Have students work with a partner to answer the questions in relation to the place they have chosen. Pair students who are working on similar places.

- When students finish, have them use all of their ideas to compose a series of three paragraphs. Have students tell *what* and *where* the place is in the first paragraph; *what it is used for* in the second paragraph; and *what it looks, sounds, smells, and feels like* in the third paragraph.

- For a complete instructional model for multiparagraph writing, see the Expedition 11 Writing lesson.

Writing Conventions
MINILESSON

Noun/Pronoun

• Write the following sentence on the board:

My best <u>friend</u> says that <u>he</u> will never have a crush on anyone.

Read the sentence aloud. **The first underlined word in this sentence is a noun. It names a person. The second is a pronoun. It stands for the noun. You could say** *My best friend says that my best friend will never have a crush on anyone,* **but that's too clunky. Instead, you use a pronoun. You say** *My best friend says HE won't have a crush.*

• Draw an arrow from the underlined pronoun back to the underlined noun. **In this sentence, the pronoun** *agrees* **with the noun. It is singular—it names one thing— just like the noun it stands for.**

• Write the following sentence on the board:

His <u>brothers</u> laugh when <u>they</u> hear this. Have students identify the noun (brothers) and the pronoun (they). **In this sentence, the pronoun also agrees with the noun. This pronoun is plural—it names more than one thing—just like the noun it stands for.**

• Write this additional sentence on the board:

The six <u>girls</u> he likes also laugh, because he calls and IMs <u>her</u> constantly.

Sometimes, if a sentence is long, it is easy to lose track of whether a noun is singular or plural. Read the sentence aloud. **Does this pronoun agree with the noun it stands for?** (no) **What should the pronoun be?** (them) Replace *her* with *them.*

▶ Write the following sentences on the board. Have students rewrite them, choosing the correct pronoun.

1. My friend Bruno likes <u>Briana</u> but is too shy to ask (them, her) out. **her**

2. He keeps picking up the <u>phone</u>, then putting (them, it) back down. **it**

3. "At least the <u>muscles</u> in your right arm are getting (its, their) daily exercise," I told him. **their**

Expedition  13

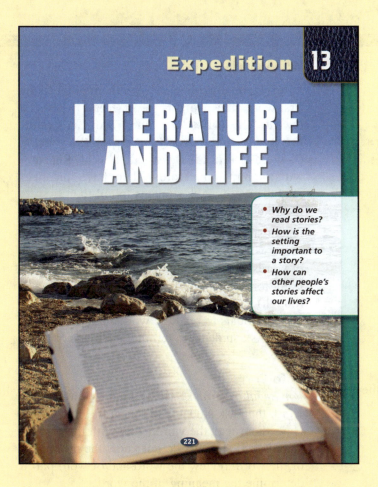

Expedition 13

LITERATURE AND LIFE

- Why do we read stories?
- How is the setting important to a story?
- How can other people's stories affect our lives?

221

DVD 13.1, 13.2

In this Expedition, the DVD segments explore the many ways in which students use and enjoy stories in their daily lives. They point out that while stories come in many styles and forms, we can all find something to inspire us in the pages of literature.

Strategic Online Learning Opportunities®

Students access the Web site http://solo.voyagerlearning.com for an interactive SOLO® session. In each session, students apply previously taught strategic skills to new readings on the student's appropriate Lexile® level. Consult the *Passport Reading Journeys™* SOLO User Guide for a comprehensive overview of this component.

Passport Reading Journeys Library

Students may select reading materials from the *Passport Reading Journeys* Library. Partner and independent reading opportunities allow students to read authentic text on their Lexile level to build fluency. Teacher resources are provided in the *Passport Reading Journeys* Library Teacher's Guide.

In This Expedition

READINGS

Lessons 1 and 2
from Holes, by Louis Sachar

Lessons 3 and 4
from The Joy Luck Club, by Amy Tan

Lessons 6 and 7
Kipling and I, by Jesús Colón
If— by Rudyard Kipling

Lesson 8
adapted from The Call of the Wild, by Jack London

Lesson 9 Assessment
A Death in the Family

SKILLS

Narrative Text Elements
- Character, Setting, Plot
- First-Person Narratives
- Character Motivation

Poetry
Elements of Description

Advanced Word Study

Prefix *pro-*

1. Write *pro-* on the board. **This word part is a prefix. Remember, a prefix is a word part that occurs at the beginning of a word and often helps us understand the meaning of the word. The sounds for this prefix are /prə/. Say the sounds for this prefix.** (/prə/) Write the word *proclaim* on the board. Underline the prefix *pro-*. **What is this prefix?** (pro-) **Use the sounds you know to read the rest of the word.** (claim) **What is the word?** (proclaim) **The prefix *pro-* means "in front of" or "forward." The meaning of *proclaim* may be difficult to determine solely from the word parts, but the prefix *pro-* gives us a hint to the word's meaning. For example, the word *proclaim* means "to claim or declare publicly or in front of people."**

   Have students turn to page E13, Lesson 1, in the back of the Student Book. Direct them to line 1 in the first box. **What is the underlined prefix in the first word?** (pro-) **Read the rest of the word.** (grammed) **What is the word?** (programmed) Repeat with the remaining words. Call on individuals to read the words in random order. Ask students to tell the meanings of the words based on the meaning of the prefix.

2. Direct students to lines 2 and 3. Have them read the words. Call on individuals to read the words in a different order. Ask students to tell the meanings of the words.

   #### ▼ To Correct
   Say the correct sound(s) or prefix/suffix, then ask students to repeat the sound(s). Have them read the words again with the correct sound(s). If students do not know the meaning of the word, review the word and/or word parts to determine the meaning of the word.

1. programmed	productive	provision	progress
2. protection	grumbled	electric	projected
3. buzzard	hastily	wasteland	counselor

Sight Words

1. Direct students to line 1. Have them point to the first word. **This word is *sweat*. Read the word.** (sweat) **This is not a regular word. Let's read the word again.** (sweat) **Let's spell the word.** (s-w-e-a-t) **What is the word?** (sweat) Repeat with the remaining words. Then, have students read the words. Ask students to tell the meanings of the words.

2. Direct students to lines 2 and 3. **Let's read these words.** Remind students that the rows of words consist of regular and irregular words. Point to the first word. **What is the word?** (bough) Repeat with the remaining words. Call on individuals to read the words in a different order. Ask students to tell the meanings of the words.

   #### ▼ To Correct
   For Regular Words: Say the sound(s) in the word, then ask students to repeat the sound(s). Have them read the word again with the correct sound(s). If students do not know the meaning of the word, review the word and/or word part to determine the meaning of the word.

   For Irregular Words: Immediately say the correct word. Then have students read the word, spell it, and read it again. If students do not know the meaning of the word, review the word.

1. sweat I	guard I	sewn I	measure I
2. bough I	originally I	relief I	unfortunately I
3. pierce I	legendary I	pathetic R	worse I

Anthology Selection

from HOLES

by Louis Sachar

Stanley Yelnats is an overweight kid from a poor family. And he's being punished for a crime he didn't commit. The judge gave him an option: Either go to jail or go to Camp Green Lake. So Stanley chose Camp Green Lake. After a long, lonely ride on a bus with no air-conditioning, Stanley has arrived at camp. What he finds is nothing like what he expected.

¹Stanley felt somewhat **dazed** as the guard unlocked his handcuffs and led him off the bus. He'd been on the bus for over eight hours.

²"Be careful," the bus driver said as Stanley walked down the steps.

³Stanley wasn't sure if the bus driver meant for him to be careful going down the steps, or if he was telling him to be careful at Camp Green Lake. "Thanks for the ride," he said. His mouth was dry and his throat hurt. He stepped onto the hard, dry dirt. There was a band of sweat around his wrist where the handcuff had been.

⁴The land was barren and **desolate**. He could see a few rundown buildings and some tents. Farther away there was a cabin beneath two tall trees. Those two trees were the only plant life he could see. There weren't even weeds.

222

⁵The guard led Stanley to a small building. A sign on the front said, YOU ARE ENTERING CAMP GREEN LAKE JUVENILE CORRECTIONAL FACILITY. Next to it was another sign which declared that it was a violation of the Texas Penal Code to bring guns, explosives, weapons, drugs, or alcohol onto the **premises**.

⁶As Stanley read the sign he couldn't help but think, *Well, duh!*

⁷The guard led Stanley into the building, where he felt the welcome relief of air-conditioning.

⁸A man was sitting with his feet up on a desk. He turned his head when Stanley and the guard entered, but otherwise didn't move. Even though he was inside, he wore sunglasses and a cowboy hat. He also held a can of soda, and the sight of it made Stanley even more aware of his own thirst.

⁹He waited while the bus guard gave the man some papers to sign.

¹⁰"That's a lot of sunflower seeds," the bus guard said.

¹¹Stanley noticed a burlap sack filled with sunflower seeds on the floor next to the desk.

¹²"I quit smoking last month," said the man in the cowboy hat. He had a tattoo of a rattlesnake on his arm, and as he signed his name, the snake's rattle seemed to wiggle. "I used to smoke a pack a day. Now I eat a sack of these every week."

¹³The guard laughed.

¹⁴There must have been a small refrigerator behind his desk, because the man in the cowboy hat produced two more cans of soda. For a second Stanley hoped that one might be for him, but the man gave one to the guard and said the other was for the driver.

¹⁵"Nine hours here, and now nine hours back," the guard grumbled. "What a day."

¹⁶Stanley thought about the long, **miserable** bus ride and felt a little sorry for the guard and the bus driver.

¹⁷The man in the cowboy hat spit sunflower seed shells into a wastepaper basket. Then he walked around the desk to Stanley. "My name is Mr. Sir," he said. "Whenever you speak to me you must call me by my name, is that clear?"

¹⁸Stanley hesitated. "Uh, yes, Mr. Sir," he said, though he couldn't imagine that was really the man's name.

¹⁹"You're not in the Girl Scouts anymore," Mr. Sir said.

²⁰Stanley had to remove his clothes in front of Mr. Sir, who made sure

223

he wasn't hiding anything. He was then given two sets of clothes and a towel. Each set consisted of a long-sleeve orange jumpsuit, an orange T-shirt, and yellow socks. Stanley wasn't sure if the socks had been yellow originally.

²¹He was also given white sneakers, an orange cap, and a canteen made of heavy plastic, which unfortunately was empty. The cap had a piece of cloth sewn on the back of it, for neck protection.

²²Stanley got dressed. The clothes smelled like soap.

²³Mr. Sir told him he should wear one set to work in and one set for relaxation. Laundry was done every three days. On that day his work clothes would be washed. Then the other set would become his work clothes, and he would get clean clothes to wear while resting.

²⁴"You are going to dig one hole each day, including Saturdays and Sundays. Each hole must be five feet deep and five feet across in every direction. Your shovel is your measuring stick. Breakfast is served at 4:30."

²⁵Stanley must have looked surprised, because Mr. Sir went on to explain that they started early to avoid the hottest part of the day. "No one is going to baby-sit you," he added. "The longer it takes you to dig, the longer you will be out in the sun. If you dig up anything interesting, you are to report it to me or any other counselor. When you finish, the rest of the day is yours."

²⁶Stanley nodded to show he understood.

²⁷"This isn't a Girl Scout camp," said Mr. Sir.

²⁸He checked Stanley's backpack and allowed him to keep it. Then he led Stanley outside into the blazing heat.

²⁹"Take a good look around you," Mr. Sir said. "What do you see?"

³⁰Stanley looked out across the **vast** wasteland. The air seemed thick with heat and dirt. "Not much," he said, then hastily added, "Mr. Sir."

³¹Mr. Sir laughed. "You see any guard towers?"

³²"No."

³³"How about an electric fence?"

³⁴"No, Mr. Sir."

³⁵"There's no fence at all, is there?"

³⁶"No, Mr. Sir."

224

³⁷"You want to run away?" Mr. Sir asked him.

³⁸Stanley looked back at him, unsure what he meant.

³⁹"If you want to run away, go ahead, start running. I'm not going to stop you."

⁴⁰Stanley didn't know what kind of game Mr. Sir was playing.

⁴¹"I see you're looking at my gun. Don't worry. I'm not going to shoot you." He tapped his holster. "This is for yellow-spotted lizards. I wouldn't waste a bullet on you."

⁴²"I'm not going to run away," Stanley said.

⁴³"Good thinking," said Mr. Sir. "Nobody runs away from here. We don't need a fence. Know why? Because we've got the only water for a hundred miles. You want to run away? You'll be buzzard food in three days."

⁴⁴Stanley could see some kids dressed in orange and carrying shovels dragging themselves toward the tents.

⁴⁵"You thirsty?" asked Mr. Sir.

⁴⁶"Yes, Mr. Sir," Stanley said gratefully.

⁴⁷"Well, you better get used to it. You're going to be thirsty for the next eighteen months."

Connect to the Author

Louis Sachar says that while he usually starts a book by thinking about the characters, he wrote *Holes* by thinking about the setting first. "The story began with the place, and the characters and plot grew out of it," says Sachar. "At the time I began the book, we had just returned from the relative coolness of a vacation in Maine to the Texas summer. Anybody who has ever tried to do yard work in Texas in July can easily imagine Hell to be a place where you are required to dig a hole five feet deep and five feet across day after day under the brutal Texas sun." Into this searing landscape Sachar introduced Stanley Yelnats. "He's a kind of pathetic kid who feels like he has no friends, feels like his life is cursed. And I think everyone can identify with that in one way or another." Sachar was born in East Meadow, New York, in 1954. He now lives in Austin, Texas.

Louis Sachar

225

Comprehension and Vocabulary *Before Reading*

Introduce the Expedition

1. Have students spend a few minutes telling a partner about something funny that happened to them recently. Ask them to make sure that they tell clearly who was involved in the story and what happened, such as: "At dinner last night, my sister proudly served homemade pudding for dessert. I took a spoonful and found that it tasted like melted tires. . . ."

2. As students tell their stories, write *Character(s)*, *Setting*, and *Plot* on the board, each within a large box. **Who heard a particularly good story just now?** Call on a student and ask him or her to tell who was in the story, where and when it took place, and what happened. List each detail on the board in the appropriate box.

3. **We tell one another stories all the time—so often, in fact, that we usually don't realize we're doing it. At the dinner table, you might share stories about your day with family members. In a phone call or e-mail to a friend, you share stories about yourself and others.**

4. **Why do you think we tell one another stories?** Write students' responses on the board. **We tell stories—real-life stories *and* made-up stories—for a lot of reasons.**

   • **People tell stories to help them remember important events and to share important information. If you win a contest, you might tell this story to many people so that they know and remember what happened to you.**

   • **People also tell stories to entertain one another. If something funny happens to you, and you tell a friend about it, you are telling a story to entertain.**

   • **Other times, we tell stories to teach a lesson. We tell what has happened to us so that someone else doesn't make the same mistake.**

   If they do not already appear, list *share and remember information*, *entertain*, and *teach a lesson* on the board.

5. **In this Expedition, we'll read some made-up, or fictional, stories and some real-life stories. We'll be looking at the different parts of the stories—like those that are listed on the board. We'll also try to figure out what each story's purpose is, and how the story relates to our own lives and experiences.**

6. Have students turn to Anthology page 221. Read the title of the Expedition. Then call on individuals to read aloud each probing question.

   • **Why do we read stories?**
   • **How is the setting important to a story?**
   • **How can other people's stories affect our lives?**

7. Tell students that they will return to these questions as they learn more about storytelling. Show DVD 13.1.

8. After students view the video, have them summarize its main points and recall supporting details. If necessary, prompt students with questions such as the following:

   • **What main message were the people in this video trying to communicate?**
   • **What did they have to say about _____?**
   • **What parts of the video helped illustrate or support this idea?**

Introduce Vocabulary

9. **We will read some new words in today's story, a selection from the novel *Holes*.**

   • Write the vocabulary words on the board. Include Challenge Words to meet the needs of students who are advancing.

630

• Read the words to students.
• Call on individuals to read the words as you point to them.
• Provide correction and feedback as needed.

▶ Have students write the words in the Vocabulary Log.

10. Tell students that knowing the meanings of these words will help them better understand the article.

For each word:

• Read the word with its definition and the sentence that follows.
• Write the sentences on the board.
• Call on students to use their own words to give the meaning and some examples of each vocabulary word.

Vocabulary

daze	*to stun or shock because of a blow*
	After being hit by the baseball, the batter seemed *dazed* but all right.
desolate	*bare and deserted*
	The movie's first scene shows a lonely, *desolate* ghost town.
premises	*grounds or locations*
	Students must leave school *premises* by 5 p.m.
miserable	*very uncomfortable*
	The campers spent a *miserable* night in a rainstorm.
vast	*covering a huge area*
	This lake seems as *vast* as an ocean.

Challenge Words
Word Meaning

searing	*burning*
	She felt a *searing* pain as soon as she put her hand on the hot pan.
pathetic	*sad, weak, or helpless*
	A small, *pathetic* group of fans gathered in the rain to watch their team lose.

Review Narrative Text Features

11. Point to the narrative elements listed on the board—*Character(s)*, *Setting*, and *Plot*. **We already know that these are the elements, or parts, of a narrative text.**

• **How is a narrative text different from an expository text?** (Most narrative texts are fictional; all narrative text tells a story. An expository text is a nonfiction text that gives information.)
• **What are characters?** (the people in a narrative, or story)
• **What is the setting?** (where and when the story takes place)
• **What is the plot?** (what happens first, next, and last in a story)

12. **In the story from *Holes*, one aspect of the setting—the place where the action happens—shapes the feeling or mood of the story. For example, details such as "hard, dry dirt," "rundown buildings," and "wasteland" create a bleak or depressing feeling and a sense of a desolate place.**

13. **As we read the story, think about how the setting affects the main character's thoughts and feelings. Also, think about how this setting affects your feelings as you read the story. Note the details in the story that make you feel this way.**

Reading for Understanding

Reading

Places and Names to Look For:
- Stanley Yelnats
- Mr. Sir
- Camp Green Lake Juvenile Correctional Facility
- Texas Penal Code
- Girl Scouts

1. **As you read this story from *Holes*, you may come across some unfamiliar places and names.**
   - Write the words on the board.
   - Point to each word as you read the following:

   You will read about a boy named *Stanley Yelnats*, who has just arrived at *Camp Green Lake Juvenile Correctional Facility*, a type of prison. What do you notice about the letters of Stanley's last name? (It is Stanley spelled backward.) **Among the sights Stanley notices at the camp is a sign announcing that bringing weapons and drugs to the camp violates the *Texas Penal Code*, a state document that lists crimes and their punishments. The head of the camp introduces himself as "*Mr. Sir*" and assures Stanley that he is not at a *Girl Scout* camp.**
   - Call on individuals to read the words.

2. **As we read this story, remember to look for ways that the setting creates a certain feeling, or mood, in the story.**

3. Read aloud the first seven paragraphs of the story. Use different pitches of voice for the narrator, bus driver, and Stanley to help students distinguish among them. **In these paragraphs, the bus driver speaks to Stanley, and Stanley responds. The quotation marks tell you where each person's words begin and end. When a different person talks, a new set of quotation marks is used. Other characters in the story will also speak. As you continue reading, try to keep track of who is saying what in the story.**

4. **Fluency** Have partners read the remainder of the story and the Connect to the Author feature. Encourage them to use different voices for different characters. If necessary, review the following fluency correction procedure with students to ensure accuracy: **Offer help when your partner comes to an unfamiliar word or makes a reading error. Pause, then say, "That word is _____. Let's read it again."** As students read, monitor for reading rate, accuracy, and expression.

5. When students have completed their reading, check for literal comprehension of the text by asking these questions: KNOWLEDGE
   - *Paragraph 12:* **What does the man in the camp office do instead of smoke cigarettes?** (eats sunflower seeds)
   - *Paragraphs 20 and 21:* **What supplies does Mr. Sir give Stanley?** (two sets of clothes, sneakers, a cap, and a canteen)
   - *Paragraph 24:* **What will Stanley have to do every day?** (dig a hole five feet wide and five feet deep)
   - *Connect to the Author:* **What was the first part of *Holes* that Louis Sachar imagined?** (the place)

Checking for Comprehension *After Reading*

ELL

1. Erase the details listed in the *Character(s)*, *Setting*, and *Plot* boxes on the board. As students provide details related to the story, write them in the appropriate box. **Let's identify some of the elements of the story we just read.**

2. **Who is the main *character*?** (Stanley) **Who are the other characters?** (the bus driver, the bus guard, and Mr. Sir)

3. **Does the story take place long ago or in the present?** (the present) **How do you know?** (because there is a bus, air conditioning, and a refrigerator, all modern conveniences) **Is this story set in the country, in a small town, or in a city?** (the country) **How can you tell?** (The land is bare and dusty, and there are few buildings on it; Mr. Sir says that they have the only water for many miles.)

4. Divide the *Plot* box into three sections and label them *Beginning*, *Middle*, and *End*. As students tell what happened during each part of the story, write what they say in the appropriate section.

   • **What are the important events at the beginning of this story?** (Possible responses: Stanley gets off the bus at Camp Green Lake. The bus guard leads Stanley into a building. Stanley meets a man wearing a cowboy hat who introduces himself as "Mr. Sir.")

   • **What are the important events in the middle of the story?** (Possible responses: Mr. Sir gives Stanley clothes and other items and tells how the clothes should be worn. Mr. Sir explains that Stanley will dig one hole each day. Mr. Sir tells Stanley that there are no guard towers or fences because if Stanley tried to run away, he'd probably die of thirst.)

   • **What are the important events at the end of the story?** (Possible responses: Stanley sees other kids at the camp. Mr. Sir asks if he is thirsty. When Stanley answers "yes," Mr. Sir tells him to get used to it because he will be thirsty for the next 18 months.)

5. With students, determine the most important events. Cross out the events that are not important. Then call on students to use the information on the board to briefly retell the story. Point out that this retelling is a summary of the plot.

Connect to Science

Use the following activity to help students investigate ways that desert animals conserve water.

Materials: 4-6 sponges, water, balance scales

• Point out that the desert area of Texas is in the far western part of the state. **Many different animals live in this region, with the exception of the yellow-spotted lizard, which exists only in the imagination of the author of *Holes*.**

• Tell students that these animals include mice, rats, rabbits, deer, foxes, snakes, lizards, toads, spiders, and many types of birds. **Desert animals have adapted to survive the hot, dry environment. Some get their water from seeds; others conserve water by being active only at night; some burrow underground for the hottest months; and others have special physiological adaptations such as kidneys that extract water from their urine.**

• For this activity, saturate a sponge and leave it exposed to the air, as a "control sponge." Then arrange students in groups and provide each group with a sponge saturated in water. Explain that the sponge represents a desert animal. Have students follow these steps:

   – Weigh your "animal" to get a baseline weight. Record the weight on a data sheet.

   – Plan a strategy to conserve the animal's water for 24 hours. The animal must be able to be in the open for 2 to 4 hours of that time, for "feeding."

   – Record observations on the data sheet for the 24-hour period.

   – Weigh the sponge at the end of the 24 hours. Compare this to the baseline weight.

• Have groups share their results. Call on individuals to make inferences about desert-animal survival, based on the activity.

To increase difficulty: Have students sketch a design for a new animal that is perfectly adapted for desert life.

Science

Anthology Selection

from HOLES

by Louis Sachar

Stanley Yelnats is an overweight kid from a poor family. And he's being punished for a crime he didn't commit. The judge gave him an option: Either go to jail or go to Camp Green Lake. So Stanley chose Camp Green Lake. After a long, lonely ride on a bus with no air-conditioning, Stanley has arrived at camp. What he finds is nothing like what he expected.

¹Stanley felt somewhat **dazed** as the guard unlocked his handcuffs and led him off the bus. He'd been on the bus for over eight hours.

²"Be careful," the bus driver said as Stanley walked down the steps.

³Stanley wasn't sure if the bus driver meant for him to be careful going down the steps, or if he was telling him to be careful at Camp Green Lake. "Thanks for the ride," he said. His mouth was dry and his throat hurt. He stepped onto the hard, dry dirt. There was a band of sweat around his wrist where the handcuff had been.

⁴The land was barren and **desolate**. He could see a few rundown buildings and some tents. Farther away there was a cabin beneath two tall trees. Those two trees were the only plant life he could see. There weren't even weeds.

222

⁵The guard led Stanley to a small building. A sign on the front said, YOU ARE ENTERING CAMP GREEN LAKE JUVENILE CORRECTIONAL FACILITY. Next to it was another sign which declared that it was a violation of the Texas Penal Code to bring guns, explosives, weapons, drugs, or alcohol onto the **premises**.

⁶As Stanley read the sign he couldn't help but think, *Well, duh!*

⁷The guard led Stanley into the building, where he felt the welcome relief of air-conditioning.

⁸A man was sitting with his feet up on a desk. He turned his head when Stanley and the guard entered, but otherwise didn't move. Even though he was inside, he wore sunglasses and a cowboy hat. He also held a can of soda, and the sight of it made Stanley even more aware of his own thirst.

⁹He waited while the bus guard gave the man some papers to sign.

¹⁰"That's a lot of sunflower seeds," the bus guard said.

¹¹Stanley noticed a burlap sack filled with sunflower seeds on the floor next to the desk.

¹²"I quit smoking last month," said the man in the cowboy hat. He had a tattoo of a rattlesnake on his arm, and as he signed his name, the snake's rattle seemed to wiggle. "I used to smoke a pack a day. Now I eat a sack of these every week."

¹³The guard laughed.

¹⁴There must have been a small refrigerator behind his desk, because the man in the cowboy hat produced two more cans of soda. For a second Stanley hoped that one might be for him, but the man gave one to the guard and said the other was for the driver.

¹⁵"Nine hours here, and now nine hours back," the guard grumbled. "What a day."

¹⁶Stanley thought about the long, **miserable** bus ride and felt a little sorry for the guard and the bus driver.

¹⁷The man in the cowboy hat spit sunflower seed shells into a wastepaper basket. Then he walked around the desk to Stanley. "My name is Mr. Sir," he said. "Whenever you speak to me you must call me by my name, is that clear?"

¹⁸Stanley hesitated. "Uh, yes, Mr. Sir," he said, though he couldn't imagine that was really the man's name.

¹⁹"You're not in the Girl Scouts anymore," Mr. Sir said.

²⁰Stanley had to remove his clothes in front of Mr. Sir, who made sure

223

he wasn't hiding anything. He was then given two sets of clothes and a towel. Each set consisted of a long-sleeve orange jumpsuit, an orange T-shirt, and yellow socks. Stanley wasn't sure if the socks had been yellow originally.

²¹He was also given white sneakers, an orange cap, and a canteen made of heavy plastic, which unfortunately was empty. The cap had a piece of cloth sewn on the back of it, for neck protection.

²²Stanley got dressed. The clothes smelled like soap.

²³Mr. Sir told him he should wear one set to work in and one set for relaxation. Laundry was done every three days. On that day his work clothes would be washed. Then the other set would become his work clothes, and he would get clean clothes to wear while resting.

²⁴"You are going to dig one hole each day, including Saturdays and Sundays. Each hole must be five feet deep and five feet across in every direction. Your shovel is your measuring stick. Breakfast is served at 4:30."

²⁵Stanley must have looked surprised, because Mr. Sir went on to explain that they started early to avoid the hottest part of the day. "No one is going to baby-sit you," he added. "The longer it takes you to dig, the longer you will be out in the sun. If you dig up anything interesting, you are to report it to me or any other counselor. When you finish, the rest of the day is yours."

²⁶Stanley nodded to show he understood.

²⁷"This isn't a Girl Scout camp," said Mr. Sir.

²⁸He checked Stanley's backpack and allowed him to keep it. Then he led Stanley outside into the blazing heat.

²⁹"Take a good look around you," Mr. Sir said. "What do you see?"

³⁰Stanley looked out across the **vast** wasteland. The air seemed thick with heat and dirt. "Not much," he said, then hastily added, "Mr. Sir."

³¹Mr. Sir laughed. "You see any guard towers?"

³²"No."

³³"How about an electric fence?"

³⁴"No, Mr. Sir."

³⁵"There's no fence at all, is there?"

³⁶"No, Mr. Sir."

224

³⁷"You want to run away?" Mr. Sir asked him.

³⁸Stanley looked back at him, unsure what he meant.

³⁹"If you want to run away, go ahead, start running. I'm not going to stop you."

⁴⁰Stanley didn't know what kind of game Mr. Sir was playing.

⁴¹"I see you're looking at my gun. Don't worry. I'm not going to shoot you." He tapped his holster. "This is for yellow-spotted lizards. I wouldn't waste a bullet on you."

⁴²"I'm not going to run away," Stanley said.

⁴³"Good thinking," said Mr. Sir. "Nobody runs away from here. We don't need a fence. Know why? Because we've got the only water for a hundred miles. You want to run away? You'll be buzzard food in three days."

⁴⁴Stanley could see some kids dressed in orange and carrying shovels dragging themselves toward the tents.

⁴⁵"You thirsty?" asked Mr. Sir.

⁴⁶"Yes, Mr. Sir," Stanley said gratefully.

⁴⁷"Well, you better get used to it. You're going to be thirsty for the next eighteen months."

Connect to the Author

Louis Sachar says that while he usually starts a book by thinking about the characters, he wrote *Holes* by thinking about the setting first. "The story began with the place, and the characters and plot grew out of it," says Sachar. "At the time I began the book, we had just returned from the relative coolness of a vacation in Maine to the Texas summer. Anybody who has ever tried to do yard work in Texas in July can easily imagine Hell to be a place where you are required to dig a hole five feet deep and five feet across day after day under the brutal Texas sun." Into this searing landscape Sachar introduced Stanley Yelnats. "He's a kind of pathetic kid who feels like he has no friends, feels like his life is cursed. And I think everyone can identify with that in one way or another." Sachar was born in East Meadow, New York, in 1954. He now lives in Austin, Texas.

Louis Sachar

225

Comprehension and Vocabulary
Before Reading

1. In Lesson 1, we read a story about a boy named Stanley Yelnats. As we reread the story from *Holes*, we'll think more about the kind of person Stanley is and why he reacts the way he does.

Vocabulary Review

2. Arrange students with partners, and have them turn to Student Book page 169. Ask students to read the vocabulary words listed in the box.

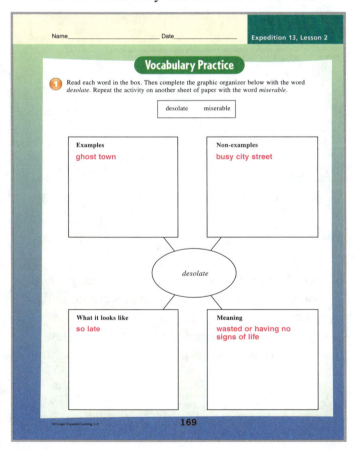

3. Display Transparency 11. Write the word *desolate* in the center oval. **Let's map this word by thinking of examples and non-examples; by telling what the word looks like; and by telling what it means.**

   • **One example of something that is *desolate* would be a ghost town. Let's write that in the Examples box.**

   • **What is another example of something that is desolate?** Write students' responses in the Examples box, and have them record the examples in the Student Book.

   • **Now let's think of some non-examples of things that are desolate. One non-example would be a busy city street.** Write this on the transparency while students record it in their books.

   • **What are some other non-examples?** Record these as students do the same.

   • **Let's move on to what the word looks like. To me, it looks like "so late," which can mean a wasted chance, or just "late," a word we sometimes use to refer to a person who has died.** Write these words on the transparency. **The word *desolate* is related to both of these, in a way. Something *desolate* can be wasted and empty of life.**

   • **Does the word *desolate* look like any other words to you?** Record and discuss students' ideas.

   • **Finally, let's write a meaning for the word. Based on our examples, non-examples, and related words, it seems to me that *desolate* means "wasted or having no signs of life." Let's write this in the Meaning box.**

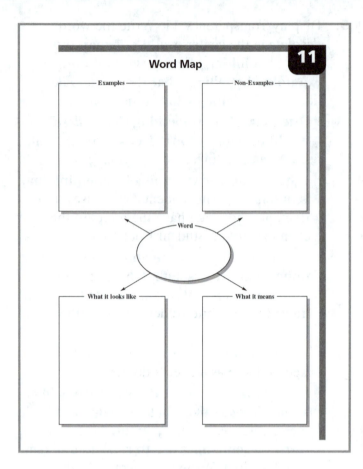

5. When students have finished this activity, read aloud the instructions on Student Book page 170. Have students complete the activity independently. Then call on individuals to read their completed sentences aloud.

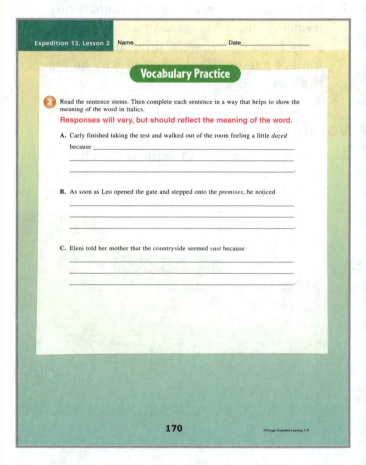

4. Distribute copies of Transparency 11 to students, and have them work with a partner to complete an additional word map for *miserable*. When all students are finished, review students' responses as a class. (Possible responses for *miserable*: Examples—someone with the flu or a cold and rainy day; Non-examples—the winner of a prize or a crisp autumn morning; Looks like—*misery*, which has to do with being uncomfortable; *miser*, which means "someone who is stingy"; Means—uncomfortable or causing discomfort)

6. **Challenge Words** Write *searing* and *pathetic* on the board, and have students create and complete a word map like the one on the Student Book page for each word. Review students' responses as a class.

Reading for Understanding

Reading

1. Have students turn to Anthology page 222 and Student Book page 171. Read the Student Book instructions for section 3 aloud.

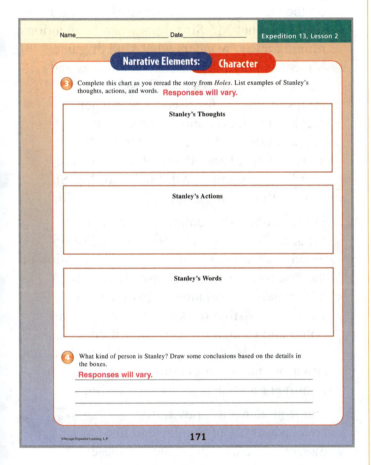

2. Draw three boxes on the board like the ones on the Student Book page, and label them *Thoughts*, *Actions*, and *Words*. **As we reread the story from *Holes*, let's pay close attention to the things Stanley thinks, does, and says. We can list his most important thoughts, actions, and words in the boxes. Then we can use these details to draw some conclusions about the kind of person Stanley is—and why he does the things he does.**

3. Read aloud the first three paragraphs of the story. **Stanley says something important in the third paragraph. As he's getting off the bus, after a long, uncomfortable ride, Stanley thanks the bus driver. This shows something important about Stanley's character. Let's write *thanks the bus driver* in the Words box on the chart.**

4. Continue reading, then pause after paragraph 16. **Stanley thinks something important in this paragraph. The narrator says Stanley "thought about the long, miserable bus ride and felt a little sorry for the guard and the bus driver." Stanley is thinking about the discomfort of the two men. Let's write *feels sorry for the guard and driver* in the Thoughts box.**

5. Have students read paragraphs 17 and 18 independently. **What does Stanley say in paragraph 18?** ("Uh, yes, Mr. Sir . . . ") **Why is this important?** (It shows that Stanley is willing to do as he is told.) **Let's write Stanley's statement in the Words box.** Remind students to use quotation marks any time they write Stanley's exact words.

6. **Fluency** Have students finish reading the story independently. Instruct them to pause to identify and record Stanley's other important thoughts, actions, and words. Tell students not to complete section 4 at this time.

7. Encourage students to monitor their own comprehension of the text by pausing occasionally to ask themselves *Am I understanding what I'm reading?* Tell students that when they do not understand what they are reading, they should reread that portion of the text.

637

ELL Provide English language learners with support in using concrete and sensory details to build mental images of what they read. As students read selections with a partner, have them stop after specific paragraphs or after every two or three paragraphs and do the following:

• Write key concrete and sensory details from the text. For example: *The land was barren and desolate. He could see a few rundown buildings and some tents. Farther away there was a cabin beneath two tall trees.* (paragraph 4)

• Use the details to draw a picture of the scene.

• Write a description of the scene.

• Describe the scene aloud to one another.

• Reread the paragraph.

For a complete model of this strategy, see Expedition 12, Lesson 3.

Checking for Comprehension *After Reading*

1. When all students are finished, call on individuals to identify the thoughts, actions, and words they listed. Write these in the boxes on the board. (Possible responses: Thoughts—wonders what Mr. Sir means when he mentions running away, wonders what kind of game Mr. Sir is playing; Actions—undresses and submits to the inspection, dresses in the jumpsuit, looks surprised to hear when breakfast is served, nods to show his understanding, takes a good look at his surroundings, sees other kids at the camp; Words—"Not much, Mr. Sir," "No, Mr. Sir," "I'm not going to run away," "Yes, Mr. Sir.")

2. Direct students' attention to section 4 on Student Book page 171. Read the question aloud, and have students use the information on the board to write a response. Then call on individuals to read aloud what they have written. (Possible responses: Stanley seems polite and thoughtful, even in difficult circumstances; he doesn't seem bitter about his situation; he doesn't complain; he seems intelligent and alert to his surroundings.)

3. Guide students to draw further conclusions about Stanley and his motives. Use questions such as these: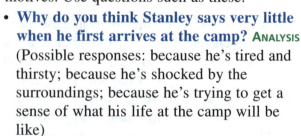

• **Why do you think Stanley says very little when he first arrives at the camp?** ANALYSIS (Possible responses: because he's tired and thirsty; because he's shocked by the surroundings; because he's trying to get a sense of what his life at the camp will be like)

• **Why do you think Stanley tells Mr. Sir that he will not run away?** ANALYSIS (Possible responses: because he does not want to get into further trouble; because he can see that he would not succeed)

- **Why do you think Stanley chose Camp Green Lake instead of going to jail?** ANALYSIS (Possible response: because the name sounded like a friendlier place than jail)

- **Why do you think the author named the facility Camp "Green Lake"?** ANALYSIS (Possible response: for humor, because there appears to be no lake anywhere near the camp)

- **What are some ways that Stanley and Mr. Sir are different?** SYNTHESIS (Possible responses: Stanley seems kind, but Mr. Sir seems cruel; Stanley is sympathetic, but Mr. Sir doesn't seem to care how others feel; Stanley is respectful, but Mr. Sir is mean.)

4. **Challenge Questions** **Based on what you know about Stanley, how do you think he feels about being punished for a crime he didn't commit?** SYNTHESIS (Possible response: He seems to accept this without bitterness.) **In what ways might this attitude be important for the rest of the plot?** (Possible responses: It will allow terrible things to happen to Stanley. Ultimately, Stanley may be forced to discover some sort of inner strength.)

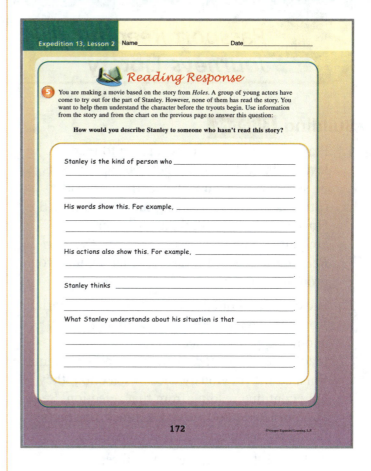

Expedition 13, Lesson 2   Name_____   Date_____

Reading Response

5 You are making a movie based on the story from *Holes*. A group of young actors have come to try out for the part of Stanley. However, none of them has read the story. You want to help them understand the character before the tryouts begin. Use information from the story and from the chart on the previous page to answer this question:

How would you describe Stanley to someone who hasn't read this story?

Stanley is the kind of person who _____
_____
_____.

His words show this. For example, _____
_____
_____.

His actions also show this. For example, _____
_____
_____.

Stanley thinks _____
_____
_____.

What Stanley understands about his situation is that _____
_____
_____
_____.

172   ©Voyager Expanded Learning, L.P.

Reading Response

Have students turn to Student Book page 172. Read the instructions aloud. Then have students use the selection, the information on Student Book page 171, and the paragraph frame to answer this question:

 How would you describe Stanley to someone who hasn't read this story?

Students may work with partners or small groups. When students have completed their responses, call on individuals to read their character descriptions aloud.

Passport Reading Journeys Library

Building Fluency

1. Place students in pairs according to reading level to build fluency. When pairing students, be sure that one student is a stronger reader (Student A) than the other student (Student B). However, do not reveal that stronger readers are paired with weaker readers. See *Passport Reading Journeys* Library Teacher's Guide for grouping guidelines.

2. Have students quickly choose reading material from the *Passport Reading Journeys* Library or another approved selection that is at the reading level of Student B. If students have not finished the previously chosen selection, they may continue reading from that selection. See *Passport Reading Journeys* Library Teacher's Guide for material selection guidelines.

3. Tell students that Student A will read one paragraph, and Student B will reread that same paragraph.

4. Have students follow this routine until the end of class.

5. If necessary, review the following practices to enhance fluency:
    - Rate and accuracy of reading
    - Expression during reading
    - Correction procedures

Library *Highlights*

Reading Independently

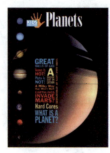

Level I

Level III

Students interested in space and telescopes may enjoy reading about the solar system in *Kids Discover: Planets* or about the history of telescopes and their role in exploring the solar system and space in *Kids Discover: Telescopes*.

Advanced Word Study

Suffix *-less*

1. Write *-less* on the board. **This word part is a suffix. Remember, a suffix is a word part that occurs at the end of a word and often helps us understand the meaning of the word. The sounds for this suffix are /les/. Say the sounds for this suffix.** (/les/) Write the word *lifeless* on the board. Underline the suffix *-less*. **What is this suffix?** (-less) **Read the rest of the word.** (life) **What is the word?** (lifeless) **The suffix *-less* means "without." The word *life* means "existence or being." The word *lifeless* means "without life or existence."**

2. Have students turn to Student Book page E13, Lesson 3. Direct them to line 1 in the first box. **What is the underlined suffix in the first word?** (-less) **Read the rest of the word.** (speech) **What is the word?** (speechless) Repeat with the remaining words. Call on individuals to read the words in a different order. Ask students to tell the meanings of the words based on the meaning of the suffix.

3. Direct students to lines 2 and 3. Have them read the words. Call on individuals to read the words in a different order. Ask students to tell the meanings of the words.

▼ To Correct
Say the correct sound(s) or prefix/suffix, then ask students to repeat the sound(s). Have them read the words again with the correct sound(s). If students do not know the meaning of the word, review the word and/or word parts to determine the meaning of the word.

1. speech<u>less</u> nam<u>eless</u> match<u>less</u> ground<u>less</u>
2. homeless unexpected professional joyless
3. luxuries relationship bestseller dumplings

Sight Words

1. Direct students to line 1. Have them point to the first word. **This word is *moths*. Read the word.** (moths) **This is not a regular word. Let's read the word again.** (moths) **Let's spell the word.** (m-o-t-h-s) **What is the word?** (moths) Repeat with the remaining words. Then, have students read the words. Ask students to tell the meanings of the words.

2. Direct students to lines 2 and 3. **Let's read these words.** Remind students that the rows of words consist of regular and irregular words. Point to the first word. **What is the word?** (stomachs) Repeat with the remaining words. Call on individuals to read the words in a different order. Ask students to tell the meanings of the words.

▼ To Correct
For Regular Words: Say the sound(s) in the word, then ask students to repeat the sound(s). Have them read the word again with the correct sound(s). If students do not know the meaning of the word, review the word and/or word part to determine the meaning of the word.

For Irregular Words: Immediately say the correct word. Then have students read the word, spell it, and read it again. If students do not know the meaning of the word, review the word.

1. moths I   sewers I peasant I   foreign I
2. stomachs I guard I   ingots I   measure I
3. favorite I   sweat I   sewn I   firecrackers R

Anthology Selection

Social Studies

from

The Joy Luck Club

by Amy Tan

In 1937 a minor clash between Japan and China quickly grew into a full-scale war. To escape the bloody fighting, many Chinese people fled to Kweilin in southern China. Among them is the speaker in this excerpt, Jing-Mei Woo. Here, Jing-Mei explains why, despite the war, she started the Joy Luck Club. The four members of the club play an ancient Chinese board game called mah jong.

¹"I thought up Joy Luck on a summer night that was so hot even the moths fainted to the ground, their wings were so heavy with the damp heat. Every place was so crowded there was no room for fresh air. **Unbearable** smells from the sewers rose up to my second-story window and the stink had nowhere else to go but into my nose. At all hours of the night and day, I heard screaming sounds. I didn't know if it was a peasant slitting the throat of a runaway pig or an officer beating a half-dead peasant for lying in his way on the sidewalk. I didn't go to the window to find out. What use would it have been? And that's when I thought I needed something to do to help me move.

²"My idea was to have a gathering of four women, one for each corner of my mah jong table. I knew which women I wanted to ask. They were all young like me, with wishful faces. One was an army officer's wife, like myself. Another was a girl with very fine manners from a rich

226

family in Shanghai. She had escaped with only a little money. And there was a girl from Nanking who had the blackest hair I have ever seen. She came from a low-class family, but she was pretty and pleasant and had married well, to an old man who died and left her with a better life.

³"Each week one of us would host a party to raise money and raise our spirits. The hostess had to serve special *dyansyin* foods to bring good fortune of all kinds—dumplings shaped like silver money ingots, long rice noodles for long life, boiled peanuts for conceiving sons, and of course, many good-luck oranges for a plentiful, sweet life.

⁴"What fine food we treated ourselves to with our **meager** allowances! We didn't notice that the dumplings were stuffed mostly with stringy squash and that the oranges were spotted with wormy holes. We ate sparingly, not as if we didn't have enough, but to protest how we could not eat another bite, we had already **bloated** ourselves from earlier in the day. We knew we had luxuries few people could afford. We were the lucky ones.

⁵"After filling our stomachs, we would then fill a bowl with money and put it where everyone could see. Then we would sit down at the mah jong table. My table was from my family and was of a very **fragrant** red wood, not what you call rosewood, but *hong mu*, which is so fine there's no English word for it. The table had a very thick pad, so that when the mah jong *pai* were spilled onto the table the only sound was of ivory tiles washing against one another.

⁶"Once we started to play, nobody could speak, except to say 'Pung!' or 'Chr!' when taking a tile. We had to play with seriousness and think of nothing else but adding to our happiness through winning. But

227

after sixteen rounds, we would again feast, this time to celebrate our good fortune. And then we would talk into the night until morning, saying stories about good times in the past and good times yet to come.

⁷"Oh, what good stories! Stories spilling out all over the place! We almost laughed to death. A rooster that ran into the house screeching on the top of dinner bowls, the same bowls that held him quietly in pieces the next day! And one about a girl who wrote love letters for two friends who loved the same man. And a silly foreign lady who fainted on a toilet when firecrackers went off next to her.

⁸"People thought we were wrong to serve banquets every week while many people in the city were starving, eating rats and, later, the garbage that the poorest rats used to feed on. Others thought we were **possessed** by demons—to celebrate when even within our own families we had lost generations, had lost homes and fortunes, and were separated, husband from wife, brother from sister, daughter from mother. Hnnn! How could we laugh, people asked.

⁹"It's not that we had no heart or eyes for pain. We were all afraid. We all had our **miseries**. But to despair was to wish back for something already lost. Or to prolong what was already unbearable. How much can you wish for a favorite warm coat that hangs in the closet of a house that burned down with your mother and father inside of it? How can you see in your mind arms and legs hanging from telephone wires

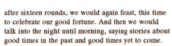

228

and starving dogs running down the streets with half-chewed hands dangling from their jaws? What was worse, we asked among ourselves, to sit and wait for our own deaths with proper **somber** faces? Or to choose our own happiness?

¹⁰"So we decided to hold parties and pretend each week had become the new year. Each week we could forget past wrongs done to us. We weren't allowed to think a bad thought. We feasted, we laughed, we played games, lost and won, we told the best stories. And each week, we could hope to be lucky. That hope was our only joy. And that's how we came to call our little parties Joy Luck."

Connect to the Author

Amy Tan's novels are inspired by her real life. They often explore the relationship between mothers and daughters who were raised in different countries, as she and her mother were. Tan, who was born in 1952 in California, never planned to become a writer. Her mother, who was born in China, wanted her daughter to be a neurosurgeon and concert pianist. Overworked, Tan turned to writing as a form of therapy. That strategy paid off in an unexpected way. Tan's very first novel, *The Joy Luck Club*, spent 9 months on the *New York Times* bestseller list. She has been a professional writer ever since.

Amy Tan

229

Comprehension and Vocabulary
Before Reading

1. In Lessons 1 and 2, we read a fictional story about a boy who is adjusting to a miserable situation. In Lesson 3, we'll read a fictional story about a group of women who find a clever way to live through their difficult circumstances.

2. Ask students to name board games they enjoy playing. Explain that they will read about four women who gather each week to play *mah jong*, a board game played with tiles that are similar to dominoes. Instead of dots, the tiles are engraved with Chinese symbols and characters and are divided into suits.

3. Have students turn to Anthology page 226 and preview the text by looking at the image and skimming the introduction.

4. Have students turn to Anthology page 229 and locate the Connect to the Author feature. Read the biography aloud as students follow along in their books. **When Amy Tan was a teenager, she and her mother, Daisy, were sometimes in conflict. Tan often escaped by reading books. "I think books were my salvation," Tan says. "They saved me from being miserable." Tan eventually wanted to understand her mother's life, which was so different from her own. Long conversations with Daisy led Tan to write *The Joy Luck Club*. We'll read a story from that book, which is based on some of the details of Daisy's life in China.**

Introduce Vocabulary

5. **We will read some new words in the Lesson 3 text, a selection from *The Joy Luck Club*.**
   - Write the vocabulary words on the board. Include Challenge Words to meet the needs of students who are advancing.
   - Read the words to students.

- Call on individuals to read the words as you point to them.
- Provide correction and feedback as needed.

▶ Have students write the words in the Vocabulary Log.

6. Tell students that knowing the meanings of these words will help them better understand the article.

   For each word:
   - Read the word with its definition and the sentence that follows.
   - Write the sentences on the board.
   - Call on students to use their own words to give the meaning and some examples of each vocabulary word.

Vocabulary

unbearable	*more than a person can stand* The heat from the blazing sun on the pavement was *unbearable*.
meager	*barely enough* Jonah's *meager* salary hardly paid his rent.
bloat	*to swell* The guests proceeded to *bloat* themselves on the huge meal.
fragrant	*having a sweet or pleasant odor* *Fragrant* cherry blossoms filled the air with their perfume.
possess	*to control or take over* The wish to return to his farm seemed to *possess* my grandfather.
misery	*great suffering or unhappiness* Steam heat can relieve the *misery* of a cold.
somber	*serious; gloomy* Leaving our beloved city was a *somber* event.

Challenge Words
Word Meaning

ingot	*a lump of metal shaped into a bar or some other form* Gold *ingots* were used as money long ago.

Content Area • Science

neurosurgeon	*a doctor trained to operate on the brain and spinal cord* Only a *neurosurgeon* can safely operate on a brain tumor.

Review Narrative Elements

7. Write *Character*, *Setting*, and *Plot* on the board. Call on students to tell what they know about each element of narrative writing.

8. Draw a box around *Setting*. **What is a story's setting?** (the time and place in which it happens) **When we read the story from *Holes*, we saw that some stories, or narratives, are set in the present. Other stories have *historical* settings. This means that the story is set during some time in the past.**

9. **Today's story is set in the past. It takes place in the late 1930s or early 1940s, at a time when China and Japan were at war with each other. Japan invaded China just before and during World War II. At the war's end, in 1945, Japan was finally forced to surrender.**

10. **The *place* where this story happens is also very important. It has a direct impact on the lives of the four women in the story. When Japan invaded China, many people fled to Kweilin, seeking safety from Japanese troops. There the people found much crowding, constant bombing, and other terrible conditions.** Direct students' attention to the introductory note on Anthology page 226, and read it aloud.

- **Where is this story set?** (in a city in southern China)
- **How do you think the story's setting—a crowded city threatened by war—might impact, or affect, a character's actions?** (Possible responses: Some characters might be frightened all the time; they might go into hiding and not have contact with others. Other characters might find something worthwhile or even fun to do to relieve the stress.)

11. **As we read the story, let's think about how a club with the words *joy* and *luck* in its name could arise in a city crowded with people experiencing the terrors of war.**

Introduce First-Person Narratives

12. **Let's look at the first sentence of our reading.** Read the sentence aloud, emphasizing the word *I*. **The word *I* is one clue that the main character is telling this story about herself.** Write the word *I* on the board.

13. **Writing that uses the words *I*, *my*, and *me* is called *first-person* writing.** Add *my* and *me* to the board. **The first-person point of view can be used in a real-life story or a made-up one. In either case, the person telling the story participates in the action and includes details of his or her thoughts and feelings. What are some other words that might be used in first-person writing?** (Possible responses: we, our, mine, myself) Add these words to the board.

14. **Think about stories you have read or heard that are told from the first-person point of view. Why is this point of view helpful for a reader or a listener?** (It helps the reader or listener get to know the speaker.) As time allows, have students briefly review the texts they read in Expeditions 11 and 12 to identify first-person writing.

15. **The speaker in this story, Jing-Mei, tells about an important time in her life. As you read, think about your own first-person writing—in letters or journals, perhaps—in which you describe your thoughts and feelings about an important time in your life, especially a difficult or challenging one. Also think about ways you might have found relief during a difficult time, as the women in the story did.**

Reading for Understanding

Reading

Places and Names to Look For:
- Japan
- China
- Kweilin
- Jing-Mei Woo
- Shanghai
- Nanking

1. **As you read this story, you may come across some unfamiliar places and names.**
   - Write the words on the board.
   - Point to each word as you read the following:

   In this story, you will learn from the story's speaker, *Jing-Mei Woo*, how she and three friends found relief from the horrors of war. The story takes place during a time when *Japan* invaded *China*. The four women have fled to *Kweilin*, a city in southern China. Jing-Mei introduces the women in her group, one of whom is from *Shanghai*, China's largest city, and one of whom is from *Nanking*, a famous ancient capital city in China.

   - Call on individuals to read the words.

2. **As we read the story, remember to think about the ways in which the setting—a city in the midst of war—affects Jing-Mei and her friends. Think also about ways that people find relief from suffering during hard times.**

3. **Fluency** Read the first paragraph aloud. Then have students read the remainder of the text and the Connect to Author feature aloud with you. If necessary, review the following fluency goal with students to practice prosody: **As we read aloud, we will use expression and combine words in phrases in a way that sounds like speech. This will show that we understand what we are reading.**

4. When students have completed their reading, check for literal comprehension of the text by asking these questions: **KNOWLEDGE**
   - *Paragraph 3:* **What is the Joy Luck club?** (a weekly gathering of four women to eat special foods and play a game)
   - *Paragraph 6:* **What were the women supposed to think about while playing the game?** (adding to their happiness through winning) **What would the women do after the game?** (tell stories)
   - *Paragraph 8:* **Why did some people think the women were wrong for playing games and eating feasts?** (because many people in the city were starving)

645

Checking for Comprehension *After Reading*

Check students' understanding of narrative elements and encourage them to apply what they understood from the text by asking the following questions:

- **How would you summarize the plot of this story in two or three sentences? SYNTHESIS** (Possible response: Jing-Mei decides to start a club with three other women to distract herself and her friends from an awful war. Once a week, the women play a game, eat treats, and tell stories. During this time, they set aside their fears and their memories of terrible losses.)

- **Jing-Mei says of the Joy Luck Club, "We were the lucky ones." Why is this surprising given the story's setting—a time and place of great suffering? ANALYSIS** (Possible responses: because they have some food and money, unlike others; because they are able to find a way to relieve their suffering)

- **How is the story's setting directly related to Jing-Mei's decision to start the Joy Luck Club? ANALYSIS** (Possible response: The city's awful heat, crowded conditions, terrible odors, and frightening sounds force Jing-Mei to find a way to survive.)

- **The women find a way to cope with a difficult situation. Why do you think others criticized them for this? ANALYSIS** (Possible responses: Others too defeated by war could not imagine having fun during such a time; some people were probably jealous of the women for finding a way out of their suffering.)

- **Do you think the Joy Luck Club was a good idea? Explain your answer. EVALUATION** (Possible responses: yes, because it was a way for them to feel better for a little while; no, because they should have been sharing their food and money with those worse off)

Connect to the Author

Have students discuss the following questions with a partner.

- **Why do you think the author includes Chinese words such as *dyansyin, hong mu,* and *pai* in the story?** (Possible response: to give readers a flavor of the culture she is writing about)

- **In the first paragraph, the author uses specific details to describe the story's setting. To what senses—sight, hearing, smell, taste, and touch—do these details appeal? Give examples from the text.** (sight—moths fainting; hearing—screaming sounds; smell—terrible odors from sewers)

- **What is the details' effect on you?** (Possible responses: It's easier to picture the setting; the details draw me into the story.)

- **Why do you think the author chose to tell the story through a first-person speaker, Jing-Mei?** (Possible response: so that readers could more easily connect to Jing-Mei's thoughts and feelings)

Listening and Speaking After all pairs have discussed the questions, call on students to present one or more of their ideas to the class. Remind students to use standard English rather than slang in their presentations. Encourage them to speak slowly, taking the time needed to choose words that will best communicate their message.

Connect to Social Studies

Use the following activity to help students appreciate the value of wartime diversions such as the Joy Luck Club.

- Remind students that the Joy Luck Club was formed as a way for the women to divert their minds from the horrors of the war between China and Japan. **Do you think people should engage in games and other pleasurable pastimes in the midst of a terrible event such as war or a natural disaster? Why or why not?**

- On the board, write these words and phrases: *escape, community, shared experiences*. Ask students how the Joy Luck Club provided all of these.

- Point out that during the 1930s and 1940s in the United States—when economic times were difficult for many and World War II had begun—many Americans found relief from their difficulties in forms of entertainment such as watching movies, listening to music, dancing, and attending plays, many of which were free or inexpensive.

- Ask students to imagine how they might find hope and joy during difficult times. For each term on the board, have them write suggestions for finding ways to escape, for maintaining a sense of community, and for sharing the experience of undergoing difficulties.

- When students have finished writing their ideas, call on individuals to share them with the class.

To increase difficulty: Have students conduct research to learn about the game of *mah jong*. Ask them to make drawings of some of the *mah jong* tiles and display these in the classroom.

Social Studies

Lesson 4

Anthology Selection

from

The Joy Luck Club

by Amy Tan

In 1937 a minor clash between Japan and China quickly grew into a full-scale war. To escape the bloody fighting, many Chinese people fled to Kweilin in southern China. Among them is the speaker in this excerpt, Jing-Mei Woo. Here, Jing-Mei explains why, despite the war, she started the Joy Luck Club. The four members of the club play an ancient Chinese board game called mah jong.

¹"I thought up Joy Luck on a summer night that was so hot even the moths fainted to the ground, their wings were so heavy with the damp heat. Every place was so crowded there was no room for fresh air. **Unbearable** smells from the sewers rose up to my second-story window and the stink had nowhere else to go but into my nose. At all hours of the night and day, I heard screaming sounds. I didn't know if it was a peasant slitting the throat of a runaway pig or an officer beating a half-dead peasant for lying in his way on the sidewalk. I didn't go to the window to find out. What use would it have been? And that's when I thought I needed something to do to help me move.

²"My idea was to have a gathering of four women, one for each corner of my mah jong table. I knew which women I wanted to ask. They were all young like me, with wishful faces. One was an army officer's wife, like myself. Another was a girl with very fine manners from a rich

226

family in Shanghai. She had escaped with only a little money. And there was a girl from Nanking who had the blackest hair I have ever seen. She came from a low-class family, but she was pretty and pleasant and had married well, to an old man who died and left her with a better life.

³"Each week one of us would host a party to raise money and raise our spirits. The hostess had to serve special *dyansyin* foods to bring good fortune of all kinds—dumplings shaped like silver money ingots, long rice noodles for long life, boiled peanuts for conceiving sons, and of course, many good-luck oranges for a plentiful, sweet life.

⁴"What fine food we treated ourselves to with our **meager** allowances! We didn't notice that the dumplings were stuffed mostly with stringy squash and that the oranges were spotted with wormy holes. We ate sparingly, not as if we didn't have enough, but to protest how we could not eat another bite, we had already **bloated** ourselves from earlier in the day. We knew we had luxuries few people could afford. We were the lucky ones.

⁵"After filling our stomachs, we would then fill a bowl with money and put it where everyone could see. Then we would sit down at the mah jong table. My table was from my family and was of a very **fragrant** red wood, not what you call rosewood, but *hong mu*, which is so fine there's no English word for it. The table had a very thick pad, so that when the mah jong *pai* were spilled onto the table the only sound was of ivory tiles washing against one another.

⁶"Once we started to play, nobody could speak, except to say '*Pung!*' or '*Chr!*' when taking a tile. We had to play with seriousness and think of nothing else but adding to our happiness through winning. But

227

after sixteen rounds, we would again feast, this time to celebrate our good fortune. And then we would talk into the night until morning, saying stories about good times in the past and good times yet to come.

⁷"Oh, what good stories! Stories spilling out all over the place! We almost laughed to death. A rooster that ran into the house screeching on the top of dinner bowls, the same bowls that held him quietly in pieces the next day! And one about a girl who wrote love letters for two friends who loved the same man. And a silly foreign lady who fainted on a toilet when firecrackers went off next to her.

⁸"People thought we were wrong to serve banquets every week while many people in the city were starving, eating rats and, later, the garbage that the poorest rats used to feed on. Others thought we were **possessed** by demons—to celebrate when even within our own families we had lost generations, had lost homes and fortunes, and were separated, husband from wife, brother from sister, daughter from mother. Hnnnh! How could we laugh, people asked.

⁹"It's not that we had no heart or eyes for pain. We were all afraid. We all had our **miseries**. But to despair was to wish back for something already lost. Or to prolong what was already unbearable. How much can you wish for a favorite warm coat that hangs in the closet of a house that burned down with your mother and father inside of it? How can you see in your mind arms and legs hanging from telephone wires

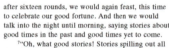

228

and starving dogs running down the streets with half-chewed hands dangling from their jaws? What was worse, we asked among ourselves, to sit and wait for our own deaths with proper **somber** faces? Or to choose our own happiness?

¹⁰"So we decided to hold parties and pretend each week had become the new year. Each week we could forget past wrongs done to us. We weren't allowed to think a bad thought. We feasted, we laughed, we played games, lost and won, we told the best stories. And each week, we could hope to be lucky. That hope was our only joy. And that's how we came to call our little parties Joy Luck."

Connect to the Author

Amy Tan's novels are inspired by her real life. They often explore the relationship between mothers and daughters who were raised in different countries, as she and her mother were. Tan, who was born in 1952 in California, never planned to become a writer. Her mother, who was born in China, wanted her daughter to be a neurosurgeon and concert pianist. Overworked, Tan turned to writing as a form of therapy. That strategy paid off in an unexpected way. Tan's very first novel, *The Joy Luck Club*, spent 9 months on the *New York Times* bestseller list. She has been a professional writer ever since.

Amy Tan

229

Comprehension and Vocabulary
Before Reading

1. In Lesson 3, we read a story from *The Joy Luck Club*.
   - **What does the speaker, Jing-Mei, do in this story?** (She starts a club for herself and three other women.)
   - **What do the women do when they meet each week?** (They eat different foods, play a game, and tell stories.)

2. **Suppose that a disaster such as a hurricane destroys your city, and your family is forced to move to a new town. You are unhappy about having to leave your home. List three things you can do to help yourself and others feel better about this situation.** (Responses will vary.)

3. **As we reread the selection from *The Joy Luck Club*, we'll think about the reasons why the women participate in the club each week.**

Vocabulary Review

4. Arrange students in pairs, and have them turn to Student Book page 173. Ask students to read the vocabulary words listed in the box. Call on students to tell what each word means and to use it in a sentence.

5. **Now, we will take a closer look at the word *unbearable*.**
   - **What other, more familiar word does the word *unbearable* contain?** (bear) **What does the word *bear* mean?** (Possible response: to stand or endure) Have students write this base word and definition in the first box.
   - **What is another meaning of the word *bear*?** (Possible response: a large, furry animal)

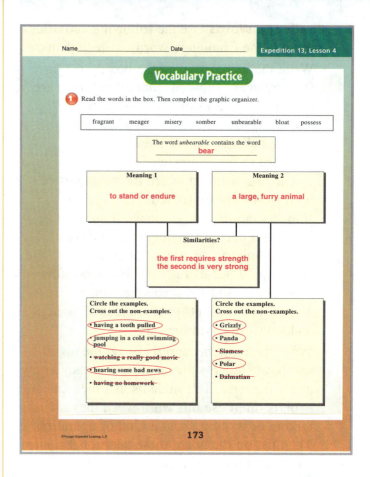

- **Are there any similarities between these meanings? Are these meanings related to each other in any way?** Have students write their thoughts in the Similarities box.
- **Now, let's look at the list in the box below each meaning. If an item is an example of that meaning of *bear*, let's circle it. If the item is *not* an example of that meaning of *bear*, let's cross it out. The first item in the box on the left is *having a tooth pulled*. This is something nobody enjoys. If your tooth must be pulled, you must endure it, or *bear* it. This is an example of the first meaning of *bear*. Let's circle it.**
- Have students complete the activity with a partner. When all pairs are finished, call on individuals to tell whether an item on one of the lists is an example or a non-example of the related meaning and to explain their thinking.

6. Challenge Words Use the following activities to review the Challenge Words with students.

- Write the word *ingot* on the board, and have students identify words that resemble or are contained within this word. (Possible responses: in, got, ignorant) Then have students choose one of these words as a keyword to the meaning of *ingot*, then visualize a scene in which the meanings of both words are illustrated. For example, students might choose the word *got*, and imagine a person standing in a shallow stream, holding up a lump of gold metal, and shouting, "I got it! I got it!" Have students draw pictures of the scene they imagine. Then invite students to share their drawings and keywords with the class.

- Write the word *neurosurgeon* on the board and have students brainstorm what they know about the term. Tell students that medical experts often use this word when they are talking or writing about a kind of operation. Then list on the board these additional related words and phrases: *neurosurgery, doctor, brain, spinal cord, tumor, epilepsy*. Have students provide sentences that contain the content area word as well as one of the other words on the board.

Introduce Character Motivation

7. In the last lesson, we talked mainly about *what* Jing-Mei and her friends do in Kweilin. In Lesson 4, we'll look more closely at the *reasons* for their actions.

SKILL ✓

8. Write *Motivation* on the board. **Characters in stories usually have reasons for their actions. These reasons are called *motivations*.**

- **Some motivations come from the outside world. For example, if you are writing with a pen and the pen runs out of ink, you would get a new pen. Your motivation, or reason, would be the empty pen.**

- **Other motivations come from inside. They are desires or feelings. For example, I might have a desire to be a famous guitar player. For this reason, I might be motivated to practice the guitar every day. Other actions that I take—such as washing my own clothes or taking out the garbage—are motivated by the good feeling I get from being helpful. Still other actions might be motivated by fear, hope, or greed.**

9. Motivations are often mixed. They might come partly from the outside and partly from the inside. For example, if you were outside and saw a flash of lightning, you would quickly find shelter. This action would be partly motivated by something in the outside world—the lightning. What inside feeling would it also be motivated by? (fear)

10. Characters in stories can have more than one reason for what they do. These reasons can also change over time. As we reread the story about Jing-Mei and her friends, let's see whether her first motivation for starting the Joy Luck Club changes or stays the same.

Reading for Understanding

Reading

1. Have students turn to Anthology page 226 and Student Book page 174. Read the Student Book instructions aloud.

2. **The first action listed is** *Jing-Mei gets the idea for the Joy Luck Club*. **As we read paragraph 1, let's look for a reason for this action.** Read the first paragraph of the story aloud. **In this paragraph, Jing-Mei describes the hot, crowded, and frightening conditions in the city she has come to. These make her feel helpless. Let's write this reason under Motivation next to** *Paragraphs 1 and 2* **in the first box.** Pause. **Now, as we read paragraph 2, let's look for another reason why Jing-Mei wants to start her club.** Read the first sentence of paragraph 2 aloud. **What reason does she give here?** (She wants a gathering of four women to play mah jong.) Have students write this under Motivation in the same box.

3. Have students finish reading the story independently, pausing to fill in the motivations for each action listed on the Student Book page. Monitor students' work, providing correction and feedback as needed.

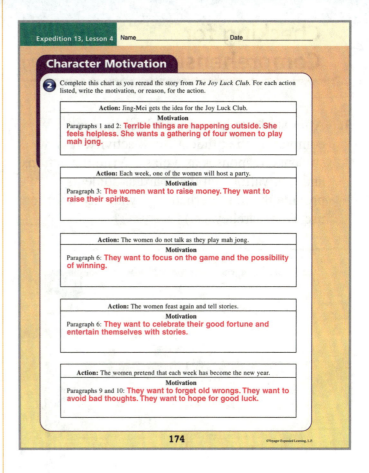

Expedition 13, Lesson 4   Name_____   Date_____

Character Motivation

2 Complete this chart as you reread the story from *The Joy Luck Club*. For each action listed, write the motivation, or reason, for the action.

Action: Jing-Mei gets the idea for the Joy Luck Club.
Motivation
Paragraphs 1 and 2: Terrible things are happening outside. She feels helpless. She wants a gathering of four women to play mah jong.

Action: Each week, one of the women will host a party.
Motivation
Paragraph 3: The women want to raise money. They want to raise their spirits.

Action: The women do not talk as they play mah jong.
Motivation
Paragraph 6: They want to focus on the game and the possibility of winning.

Action: The women feast again and tell stories.
Motivation
Paragraph 6: They want to celebrate their good fortune and entertain themselves with stories.

Action: The women pretend that each week has become the new year.
Motivation
Paragraphs 9 and 10: They want to forget old wrongs. They want to avoid bad thoughts. They want to hope for good luck.

174   ©Voyager Expanded Learning, L.P.

Checking for Comprehension *After Reading*

1. After students have finished reading and completing the Student Book activity, review students' responses as a class. Write the actions and motivations on the board as students provide them. (Alternatively, you may want to use Transparency 15.)

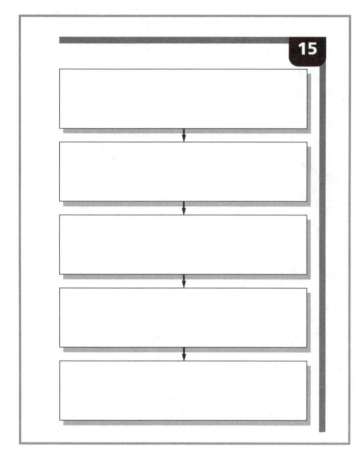

2. **Earlier, we discussed that some motivations come from the inside, and some come from the outside. Do any of the motivations we've listed come from the outside?** (Possible responses: yes, the terrible conditions of the city; the lack of enough food and money) **Do any come from the inside?** (All come at least partly from the inside, such as the desire for lifted spirits and the hope of getting lucky.)

3. **Near the end of the story, Jing-Mei says that people think the women are wrong or even demon possessed to have their weekly parties.**
   - **What do you think is the motivation for these remarks from others?** (Possible responses: Terrible things are happening in their land; they are jealous of the women's fun.)
   - **Is this motivation from the inside, or outside, or both? Explain.** (Possible responses: outside, because conditions are so bad; inside, because they are unhappy and are upset by the women's fun; both, because conditions are bad, but they can't find the inner strength as Jing-Mei and her friends have)

4. **Challenge Questions Do you think the women's reasons for having the parties change over the course of the story? How so?** ANALYSIS (Possible responses: no, because the basic reason—companionship—stays the same; yes, because they discover many things to enjoy besides playing the game, such as telling stories) **In your opinion, do these reasons make it okay for the women to play and eat together, despite other people's misery?** EVALUATION (Responses will vary.)

Reading Response

Have students turn to Student Book page 175. Read the instructions aloud. Ask students to imagine that they are Jing-Mei. Then instruct them to look back in the story and to the previous Student Book page to help them find answers to this question:

 How and why did I start the Joy Luck Club?

Have students complete their paragraphs independently. When all students are finished, call on individuals to read aloud what they have written.

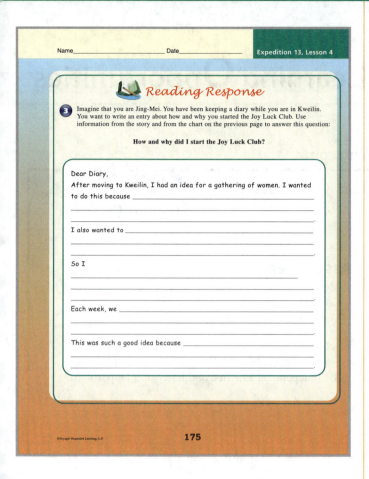

Name_____ Date_____ Expedition 13, Lesson 4

Reading Response

3 Imagine that you are Jing-Mei. You have been keeping a diary while you are in Kweilin. You want to write an entry about how and why you started the Joy Luck Club. Use information from the story and from the chart on the previous page to answer this question:

How and why did I start the Joy Luck Club?

Dear Diary,
After moving to Kweilin, I had an idea for a gathering of women. I wanted to do this because _____

I also wanted to _____

So I _____

Each week, we _____

This was such a good idea because _____

©Voyager Expanded Learning, L.P.

175

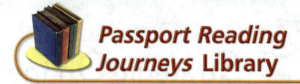

Passport Reading Journeys Library

Building Fluency

1. Place students in pairs according to reading level to build fluency. When pairing students, be sure that one student is a stronger reader (Student A) than the other student (Student B). However, do not reveal that stronger readers are paired with weaker readers. See *Passport Reading Journeys* Library Teacher's Guide for grouping guidelines.

2. Have students quickly choose reading material from the *Passport Reading Journeys* Library or another approved selection that is at the reading level of Student B. If students have not finished the previously chosen selection, they may continue reading from that selection. See *Passport Reading Journeys* Library Teacher's Guide for material selection guidelines.

3. Tell students that Student A will read one paragraph, and Student B will reread that same paragraph.

4. Have students follow this routine until the end of class.

5. If necessary, review the following practices to enhance fluency:
   - Rate and accuracy of reading
   - Expression during reading
   - Correction procedures

Library Highlights

Spotlight on an Author

Level I

Sharon Creech received the Newbery Medal for *Walk Two Moons* in 1995. *Heartbeat* is included in the *Passport Reading Journeys II* Library. Creech has written several other books for young adult readers. Her books often have a realistic theme of self-discovery and growth.

Lesson 5

Strategic Online Learning Opportunities®

Session 1   http://solo.voyagerlearning.com

Students read a passage about hoaxes, such as Bigfoot and ghosts, which have intrigued people.

Content Connection
Language Arts

The "Paranormal" Hoax
by Joe Nickell

Lexile Levels
Passage B 910L
Passage C 980L

Assessment

- Metacognition
- Content
- Vocabulary
- Main Idea
- Summary

SKILL ✓

Based on their assessment scores, students automatically are assigned either the Skills Practice for reinforcement or the Independent Practice and Extension Opportunities.

SKILLS PRACTICE

Vocabulary Strategies
- Context
- Word Parts: Prefixes and Suffixes
- Word Parts: Compound Words

Dictionary Skills

Main Idea Strategy: W–I–N
- Identifying the Most Important *Who* or *What*
- Identifying the Most Important *Information*
- Stating the Main Idea in a Small *Number* of Words

Questioning

Writing
- Writing a Summary Statement

INDEPENDENT PRACTICE

Vocabulary Strategies

Writing
- Writing a Summary Statement

EXTENSION OPPORTUNITIES

- Online Books
- Book Cart
- Review of Previous Passages

Advanced Word Study

Multisyllabic Words

1. **Remember, sometimes it's easier to read parts of a longer word before reading the entire word. One way is to use what we know about open and closed syllables.** Write *titanic* on the board. Underline the word part *ti*. **What is the first word part?** (ti) **What kind of syllable is this word part?** (open) **How do we know?** (It has one long vowel sound without any consonants following it, or closing it in.) **What long vowel sound does the vowel make?** (/ī/) Underline the word part *tan*. **What is the next part?** (tan) **What kind of syllable is this?** (closed) **How do we know?** (It has one short vowel sound followed by one or more consonants.) **What short sound does the vowel make?** (/a/) Underline the suffix *-ic*. **What is this suffix?** (-ic) **What is the word?** (titanic) *Titanic* means "relating to being huge or gigantic."

2. Have students turn to Student Book page E13, Lesson 6. Direct students to line 1. **Point to the first word. What is the prefix?** (un-) **What is the next word part?** (em) **What is the next word part?** (ploy) **What is this suffix?** (-ment) **What is the word?** (unemployment) **The word** *unemployment* **means "the quality of not being employed or having a job."** Repeat with the remaining words. Call on individuals to read the words in random order. Ask students to tell the meanings of the words.

3. Direct students to lines 2 and 3. Have them read the words. Then, call on individuals to read the words in a different order. Ask students to tell the meanings of the words.

▼ **To Correct**

For Multisyllabic Words: **What is the first word part? What is the next part? What is the word?** If students do not know the meaning of the word, review the word and/or word parts to determine the meaning of the word.

For Sounds in Words: Say the correct sound(s), then ask students to repeat the sound(s). Have students read the words again with the correct sound(s).

If students do not know the meaning of the word, review the word and/or word parts to determine the meaning of the word.

1.	unemployment	inspiration	summarize	conversations
2.	eternity	resolution	overwhelm	disillusionment
3.	immigrants	glimmering	literature	combinations

Sight Words

1. Direct students to line 1. Have them point to the first word. **This word is** *sinew*. **Read the word.** (sinew) **This is not a regular word. Let's read the word again.** (sinew) **Let's spell the word.** (s-i-n-e-w) **What is the word?** (sinew) Repeat with the remaining words. Then, have students read the words. Ask students to tell the meanings of the words.

2. Direct students to lines 2 and 3. **Let's read these words.** Remind students that the rows of words consist of regular and irregular words. Point to the first word. **What is the word?** (crimson) Repeat with the remaining words. Call on individuals to read the words in a different order. Ask students to tell the meanings of the words.

▼ **To Correct**

For Regular Words: Say the sound(s) in the word, then ask students to repeat the sound(s). Have them read the word again with the correct sound(s). If students do not know the meaning of the word, review the word and/or word part to determine the meaning of the word.

For Irregular Words: Immediately say the correct word. Then have students read the word, spell it, and read it again. If students do not know the meaning of the word, review the word.

1.	sinew I	frigid I	poetical I	descent I
2.	crimson R	moths I	continued I	peasant I
3.	sewers I	pieces I	foreign I	intimate I

Anthology Selection

Expedition 13, Lessons 6 and 7

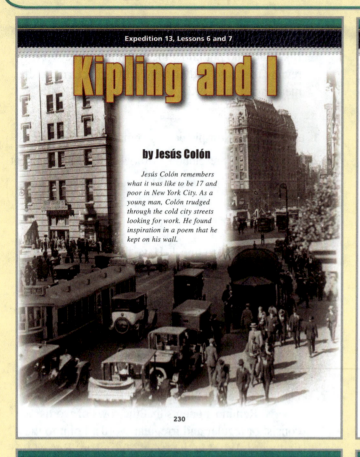

Kipling and I

by Jesús Colón

Jesús Colón remembers what it was like to be 17 and poor in New York City. As a young man, Colón trudged through the cold city streets looking for work. He found inspiration in a poem that he kept on his wall.

230

Expedition 13, Lessons 6 and 7

¹Sometimes I pass Debevoise Place at the corner of Willoughby Street . . . I look at the old wooden house, gray and ancient, the house where I used to live some forty years ago . . .

²My room was on the second floor at the corner. On hot summer nights I would sit at the window reading by the electric light from the street lamp which was almost at a level with the windowsill.

³It was nice to come home late during the winter, look for some scrap of old newspaper, some bits of wood and a few chunks of coal, and start a sparkling fire in the chunky fourlegged coal stove. I would be rewarded with an intimate warmth as little by little the pigmy stove became alive puffing out its sides, hot and red, like the crimson cheeks of a Santa Claus.

⁴My few books were in a soap box nailed to the wall. But my most prized possession in those days was a poem I had bought in a five-and-ten-cent store on Fulton Street. (I wonder what has become of these poems, maxims and sayings of wise men that they used to sell at the five-and-ten-cent stores?) The poem was printed on gold paper and mounted in a gilded frame ready to be hung in a **conspicuous** place in the house. I bought one of those fancy silken picture cords finishing in a rosette to match the color of the frame.

maxims: short sayings that express a truth

⁵I was seventeen. This poem to me then seemed to summarize, in one poetical nutshell, the wisdom of all the sages that ever lived. It was what I was looking for, something to guide myself by, a way of life, a compendium of the wise, the true and the beautiful. All I had to do was to live according to the counsel of the poem and follow its instructions and I would be a perfect man—the useful, the good, the true human being. I was very happy that day, forty years ago.

compendium: collection

counsel: advice

⁶The poem had to have the most **prominent** place in the room. Where could I hang it? I decided that the best place for the poem was on the wall right by the entrance to the room. No one coming in and out would miss it. Perhaps someone would be interested enough to read it and drink the profound waters of its message . . .

231

Expedition 13, Lessons 6 and 7

⁷Every morning as I prepared to leave, I stood in front of the poem and read it over and over again, sometimes half a dozen times. I let the sonorous music of the verse carry me away. I brought with me a handwritten copy as I stepped out every morning looking for work, repeating verses and stanzas from memory until the whole poem came to be part of me. Other days my lips kept repeating a single verse of the poem at intervals throughout the day.

intervals: times between one event and another

⁸In the subways I loved to compete with the shrill noises of the many wheels below by chanting the lines of the poem. People stared at me moving my lips as though I were in a trance. I looked back with pity. They were not so fortunate as I who had as a guide to direct my life a great poem to make me wise, useful and happy.

⁹And I chanted:

> If you can keep your head when all about you
> Are losing theirs and blaming it on you . . .
>
> If you can wait and not be tired by waiting,
> Or being lied about, don't deal in lies,
> Or being hated don't give way to hating . . .
>
> If you can make one heap of all your winnings
> And risk it on one turn of pitch-and-toss,
> And lose, and start again at your beginnings . . .

¹⁰"If —," by Kipling, was the poem. At seventeen, my evening prayer and my first morning thought. I repeated it every day with the resolution to live up to the very last line of that poem.

¹¹I would visit the government employment office on Jay Street. The conversations among the Puerto Ricans on the large wooden benches in the employment office were always on the same subject. How to find a decent place to live. How they would not rent to Negroes or Puerto Ricans. How Negroes and Puerto Ricans were given the pink slips first at work.

¹²From the employment office I would call door to door at the piers, factories and storage houses in the streets under the

232

Expedition 13, Lessons 6 and 7

Brooklyn and Manhattan bridges. "Sorry, nothing today." It seemed to me that that "today" was a continuation and combination of all the yesterdays, todays and tomorrows.

¹³From the factories I would go to the restaurants, looking for a job as a porter or dishwasher. At least I would eat and be warm in a kitchen.

¹⁴"Sorry" . . . "Sorry" . . .

¹⁵Sometimes I was hired at ten dollars a week, ten hours a day including Sundays and holidays. One day off during the week. My work was that of three men: dishwasher, porter, busboy. And to clear the sidewalk of snow and slush "when you have nothing else to do." I was to be appropriately humble and grateful not only to the owner but to everybody else in the place.

¹⁶If I rebelled at insults or at a pointed innuendo or just the inhuman amount of work, I was unceremoniously thrown out and told to come "next week for your pay." "Next week" meant weeks of calling for the **paltry** dollars owed me. The owners relished this "next week."

innuendo: a hint with an undertone of rudeness

¹⁷I clung to my poem as to a faith. Like a **potent** amulet, my precious poem was clenched in the fist of my right hand inside my secondhand overcoat. Again and again I declaimed aloud a few precious lines when discouragement and disillusionment threatened to overwhelm me.

amulet: item that protects against evil

declaimed: read or repeated from memory

> If you can force your heart and nerve and sinew
> To serve your turn long after they are gone . . .

¹⁸The weeks of unemployment and hard knocks turned into months. I continued to find two or three days of work here and there. And I continued to be thrown out when I rebelled at the ill treatment, overwork and insults. I kept pounding the streets looking for a place where they would treat me half decently, where my devotion to work and faith in Kipling's poem would be appreciated. I remember the worn-out shoes I bought in a secondhand store on Myrtle Avenue at the corner of Adams

233

Street. The round holes in the soles that I tried to cover with pieces of carton were no match for the frigid knives of the unrelenting snow.

[19]One night I returned late after a long day of looking for work. I was hungry. My room was dark and cold. I wanted to warm my numb body. I lit a match and began looking for some scraps of wood and a piece of paper to start a fire. I searched all over the floor. No wood, no paper. As I stood up, the glimmering flicker of the dying match was reflected in the glass surface of the framed poem. I unhooked the poem from the wall. I reflected for a minute, a minute that felt like an eternity. I took the frame apart, placing the square glass upon the small table. I tore the gold paper on which the poem was printed, threw its pieces inside the stove and, placing the small bits of wood from the frame on top of the paper, I lit it, adding soft and hard coal as the fire began to gain strength and brightness.

[20]I watched how the lines of the poem withered into ashes inside the small stove.

Connect to the Author

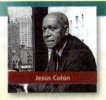

Jesús Colón

Jesús Colón arrived in New York City in 1918, when he was 17 years old. To get there, he had hidden on a boat leaving from his home country of Puerto Rico. Colón, who was of African descent, spoke only Spanish. He worked low-paying jobs to support himself. Meanwhile, he wrote articles for Puerto Rican newspapers. He soon became well known and respected in both New York and Puerto Rico for his journalism. His 1961 book *A Puerto Rican in New York*, from which this story is taken, was one of the first works of Latino literature to talk about the experience of immigrants in this country. Colón died in 1974.

234

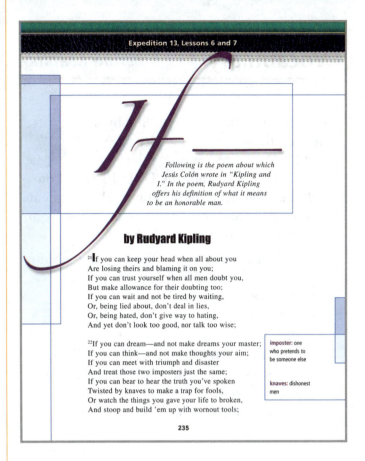

Following is the poem about which Jesús Colón wrote in "Kipling and I." In the poem, Rudyard Kipling offers his definition of what it means to be an honorable man.

by Rudyard Kipling

[21]If you can keep your head when all about you
Are losing theirs and blaming it on you;
If you can trust yourself when all men doubt you,
But make allowance for their doubting too;
If you can wait and not be tired by waiting,
Or, being lied about, don't deal in lies,
Or, being hated, don't give way to hating,
And yet don't look too good, nor talk too wise;

[22]If you can dream—and not make dreams your master;
If you can think—and not make thoughts your aim;
If you can meet with triumph and disaster
And treat those two imposters just the same;
If you can bear to hear the truth you've spoken
Twisted by knaves to make a trap for fools,
Or watch the things you gave your life to broken,
And stoop and build 'em up with wornout tools;

imposter: one who pretends to be someone else

knaves: dishonest men

235

---

[23]If you can make one heap of all your winnings
And risk it on one turn of pitch-and-toss,
And lose, and start again at your beginnings
And never breathe a word about your loss;
If you can force your heart and nerve and sinew
To serve your turn long after they are gone,
And so hold on when there is nothing in you
Except the Will which says to them: "Hold on";

[24]If you can talk with crowds and keep your virtue,
Or walk with kings—nor lose the common touch;
If neither foes nor loving friends can hurt you;
If all men count with you, but none too much;
If you can fill the unforgiving minute
With sixty seconds' worth of distance run—
Yours is the Earth and everything that's in it,
And—which is more—you'll be a Man my son!

sinew: tissue that connects bone to muscle

Connect to the Author

Rudyard Kipling

Between 1890 and 1920, Rudyard Kipling was the most popular writer in the English-speaking world. Kipling was born in India in 1865. His parents were English. When Kipling was six, his parents sent him and his sister to live with strangers in England. His parents wanted to keep him away from the illness that had killed his newborn brother. They also wanted him to get an English education. But Kipling's caretaker beat him, and he was often miserable. He returned to India when he was about 17 and began his writing career. He later traveled back to England and then to America. In his lifetime, Kipling published hundreds of short stories and poems. He is especially well known for his children's stories. He wrote *The Jungle Book* and *The Second Jungle Book*, stories of a boy named Mowgli who was raised by wolves, while he lived in the United States. The stories remain popular to this day. Kipling died in 1936.

236

Comprehension and Vocabulary *Before Reading*

1. Review the topic of storytelling by using the questions from Anthology page 221 and DVD 13.1 to generate prior knowledge. After showing DVD 13.1, call on individuals to read the questions. Have students discuss their responses using information from the DVD and the Lessons 1–4 stories.

2. **In this Expedition, we've been talking about stories—both real-life and made up—and why people tell them.**

   • **In Lessons 1 and 2, we read a story from *Holes*. What was that story about?** (a boy who just arrived at a type of prison) **What conclusions did we draw about the main character, Stanley?** (that he seems polite and thoughtful; that he seems careful and intelligent)

   • **In Lessons 3 and 4, we read a story from *The Joy Luck Club*. What story did the speaker, Jing-Mei, tell in that selection?** (how and why she started the Joy Luck Club)

   • **What were her reasons, or motivations, for starting the club?** (She wanted to overcome feelings of helplessness, find some happiness in the midst of suffering, and provide hope for herself and her friends.)

3. **These earlier stories were fictional, or made up. Now we're going to read a real-life story about a young man who, like Stanley and Jing-Mei, finds himself in a new place, faced with difficult challenges.**

Introduce Vocabulary

4. **We will read some new words in today's story, "Kipling and I."**

   • Write the vocabulary words on the board. Include Challenge Words to meet the needs of students who are advancing.
   • Read the words to students.
   • Call on individuals to read the words as you point to them.
   • Provide correction and feedback as needed.
   ▶ Have students write the words in the Vocabulary Log.

5. Tell students that knowing the meanings of these words will help them better understand the article.

   For each word:
   • Read the word with its definition and the sentence that follows.
   • Write the sentences on the board.
   • Call on students to use their own words to give the meaning and some examples of each vocabulary word.

Vocabulary

conspicuous *easily seen or noticed*
The car had a *conspicuous* dent in its front fender.

prominent *important or outstanding; standing out or easily noticed*
My uncle displays his bowling trophies in a *prominent* place in his house.

paltry *very small*
I bought this used bicycle for a *paltry* sum.

potent *powerful*
Some cheeses have a *potent* odor.

Challenge Words
Word Meaning

maxim *a common saying that has some truth to it*
My mother's favorite *maxim* is "Better safe than sorry."

gilded *covered in a thin layer of gold or gold paint*
My aunt has a small *gilded* box that she keeps treasures in.

Review Narrative Elements

6. **In this Expedition, we've been reading narrative texts.**

- **What is the purpose of a narrative?** (to tell a story)

- **What are the three main elements of a narrative?** (character, setting, and plot) Write *Character*, *Setting*, and *Plot* on the board, each inside a large box.

- **What are a story's characters?** (the people in it) Write *Who?* under *Character*.

- **What is a story's setting?** (the time and place it occurs) Write *When?* and *Where?* under *Setting*.

- **What is the plot of a story?** (what happens in the story; the series of events that make up the story) Write *What?* under *Plot*.

7. Have students return to Anthology page 230. **We can tell some things about the *who*, *where*, and *when* of this story just by previewing it.** Have students read the title and look at the image.

- **Who do you think is the story's main character?** (a teenage boy) Write *teenage boy* under *Who?* in the Character box.

- **Where do you think at least some of this story will take place?** (in a big city) Write *big city* under *Where?* in the Setting box.

- **When do you think it will take place—long ago or in current times?** (long ago) Write *long ago* under *When?* in the Setting box.

8. **Based on the image, what do you predict the story will be about?** (Responses will vary, but students may say that the story is about a boy who is trying to find a job in the city.) **To learn more about the *what* of the story, or its plot, we'll have to read the story. As we read, let's notice the series of events that occur.**

Introduce Poetry

9. Direct students' attention to the introductory text on Anthology page 230. Read the text aloud.

10. **As we read this story, we will come across some lines of poetry.**

SKILL ✓

- Have students look at paragraph 9. **This paragraph contains eight lines of poetry. They look different from the other lines of the story. They are shorter, and they are set off from the rest of the text. They also appear in italics.**

- Have students scan the rest of the story. **In what other paragraph do you see lines of poetry?** (paragraph 17)

11. **When we come to the lines of poetry, don't worry about what they mean. Just remember that they are lines from a longer poem that the author is reading.**

Reading for Understanding

Reading

Places and Names to Look For:
- New York City
- Brooklyn
- Kipling
- Manhattan
- Puerto Rican

1. **As you read this story, you may come across some unfamiliar places and names.**
- Write the words on the board.
- Point to each word as you read the following:

The author of this story tells about his experiences as a young *Puerto Rican*—someone from the Caribbean island of Puerto Rico. He has come to *New York City* to search for a job. His search takes him to factories and businesses under the *Brooklyn* and *Manhattan* bridges. A poem by Rudyard *Kipling* is the author's inspiration during some difficult months.
- Call on individuals to read the words.

2. **As we read, remember to pay attention to the series of events that make up the plot. Remember also to watch for the lines of poetry.**

3. **Fluency** Read the first two paragraphs aloud while students follow along in their books. Then have students read the remainder of the story aloud with you. If necessary, review the following fluency goal with students to practice prosody: **As we read aloud, we will use expression and combine words in phrases in a way that sounds like speech. This will show that we understand what we are reading.** As you read aloud the lines of poetry, alter your pitch and tone slightly to signal the change in genre.

English Language Learners

Understanding Figurative Language
English language learners tend to interpret figurative language literally. Use the following activity to help students identify and decipher figurative language.

Write the following sentence on the board: *The cat's eyes glinted in the night like tiny mirrors.* Read it aloud.
- **The author of this sentence wants you to know what the cat's eyes looked like. To help you see the cat's eyes in your own mind, she compares them to tiny mirrors. The cat's eyes probably did not look *exactly* like tiny mirrors. By comparing the two, she creates a certain picture in your mind.**
- Circle the word *like.* **When you see this word, it may signal that two things are being compared.** Write the word *as* on the board. **The word *as* is also used to signal a comparison. A person's nose might be *as* red *as* a cherry, or someone might move *as if* she were sleepwalking.** Write these examples on the board, and circle the word *as* in each.
- List these paragraph numbers on the board: 8, 3, 17. **As you read "Kipling and I" with your partner, stop after each of these paragraphs and look for a comparison that uses the word *like* or *as*. Then decide what two things are being compared, and why. Let's try one together.** Read paragraph 2 aloud with students, then model the process. **The narrator says the sides of the stove puffed out "hot and red, like the crimson cheeks of a Santa Claus." He compares the sides of the stove to the red cheeks of Santa. The stove doesn't look *exactly* like Santa's cheeks. The author just wants us clearly to see in our minds the hot, puffed-up oven, and the image of Santa's cheeks helps us do that.**
- Have students work with their partner to find comparisons and discuss them in a similar way in each of the remaining paragraphs. Before students reach paragraph 17, explain that an *amulet* is a charm, or an object thought to give good luck.

ELL

Checking for Comprehension *After Reading*

1. Check students' comprehension of content and narrative elements with the following questions: **KNOWLEDGE**

   - **What is going on when the story begins?** (The author is recalling his new life in a new city. He explains that his prized possession is a copy of a poem.) Erase the question mark in the *Plot* box on the board, and write these responses in its place.

   - **Why is the poem so important to the author?** (It gives him a guide for how to live.)

   - **What happens as the author searches for a job?** (He is unable to find work for long periods. When he does get a job, the pay is low, the work is hard, and his bosses are mean.)

   - **What events happen next?** (The author comes home cold, hungry, and discouraged. He cannot find wood or paper to start a fire. He looks at the framed copy of the poem, thinks for a long moment, then burns the poem.)

2. Direct students' attention to the biography of Rudyard Kipling on Anthology page 236, and read it aloud. Then discuss these questions as a class:

   SKILL ✓

   - **Kipling was the same age as the author of "Kipling and I" when he returned to India to begin his career as a writer. How were the two writers' lives alike and different by the age of 17? SYNTHESIS** (Alike: both writers had suffered mistreatment—Kipling by his caretaker and Colón by his employers—and both had left their families to live in a different country; Different: at 17, Kipling returned home to India to begin writing; Colón left Puerto Rico to find work in the United States)

   - **Unlike Kipling and Colón, many 17-year-olds nowadays still live at home and attend school. What kinds of things can you imagine yourself doing at age 17? APPLICATION** (Responses will vary.)

3. **Challenge Questions** Have students write answers to the following questions. Explain that this writing will be private, as in a diary, and that they will not be asked to share their answers with you or with the class.

   - **Have you ever felt that you were being treated unfairly, as Kipling and Colón were when they were young? Describe the event and how it felt. APPLICATION**

   - **When you have gone through a difficult time, as Colón did in New York City, what are some sayings, lines of poetry, or other words of wisdom that have helped you get through the difficulty? APPLICATION**

When all students are finished, discuss generally a few sayings, poems, or other written works that can be used as guides for living.

Anthology Selection

Kipling and I

by Jesús Colón

Jesús Colón remembers what it was like to be 17 and poor in New York City. As a young man, Colón trudged through the cold city streets looking for work. He found inspiration in a poem that he kept on his wall.

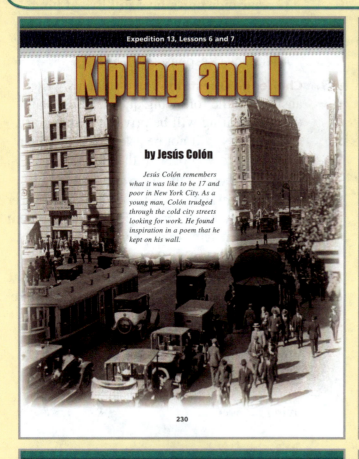

230

¹Sometimes I pass Debevoise Place at the corner of Willoughby Street . . . I look at the old wooden house, gray and ancient, the house where I used to live some forty years ago . . .

²My room was on the second floor at the corner. On hot summer nights I would sit at the window reading by the electric light from the street lamp which was almost at a level with the windowsill.

³It was nice to come home late during the winter, look for some scrap of old newspaper, some bits of wood and a few chunks of coal, and start a sparkling fire in the chunky fourlegged coal stove. I would be rewarded with an intimate warmth as little by little the pigmy stove became alive puffing out its sides, hot and red, like the crimson cheeks of a Santa Claus.

⁴My few books were in a soap box nailed to the wall. But my most prized possession in those days was a poem I had bought in a five-and-ten-cent store on Fulton Street. (I wonder what has become of these poems, maxims and sayings of wise men that they used to sell at the five-and-ten-cent stores?) The poem was printed on gold paper and mounted in a gilded frame ready to be hung in a **conspicuous** place in the house. I bought one of those fancy silken picture cords finishing in a rosette to match the color of the frame.

⁵I was seventeen. This poem to me then seemed to summarize, in one poetical nutshell, the wisdom of all the sages that ever lived. It was what I was looking for, something to guide myself by, a way of life, a compendium of the wise, the true and the beautiful. All I had to do was to live according to the counsel of the poem and follow its instructions and I would be a perfect man—the useful, the good, the true human being. I was very happy that day, forty years ago.

⁶The poem had to have the most **prominent** place in the room. Where could I hang it? I decided that the best place for the poem was on the wall right by the entrance to the room. No one coming in and out would miss it. Perhaps someone would be interested enough to read it and drink the profound waters of its message . . .

maxims: short sayings that express a truth

compendium: collection

counsel: advice

231

⁷Every morning as I prepared to leave, I stood in front of the poem and read it over and over again, sometimes half a dozen times. I let the sonorous music of the verse carry me away. I brought with me a handwritten copy as I stepped out every morning looking for work, repeating verses and stanzas from memory until the whole poem came to be part of me. Other days my lips kept repeating a single verse of the poem at intervals throughout the day.

⁸In the subways I loved to compete with the shrill noises of the many wheels below by chanting the lines of the poem. People stared at me moving my lips as though I were in a trance. I looked back with pity. They were not so fortunate as I who had as a guide to direct my life a great poem to make me wise, useful and happy.

⁹And I chanted:

*If you can keep your head when all about you
Are losing theirs and blaming it on you . . .*

*If you can wait and not be tired by waiting,
Or being lied about, don't deal in lies,
Or being hated don't give way to hating . . .*

*If you can make one heap of all your winnings
And risk it on one turn of pitch-and-toss,
And lose, and start again at your beginnings . . .*

¹⁰"If —," by Kipling, was the poem. At seventeen, my evening prayer and my first morning thought. I repeated it every day with the resolution to live up to the very last line of that poem.

¹¹I would visit the government employment office on Jay Street. The conversations among the Puerto Ricans on the large wooden benches in the employment office were always on the same subject. How to find a decent place to live. How they would not rent to Negroes or Puerto Ricans. How Negroes and Puerto Ricans were given the pink slips first at work.

¹²From the employment office I would call door to door at the piers, factories and storage houses in the streets under the

intervals: times between one event and another

232

Brooklyn and Manhattan bridges. "Sorry, nothing today." It seemed to me that that "today" was a continuation and combination of all the yesterdays, todays and tomorrows.

¹³From the factories I would go to the restaurants, looking for a job as a porter or dishwasher. At least I would eat and be warm in a kitchen.

¹⁴"Sorry" . . . "Sorry" . . .

¹⁵Sometimes I was hired at ten dollars a week, ten hours a day including Sundays and holidays. One day off during the week. My work was that of three men: dishwasher, porter, busboy. And to clear the sidewalk of snow and slush "when you have nothing else to do." I was to be appropriately humble and grateful not only to the owner but to everybody else in the place.

¹⁶If I rebelled at insults or at a pointed innuendo or just the inhuman amount of work, I was unceremoniously thrown out and told to come "next week for your pay." "Next week" meant weeks of calling for the **paltry** dollars owed me. The owners relished this "next week."

¹⁷I clung to my poem as to a faith. Like a **potent** amulet, my precious poem was clenched in the fist of my right hand inside my secondhand overcoat. Again and again I declaimed aloud a few precious lines when discouragement and disillusionment threatened to overwhelm me.

*If you can force your heart and nerve and sinew
To serve your turn long after they are gone . . .*

¹⁸The weeks of unemployment and hard knocks turned into months. I continued to find two or three days of work here and there. And I continued to be thrown out when I rebelled at the ill treatment, overwork and insults. I kept pounding the streets looking for a place where they would treat me half decently, where my devotion to work and faith in Kipling's poem would be appreciated. I remember the worn-out shoes I bought in a secondhand store on Myrtle Avenue at the corner of Adams

innuendo: a hint with an undertone of rudeness

amulet: item that protects against evil

declaimed: read or repeated from memory

233

Street. The round holes in the soles that I tried to cover with pieces of carton were no match for the frigid knives of the unrelenting snow.

¹⁹One night I returned late after a long day of looking for work. I was hungry. My room was dark and cold. I wanted to warm my numb body. I lit a match and began looking for some scraps of wood and a piece of paper to start a fire. I searched all over the floor. No wood, no paper. As I stood up, the glimmering flicker of the dying match was reflected in the glass surface of the framed poem. I unhooked the poem from the wall. I reflected for a minute, a minute that felt like an eternity. I took the frame apart, placing the square glass upon the small table. I tore the gold paper on which the poem was printed, threw its pieces inside the stove and, placing the small bits of wood from the frame on top of the paper, I lit it, adding soft and hard coal as the fire began to gain strength and brightness.

²⁰I watched how the lines of the poem withered into ashes inside the small stove.

Connect to the Author

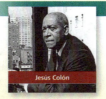
Jesús Colón

Jesús Colón arrived in New York City in 1918, when he was 17 years old. To get there, he had hidden on a boat leaving from his home country of Puerto Rico. Colón, who was of African descent, spoke only Spanish. He worked low-paying jobs to support himself. Meanwhile, he wrote articles for Puerto Rican newspapers. He soon became well known and respected in both New York and Puerto Rico for his journalism. His 1961 book *A Puerto Rican in New York*, from which this story is taken, was one of the first works of Latino literature to talk about the experience of immigrants in this country. Colón died in 1974.

234

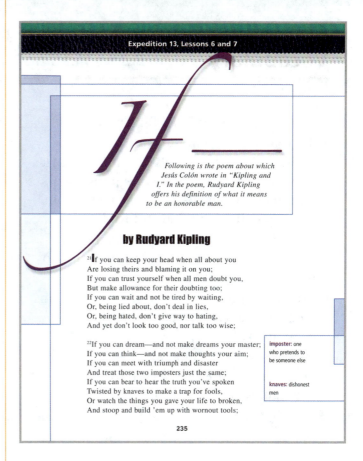

Following is the poem about which Jesús Colón wrote in "Kipling and I." In the poem, Rudyard Kipling offers his definition of what it means to be an honorable man.

by Rudyard Kipling

²¹If you can keep your head when all about you
Are losing theirs and blaming it on you;
If you can trust yourself when all men doubt you,
But make allowance for their doubting too;
If you can wait and not be tired by waiting,
Or, being lied about, don't deal in lies,
Or, being hated, don't give way to hating,
And yet don't look too good, nor talk too wise;

²²If you can dream—and not make dreams your master;
If you can think—and not make thoughts your aim;
If you can meet with triumph and disaster
And treat those two imposters just the same;
If you can bear to hear the truth you've spoken
Twisted by knaves to make a trap for fools,
Or watch the things you gave your life to broken,
And stoop and build 'em up with wornout tools;

imposter: one who pretends to be someone else

knaves: dishonest men

235

sinew: tissue that connects bone to muscle

²³If you can make one heap of all your winnings
And risk it on one turn of pitch-and-toss,
And lose, and start again at your beginnings
And never breathe a word about your loss;
If you can force your heart and nerve and sinew
To serve your turn long after they are gone,
And so hold on when there is nothing in you
Except the Will which says to them: "Hold on";

²⁴If you can talk with crowds and keep your virtue,
Or walk with kings—nor lose the common touch;
If neither foes nor loving friends can hurt you;
If all men count with you, but none too much;
If you can fill the unforgiving minute
With sixty seconds' worth of distance run—
Yours is the Earth and everything that's in it,
And—which is more—you'll be a Man my son!

Connect to the Author

Rudyard Kipling

Between 1890 and 1920, Rudyard Kipling was the most popular writer in the English-speaking world. Kipling was born in India in 1865. His parents were English. When Kipling was six, his parents sent him and his sister to live with strangers in England. His parents wanted to keep him away from the illness that had killed his newborn brother. They also wanted him to get an English education. But Kipling's caretaker beat him, and he was often miserable. He returned to India when he was about 17 and began his writing career. He later traveled back to England and then to America. In his lifetime, Kipling published hundreds of short stories and poems. He is especially well known for his children's stories. He wrote *The Jungle Book* and *The Second Jungle Book*, stories of a boy named Mowgli who was raised by wolves, while he lived in the United States. The stories remain popular to this day. Kipling died in 1936.

236

Comprehension and Vocabulary
Before Reading

1. **In Lesson 6, we read "Kipling and I."**
   - **As a teenager from Puerto Rico, the author of the story finds life in New York City difficult. What helps keep his spirits up during his hardships?** (the message in the poem "If—" by Rudyard Kipling)
   - **Why does the author repeat the lines of the poem so often?** (He strongly wishes to follow its message.)
   - **Why does the author lose some of the jobs he gets?** (He rebels when he thinks he is badly treated.)
   - **How does the poem finally help the author at the end of the story?** (It provides warmth and light when he burns it.)

2. **As we reread "Kipling and I," we'll examine more closely the author's attempt to live up to the poem's message.**

Vocabulary Review

3. Arrange students with partners, and have them turn to Student Book page 176. Read the vocabulary words aloud. Call on individuals to tell what each word means. Then read the instructions aloud.

4. **Let's look at the first item. The word is *potent*. One of the sentences below will be an example of something that is *potent*, and the other will not. Before we read the sentences, let's remind ourselves what *potent* means. It means "powerful." Let's see which sentence gives an example of something that is powerful.** Read the first sentence. **If I read a poem that didn't make sense, the poem wouldn't be powerful.** Read the second sentence. **If I read a poem that changed my life, it would definitely be a powerful poem. It would be a *potent* poem. Let's write *E* (for *example*) on the second line, and *NE* (for *non-example*) on the first line.**

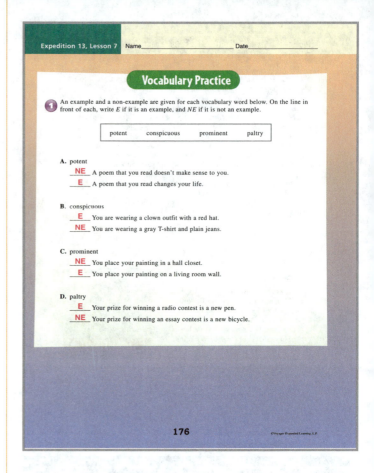

Expedition 13, Lesson 7 Name_____ Date_____

Vocabulary Practice

1. An example and a non-example are given for each vocabulary word below. On the line in front of each, write *E* if it is an example, and *NE* if it is not an example.

| potent | conspicuous | prominent | paltry |

A. potent
  - NE A poem that you read doesn't make sense to you.
  - E A poem that you read changes your life.

B. conspicuous
  - E You are wearing a clown outfit with a red hat.
  - NE You are wearing a gray T-shirt and plain jeans.

C. prominent
  - NE You place your painting in a hall closet.
  - E You place your painting on a living room wall.

D. paltry
  - E Your prize for winning a radio contest is a new pen.
  - NE Your prize for winning an essay contest is a new bicycle.

176 ©Voyager Expanded Learning, L.P.

5. Have students complete the remaining items with partners. When all students are finished, call on students to report their responses and to explain their thinking.

6. **Challenge Words** Write the following items on the board, and have students complete them along with those in the Student Book.

maxim

_____ *Look before you leap.*

_____ *Look at these great pictures I took at the party.*

gilded

_____ *wooden frame*

_____ *gold frame*

Call on students to tell whether each item is an example or a non-example of the Challenge Word and to explain their thinking.

Review Narrative Elements: Plot

7. Write *Plot* on the board and write *Beginning*, *Middle*, and *End* underneath. **Stories usually begin because someone has a problem, or a conflict.** Underline *Beginning*, and write *Problem* next to it. **Think about the very first *Star Wars* movie. What would happen if Luke Skywalker had no problem in the story? What if there were no Darth Vader?** (Possible responses: The story wouldn't be very interesting. It wouldn't really *be* a story.)

8. **In *Star Wars*, the main character's problem—Darth Vader—comes from the outside. In other stories, a character's problem can come from the inside. A character's thoughts or feelings about something can be causing a battle in his or her mind.**

9. Underline *Middle*. **Most of the action takes place in the middle of a story.** Write *Action* next to *Middle*. **The character takes certain actions, or is acted upon by people or events. What kinds of things happen in the middle of *Star Wars*?** (Luke and his friends fight Darth Vader and his forces.) **In the middle part of a good story, the reader (or viewer) is eager to see what will happen next.**

10. Underline *End*. **Stories usually end when the main character's problem is solved.** Write *Solution* next to *End*. **How does Luke Skywalker solve his problem?** (He destroys the Death Star.)

11. **As we reread "Kipling and I," let's look for the author's problem and try to decide whether it comes from the inside or the outside. Let's also look for events that lead him to a solution.**

Review Poetry

12. **Fluency** **Kipling's poem "If—" is both a problem and a solution for the author. Let's take a brief look at the lines of this poem that appear in the story.** Have students turn to Anthology page 232, and direct their attention to the poetry lines contained in paragraph 9.

- **I'm going to read each line aloud, then I'd like for you to repeat it.** Read each line slowly, slightly exaggerating the natural pauses. Repeat lines as needed until students' repetition is smooth.

- **In these lines of the poem, the poet is setting up an *if/then* condition. We don't yet know the *then* part. What we do know, though, is that the poet seems to be sending this message: being calm, patient, tolerant, and willing to take risks is important.**

- Direct students' attention to the lines of poetry in paragraph 17. Again, read each line aloud, and have students repeat it.

- After students achieve fluency with each line or set of lines, briefly discuss the lines. **When you read or hear this line, what thought or image does it spark in you? Which word or words in the line strike a chord in you?** (Responses will vary.)

Reading for Understanding

Reading

1. Display Transparency 10, and have students turn to Student Book page 177. Read the Student Book instructions aloud.

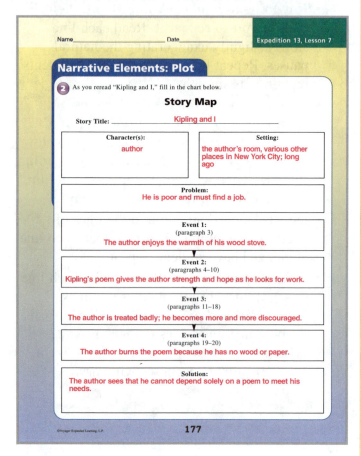

2. **Before we begin reading, let's fill in a few parts of the chart. First, let's write the story's title in the top line.** Pause. **Who are the main characters in this story?** (the author) **Write this name in the Character(s) box. Where and when does this story take place?** (in the author's room; in various other places in New York City; long ago) **Write this in the Setting box.**

3. Read the introduction to the story aloud. **This introduction describes the author's problem. What is it?** (He is poor and must find a job.) **Earlier, we discussed that some problems come from the outside, and others from the inside. Where does the author's problem come from?** (the outside) **How do you know?** (because conditions outside of him—lack of jobs and harsh weather—are problems for him; inside, he feels hopeful—at least for a while—because of the poem's message)

4. Have students finish reading the story independently. Instruct them to pause after the paragraphs indicated to record an event in one of the boxes. Tell students to leave the Solution box empty for now. Encourage students to monitor their comprehension of the text by pausing occasionally to ask themselves *Am I understanding what I'm reading?* Tell students that when they do not understand what they are reading, they should reread that portion of the text.

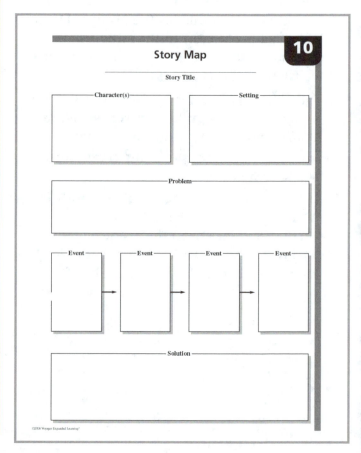

Checking for Comprehension *After Reading*

1. When all students are finished reading and filling in the Event boxes, call on students to name the events they listed. Provide correction and feedback as needed. List the four main events in the boxes on the transparency.

2. **For most of this story, the author's problems come from the outside—the weather, the lack of jobs, the cruel treatment by employers and others. At the end of the story, though, the author faces a problem that comes from both the inside and outside. What is this problem?** (whether to destroy the poem that has meant so much to him) **The author burns the poem for warmth, but what does he also realize about it?** (Possible responses: The poem hasn't been helpful in getting a job; the poem asks too much of a person; he cannot depend on the poem for his needs.) **The author sees that he can't rely solely on the poem to meet his needs. Let's write this solution in the chart.**

3. **In the last lesson, we talked about reasons that characters take certain actions. These reasons are called** *motivations*. **We said that a character's motivations—just like his or her problems—can come from the inside or the outside.**
   - **In "Kipling and I," what or who motivates the author to change his thinking about the poem?** (his lack of success in getting a job; his worsening situation)
   - **Are these outside motivations or inside motivations?** (outside)
   - **What inside feelings also motivate the author?** (his anger, discomfort, and discouragement)

4. Direct students' attention to the poem "If—" on Anthology page 235. Remind students that they are already familiar with some of the lines from the selection. Point out that the poem is divided into four sets of lines. **I'm going to read each set of lines aloud. Then we'll read the set of lines together.**

5. **The last two lines of the poem are the** *then* **part of the** *if/then* **message. If you read the poem slowly, thinking about the message in each line, you begin to see that the poet gives readers a choice between two opposites.** Call on individuals to name the opposites.

6. Read aloud and discuss the Connect to the Author feature on Anthology page 236. Then encourage students to share their opinion of the poem and its message.

7. **Challenge Question** Write the following on the board:

   If you _____,

   then _____.

   What words of wisdom would you put in the blanks? APPLICATION (Responses will vary.)

Reading Response

Have students turn to Student Book page 178. Read the instructions aloud. Explain to students that their message can take the form of a poem or an essay. Encourage students to reread the poem for ideas and to think about what they already know about virtues such as honesty and patience. Then have students work individually to write a response to these questions:

 What are some important virtues in life? Why are they important?

When students are finished, invite them to read their responses aloud.

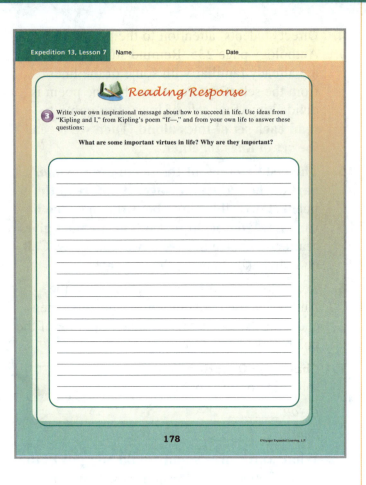

Expedition 13, Lesson 7   Name_____ Date_____

Reading Response

3 Write your own inspirational message about how to succeed in life. Use ideas from "Kipling and I," from Kipling's poem "If—," and from your own life to answer these questions:

What are some important virtues in life? Why are they important?

178

©Voyager Expanded Learning, L.P.

Passport Reading Journeys Library

Building Fluency

1. Place students in pairs according to reading level to build fluency. When pairing students, be sure that one student is a stronger reader (Student A) than the other student (Student B). However, do not reveal that stronger readers are paired with weaker readers. See *Passport Reading Journeys* Library Teacher's Guide for grouping guidelines.

2. Have students quickly choose reading material from the *Passport Reading Journeys* Library or another approved selection that is at the reading level of Student B. If students have not finished the previously chosen selection, they may continue reading from that selection. See *Passport Reading Journeys* Library Teacher's Guide for material selection guidelines.

3. Tell students that Student A will read one paragraph, and Student B will reread that same paragraph.

4. Have students follow this routine until the end of class.

5. If necessary, review the following practices to enhance fluency:
   - Rate and accuracy of reading
   - Expression during reading
   - Correction procedures

Library Highlights

Student Assessment

Level II

The assessments for some of the books and magazines are extended response questions. Some of the questions require more than three complete sentences for an answer. The assessments may be given to students to complete while they are read or after they have completed the book or magazine.

Advanced Word Study

Spelling

1. Direct students to Student Book page E13, Lesson 8. **We use the sounds we know and hear in a word to spell the word.** *Pro-* **is a prefix. Remember, a prefix is a word part that occurs at the beginning of a word.** *-Less* **is a suffix. Remember, a suffix is a word part that occurs at the end of a word. Prefixes and suffixes often help us understand the meaning of a word. Let's spell words with this prefix and suffix. The first word is** *proclaim.* **Say the word parts in the word** *proclaim.* (pro, claim) **What is the prefix?** (pro-) **What are the sounds in** *pro-?* (/p/ /r/ /ō/) **Write those sounds. What is the next syllable?** (claim) **What are the sounds in** *claim?* (/k/ /l/ /ā/ /m/) **Write those sounds.** Repeat with *promote, profile, endless, helpless,* and *restless.*

2. Write the words on the board as students check and correct their words. Have them read the list of words.

   1. proclaim   4. endless
   2. promote   5. helpless
   3. profile   6. restless

Sight Words

1. Direct students to line 1. Have them point to the first word. **This word is** *lunged.* **Read the word.** (lunged) **This is not a regular word. Let's read the word again.** (lunged) **Let's spell the word.** (l-u-n-g-e-d) **What is the word?** (lunged) Repeat with the remaining words. Then, have students read the words. Ask students to tell the meanings of the words.

2. Direct students to lines 2 and 3. **Let's read these words.** Remind students that the rows of words consist of regular and irregular words. Point to the first word. **What is the word?** (foreign) Repeat with the remaining words. Call on individuals to read the words in a different order. Ask students to tell the meanings of the words.

▼ To Correct

For Regular Words: Say the sound(s) in the word, then ask students to repeat the sound(s). Have them read the word again with the correct sound(s). If students do not know the meaning of the word, review the word and/or word part to determine the meaning of the word.

For Irregular Words: Immediately say the correct word. Then have students read the word, spell it, and read it again. If students do not know the meaning of the word, review the word.

1. lunged I   rescue I   seized I   bully I
2. foreign I   frigid I   opportunity R   leadership R
3. troubled I   sinew I   instinct R   calculating I

Building to Fluency

1. Direct students to the phrases in the Student Book. Have them read through each phrase for accuracy. Then, have students reread the phrases to increase their accuracy and fluency so that the phrases sound like natural speech.

2. Direct students to the Anthology article to locate the sentences containing the phrases. Have them read the sentences in the article accurately and fluently. Remind students to read in a way that sounds like natural speech.

▼ To Correct

Immediately say the correct word. Have students reread the word, then read the phrase or sentence again.

1. . . . panting and frothing one leap behind . . . *paragraph 2*
2. . . . because of the wild beast inside . . . *paragraph 6*
3. . . . even in sheer joy of the chase . . . *paragraph 12*

Anthology Selection

adapted from
THE CALL OF THE WILD

by Jack London

Buck is a cross between a Saint Bernard and a Scottish shepherd dog. He has lived the first four years of his life in the sun-kissed Santa Clara Valley of California. One day he is stolen and sold to a man who takes him to Alaska. Gold has been discovered there, and prospectors need dogs to pull sleds across the frozen tundra. In Alaska, Buck becomes a member of a dogsled team owned by Perrault and François. The team is led by Spitz, a fierce husky, and includes Dolly, Pike, and several other dogs.

237

---

¹The wild beast was strong in Buck. During his terrible life on the trail, the beast grew and grew. But it was a secret growth. Buck avoided fights whenever possible. Spitz, on the other hand, sensed that Buck was a challenge to his leadership. He went out of his way to bully Buck, hoping to start a fight that could end only in the death of one or the other.

²One morning, as Perrault and François were harnessing the dogs, Dolly suddenly went mad. She let out a long wolf howl and lunged at Buck. He fled in panic with Dolly panting and frothing one leap behind him. Buck plunged into the woods and crossed the icy river with Dolly snarling at his heels. François called to him and Buck doubled back, gasping painfully for air. François held an axe. As Buck shot past him the axe crashed down on mad Dolly's head.

³Buck staggered over against the sled, exhausted, sobbing for breath. Spitz realized that this was no time for **restraint**. He sprang at Buck and sank his teeth into his helpless foe, ripping and tearing the flesh. Again, François came to his rescue, driving Spitz away with a whip.

⁴"Spitz is one devil," Perrault said. "He's going to kill Buck."

⁵"That Buck is two devils," François said. "Someday he'll chew Spitz up and spit him out on the snow."

⁶From then on, Spitz and Buck were at war. They were destined to fight it out for leadership of the pack. Buck wanted it. He wanted it because it was his nature. He wanted it because of the wild beast inside him.

⁷Buck began to openly challenge Spitz's leadership. One morning, after a heavy snowfall, Pike hid from François. Spitz, wild with anger, searched the camp. When he at last found Pike, Spitz flew at him to punish him for hiding. Buck flew with equal rage at Spitz and knocked him off his feet. Pike, who had been trembling with fear, took heart at this challenge and leaped on Spitz. François broke up the fight with his whip. Buck kept challenging Spitz, but he was careful to only confront Spitz when François was not around. The other dogs began to disobey Spitz, and there was constant fighting. Trouble was brewing, and at the bottom of it was Buck.

⁸One dreary afternoon the sled team pulled into the town of Dawson. The streets were filled with men and dogs hard at work. All day, sled teams pulled loads up and down the main street. At night, with the stars leaping in the frigid sky and the land numb and frozen under the snow, the dogs howled an eerie song of pain as old as their breed. Their wolf song stirred the wild beast in Buck, and he eagerly joined their howling. With each howl, Buck

238

---

moved further away from the warmth and comfort of his life in California and deeper into the wild beginnings of his breed.

⁹After resting in Dawson for a week, Buck and his sled team set out again, but the trip was troubled. The revolt led by Buck had destroyed the team's **discipline**. The dogs no longer feared Spitz, and challenged him at every opportunity. Many nights, the camp was a howling madhouse. François swore and stamped the snow in anger and beat the dogs with his whip, but it was no use. As soon as he turned his back, they were at it again.

¹⁰One night after supper, one of the dogs spotted a rabbit. In a second, the whole team was tearing across the barren **landscape** in full pursuit. The heat of the chase stirred the wild beast in Buck, and he whined eagerly as he bounded through the pale moonlight after the rabbit. He ran with but one thought, to kill the rabbit with his own teeth. Buck felt the beast surging inside him and howled the old wolf-cry.

¹¹There is an **infinite** joy that comes when one is living completely in the moment, with no thought for the past or the future. It comes to the artist caught up in fever of work and to the war-mad soldier fighting without mercy. It came to Buck, leading the pack, sounding the old wolf-cry, straining after the food that was alive and fleeing before him through the moonlight. He was seized by a surge of life, by the perfect joy of every muscle, of every joint, of everything that was not death.

¹²Spitz, cold and calculating even in sheer joy of the chase, saw his chance. He split off from the pack and took a shortcut. Buck did not know this, and as he rounded a bend he saw Spitz leap from a high bank into the path of the rabbit. The rabbit had nowhere to turn. As Spitz's white teeth broke its back, the rabbit shrieked as loudly as a man. At this sound—the cry of Life plunging down into the grip of Death—the pack at Buck's heels howled in wild, irrational delight.

¹³Buck did not howl. Instead, he threw himself at Spitz, shoulder to shoulder, so hard that he missed the throat. They rolled over and over in the powdery snow. Spitz scrambled to his feet, slashing Buck down the shoulder and leaping clear. Spitz snapped his teeth together twice, like the steel jaws of a trap, as he backed away for better footing. His lean lips curled back, baring his teeth.

¹⁴In a flash Buck knew it. The time had come. This was a fight to the death. The dogs circled each other, snarling, ears laid back. A ghostly calm came over the whiteness. The rest of the pack had made short work of the

239

---

rabbit, and now they circled Buck and Spitz, watching silently with gleaming eyes. Their visible breath rose slowly in the frosty air.

¹⁵Buck sprang forward, **endeavoring** to sink his teeth into Spitz's neck. Fang clashed against fang, and lips were cut and bleeding. Time and time again Buck lunged for the snow-white throat. Each time Spitz slashed him and leaped lightly away. Spitz was untouched, while Buck was streaming with blood and panting hard. The fight was growing desperate. And all the while the silent, wolfish circle waited to finish off whichever dog went down. With Buck winded, Spitz rushed him and knocked him off balance. Buck almost went down, and the circle of dogs started to close in. But Buck recovered in midair and landed on his feet. The dogs pulled back and waited.

¹⁶Buck possessed a quality that made for greatness—imagination. He fought by instinct, but he could use his head as well. Buck lunged for Spitz's throat, but at the last instant he dropped to the snow and clamped his teeth into Spitz's left foreleg. There was a crunch of breaking bone, and Spitz howled in agony. Three times Buck tried to knock Spitz over, then he repeated his trick and broke the right foreleg. Despite the pain and helplessness, Spitz struggled madly to keep up. The pack **detected** his fear. Spitz watched the silent circle closing in on him as he had watched similar circles close in on beaten dogs in the past. Only this time Spitz knew he was the one who was beaten.

Connect to the Author

Jack London was born in 1876 in San Francisco, California. He was an adventurer by nature. As a young man, London sailed to Japan and traveled widely throughout the United States. Then in 1897 he headed to Alaska in search of gold, but he got there too late. Most of the gold was gone, and London returned to San Francisco poorer than when he left. Though London didn't find gold in Alaska, he turned his adventures into gold. London's books and novels based on his experiences made him the highest paid writer in the United States. Among London's 50 novels are *White Fang* and *The Call of the Wild*.

Jack London

240

670

Comprehension and Vocabulary
Before Reading

1. **We've read several narratives, or stories, in this Expedition. In each, the main character's words and actions gave us major clues about the character's personality.**

   - **Which character found a way to create happiness and hope in the midst of great suffering?** (Jing-Mei in the excerpt from *The Joy Luck Club*) **How so?** (She started a weekly gathering of women to play mah jong, eat, and tell stories.)

   - **Which character found more than one way to put an inspirational poem to use?** (the author of "Kipling and I") **How so?** (He tried to live by the poem's message, and also ended up burning the poem for warmth and light.)

   - **Which character had to accept the unexpected—and unpleasant—consequences of a choice that he had made?** (Stanley Yelnats in the excerpt from *Holes*) **How so?** (His choice of Camp Green Lake over jail was beginning to look worse than jail.)

2. **Like Stanley, Jing-Mei, and Jesús Colón, the main character in the story for Lesson 8 finds himself in new surroundings, facing many challenges. Like Stanley, he must accept another's authority—at least for now. Like Jing-Mei, he is clever. Like Jesús Colón, he is unafraid to take drastic measures at a time when it matters most.**

Introduce Vocabulary

Vocabulary

Review Words

restraint	*using control; holding back*
discipline	*self-control*
landscape	*natural scenery in an area*
infinite	*going on forever; without an end*
endeavor	*to make an effort to try something*
detect	*to discover or figure out*

Challenge Words

Word Meaning

calculating	*determined to get something* My *calculating* cousin always insists on going first in tic-tac-toe.
irrational	*lacking logic or clear thinking* It is *irrational* to go swimming during an ice storm.

3. **Our next story, adapted from *The Call of the Wild*, contains words with meanings we have already learned.** We will review these words within the text we are reading.

4. Write each Review Word on the board. Ask students to locate the word in the story. Instruct them to read aloud the sentence containing the word and any other sentences that provide context.

   - **What can you tell me about the word?**

   - Ask other questions that allow students to explore the word's meaning. (For example: **Does *infinite* mean the same as *limited*? What is a synonym for *restraint*?**).

5. Ask students to respond to the following questions. Provide correction and feedback as necessary.

   - **Why should we use *restraint* in arguments? What's an example of not using *restraint*?**

   - **Do you use *discipline* when eating snacks? What could happen if you didn't use *discipline*?**

   - **What's an unusual thing you've seen in a *landscape*? What do you expect to see in a *landscape*?**

- **What would you like an *infinite* supply of? What are you glad there's not an *infinite* supply of?**
- **What new skill have you *endeavored* to learn? Did you succeed at it? Explain.**
- **What is a food odor that's easy to *detect*?**

6. Work with students to write a definition for each word on the board.

7. Include the Challenge Words to meet the needs of students who are advancing.

Extending Vocabulary

Affix Review

- Write *ir-* on the board. Ask students to tell the meaning of the word part. (not) Provide correction and feedback as necessary.
- Have students scan paragraph 12 for a word that contains the prefix *ir-*. (irrational)
- Write the word on the board. **How does the prefix *ir-* help you figure out the meaning of *irrational*?** (*Ir-* means "not," so *irrational* must mean "not rational.") Point out that *rational* means "able to use reason."
- Have students name other words they know containing the word part *ir-* and use the meaning of the word part to determine the meanings of the words.
- ▶ Have students record *irrational* and its meaning, as well as other words that use the prefix *ir-* and their meanings, in the Vocabulary Log.

Review Narrative Elements

8. **In this Expedition, we've been looking at the elements of narrative texts. What are the three main elements?** (character, setting, and plot) Write these on the board, one next to the other. **In today's story, you will see how a writer and adventurer—Jack London—combines these three elements to create a powerful and violent tale.**

9. Have students turn to Anthology page 240 and locate the biography of Jack London in the Connect to the Author feature. Read the biography aloud while students follow along.

10. **One reason that Jack London's stories are so powerful is because he knows how to build suspense in them.** Write *Suspense* on the board, under *Character*, *Setting* and *Plot*. *Suspense* **is a feeling of tension or uncertainty about what is going to happen next in a story. An author can create suspense in several ways.**

    - **The author can make a character act in strange or unpredictable ways.** Draw an arrow from *Character* to *Suspense*.
    - **The author can use a setting that makes the reader feel nervous or trapped.** Draw an arrow from *Setting* to *Suspense*.
    - **He or she can include plot events that seem to be leading to danger.** Draw an arrow from *Plot* to *Suspense*.

11. Have students name movies they've seen that kept their attention through suspense. Choose the movie that most students have seen, and ask them to identify character behaviors, settings, and plot events that helped to build the suspense.

Review Elements of Description

12. In the last Expedition, we learned about the different elements of descriptive writing. Under *Suspense* on the board, write *Descriptive Details*. We learned that authors use lively details to bring a scene to life for the reader. What kinds of details did we learn about? (concrete, telling how things really are; figurative, telling how they seem; sensory, appealing to one of the five senses; details that compare one thing to another) Lead students to recall and describe each type of detail.

13. To create suspense, authors have to make the reader feel as if he or she is actually there. Think about the movie we discussed. Suspenseful movies often show objects or faces in close-up. They might distort how something looks, make it seem much bigger than it really is, or return to a scene or object over and over. Was this true of the movie we discussed a minute ago? How? (Responses will vary.)

14. In suspenseful stories, authors use descriptive details to achieve the same effects. The author might focus on a detail, make it seem larger than it really is, or return to it over and over. The author also might use chilling language to describe an object or situation.

15. As we read the adaptation from *The Call of the Wild*, we'll look for descriptive details that help build suspense. We'll also see how character, setting, and plot work together to create tension.

Reading for Understanding
Reading

1. **Fluency** Read the first two paragraphs of the adapted story from *The Call of the Wild* aloud, while students follow along in their books. Pause to discuss with students that the main character in this story is a dog. Then have students read the remainder of the story and the Connect to the Author feature aloud with you. If necessary, review fluency goals with students and monitor for reading rate, accuracy, and expression.

2. Have students reread the story independently.

Checking for Comprehension *After Reading*

1. When all students have finished rereading the story, guide them to identify the main plot events in the story. List these paragraphs on the board, and have students find an important plot event in each: 3, 7, 8, 9, 10, 12, 13, 16. (3—Spitz attacks Buck for the first time; 7—Buck begins challenging Spitz's leadership and the other dogs begin disobeying Spitz; 8—The beast in Buck stirs more strongly; 9—The dogs now challenge Spitz all the time; 10—The dogs begin chasing a rabbit; 12—Spitz gets the rabbit; 13—Buck attacks Spitz; 16—Buck defeats Spitz.)

2. Call on individuals to use the most important events listed on the board to retell the story. Ask students which events, in their opinion, added the most to the story's suspense. (Responses will vary, but may include the growing tension between Spitz and the other dogs, the rabbit chase, or the fight between Buck and Spitz.)

3. Arrange students in either three or six groups, and assign each group paragraphs 1–6, 7–12, or 13–16. Then have students turn to Student Book page 179, and read the instructions aloud.

4. **Let's look at paragraph 1. It begins with a description of the wild beast that is secretly growing in Buck. This detail makes me uneasy right away. It creates suspense and even dread.** Have the group assigned to paragraph 1 write this detail in an oval on the Student Book page.

5. Repeat modeling with the details "the axe crashed down on mad Dolly's head" in paragraph 2, and "stars leaping in the frigid sky" and "eerie song of pain" in paragraph 8, and "A ghostly calm came over the whiteness." in paragraph 14. Instruct students in each group to record in the Student Book the detail you identify.

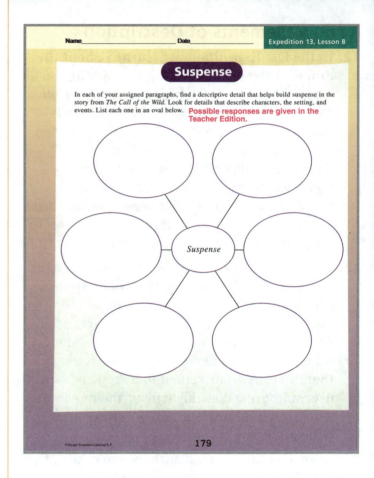

6. Have group members work together to find details in their remaining two paragraphs. Remind students to look for details that describe characters, settings, and events. Before they decide on a detail, have them ask, "Does this detail make the reader nervous?" Monitor students as they work, providing guidance and feedback as needed.

7. When all groups are finished, review their responses as a class. (Possible responses: 2—"François held an axe"; 5—"'he'll chew Spitz up and spit him out on the snow'"; 6—"He wanted it because of the wild beast inside him."; 7—"trouble was brewing"; 9—"howling madhouse"; 10—"kill the rabbit with his own teeth" and "the beast surging inside him"; 11—"everything that was not death"; 12—"the rabbit shrieked as loudly as a man," "life plunging down into the grip of Death," and "wild, irrational delight"; 13—"steel jaws of a trap"; 14—"watching silently with gleaming eyes"; 16—"Spitz watched the silent circle closing in on him . . . ")

8. **Think about the events in this story and the level of suspense London creates. In your opinion, what was his purpose for writing this story?** (to entertain) **Do you think he succeeds? Why?** EVALUATION (Responses will vary.)

9. **Challenge Question One of London's purposes for writing this "animal story" might have been to get his human readers to see *themselves* more clearly. London writes that "There is an infinite joy that comes when one is living completely in the moment, with no thought for the past or the future. It comes to the artist caught up in the fever of work and to the war-mad soldier fighting without mercy." Have you ever had this feeling when creating an artwork, playing a sport, or doing something else that you love? Describe the feeling in your own words.** APPLICATION (Responses will vary.)

675

Lesson 9

Anthology Selection

A Death in the Family

¹Catfish was a heavy sleeper. Somebody had to shake him awake every morning, and that morning it was my job. I shook him, hollered at him, kicked him playfully, but he wouldn't move. When I yanked his filthy woolen Army blanket off of him, I realized that Catfish wasn't ever going to wake up again. He lay face down, blood flowing from an ugly red gash on his temple.

²"Please," I thought, "let this be another nightmare." I had slept fitfully all night, scared awake by one bad dream after another. We usually slept outside, but Preacher knew about this abandoned farmhouse not far from where we had jumped off of the boxcar. It was already sprinkling, so a roof

241

over our heads seemed like a good idea. When we rounded a bend and I saw the house, though, I remember thinking that I might rather sleep in the rain. The whole place was overgrown with weeds, and the house looked like it might fall down any minute. The windows were shattered, the roof sagged dangerously, and the door hung on one hinge. When we walked in, I swear I saw a half dozen rats scurry for cover. The place smelled like death, and as it turns out, death was indeed spending the night there.

³I guess I should back up and tell you a bit about myself. My name is Jacob, and my folks were wheat farmers. Things started getting hard for us in 1931. Millions of people had lost their jobs, and wheat prices fell so low that we couldn't make our loan payments on the farm. The bank kicked us off our land and sent a bulldozer over to knock our house down. I can still see Pa's eyes filled with fear and guilt as he watched. We lived in our truck for a while, driving around and looking for work. But there wasn't much work to be had, and I figured Ma and Pa had their hands full feeding my little brothers and sisters. One morning I got up early, packed a few things, and started walking. I've been on the road ever since.

⁴The roads were filled with people in the same situation as me. We'd sneak rides on boxcars, traveling from town to town, looking for a day's work or maybe a bite to eat. We weren't welcome in most places, so we had to keep moving. The nicest thing people called us was "hobos," but most just called us "beggars" or "thieves."

⁵I joined up with Catfish and his group about three months ago. We took care of each other, sharing whatever food we came across. It was the closest thing to a family I'd had since I left Ma and Pa. Besides me and Catfish, there was Martino, Nick, Joe, and Preacher. That morning in that death-smelling shack, my first thought was that Martino had done it. Martino had a short fuse, and just a couple of days earlier, he and Catfish had gotten into a screaming argument over something Catfish had said. But it wasn't like Martino to sneak up on a sleeping man in the middle of the night. Martino

242

always fought people face to face, fair and square. Besides, as the guys gathered around Catfish's lifeless body, Martino looked as shocked as I did.

⁶"We should get the cops," I said.

⁷"No," Nick said softly.

⁸"He's right," Martino said. "Cops don't care nothin' about hobos, livin' or dead."

⁹Joe nodded and said, "We get the cops in on this, we'll all end up in jail."

¹⁰"Are you guys crazy?" I said. "One of us standing here is a cold-blooded killer. We can't just pretend nothing happened." I looked over at Preacher. He was the oldest and had been on the road the longest. He was as close as we had to a leader. "You know I'm right, don't you?" I said.

¹¹"Yeah, kid, you're right, but so are the other guys," Preacher said. "We'll have to handle this ourselves. Grab some of them cans off that trash pile and let's go dig Catfish a grave."

¹²We found a nice place near some trees and started digging. The ground was pretty sandy, but digging a grave with nothing but tin cans still took most of the morning. We took turns digging and telling stories about Catfish. Nick, who had been with us only a week, seemed to be taking Catfish's death harder than the rest of us. You never know how people are going to react to a tragedy.

¹³When we finished digging, Preacher spread Catfish's blanket in the grave. We went back inside and split up Catfish's meager belongings, seeing as how he didn't have any use for them anymore. Martino got his shoes, Joe got his jacket, Nick got his knife, and I got his pocket watch with a jumping, twisting catfish carved into the hinged lid. It didn't work, of course, but it reminded me of Catfish, so I was glad to have it.

¹⁴Me and Preacher carried Catfish out and laid him in his grave. That's when I remembered the locket. Catfish had this heart-shaped locket that he always wore on a chain around his neck. Inside the locket was a picture of

243

his girlfriend, Tess, whom he hadn't seen since he and his family had been forced off their farm in Alabama. I had never seen Catfish take that locket off, but now it was nowhere to be seen.

¹⁵"Where's his locket?" I said. "We can't bury him without his locket."

¹⁶"Must have fell off when we was carrying him out," Preacher said.

¹⁷Everyone started looking around on the ground. Everyone, that is, except Nick. He just stood there, looking at his clinched fist and shaking his head slowly. His eyes looked just like Pa's the day our house was bulldozed. Nick opened his fist and a chain started slithering out. Then the locket fell to the ground.

¹⁸"Tess was my girl," Nick said. "I knew her back in Kentucky, long before she ever moved to Alabama. I'd stayed behind to make some money for us to get married, but when I caught up with her, she told me she had a new boy. That's when I hit the road. I never asked who her new boy was. I didn't think I cared. Then yesterday, Catfish showed me his locket."

¹⁹Nick fell to his knees, picked up the locket, and laid it on Catfish's chest.

²⁰"I'm sorry, Catfish," he sobbed. "I'm so sorry."

²¹Nobody said anything. What was there to say? We all knelt around Catfish's grave and said a silent prayer. Then we pushed the sandy dirt over him. When we were done, Preacher put his hand on Nick's heaving shoulder.

²²"Come on, Nick," he said. "We'd better get moving."

244

Expedition Review

1. **In the last lesson, we read a story about a brutal rivalry between two dogs.**
   - **What reason does the author give for Buck's wish to defeat Spitz?** (It's in his nature; the wild beast in him desires it.)
   - **What events take place after Buck decides to go to war with Spitz?** (Buck challenges Spitz's authority every chance he gets. Buck and Spitz fight often. More and more, Buck feels his wild nature. Buck and Spitz finally fight to the death, and Buck defeats Spitz.)
   - **The author says that Buck and Spitz were "destined to fight it out for leadership of the pack." Do you think this is so? Why?** (Possible responses: yes, because both dogs were natural leaders) **Which particular actions or events make you think so?** (Possible responses: Spitz bullies Buck and tries to start fights; Buck leads revolts against Spitz; Buck uses imagination in his final fight with Spitz.)

2. **Now, let's compare this story and its main character with some of the others in this Expedition.** Arrange students in three or six groups, and assign each group one of the other stories in this Expedition (the excerpt from *Holes*, the excerpt from *The Joy Luck Club*, or "Kipling and I.") Then have students discuss ways that the main character of their assigned story is similar to or different from the main character in the adapted story from *The Call of the Wild*.

Have students use these questions to guide their discussion:
- **What problem does each character have?**
- **How does each character solve his or her problem?**
- **Does each character's motivations (or reasons for acting) come from the inside, or the outside?**
- **Does each character see himself or herself clearly, or learn to?**

3. Have students sum up the similarities or differences in the characters in two or three written sentences. Write the following vocabulary words on the board: *desolate, miserable, dazed, vast, misery, fragrant, somber, meager, unbearable, potent, prominent, paltry.* Instruct students to use at least two of these vocabulary words in their sentences.

4. **Challenge Words** If students have learned the Challenge Words, instruct them to include at least one of those words in their sentences.

5. **Listening and Speaking** Invite a representative from each group to read the group's summary aloud. Remind students to speak loudly, clearly, and slowly. Encourage them to "aim" their words at listeners near the back of the room. After each presentation, have audience members evaluate the speaker's delivery by identifying one thing that was done well and making one suggestion for improvement.

6. After each summary is read, call on other students to identify and define the vocabulary words that were used.

677

Assessment

1. Have students turn to Student Book page 180. Then have them turn to Anthology page 241. Explain to students that they will read the story "A Death in the Family" before they answer the questions on the Student Book page.

2. Read aloud the Tips for Success and assessment instructions. Then have students complete the assessment independently.

SKILL

Reteaching Guidelines

Comprehension

If students incorrectly answer more than 2 out of 11 questions on the Comprehension Assessment, refer to the Reteach lesson on page 681a. Using the Comprehension section, reteach the skills, guide students in completing the practice activity, and reassess comprehension.

Vocabulary

If more than 20 percent of the students miss certain vocabulary items, reteach and practice those words using the Vocabulary section of the Reteach lesson on page 681c.

Expedition 13, Lesson 9   Name_____ Date_____

Comprehension Assessment

Tips for Success! **Think About Narrative Elements:** Often on a test, you will answer questions about story elements such as character, setting, and plot. As you read a story, try to picture the characters and setting. Think about which events seem most important. These are clues to the plot of the story. Notice important details about the *who, what, where,* and *when* of a story. These will help you infer the answers to the questions.

Multiple Choice 3 points each
Read "A Death in the Family" to answer questions 1–5. Look back in the story. Fill in the bubble next to the best answer.

1. Where does this story mainly take place?
   Ⓐ in a boxcar
   Ⓑ in a campground
   Ⓒ in a farmhouse
   Ⓓ in a field

2. Why has Jacob left his family?
   Ⓐ He did not enjoy traveling with them.
   Ⓑ He had grown tired of living on a farm.
   Ⓒ He was angry at his father for losing the farm.
   Ⓓ He felt that he was a burden to his parents.

3. Why does Nick kill Catfish?
   Ⓐ He realizes that he lost his girlfriend to Catfish.
   Ⓑ Catfish stole a locket that belonged to his girlfriend.
   Ⓒ Catfish and Nick had a disagreement over an issue.
   Ⓓ Catfish refused to share some food with Nick.

4. Which story detail helps build suspense?
   Ⓐ The whole place was overgrown with weeds.
   Ⓑ Martino looked as shocked as I did.
   Ⓒ One of us standing here is a cold-blooded killer.
   Ⓓ Then yesterday, Catfish showed me his locket.

5. In the following sentence, which underlined word is a clue that Jacob is telling a story about his life? Somebody had to shake him awake every morning, and that morning it was my job.
   Ⓐ Somebody
   Ⓑ him
   Ⓒ it
   Ⓓ my

180   ©Voyager Expanded Learning, L.P.

Name_____ Date_____   Expedition 13, Lesson 9

Short Response 4 points each
Read "A Death in the Family" to answer questions 6–10. Look back in the story. Then write your answer on the line(s).

6. Is this story set in modern times or long ago? __long ago__
   How do you know? List one detail from the photograph and one from paragraph 3 that tells when the story takes place.
   Detail from photograph: Possible response: The clothes on the people are not like those worn today.
   Detail from paragraph 3: Possible responses: Jacob's mention of the year 1931; Jacob's use of "Ma" and "Pa" to refer to his parents

7. Jacob says that the men were "the closest thing to a family I'd had since I left Ma and Pa." List two details from the story that show this.
   Detail 1: Possible responses: The men travel and sleep together; they share food.
   Detail 2: Possible response: The men protect one another, as when they do not call the police after Catfish is murdered.

8. Jacob wants to call the police when Catfish is found dead, but the other men are against this. What is their reason, or motivation, for not calling the police?
   Possible responses: Because the men are considered "hobos" or "thieves," they might all be put in jail; one or all of them might be accused of murder and sent to prison.

9. At first, Jacob thinks that Martino killed Catfish. Then he thinks this is unlikely. List two reasons Jacob gives to show that Martino is not the likely killer.
   Reason 1: Martino fights with people face to face rather than sneaking up on them.
   Reason 2: Martino seems as shocked as Jacob is to see that Catfish is dead.

10. What is the problem, or conflict, that Nick is likely struggling with at the end of the story?
   He feels guilty for killing Catfish.

©Voyager Expanded Learning, L.P.   181

Extended Response 20 points

Read "A Death in the Family" to plan your answer to question 11. Look back in the story. Use the information you find to complete the chart.

11. What narrative elements make up "A Death in the Family"?

Possible events are provided. Accept all reasonable responses.

Story Title: _____ **A Death in the Family** _____

Character(s):	Setting:
Catfish, Preacher, Jacob, Martino, Nick, Joe	**Time: long ago** **Place: an abandoned farmhouse**

Event 1:
Jacob finds that Catfish is dead.

▼

Event 2:
The men gather around Catfish's body.

▼

Event 3:
The men dig a grave for Catfish and divide his belongings.

▼

Event 4:
Jacob notices the locket is missing.

▼

Event 5:
Nick shows the locket and admits to killing Catfish.

▼

Event 6:
Nick apologizes to Catfish.

▼

Event 7:
The men bury Catfish and leave.

182
©Voyager Expanded Learning, L.P.

Vocabulary Assessment 3 points each

For questions 12–26, read each sentence. Fill in the bubble next to the correct meaning for the underlined word.

12. We had already <u>bloated</u> ourselves from earlier in the day.
What does the word *bloat* mean?
- Ⓐ entertain
- Ⓑ stuff ●
- Ⓒ gather
- Ⓓ bathe

13. The poem was hung in a <u>conspicuous</u> place in the house.
What does the word *conspicuous* mean?
- Ⓐ easily seen ●
- Ⓑ safe
- Ⓒ high
- Ⓓ easily reached

14. Stanley felt somewhat <u>dazed</u> as the guard unlocked his handcuffs.
What does the word *dazed* mean?
- Ⓐ silly
- Ⓑ shocked ●
- Ⓒ tired
- Ⓓ free

15. The land was barren and <u>desolate</u>.
What does the word *desolate* mean?
- Ⓐ deserted ●
- Ⓑ hilly
- Ⓒ covered with plants
- Ⓓ dangerous

16. My table was of a very <u>fragrant</u> red wood.
What does the word *fragrant* mean?
- Ⓐ being very strong
- Ⓑ having a bright color
- Ⓒ costing a lot of money
- Ⓓ having a pleasant odor ●

17. What fine food we treated ourselves to with our <u>meager</u> allowances!
What does the word *meager* mean?
- Ⓐ badly needed
- Ⓑ barely enough ●
- Ⓒ saved
- Ⓓ combined

18. We all had our <u>miseries</u>.
What does the word *misery* mean?
- Ⓐ suffering ●
- Ⓑ favorite
- Ⓒ curiosity
- Ⓓ memory

19. "Next week" meant weeks of calling for the <u>paltry</u> dollars owed me.
What does the word *paltry* mean?
- Ⓐ stolen
- Ⓑ few ●
- Ⓒ borrowed
- Ⓓ earned

©Voyager Expanded Learning, L.P.
183

---

20. Others thought we were <u>possessed</u> by demons.
What does the word *possess* mean?
- Ⓐ advise
- Ⓑ amuse
- Ⓒ control ●
- Ⓓ help

21. The <u>potent</u> odor made everyone run from the kitchen.
What does the word *potent* mean?
- Ⓐ powerful ●
- Ⓑ valuable
- Ⓒ delicious
- Ⓓ burned

22. Guns, weapons, and drugs are not allowed on the <u>premises</u>.
What does the word *premises* mean?
- Ⓐ a type of bus
- Ⓑ a type of prison
- Ⓒ a long trip
- Ⓓ a certain property ●

23. The poem had to have the most <u>prominent</u> place in the room.
What does the word *prominent* mean?
- Ⓐ easy to see ●
- Ⓑ comfortable
- Ⓒ safe
- Ⓓ easy to reach

24. Were we to wait for our own deaths with proper <u>somber</u> faces?
What does the word *somber* mean?
- Ⓐ frightened
- Ⓑ gloomy ●
- Ⓒ nervous
- Ⓓ eager

25. <u>Unbearable</u> smells from the sewers rose up to my window.
What does the word *unbearable* mean?
- Ⓐ lasting a short while
- Ⓑ not easy to identify
- Ⓒ greater than someone can stand ●
- Ⓓ causing slight discomfort

26. Stanley looked out across the <u>vast</u> wasteland.
What does the word *vast* mean?
- Ⓐ having few trees and plants
- Ⓑ filled with garbage
- Ⓒ not worth a great amount
- Ⓓ stretching out for a long way ●

184
©Voyager Expanded Learning, L.P.

Expedition Wrap-Up

1. After students have completed the assessment, bring them together to discuss the probing questions as a way to provide closure for Expedition 13. Briefly discuss each of the Expedition stories. Then watch DVD 13.2 together as a class. Have students turn to Anthology page 221. Ask students to summarize the response to each probing question that was given on the DVD.

2. Conclude the Expedition by reviewing with students some of the purposes of storytelling that were discussed in this Expedition (to tell about, record, or remember important events; to entertain; to share a message or teach a lesson). Write these purposes on the board. Then have students brainstorm story ideas that relate to each purpose. Encourage students to draw ideas from their lives and experiences, as well as from what they know about the world. Have students record and save these ideas as possible future writing topics.

Strategic Online Learning Opportunities®

Students read a passage about the mysterious disappearance of a colony on Roanoke Island in Virginia.

Content Connection
Social Studies

Lost Colony of the New World

Lexile Levels
Passage B 860L
Passage C 960L

Assessment

- Metacognition
- Content
- Vocabulary
- Main Idea
- Summary

Based on their assessment scores, students automatically are assigned either the Skills Practice for reinforcement or the Independent Practice and Extension Opportunities.

SKILLS PRACTICE

Vocabulary Strategies
- Context
- Word Parts: Prefixes and Suffixes
- Word Parts: Compound Words

Dictionary Skills

Main Idea Strategy: W–I–N
- Identifying the Most Important *Who* or *What*
- Identifying the Most Important *Information*
- Stating the Main Idea in a Small *Number* of Words

Questioning

Writing
- Responding to Texts
- Writing a Summary Statement

INDEPENDENT PRACTICE

Vocabulary Strategies

Writing
- Writing a Summary Statement
- Responding to Texts

EXTENSION OPPORTUNITIES

- Online Books
- Book Cart
- Review of Previous Passages

■ Reteach

Reteach Skills

✔ **Narrative Text Elements: Character, Setting, Plot**   Lesson 1

✔ **Character Motivation**   Lesson 4

Before Reading

Narrative Text Elements: Character, Setting, Plot

1. **The purpose of a narrative text is to tell a story.**

2. **One important element of a narrative text are the *characters*. What are characters?** (the people or animals that take part in the story)

3. **Two more elements of narratives are *setting* and *plot*. What is a story's setting?** (where and when it takes place) **What is a story's plot?** (the series of events that make up the story)

4. Write on the board *Craig had already missed track three times. If it happened again, he would be benched for the next meet. It was the worst possible day for his friend Marcus to be waiting for him at his locker after school.* Read aloud the sentences. **This is the beginning of a narrative.**

   • **Who are the characters in this story?** (Craig and Marcus)

   • **What is the setting?** (after school, at Craig's locker)

   • **What problem does Craig have?** (If he misses track he will be benched for the next meet.)

5. **The problem presented at the beginning of a story sets a chain of events in motion. These events make up the middle of the story. What kinds of events do you think might happen in the middle of this story?** (Responses will vary.)

6. **At the end of a story, the problem might be solved. This makes a happy ending. Other times, the problem isn't solved, and the ending isn't so happy. How do you think the story about Craig will end?** (Responses will vary.)

Reading for Understanding

1. Have students turn to Anthology page 241. **As we read this story, let's think about its characters, setting, and plot.**

2. Read aloud the first paragraph of the story, then have students read the remainder with you.

After Reading

Character Motivation

1. Distribute copies of Reteach page 25, and draw the graphic organizer on the board. Read the instructions for section 1 aloud. Guide students to fill in the story map.

2. **Usually, characters in stories have reasons, or *motivations*, for what they do.** Write *Character Motivation* on the board.

   • **Sometimes these reasons come from the outside. If a character steals firewood to stay warm, her motivation is the cold weather. This comes from the outside.**

   • **Other times, a motivation comes from the inside. These motivations are desires or feelings. If a character gives someone a gift because he loves her, his motivation comes from the inside.**

   • **Sometimes motivations are mixed. For example, a character might train to become a firefighter because of a firefighter shortage, which is an outside motivation. She might also love adventure, which is an inside motivation.**

3. Direct students' attention to section 2 of Reteach page 25. Discuss each question as a class before students write an answer to it.

Name_____ Date_____

Narrative Text Elements

1. Fill in the story map.

Story Title: _____A Death in the Family_____

SETTING

Place: _____an abandoned farmhouse_____ Time: _____long ago_____

CHARACTERS

Catfish, Preacher, Jacob, Martino, Nick, Joe

PLOT

Beginning (Problem)	Middle (Chain of Events)	End (Problem Solved?)
Catfish gets killed, but nobody knows who did it.	• The men dig a grave for Catfish. • Jacob notices the locket is missing. • Nick shows the locket and admits to killing Catfish. • The men bury Catfish.	The problem is solved. Preacher suggests they "get moving."

2. Answer these questions.

A. What was Nick's motivation for killing Catfish? _____
    Possible response: He was jealous.

B. Does this motive come from the inside, the outside, or both? _____
    the inside

©Voyager Expanded Learning, L.P.

Expedition 13

Extra Support

Narrative Text Elements

If students need additional support, write the following sentences on strips of paper: *Alma argues with stepsister. Alma runs out of the apartment into the rainstorm. Alma slips and hurts her ankle. Alma's stepsister finds her and helps her back inside. Alma and her stepsister make up.* Shuffle the strips and have students arrange them in the correct story order. Then lay out three index cards that say *Beginning*, *Middle*, and *End*, and have students place the strips under the appropriate heading. Finally, have students underline the names of the characters with one colored marker, and words that indicate setting with another colored marker.

Checking for Comprehension

1. Distribute to students copies of Reteach page 26. Then have students turn to "A Death in the Family" on Anthology page 241. Explain to students that they will read this text before answering the questions on Reteach page 26.

2. Read aloud the Keys to Comprehension section and the assessment instructions. Then have students complete the assessment independently.

3. Review the correct answers and discuss any questions that students answered incorrectly.

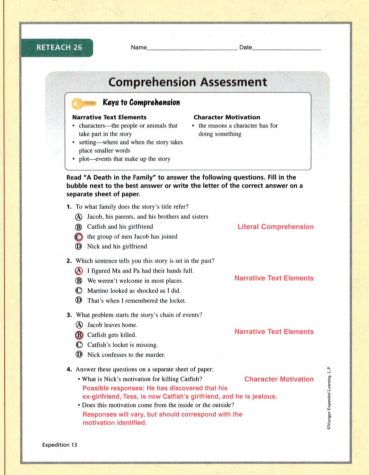

Name_____ Date_____

Comprehension Assessment

🔑 **Keys to Comprehension**

Narrative Text Elements
• characters—the people or animals that take part in the story
• setting—where and when the story takes place smaller words
• plot—events that make up the story

Character Motivation
• the reasons a character has for doing something

Read "A Death in the Family" to answer the following questions. Fill in the bubble next to the best answer or write the letter of the correct answer on a separate sheet of paper.

1. To what family does the story's title refer?
- Ⓐ Jacob, his parents, and his brothers and sisters
- Ⓑ Catfish and his girlfriend   Literal Comprehension
- Ⓒ the group of men Jacob has joined
- Ⓓ Nick and his girlfriend

2. Which sentence tells you this story is set in the past?
- Ⓐ I figured Ma and Pa had their hands full.
- Ⓑ We weren't welcome in most places.   Narrative Text Elements
- Ⓒ Martino looked as shocked as I did.
- Ⓓ That's when I remembered the locket.

3. What problem starts the story's chain of events?
- Ⓐ Jacob leaves home.
- Ⓑ Catfish gets killed.   Narrative Text Elements
- Ⓒ Catfish's locket is missing.
- Ⓓ Nick confesses to the murder.

4. Answer these questions on a separate sheet of paper:
- • What is Nick's motivation for killing Catfish?   Character Motivation
    Possible responses: He has discovered that his ex-girlfriend, Tess, is now Catfish's girlfriend, and he is jealous.
- • Does this motivation come from the inside or the outside?
    Responses will vary, but should correspond with the motivation identified.

©Voyager Expanded Learning, L.P.

Expedition 13

■ Vocabulary

1. Write on the board the specific words that students have missed, along with a synonym web such as the one below. Then guide students in completing the graphic organizer for each of the words.
   - First, have students think of synonyms for the word. Write these in the inner ovals.
   - Next, have students think of additional synonyms, and help them categorize these according to the different meanings of the words. Write these in the outer ovals.

2. When students have completed the synonym maps, check comprehension by having them write in their own words the meaning of each vocabulary word.

■ Narrative

Teach and Model

1. **Everybody loves a good story. You have probably heard stories—about three bears or a big bad wolf, about relatives and friends—since you were a child. Writing stories can be especially fun. The writing you have done so far has been expository writing. Expository texts are nonfiction and give information about things and ideas. They can be organized in a variety of ways. For example, you can tell how to do things in sequential order or you can explain causes and effects. When you write stories, however, you are writing narrative texts. A narrative is a piece of fictional writing that tells a story. Writers use three main elements to write narratives: character, setting, and plot.** Write *Character, Setting, Plot* on the board.

2. **Let's write a short narrative that has characters, a setting, and a plot. We will write about our fictional friend, Ellen.** Write this prompt on the board: *Ellen is in her room. She decides to read a book but cannot find the book on her desk.*

3. **Let's look at the first narrative element: character. *Character* is the person in the story. Who is in our story?** (Ellen) Write her name next to *Character*. **The second narrative element is setting. The *setting* is where and when a story happens. We know at least one thing about the setting of our story: the place. Where does the story take place?** (in Ellen's room) **We can add details to tell more about the setting. For example, we can make up details to tell when the story happens.** (Possible response: in current times; in the evening after supper) Write these details next to *Setting*. **The third narrative element is plot. The *plot* is what happens in the story. What happens in this story?** (Ellen decides to read a book but cannot find the book.) Write this detail next to *Plot*.

4. **So far we have the basic elements of a story. We know who is in the story, where and when the story takes place, and what happens. Now let's learn more about the plot. The plot tells about an action that has a beginning, middle, and end.** Under *Plot* in the chart, write *Beginning, Middle, End*. **Stories that are interesting usually have some complication, or problem, that the characters must overcome. The beginning of the plot presents that problem. What is the problem in our story?** Next to *Beginning*, write: *Ellen wants her book but can't find it.* **Next we have to add information that tells us more about the actions that happened next. What do you think Ellen does when she can't find the book?** (Ellen takes everything off of her desk. She puts an empty plate, a box of tissues, a comb, and a notebook on the floor.) Write these details next to *Middle*. **The plot, and the story, come to an end when the problem is resolved. Here's what happens to Ellen.** Next to *End*, write: *Ellen smiles when she finds the book hidden under a pair of jeans.*

5. **Now I can write my narrative. I will use our ideas to write sentences about the character, setting, and plot. I'll need to add words and details as I flesh out the narrative elements. The plot should present a string of events that have a beginning, middle, and end.** Write these sentences on the board and read them aloud: *Ellen wanders into her room one evening after supper. She has finished her homework, so she decides to read more of the novel she got from the library. Where did she leave the book? She can't find it. Ellen takes everything off of her desk. She puts an empty plate, a box of tissues, a comb, and a notebook on the floor. Ellen smiles as she finds the book hidden under a pair of jeans.* Go through the list of narrative and plot elements, and ask students to identify them. Underline each part of the narrative as they respond.

 **Anthology Connection**

Review the topic of "literature and life" by revisiting the reading selections from Expedition 13. Pay special attention to the following passages:

from *Holes*

from *The Joy Luck Club*

"Kipling and I"

from *The Call of the Wild*

Next, have students list three or four main characters they have read about in this Expedition. Then have them take turns reading one of the names aloud to a partner. The partner should then describe the problem that character faced, and how—or whether—he or she solved the problem.

Writing Sample

Name_____ Date_____   **WRITING 45**

Narrative

A Big Flash

Morgan walked up to the soccer field at the park with her little dog, Flash, who was a whopping twelve inches tall. The morning sun sparkled through the leaves on the trees. The other contestants were already warming up their dogs–their big dogs. People sent disks sailing through the air. Their dogs ran, turned, and jumped, catching the disks in mid-flight. Morgan unpacked her gear and began gently tossing a disk to Flash. Jay and Patricia saw Morgan and burst into laughter. They realized that Morgan was there to compete with Flash in the contest. Jay and Patricia weren't even sure the rules allowed dogs as small as Flash to enter. Morgan was sure, though. She knew that Flash could compete and she knew he would win. She scooped up her disks, called her dog, and marched onto the field.

Expedition 13

1. Distribute Writing page 45, and read the passage aloud. **This paragraph is the introduction to a longer piece narrative writing. Let's look at how the writer presents the characters, setting, and plot.**

2. **The characters are the people in the story. Who are the characters?** (Morgan, Flash, Jay, Patricia)

3. **The setting is where and when the story takes place. What is the setting of this story?** (soccer field at a park in current times; during a sunny morning) **What words and phrases helped you identify the setting?** (soccer field, park, morning sun)

4. **The plot is what happens in the story. Usually a plot has a beginning that presents a problem, a middle that develops the action, and an end that resolves the problem. This passage is only the introduction to the story, so only the beginning of the plot is given here. What problem is presented in this paragraph?** (Morgan and Flash want to compete in the disk contest, but other contestants laugh at them and question whether they can enter because Flash is small.) **Circle the words and phrases that helped you identify the problem.** (Flash was a whopping twelve inches tall; The other contestants were already warming up their big dogs; Morgan unpacked her gear and began gently tossing a disk to Flash; Jay and Patricia saw Morgan and burst into laughter; They realized that Morgan was there to compete; They weren't even sure the rules allowed dogs as small as Flash to enter.)

Evaluating Writing

1. Distribute Writing page 46. Read the rubric. **This rubric focuses on narrative texts: fictional writing that tells a story with characters, a setting, and a plot.**

2. Call on an individual to reread the paragraph from Writing page 45. Have students use the criteria on the rubric to evaluate the story, identifying the following:

   • the characters

   • the setting

   • the beginning of the plot

3. **Using the rubric, what score would you give this paragraph?** (5) **Why?** (because it clearly describes the characters, the place where the action occurs, and the time of the story; the beginning of the plot, the problem, is clearly defined)

Guided Practice

1. **Now we'll work together to write the first paragraph of a story.** Distribute Writing page 47. Draw the contents of the page on the board. Read the directions above the graphic organizer. **First let's read the prompt. Remember that we can use our PLAN to help us think about what we are writing. What part of the PLAN can help us with the prompt?** (the P) Write *Pay attention to the prompt.* on the board. **What kind of paragraph are you being asked to write?** (a narrative one) **What are you being asked to write about?** (events that happen as a vacant lot is cleaned up) **How does the prompt suggest you organize your paragraph?** (by creating characters, a setting, and plot that presents a problem)

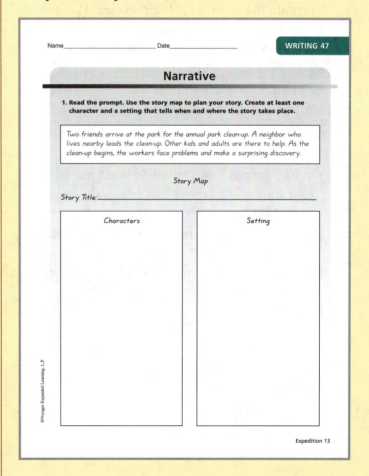

2. We will use the story map on page 47, as well as a plot map, to plan our stories. A story map lays out the key narrative elements in a piece of fiction. First think about characters. Will your characters be male or female? What are their names? How old are they? Write the names of your characters on your graphic organizer. You can include brief details about them in the box. If I were writing a story based on this prompt, I would write about two boys, Jesse and David, who are both 15 years old. Write *Jesse and David; 15 years old* on the board. Remember that you will write names and details of *your* characters on your chart. Now you will work together to create the setting of your story.

3. Have students work in small groups or in pairs to create the setting for their stories. Have them write their ideas in the graphic organizer on page 47. Guide students by asking these questions:

• Part of the setting is the location. Where will your story take place?

• Time is also part of the setting. When does your story take place?

• What details can you add about the place and time of your story to bring the setting to life for the reader?

4. Have students share their settings with the class. Write students' responses on the board. Be sure all students have listed their characters and setting in the graphic organizer before moving on.

Independent Practice

1. Have students turn to the rubric they used on Writing page 46. Review the criteria for narrative writing that scores a 5 on the rubric.

WRITING 48   Name_____ Date_____

Narrative

2. Continue planning your story by creating your plot. Tell what the problem is, what events happen to develop it, and how it is resolved.

Plot Map

Beginning: What is the problem?

Middle: What events happen?

End: How is the problem solved?

3. Write the first paragraph of your story on your own paper. Use the narrative elements you described above, and add as many descriptive details as you can.

Expedition 13

©Voyager Expanded Learning, L.P.

2. Distribute Writing page 48. **This is your plot map. Read aloud the instructions for section 2. Continue planning your paragraph on your own by writing about the plot. Although you will only write about the beginning of the plot (the problem) in your paragraph, you should decide what happens in the middle and end of the story as though you were going to write the whole narrative. Remember that in the middle of the story, the plot is developed through a series of events or actions. The end of the story shows how the problem is resolved.**

3. Read aloud the instructions for section 3 on Writing page 48. **Now you're ready to write the first paragraph in your story. On your own paper, write a sentence that presents the characters in your story.**

4. Have students use the narrative elements they created as they write their paragraphs. Monitor students as they write, and provide correction and feedback as needed.

5. After students complete their narrative paragraphs, have them share their work with the class. Discuss which paragraphs present the clearest, most interesting characters, settings, and plots.

6. Have students return to their paragraphs and strengthen their details, which will make the narrative elements more specific and interesting to the reader. Remind students that this step is called revision and explain that they should revise their fictional writing just as they did their nonfiction texts. **When you *revise*, you go back over your writing and make changes to improve it. Descriptive writing is important in narratives. Remember that descriptive details can be concrete, appeal to the senses, or use figurative language. Replacing vague or boring details with descriptive details is a good way to revise. You should use the most vivid descriptive details you can think of.** Have students read their paragraphs again and replace any nonspecific details with descriptive details.

7. Then have students get into pairs for peer editing. Instruct them to exchange stories, then read each other's work aloud. Students should first tell one thing the writer did well. Then students should choose a score for the story based on the rubric on Writing page 46. Finally, students should offer one idea for improving the story. Remind students that they should treat each other with respect as they work together.

8. Close the lesson by reminding students that narrative writing tells a fictional story using characters, setting, and plot. **Like other kinds of writing, narrative depends on organization. The plot should be organized around the beginning, middle, and end of the action.**

Extended Writing

Elaborating Plot Events in Narrative Writing

Use this activity to help students complete the story they began writing in Independent Practice.

- **On Writing page 48, we mapped out the plot for our story. We have already written the first paragraph of the story. Now let's elaborate what we've written on the plot map, then use these ideas to finish the story.**

- Write the following questions on the board:
  - *As each event happens, what are the characters thinking? What are they feeling?*
  - *How does the setting contribute to the events? Does something or someone in the setting help cause one of the events?*
  - *How can I add suspense to the series of events? Can I add details that seem ominous? Can I have other characters say mysterious things?*
  - *How do the characters feel at the end of the story? What will they do next? Would they relive the experience if they could? Why?*

- Have partners read their opening paragraphs to one another, then discuss the questions on the board. Encourage students to offer possible story ideas to their partners. Tell students to add new ideas to the graphic organizer on Writing page 48.

- When students are finished, have them use all of their ideas to complete their story. Suggest that students write four additional paragraphs: one for each plot event, and one for the conclusion.

- Invite students to read their completed stories aloud.

- For a complete instructional model for multiparagraph writing, see the Expedition 11 Writing lesson.

Writing Conventions
MINILESSON

Possessives

- Write the following sentence on the board:

  Stanley's orange jumpsuits are faded.

  Read the sentence aloud. **In this sentence, the word *Stanley* is in the possessive form. What does it mean to *possess* something?** (to have it or own it) **When a word is in the possessive form, it indicates ownership. In this case, what does Stanley own?** (the jumpsuits)

- Circle the apostrophe *s* in *Stanley's*. **If a noun is singular—if it names just one person, place, or thing, an apostrophe *s* is added to the end of it to show ownership.** Write *the jumpsuits' buttons* on the board. **However, if a noun is plural—if it names more than one person, place, or thing—and it already ends in an *s*, you simply add an apostrophe to show possession.** Circle the apostrophe.

- Write *Where are the boys socks?* on the board twice. **In the first sentence, let's say we were talking about one boy. Where would we place the apostrophe to show ownership in the first sentence?** (between the *y* and the *s* in *boys*) **In the second sentence, we are talking about 12 boys. Where would we place the apostrophe to show possession?** (after the *s* in *boys*)

▶ Write the following sentences on the board. Have students rewrite them, adding an apostrophe where needed to show possession.

1. Mr. Sirs keys rattled on two big rings. **Mr. Sir's**

2. His boots heels thudded across the wood floor. **boots'**

3. His eyes pupils were two small black dots. **eyes'**

4. Stanleys future looked bleak. **Stanley's**

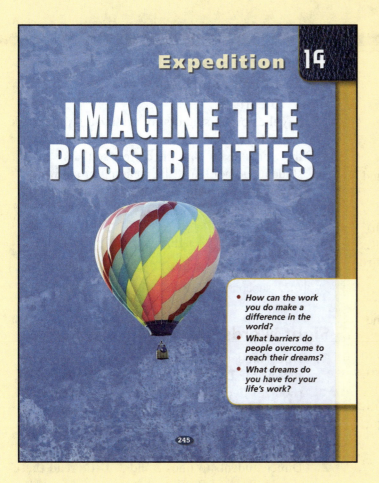

Expedition 14

IMAGINE THE POSSIBILITIES

- *How can the work you do make a difference in the world?*
- *What barriers do people overcome to reach their dreams?*
- *What dreams do you have for your life's work?*

245

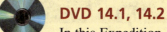

DVD 14.1, 14.2

In this Expedition, DVD segments investigate the ways in which people's dreams for the future can influence not only their lives, but also the lives of others. They point out how those who have broken through barriers to achieve many forms of success have made meaningful differences in the world.

Strategic Online Learning Opportunities®

Students access the Web site http://solo.voyagerlearning.com for an interactive SOLO® session. In each session, students apply previously taught strategic skills to new readings on the student's appropriate Lexile® level. Consult the *Passport Reading Journeys*™ SOLO User Guide for a comprehensive overview of this component.

Passport Reading Journeys Library

Students may select reading materials from the *Passport Reading Journeys* Library. Partner and independent reading opportunities allow students to read authentic text on their Lexile level to build fluency. Teacher resources are provided in the *Passport Reading Journeys* Library Teacher's Guide.

In This Expedition

READINGS

Lessons 1 and 2
Dolores Huerta: Striking for Justice
from A Migrant Family,
   by Larry Dane Brimner

Lessons 3 and 4
from Gig: Americans Talk About Their Jobs
from Keeping the Moon, by Sarah Dessen

Lessons 6 and 7
The Fast Track
Making History at Indianapolis

Lesson 8
Out of Many, One, by Barack Obama

Lesson 9 Assessment
From Sitcom Junkie to King of Bling

SKILLS

Narrative and Expository Texts Review
- Biography
- First-Person Narratives
- Interviews
- Direct Quotations
- Description
- Persuasion
- Compare/Contrast Across Texts

Advanced Word Study

Suffix -*en* and Prefix *sub-*

1. Write -*en* on the board. **This word part is a suffix. Remember, a suffix is a word part that occurs at the end of a word and often helps us understand the meaning of the word. The sounds for this suffix are /en/. Say the sounds for this suffix.** (/en/) Write the words *frighten* and *ashen* on the board. Underline the suffix -*en*. **What is the suffix?** (-en) **Use the sounds you know to read the rest of the words.** (fright, ash) **What are the words?** (frighten, ashen) **The suffix -*en* means "relating to" or "to make." The word *frighten* means "to make scared"; the word *ashen* means "relating to a gray or pale color."**

   Have students turn to page E14, Lesson 1, in the back of the Student Book. Direct them to line 1 in the first box. **What is the underlined suffix in the first word?** (-en) **Read the rest of the word.** (unbeat) **What is the word?** (unbeaten) Repeat with the remaining words. Call on individuals to read the words in random order. Ask students to tell the meanings of the words based on the meaning of the suffix.

2. Write *sub-* on the board. **This word part is a prefix. Remember, a prefix is a word part that occurs at the beginning of a word and often helps us understand the meaning of the word. The sounds for this prefix are /sub/. Say the sounds for this prefix.** (/sub/) Write the word *substandard* on the board. Underline the prefix *sub-*. **What is this prefix?** (sub-) **Use the sounds you know to read the rest of the word.** (standard) **What is the word?** (substandard) **The prefix *sub-* means "under" or "below." It can refer to location or rank. The word *standard* means "average." The word *substandard* means "below average" or "inferior."** Direct students to line 2. **What is the underlined prefix in the first word?** (sub-) **Read the rest of the word.** (jective) **What is the word?** (subjective) Repeat with the remaining words. Call on individuals to read the words in a different order. Ask students to tell the meanings of the words based on the meaning of the prefix.

3. Direct students to line 3. Have them read the words. Call on individuals to read the words in a

different order. Ask students to tell the meanings of the words.

▼ To Correct

Say the correct sound(s) or prefix/suffix, then ask students to repeat the sound(s). Have them read the words again with the correct sound(s). If students do not know the meaning of the word, review the word and/or word parts to determine the meaning of the word.

1. unbeat<u>en</u>	length<u>en</u>	rip<u>en</u>	retak<u>en</u>
2. <u>sub</u>jective	<u>sub</u>way	<u>sub</u>stantial	<u>sub</u>missive
3. subcontract	lessen	harvesting	brutality

Sight Words

1. Direct students to line 1. Have them point to the first word. **This word is *lionize*. Read the word.** (lionize) **Let's read the word again.** (lionize) **Let's spell the word.** (l-i-o-n-i-z-e) **What is the word?** (lionize) Repeat with the remaining words. Then have students read the words.

2. Direct students to lines 2 and 3. **Let's read these words.** Remind students that the rows of words consist of regular and irregular words. Point to the first word. **What is the word?** (legend) Repeat with the remaining words. Call on individuals to read the words in a different order. Ask students to tell the meanings of the words.

▼ To Correct

For Regular Words: Say the sound(s) in the word, then ask students to repeat the sound(s). Have them read the word again with the correct sound(s). If students do not know the meaning of the word, review the word and/or word part to determine the meaning of the word.

For Irregular Words: Immediately say the correct word. Then have students read the word, spell it, and read it again. If students do not know the meaning of the word, review the word.

1. lionize **I**	muscle **I**	urgent **I**	threaten **I**
2. legend **I**	seized **I**	lunged **I**	influential **I**
3. rescue **I**	foreseeable **I**	bully **I**	political **R**

Anthology Selection

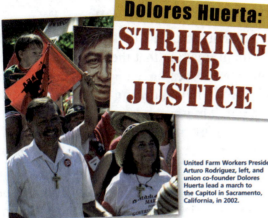

Dolores Huerta:
STRIKING FOR JUSTICE

United Farm Workers President Arturo Rodriguez, left, and union co-founder Dolores Huerta lead a march to the Capitol in Sacramento, California, in 2002.

[1]Dolores Fernandez Huerta is a living legend.

[2]She's been lionized in songs. She's been memorialized in paintings. She's been arrested more than 20 times and has been beaten almost to death by police. She was one of the most influential labor leaders of the 20th century. And she continues to work for justice in the 21st. Huerta has dedicated her life to the struggle for justice, dignity, and decent working conditions for the men, women, and children who pick the food we eat every day.

[3]Huerta was born in 1930, in the middle of the Great Depression, in a small mining town in northern New Mexico. After her parents divorced, her mother moved Dolores and her two brothers to California. Huerta's mother worked two jobs—literally day and night—to support her children.

[4]After high school, Huerta got her teaching certificate. But she wasn't satisfied teaching. "I realized one day that as a teacher I couldn't do anything for the kids who came to school barefoot and hungry," she says. After only a few months in the classroom, Huerta decided she should fight poverty more directly. She helped found a group to fight for the rights of Mexican Americans.

[5]As she became more active in social and labor organizations, her marriage **faltered**. "I knew I wasn't comfortable in a wife's role, but I wasn't clearly facing the issue. I hedged, I made excuses. I didn't come out and tell my husband that I cared more about helping other people than cleaning our house and doing my hair," she says.

[6]It was during her work for social justice that Huerta met Cesar Chavez. Chavez had worked in the California fields picking fruits and vegetables. He knew firsthand how hard it was to stoop over all day, gathering produce in the broiling sun, for just a few dollars. Though farm workers were crucial to the economy, they were treated terribly. They worked with no protection against the dangerous pesticides sprayed on the food they picked. Earning so little money, they were forced to live in shacks with no running water or electricity. Growers sometimes cheated them out of their wages. The farm workers were powerless to fight back.

[7]Huerta teamed up with Cesar Chavez in the early 1960s. "I think we really built on each other's strengths a lot," Huerta says. They worked together to form the National Farm Workers Association (later called the United Farm Workers). As second in command, Huerta led workers on strikes against growers. She organized a **boycott** too. In the boycott, she urged consumers not to buy grapes from growers who would not bargain with workers or protect them. Her efforts led directly to laws that allowed workers to bargain with growers.

[8]Huerta comments, "I think we brought to the world, the United States anyway, the whole idea of boycotting as a nonviolent tactic. I think we showed the world that nonviolence can work to make social change. . . . I think we have laid a pattern of how farm workers are eventually going to get out of their bondage. It may not happen right now in our foreseeable future, but the pattern is there and farm workers are going to make it."

[9]Though she is committed to changing the system with peaceful means, she herself has been the target of brutality. During a protest in 1988, baton-wielding police beat her so severely she was rushed to the emergency room.

wielding police beat her so severely she was rushed to the emergency room. The beating was captured on tape. The tape shows the officer hitting the small, 58-year-old woman with his baton again and again, though she was not threatening him. The officer broke her ribs and ruptured her spleen. Later, she reached a settlement with the police department. In addition to giving her money, they agreed to change their policy about how to control crowds during marches.

[10]Throughout her career, Huerta has worked long hours. Traveling often, she has had to spend much time away from her 11 children. Reflecting on the sacrifices her children have made for her political work, Huerta says, "I guess the political and the work has always come first with me and then I just tried to catch up on the other because I often felt that for every unmade bed and for every unwashed dish some farm worker got one dollar more in wages somewhere."

[11]In fact, Huerta believes that mothers have responsibilities to their children that go beyond cooking dinner and making the bed. In a 2005 editorial, Huerta urged mothers—and their children—to get involved in politics:

> The situation today for children and mothers in America is urgent.
> Asthma and autism rates in some places are up 400%; one of every six American moms has unsafe levels of mercury in their bodies; 200 species become extinct every day; our water, food and air are becoming more toxic instead of less for the first time since 1968; and more children fall into poverty and homelessness each year than ever since the Great Depression.
> Our children's future is bleak unless far more of us act now. Now more than ever is the time to get involved—and get our children involved with us.

[12]At age 75, Dolores Huerta continues her work. "We mothers have to help make the world safer not only for our children, but for other people's children too. Because if all children are not safe, no child is safe."

from A MIGRANT FAMILY

by Larry Dane Brimner

Twelve-year-old Juan Medina and his family live in a camp along a highway in Southern California. They share the camp with 300 other migrant workers. The houses in the camp are, at best, shacks, built with whatever plastic and plywood can be found. Sometimes the shelters are no more than plastic sheets draped over shrubs. The houses have dirt floors, no running water, and no electricity.

[13]As darkness bleeds from the sky, Juan shivers at the 6:00 A.M. chill. The 12-year-old tugs at the blanket, wishing for a little more warmth and a few extra minutes of sleep. But it's no use. The blanket he shares with his brothers, eight-year-old Alejandro and four-year-old Martin, is just as quickly snatched back, so Juan stretches and gives in to another day.

Expedition 14, Lessons 1 and 2

¹⁴Juan Medina is used to getting up with the sun. "Es el reloj de alarma," he explains in Spanish. Then in English he interprets: "Alarm clock." He nods toward a **sliver** of sun peeking above the California hillside and buries his bare hands in his pockets.

¹⁵Juan is a **migrant**. He was born in Mexico, but he has lived in Indiana, Illinois, and Iowa, where his stepfather, Joel Ruiz, has worked on farms. For the last three years, however, Juan and his family have been in California. During the winter and spring, they stay in the coastal community of Encinitas, near San Diego. Juan's stepfather works as a day laborer—someone hired for one day's work at a time—in construction, harvesting flowers, or doing odd jobs. But when it's time to pick melons, tomatoes, and other crops, the family heads north to Fresno, a city in California's great Central Valley.

¹⁶Just as migratory birds fly north or south depending on the season and the weather, migrant farm workers have their own patterns of migration. For these people, it is the promise of earning minimum wages that keeps them on the move. Workers and their families **trek** to *el norte* (the north) as the days grow warmer and the crops reach their peak. There is food to be pulled from the ground or plucked from the trees and vines, and migrant farm workers provide the muscle to do the pulling and the plucking. When a job is done, they move on to the next crop and the next harvest in an annual cycle.

Connect to the Author

Award-winning writer Larry Dane Brimner is the author of more than 120 books for young readers. Born in Florida in 1949, Brimner spent his early years in Alaska. There, without television to keep him entertained, Brimner developed his love of reading and telling stories. In addition to being a writer, Brimner has worked as a waiter, ditch-digger, clothing model, teacher, interior designer, and house builder.

Larry Brimner

250

Comprehension and Vocabulary
Before Reading

Introduce the Expedition

1. Ask students to take a look at their shoes. Then have them imagine that the shoes can talk to them. **Your shoes have an important job to do every day. They show up, whether they want to or not. They work hard. They don't even get paid! How might they describe what they do on a typical day? Let's look at life from a shoe's point of view.**

2. Ask willing students to discuss—from the point of view of their shoes—the work they do and how they feel about it. Allow several students to take turns discussing the work of shoes.

3. **Now let's change the focus from shoes to humans. At any given moment, millions of people are at work in the world. Some—like restaurant cooks or TV reporters—get paid for their work. Others—like homemakers and volunteers—do not get paid.** Ask students to describe jobs they do or have done, paid or unpaid. **What parts of the work did you enjoy? What parts did you not enjoy?**

4. Write *What you do* and *Who you are* on the board. **For some people, their work is *what they do* in order to pay their bills and buy the things they want. For others, their work is both *what they do* and *who they are*, whether they receive payment for it or not. The work expresses their deepest beliefs and hopes. Those are very lucky people. What are some possible examples of this?** (Responses may vary, but could include artists, actors, ministers, doctors, homemakers, or child-care workers.)

5. **In this Expedition, we'll read about the work that some people do and how they feel about it. We'll get a sense of whether the work is *what they do, who they are*, or both. We'll learn how the work has changed their lives and, in some cases, the lives of others.**

6. Have students turn to Anthology page 245. Read the title of the Expedition. Then call on individuals to read aloud each probing question.

> • **How can the work you do make a difference in the world?**
> • **What barriers do people overcome to reach their dreams?**
> • **What dreams do you have for your life's work?**

7. Tell students that they will return to these questions as they learn more about the kinds of work that people do. Show DVD 14.1.

8. After students view the video, have them summarize its main points and recall supporting details. If necessary, prompt students with questions such as the following:

> • **What main message were the people in this video trying to communicate?**
> • **What did they have to say about _____?**
> • **What parts of the video helped illustrate or support this idea?**

Introduce Vocabulary

9. **We will read some new words in this and the next lesson's texts.**

• Write the vocabulary words on the board. Include Challenge Words to meet the needs of students who are advancing.

• Read the words to students.

• Call on individuals to read the words as you point to them.

• Provide correction and feedback as needed.

▶ Have students write the words in the Vocabulary Log.

10. Tell students that knowing the meanings of these words will help them better understand the article.

For each word:

• Read the word with its definition and the sentence that follows.

• Write the sentences on the board.

• Call on students to use their own words to give the meaning and some examples of each vocabulary word.

Vocabulary

falter *to become unsteady; to begin to fall apart*
Dolores's marriage began to *falter* as she became more active in social causes.

boycott *the refusal to buy something as a form of protest*
Huerta organized a *boycott* to force grape growers to treat workers fairly.

sliver *a small, narrow piece of something*
The child needed help in pulling the *sliver* of glass from his foot.

migrant *a person who moves from place to place to get work*
As a *migrant*, Juan travels with his family to pick crops.

trek *to hike or travel*
Workers and their families *trek* northward for the harvest.

Challenge Words

Word Meaning

literally *meaning exactly what is said*
He *literally* won the race by a mile.

crucial *extremely important*
It is *crucial* that we leave by 7:00 if we want to make it to the competition by 9:00.

Introduce Biography

11. **Picture yourself, some years from now, working at the perfect job. Perhaps you're a record producer or a teacher or a professional athlete. Now imagine that you're so amazing at what you do that someone wants to write a story about your life. The story would be a biography.**

12. Write the word *biography* on the board. **SKILL** ✓ **A biography is the story of all or part of someone's life. It's a story written by a person about another person. A biography is different from an autobiography.** Write the word *autobiography* on the board. **In an autobiography, a person writes about his or her own life and experiences. For example, the story "Kipling and I," which we read in Expedition 13, is an autobiography. Now, we'll read a biography of a person whose life's work has helped many others.**

13. Have students turn to Anthology page 246 and preview the text. **Who will this biography be about?** (Dolores Huerta) **What can you tell about Dolores Huerta, based on the photograph?** (Responses will vary.)

Review Narrative and Expository Texts

14. **Biographies tell the stories of people's lives.** **SKILL** ✓

- **What do we call texts that tell stories?** (narratives) Erase *autobiography* from the board, and write *narrative* under *biography*.
- **What are some of the elements of narratives, or stories?** (character, setting, plot) List and bullet these under *narrative*.

15. **Biographies tell stories, but they also give information—not only about the person, but also about the time and place in which the person lives or lived. What kind of text explains or gives information?** (expository) Write *expository* on the board.

16. **Biographies are narrative *and* expository texts. They have some of the elements of each. As we read "Dolores Huerta: Striking for Justice," let's watch for these story elements.** Point to the elements listed on the board. **Let's also think about the kinds of information presented in the text.**

Reading for Understanding
Reading

> **Places and Names to Look For:**
> - Dolores Fernandez Huerta
> - Great Depression
> - New Mexico
> - California
> - Mexican Americans
> - Cesar Chavez
> - National Farm Workers Association

1. **As you read "Dolores Huerta: Striking for Justice," you may come across some unfamiliar places and names.**

- Write the words on the board.
- Point to each word as you read the following:

Born during the *Great Depression*—an economic crisis that occurred in the 1930s—*Dolores Fernandez Huerta* moved with her mother and brothers from *New Mexico* farther west to *California*. After becoming a teacher, Huerta worked with labor leader *Cesar Chavez* through the *National Farm Workers Association* to protect the rights of *Mexican Americans* who were farm workers.

- Call on individuals to read the words.

2. **Fluency** Read aloud the first two paragraphs as students follow along in their books. Then have students read paragraphs 3 through 8 aloud with you. If necessary, review the following fluency goal with students to practice prosody: **As we read aloud, we will use expression and combine words in phrases in a way that sounds like speech. This will show that we understand what we are reading.**

3. Read paragraphs 9 through 12 aloud as students follow along. Use a firm, commanding tone of voice for Dolores Huerta's editorial.

4. Check for literal comprehension of the text by asking these questions after the appropriate paragraph as you read: KNOWLEDGE

- *Paragraph 2:* **What cause has Dolores Huerta dedicated her life to?** (justice for the people who pick our food)

- *Paragraph 4:* **Why was teaching an unsatisfying job for Huerta?** (because she couldn't do anything to help the kids who came to school hungry and barefoot)

- *Paragraph 6:* **What challenges did farm workers face?** (They had to stoop over all day for just a few dollars. They were treated terribly. They had no protection from the pesticides on the crops. They lived in shacks with no water or electricity.)

- *Paragraph 7:* **What group did Huerta form, along with Cesar Chavez?** (the National Farm Workers Association) **What did Huerta do as a leader in this group?** (organized boycotts against growers who would not bargain with workers)

- *Paragraph 11:* **What does Huerta believe all mothers should do?** (get involved in politics to help all children)

Checking for Comprehension *After Reading*

1. Have students turn to Student Book page 185. Read the instructions for section 1 aloud. Then have students work in groups to complete the activity. When all groups are finished, review students' responses as a class. Before discussing item D, point out that the narrative tells about the beginning, middle, and later years of Dolores Huerta's life. Then ask students to give one or two events from each, and list these on the board.

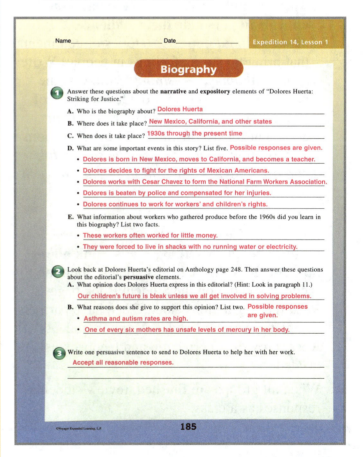

2. Have students turn to the editorial within the text on Anthology page 248. **This biography includes an excerpt from an editorial that Dolores Huerta wrote in 2005. To whom is this message directed?** (American mothers)

3. **In an earlier Expedition, we learned about persuasive texts.**

   • **What is the purpose of a persuasive text?** (to convince someone to believe or do something)

   • **What are some of the elements of a persuasive text?** (opinion statement, supporting reasons, counterarguments, conclusion) List these on the board. Ask students briefly to define each element, providing support as needed.

   • Have students use these elements to make a persuasive argument for playing music in the classroom each day. Provide correction and feedback as necessary.

   • **Authors and speakers also use emotional appeals to persuade their audience. What are emotional appeals?** (stories or comments that bring up strong feelings in people) Write *emotional appeal* → *strong feelings* on the board. Ask students to provide examples of emotional appeals they could add to their argument for playing music in the classroom (for example, *You want us to be successful, and listening to music will inspire us to reach our goals*).

4. **Dolores Huerta's editorial is a persuasive text. In it, Huerta tries to persuade American mothers to do something. Let's think about how she does this.** Direct students' attention to sections 2 and 3 on the Student Book page. Read the instructions aloud. Then have partners complete sections 2 and 3. Monitor students' work, providing correction and feedback as needed.

5. When all groups are finished, review students' responses as a class.

Connect to Science

Use the following activity to help students learn more about pesticide use in the United States.

• Call on individuals who are familiar with the names and uses of common pesticides to describe them as you record the information on the board. Explain that a pesticide is any substance or mixture of substances used to prevent, destroy, or otherwise discourage pests. **Pesticides can be chemicals or biological agents such as bacteria or viruses.**

• Draw a word web on the board with the word *pests* in the center. Have students suggest words or phrases they associate with pests, including examples of pests. (Possible responses: icky, gross, bothersome, scary, bugs, rats, mice, bacteria, viruses)

• Explain that many household products are considered pesticides, such as cockroach sprays, rat poisons, and pet collars.

• Tell students that many of the foods they eat, such as lettuce and apples, contain pesticides even after washing or peeling them unless their food sources are certified to be pesticide-free.

• Draw two columns with the headings *Benefits of Pesticides* and *Risks of Pesticides* on the board. Call on individuals to provide information for each column. (Possible responses: Benefits—They kill disease-causing pests; they control pests; Risks—They can harm the health of humans and animals; they can harm the environment.)

• Arrange students in groups and assign one of these topics to each group: effects of pesticides found in lakes, rivers, and streams; effects of pesticides on children; the pesticide DDT; bugs that resist pesticides; safe use of pesticides; alternatives to pesticides.

• Have each group research its topic and write a brief report on it. Then have students come together as a class to share what they learned.

To increase difficulty: Have students devise a creative way to control pests without the use of harmful pesticides.

Science

Lesson 2

Anthology Selection

Dolores Huerta: STRIKING FOR JUSTICE

United Farm Workers President Arturo Rodriguez, left, and union co-founder Dolores Huerta lead a march to the Capitol in Sacramento, California, in 2002.

[1]Dolores Fernandez Huerta is a living legend.

[2]She's been lionized in songs. She's been memorialized in paintings. She's been arrested more than 20 times and has been beaten almost to death by police. She was one of the most influential labor leaders of the 20th century. And she continues to work for justice in the 21st. Huerta has dedicated her life to the struggle for justice, dignity, and decent working conditions for the men, women, and children who pick the food we eat every day.

[3]Huerta was born in 1930, in the middle of the Great Depression, in a small mining town in northern New Mexico. After her parents divorced, her mother moved Dolores and her two brothers to California. Huerta's mother worked two jobs—literally day and night—to support her children.

[4]After high school, Huerta got her teaching certificate. But she wasn't satisfied teaching. "I realized one day that as a teacher I couldn't do anything for the kids who came to school barefoot and hungry," she says. After only a few months in the classroom, Huerta decided she should fight poverty more directly. She helped found a group to fight for the rights of Mexican Americans.

[5]As she became more active in social and labor organizations, her marriage **faltered**. "I knew I wasn't comfortable in a wife's role, but I wasn't clearly facing the issue. I hedged, I made excuses. I didn't come out and tell my husband that I cared more about helping other people than cleaning our house and doing my hair," she says.

[6]It was during her work for social justice that Huerta met Cesar Chavez. Chavez had worked in the California fields picking fruits and vegetables. He knew firsthand how hard it was to stoop over all day, gathering produce in the broiling sun, for just a few dollars. Though farm workers were crucial to the economy, they were treated terribly. They worked with no protection against the dangerous pesticides sprayed on the food they picked. Earning so little money, they were forced to live in shacks with no running water or electricity. Growers sometimes cheated them out of their wages. The farm workers were powerless to fight back.

[7]Huerta teamed up with Cesar Chavez in the early 1960s. "I think we really built on each other's strengths a lot," Huerta says. They worked together to form the National Farm Workers Association (later called the United Farm Workers). As second in command, Huerta led workers on strikes against growers. She organized a **boycott** too. In the boycott, she urged consumers not to buy grapes from growers who would not bargain with workers or protect them. Her efforts led directly to laws that allowed workers to bargain with growers.

[8]Huerta comments, "I think we brought to the world, the United States anyway, the whole idea of boycotting as a nonviolent tactic. I think we showed the world that nonviolence can work to make social change. . . . I think we have laid a pattern of how farm workers are eventually going to get out of their bondage. It may not happen right now in our foreseeable future, but the pattern is there and farm workers are going to make it."

[9]Though she is committed to changing the system with peaceful means, she herself has been the target of brutality. During a protest in 1988, baton-wielding police beat her so severely she was rushed to the emergency room.

wielding police beat her so severely she was rushed to the emergency room. The beating was captured on tape. The tape shows the officer hitting the small, 58-year-old woman with his baton again and again, though she was not threatening him. The officer broke her ribs and ruptured her spleen. Later, she reached a settlement with the police department. In addition to giving her money, they agreed to change their policy about how to control crowds during marches.

[10]Throughout her career, Huerta has worked long hours. Traveling often, she has had to spend much time away from her 11 children. Reflecting on the sacrifices her children have made for her political work, Huerta says, "I guess the political and the work has always come first with me and then I just tried to catch up on the other because I often felt that for every unmade bed and for every unwashed dish some farm worker got one dollar more in wages somewhere."

[11]In fact, Huerta believes that mothers have responsibilities to their children that go beyond cooking dinner and making the bed. In a 2005 editorial, Huerta urged mothers—and their children—to get involved in politics:

> The situation today for children and mothers in America is urgent.
> Asthma and autism rates in some places are up 400%; one of every six American moms has unsafe levels of mercury in their bodies; 200 species become extinct every day; our water, food and air are becoming more toxic instead of less for the first time since 1968; and more children fall into poverty and homelessness each year than ever since the Great Depression.
> Our children's future is bleak unless far more of us act now. Now more than ever is the time to get involved—and get our children involved with us.

[12]At age 75, Dolores Huerta continues her work. "We mothers have to help make the world safer not only for our children, but for other people's children too. Because if all children are not safe, no child is safe."

from A MIGRANT FAMILY

by Larry Dane Brimner

Twelve-year-old Juan Medina and his family live in a camp along a highway in Southern California. They share the camp with 300 other migrant workers. The houses in the camp are, at best, shacks, built with whatever plastic and plywood can be found. Sometimes the shelters are no more than plastic sheets draped over shrubs. The houses have dirt floors, no running water, and no electricity.

[13]As darkness bleeds from the sky, Juan shivers at the 6:00 A.M. chill. The 12-year-old tugs at the blanket, wishing for a little more warmth and a few extra minutes of sleep. But it's no use. The blanket he shares with his brothers, eight-year-old Alejandro and four-year-old Martin, is just as quickly snatched back, so Juan stretches and gives in to another day.

Expedition 14, Lessons 1 and 2

[14]Juan Medina is used to getting up with the sun. "Es el reloj de alarma," he explains in Spanish. Then in English he interprets: "Alarm clock." He nods toward a **sliver** of sun peeking above the California hillside and buries his bare hands in his pockets.

[15]Juan is a **migrant**. He was born in Mexico, but he has lived in Indiana, Illinois, and Iowa, where his stepfather, Joel Ruiz, has worked on farms. For the last three years, however, Juan and his family have been in California. During the winter and spring, they stay in the coastal community of Encinitas, near San Diego. Juan's stepfather works as a day laborer—someone hired for one day's work at a time—in construction, harvesting flowers, or doing odd jobs. But when it's time to pick melons, tomatoes, and other crops, the family heads north to Fresno, a city in California's great Central Valley.

[16]Just as migratory birds fly north or south depending on the season and the weather, migrant farm workers have their own patterns of migration. For these people, it is the promise of earning minimum wages that keeps them on the move. Workers and their families **trek** to *el norte* (the north) as the days grow warmer and the crops reach their peak. There is food to be pulled from the ground or plucked from the trees and vines, and migrant farm workers provide the muscle to do the pulling and the plucking. When a job is done, they move on to the next crop and the next harvest in an annual cycle.

Connect to the Author

Award-winning writer Larry Dane Brimner is the author of more than 120 books for young readers. Born in Florida in 1949, Brimner spent his early years in Alaska. There, without television to keep him entertained, Brimner developed his love of reading and telling stories. In addition to being a writer, Brimner has worked as a waiter, ditch-digger, clothing model, teacher, interior designer, and house builder.

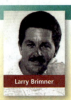

Larry Brimner

250

Comprehension and Vocabulary
Before Reading

1. **In Lesson 1, we read a biography of a woman named Dolores Huerta.**
    - **What has been Dolores Huerta's life's work?** (fighting for rights for farm workers)
    - **What peaceful means has Huerta used to bring about changes for farm workers?** (strikes and boycotts)

2. **Our next reading will give us a close-up look at the lives of farm workers and their families—the people whom Dolores Huerta has devoted her life to helping.**

Vocabulary Review

3. Arrange students with partners, and have them turn to Student Book page 186. Read the instructions aloud. Then call on individuals to read one vocabulary word and to provide a definition for it.

4. Read aloud the first item and model a response. *Sliver* **means "a small, narrow piece of something." So, if I were hungry and ate a small, narrow piece of pizza, I would most likely still be hungry, because a sliver of pizza isn't much food.** Have students write this explanation in their Student Books.

5. Have students work with their partners to discuss and write answers to the remaining items. When all partners are finished, call on students to share their responses.

6. **Challenge Words** Write the following items on the board and have students complete them along with those on the Student Book page.
    - *Have you ever felt so happy that you were <u>literally</u> walking on air? Explain.*
    - *What is the most <u>crucial</u> part of your daily routine? Explain.*

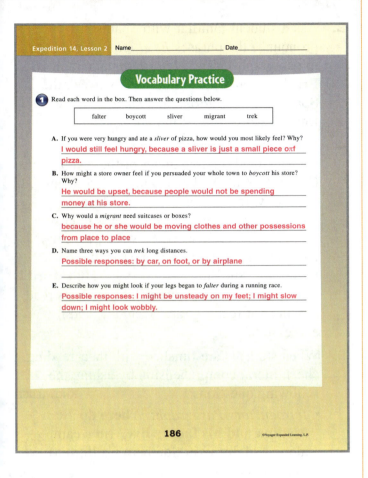

Expedition 14, Lesson 2   Name_____ Date_____

Vocabulary Practice

1   Read each word in the box. Then answer the questions below.

| falter | boycott | sliver | migrant | trek |

A. If you were very hungry and ate a *sliver* of pizza, how would you most likely feel? Why?
I would still feel hungry, because a sliver is just a small piece of pizza.

B. How might a store owner feel if you persuaded your whole town to *boycott* his store? Why?
He would be upset, because people would not be spending money at his store.

C. Why would a *migrant* need suitcases or boxes?
because he or she would be moving clothes and other possessions from place to place

D. Name three ways you can *trek* long distances.
Possible responses: by car, on foot, or by airplane

E. Describe how you might look if your legs began to *falter* during a running race.
Possible responses: I might be unsteady on my feet; I might slow down; I might look wobbly.

186   ©Voyager Expanded Learning, L.P.

Extending Vocabulary

Word Building

- Write *migrant* on the board.
- Have students scan the last paragraph of the excerpt from *A Migrant Family* to find two words that are similar to *migrant*. (migratory, migration) Write these words on the board. **Let's see how we can use the meaning of the word *migrant* to figure out the meanings of *migratory* and *migration*.**
- **You will soon read about a boy who is a migrant. What does the word *migrant* mean?** (a person who moves from place to place to find work) **Based on that, what do you think *migratory* and *migration* mean? Here are some hints: *migratory* is an adjective, a word that describes something or someone; *migration* is a noun, a word that names something.** (migratory: moving from place to place; migration: a movement from one place to another place)
- Write students' responses on the board and discuss the words' meanings. **If you wrote a paper about *migratory* birds, what behavior would you describe in the paper?** (birds flying north or south with weather changes) **If you photographed a buffalo *migration*, what would the picture show?** (buffalo moving from one place to another)
► Have students write *migratory* and *migration,* and their meanings, in the Vocabulary Log.

Reading for Understanding

Reading

Places and Names to Look For:
- Juan Medina
- Alejandro
- Joel Ruiz
- Encinitas
- San Diego
- Fresno

1. Have students turn to Anthology page 249. **As you read this story from *A Migrant Family*, you may come across some unfamiliar places and names.**

   - Write the words on the board.
   - Point to each word as you read the following:

   You will read about a boy named *Juan Medina*, who—with his brothers, *Alejandro* and Martin, and stepfather *Joel Ruiz*— travels around the United States to pick crops for a living. Juan was born in Mexico and still speaks Spanish but has learned English as well, from having lived in places such as Indiana, Illinois, and Iowa. The migrant family spends part of the year in *Encinitas*, near *San Diego*, California. When crops are ready to be picked farther north, the family heads to *Fresno*, in the Central Valley.

   - Call on individuals to read the words.

2. Read the introductory text aloud. Then call on a student to restate the situation. (Possible response: Juan and his family live with 300 other people in a camp for workers in California. Their houses are shacks made of plastic or plywood. The floors are dirt. There's no running water or electricity. Sometimes their houses are plastic sheets hung over bushes.)

3. Ask a student familiar with Spanish to pronounce the phrases *Es el reloj de alarma* in paragraph 14 and *el norte* in paragraph 16. Briefly discuss the similarities between the Spanish words *alarma* and *norte*, and the English words *alarm* and *north*.

4. Read the first paragraph aloud. Then have students read the remainder of the text and the Connect to the Author feature independently. If necessary, review the following fluency correction procedure with students to ensure accuracy: **Offer help when your partner comes to an unfamiliar word or makes a reading error. Pause, then say, "That word is _____. Let's read it again."** As students read, monitor for reading rate, accuracy, and expression.

5. When students are finished with their reading, check literal comprehension by asking the following questions: KNOWLEDGE

   - *Introductory Paragraph:* **Where do Juan Medina and his family live?** (in a camp along a highway in Southern California)
   - *Paragraph 15:* **What does Juan's stepfather do for a living?** (He is a day laborer. He does farm work, construction work, or odd jobs.)
   - *Paragraph 16:* **What keeps migrant workers moving from place to place?** (the hope of earning minimum wage)
   - *Connect to the Author:* **Why did Brimner develop a love of reading and storytelling?** (While living in Alaska, he did not have TV to keep him entertained.)

Checking for Comprehension *After Reading*

1. Have students apply what they understood from the text by asking the following questions:

   - **Why do you think the author wrote this text?** ANALYSIS (to describe the life of a migrant family)

   - **Is the text narrative, expository, or both? How do you know?** COMPREHENSION (both, because it gives information while telling a story)

   - **As you read about Juan and his family, what feelings did you have about their life?** ANALYSIS (Possible responses: I felt sad that they had to work so hard and travel so much; I felt angry that they didn't have a proper house and better living conditions.)

2. **Challenge Questions Does the text about Juan Medina help you better understand why Dolores Huerta has devoted her life to helping migrants? How?** SYNTHESIS (Possible response: Yes, because it tells about the harsh conditions under which migrants live.) **What problem in today's world do you feel passionately about?** APPLICATION (Responses will vary.)

3. **This text uses descriptive details to bring to life a particular scene. These details help you picture Juan's life.** Write *descriptive text* on the board. **Writers often use descriptive details to capture readers' attention and help them picture a scene.**

4. **When we discussed descriptive writing in an earlier Expedition, we learned about two different kinds of details.**

   - **What were the two kinds of details?** (concrete and sensory) Write *concrete details* and *sensory details* on the board.

   - **What are concrete details?** (They are details that describe something in clear, vivid language.)

   - **What are sensory details?** (They are details that appeal to one or more of the five senses.)

5. Have students work with a partner to locate one detail in the text that creates a powerful picture in their minds. When all pairs have finished, ask each to share their details with the class. Discuss whether each detail is concrete or sensory, and what feelings each detail calls up in the reader.

Connect to the Author

Discuss the following questions with the class:

- **Why do you think Larry Dane Brimner makes sure to explain Spanish phrases, the work of a day laborer, and the pattern of migration for families such as Juan's?** (so that the reader can more fully understand the life and culture the author is describing)

- **If you could visit Dolores Huerta, what questions would you like to ask her?** (Responses will vary.)

Listening and Speaking Have students write their questions for Dolores Huerta and take turns role-playing interviews with her. As students conduct their interviews, ask them to listen closely to their partner's words and also to pay close attention to his or her body language. Encourage them to respond to both the spoken messages and the unspoken messages with appropriate follow-up statements or questions, such as *You seem to feel strongly about the problems farm workers endure. What else can you tell me about this issue?* Monitor student interviews for appropriate responses to verbal and nonverbal cues, providing additional modeling or feedback when needed.

Reading Response

Have students turn to Student Book page 187. Read the instructions aloud. Then have students use the information about Dolores Huerta and the text about Juan Medina to answer these questions:

 What is Dolores Huerta trying to do? Why is she trying to do it?

Students may work with partners or small groups. When students have completed their responses, call on individuals to read their news reports aloud.

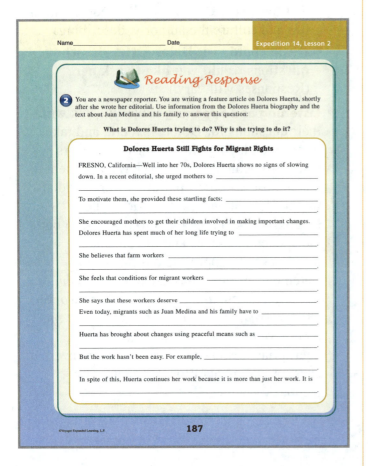

Name_____ Date_____ Expedition 14, Lesson 2

Reading Response

2 You are a newspaper reporter. You are writing a feature article on Dolores Huerta, shortly after she wrote her editorial. Use information from the Dolores Huerta biography and the text about Juan Medina and his family to answer this question:

What is Dolores Huerta trying to do? Why is she trying to do it?

Dolores Huerta Still Fights for Migrant Rights

FRESNO, California—Well into her 70s, Dolores Huerta shows no signs of slowing down. In a recent editorial, she urged mothers to _____

To motivate them, she provided these startling facts: _____

She encouraged mothers to get their children involved in making important changes. Dolores Huerta has spent much of her long life trying to _____

She believes that farm workers _____

She feels that conditions for migrant workers _____

She says that these workers deserve _____

Even today, migrants such as Juan Medina and his family have to _____

Huerta has brought about changes using peaceful means such as _____

But the work hasn't been easy. For example, _____

In spite of this, Huerta continues her work because it is more than just her work. It is _____

©Voyager Expanded Learning, L.P.

187

Passport Reading Journeys Library

Building Fluency

1. Place students in pairs according to reading level to build fluency. When pairing students, be sure that one student is a stronger reader (Student A) than the other student (Student B). However, do not reveal that stronger readers are paired with weaker readers. See *Passport Reading Journeys* Library Teacher's Guide for grouping guidelines.

2. Have students quickly choose reading material from the *Passport Reading Journeys* Library or another approved selection that is at the reading level of Student B. If students have not finished the previously chosen selection, they may continue reading from that selection. See *Passport Reading Journeys* Library Teacher's Guide for material selection guidelines.

3. Tell students that Student A will read one paragraph, and Student B will reread that same paragraph.

4. Have students follow this routine until the end of class.

5. If necessary, review the following practices to enhance fluency:
   • Rate and accuracy of reading
   • Expression during reading
   • Correction procedures

Library Highlights

Content Connection

Kids Discover: Moon provides scientific information about the moon through pictures, illustrations, and charts. A bibliography lists books about the moon for additional reading.

Level II

Advanced Word Study

Multisyllabic Words

1. **Remember, sometimes it's easier to read parts of a longer word before reading the entire word. One way is to use what we know about prefixes and suffixes.** Write *impossible* on the board. Underline the prefix *im-*. **What is this prefix?** (im-) Underline *poss*. **What is the next word part?** (poss) Underline the suffix *-ible*. **What is this suffix?** (-ible) **What is the word?** (impossible) **The word** *impossible* **means "not possible or not practical."**

   Another way to read longer words is to use what we know about open and closed syllables. Write *fantastic* on the board. Underline the word part *fan*. **What is the first word part?** (fan) **What kind of syllable is this word part?** (closed) **How do we know?** (It has one short vowel sound followed by one or more consonants.) **What short sound does the vowel make?** (/a/) Underline the word part *tas*. **What kind of syllable is this word part?** (closed) **How do we know?** (It has one short vowel followed by one or more consonants.) Underline the word part *-tic*. **Read the rest of the word.** (tic) **What is the word?** (fantastic) **The word** *fantastic* **means "great or excellent."**

2. Have students turn to Student Book page E14, Lesson 3. Direct students to line 1. **What is the first word part?** (met) **What is the next word part?** (ic) **What is the next word part?** (u) **What is the suffix?** (-lous) **What is the word?** (meticulous) **The word** *meticulous* **means "careful or thorough."** Repeat with the remaining words. Call on individuals to read the words in random order. Ask students to tell the meanings of the words.

3. Direct students to lines 2 and 3. Have them read the words. Then call on individuals to read the words in a different order. Ask students to tell the meanings of the words.

   ▼ **To Correct**
   For Multisyllabic Words: **What is the first word part? What is the next part? What is the word?** If students do not know the meaning of the word, review the word and/or word parts to determine the meaning of the word.

For Sounds in Words: Tell students the correct sound(s), then ask them to repeat the sound(s). Have students read the word again with the correct sound(s). If students do not know the meaning of the word, review the word and/or word parts to determine the meaning of the word.

1. meticulous	communicate	majority	customers
2. personally	schoolwork	sanitizing	waitresses
3. straightforward	demonstrating	garnish	carnivals

Sight Words

1. Direct students to line 1. Have them point to the first word. **This word is** *instance*. **Read the word.** (instance) **This is not a regular word. Let's read the word again.** (instance) **Let's spell the word.** (i-n-s-t-a-n-c-e) **What is the word?** (instance) Repeat with the remaining words. Then have students read the words. Ask students to tell the meanings of the words.

2. Direct students to lines 2 and 3. **Let's read these words.** Remind students that the rows of words consist of regular and irregular words. Point to the first word. **What is the word?** (urgent) Repeat with the remaining words. Call on individuals to read the words in a different order. Ask students to tell the meanings of the words.

   ▼ **To Correct**
   For Regular Words: Say the sound(s) in the word, then ask students to repeat the sound(s). Have them read the word again with the correct sound(s). If students do not know the meaning of the word, review the word and/or word part to determine the meaning of the word.

   For Irregular Words: Immediately say the correct word. Then have students read the word, spell it, and read it again. If students do not know the meaning of the word, review the word.

1. instance I	obey I	mayonnaise I	ritual I
2. urgent I	hostess I	threaten I	immortalize R
3. muscle I	measurement I	lionize I	hospital R

Anthology Selection

from Gig, Americans Talk About Their Jobs

To create the book Gig, *interviewers sat down with several dozen Americans and asked them about their jobs. They taped the interviews, transcribed them, and then cut them down to create personal essays. In this essay, Kysha Lewin describes her job at McDonald's.*

251

McDonald's Crew Member Kysha Lewin

¹I'm 16 and a half. I go to Red Bank Regional High School in Little Silver, New Jersey. I'm in tenth grade. Last year I decided I needed a job because it's like only my mom, you know? She's trying to take care of the bills, and it's hard for her. So I don't get allowance, and I'm still a child, I want to have fun, to go out, not just sit on the porch crying. So when I turned fifteen, I decided that I wanted to work. I heard that McDonald's would hire you at fifteen and I came and talked to the managers.

²They asked what kind of things you do—do you communicate with people well? Are you good at talking to them, understanding what they're saying? You know? They asked me do I like kids because they wanted me to do birthday parties for little kids. I'm like the hostess sometimes. And I love kids. And I guess they liked me, because they hired me.

³It was kind of difficult at first. I had to get to know the register, to listen and concentrate on what the person's ordering and then find the buttons on the board—it took me like two days or so to really get to understand it. But everybody was very relaxed, kinda like, "It's just gonna take you some time to get used to it." They were very patient with me, even the customers were patient. And now it's a breeze. I just pick up stuff easily. I'm a good listener, a person that loves to follow directions.

⁴The only real thing with this job is you have to make sure you're always busy. Because McDonald's is always busy. Make sure everything is stocked, cleaned—if you don't have a customer to serve, maybe somebody else has a customer, try to help them out, back them up, get the food, you know? Look at the screen on their register and see what food they don't already have. Go get it. Work together.

⁵They have a lot of rules, but it's not like rule crazy. . . . It's really pretty straightforward, like with the balloon situation—we just always have to make sure there's balloons in the lobby 'cause, you know, we want to make the kids happy. And we have to sweep and mop every hour. And we have this thing, it's like a timer, and when it goes off, everybody in the place has to go and **sanitize** their hands. There's like a liquid that you rub on that dries off real quick. You have to make sure you go do that or you get in trouble.

252

---

⁶The other rules are basically you have to be on time, you have to stock, clean up, help out. They also have a rule for fries. You have to be sixteen to make fries. If you're fifteen you can only stuff 'em, you can't pick 'em up outta the fryer. I think it's a dumb rule—I mean, what are we supposed to do if it gets busy and there's nobody at the fries but you and you're fifteen? Sit and wait? Then the customer gets mad. Dumb rule, but whatever. Now I'm sixteen, so I make fries sometimes. I just started doing that. . . .

⁷Some of the customers can be friendly, some can just have an attitude, and some try to make you a fool. I've seen it many a time. Like, for instance, I was working the drive-through and the guy said he was missing his fries, right? So I gave him a fry. He came back into McDonald's and told the manager that he was missing his fries. He was trying to just get another fry for free. I went and told the manager. I don't know why they think they can get over like that. These people are crazy. They say the customer is always right, but personally, me, I don't let 'em get away with that. It makes me mad. I mean, it's costing the boss money and if he loses money then we lose money because we lose our hours and I can't have that.

⁸I work about twenty hours a week, after school and weekends. When I turned sixteen they wanted me to take more hours but my mom didn't want me to mess up my school. So I just stayed around twenty. With schoolwork, I guess it's a lot. But I got God in my life, I have a lot of faith, I'm not tired. I'm young and have a lot of energy.

⁹I make five-fifteen an hour and I give my mother about half of my check because it helps. I mean, I live with my eleven-year-old brother, my four-year-old sister, and my eight-month-old baby sister and we get along real well, but my mother works hard. I see how hard. . . .

¹⁰I got a lot of friends here. They're real cool to talk to, chill with, go out with. There's turnover—some people aren't used to working and they get lazy or they don't come to work and get fired, or if they don't obey the rules they have to go—but still, the majority of my friends work here. And cute boys come through the drive-through and flirt. Like you catch their eye or whatever and they ask you for your phone number. [Laughs] I don't ever give out my number. I ask them for theirs, and I decide if I want to call them or not. I'm not giving my number 'cause eehhhhh, you know, some people

253

---

like to play on the phone and some boys are just disgusting. But it's nice sometimes. It makes me happy.

¹¹I know work won't be fun my whole life. 'Cause work is not always about fun and games. There comes a time when you have to be serious about what you're doing, you know? . . .

¹²But I'll always be grateful to McDonald's, you know? The majority of people I know first started here or some other kind of fast-food place before they got to a good job, a better job. I'd like to do something with hair or maybe clothes. Or I want to get a job working in the hospital—in the nursery with the little babies. I love little kids. I can't wait till I get older so I can have kids. I adore my sisters and my brothers, spoil them. So I'd like the hospital. But whatever happens, a year from now, I'm gonna have a better job. I have a lot of confidence in myself. There's nothing I can't do. I'm fine.

Connect to the Author

About 40 interviewers contributed to *Gig.* One of the interviewers was John Bowe, who also is an editor of the book. Bowe traveled around the country talking to a wide variety of people, including a carnival worker in Appalachia, a supermodel between flights at an airport, and truck drivers at a truck stop in Wyoming. The editors of the book wanted Americans to speak for themselves. "Our goal was to take accurate snapshots, person by person, of work as it is today in this country," writes Marisa Bowe, John's sister, another of the book's editors. "We were very moved by the wholehearted diligence that people bring to their work."

254

from

Keeping the Moon

by Sarah Dessen

Fifteen-year-old Colie Sparks is a loner. When her glamorous, outgoing mother leaves for Europe, Colie is forced to spend the summer with her oddball aunt Mira in the seaside town of Colby, South Carolina. There, Colie finds a job at the Last Chance Café. Her coworkers, Morgan and Isabel, teach her the ropes.

[13] "Mayonnaise," Morgan said, "is a lot like men."

[14] It was nine-thirty in the morning on my first day of work, but I'd been up since six. I kept thinking Morgan would forget me or change her mind but at nine-fifteen she pulled up in front of Mira's steps and beeped her horn, just as we'd planned.

[15] The restaurant was empty except for us and the radio, tuned to an oldies station. "Twisting the Night Away" was playing, and we were making salad dressing, both of us up to our elbows in thick, smelly mayonnaise.

[16] "It can," she went on, plopping another scoop into the bowl, "make everything much better, adding flavor and ease to your life. Or, it can just be sticky and gross and make you nauseous."

[17] I smiled, stirring my mayonnaise while I considered this. "I hate mayonnaise."

[18] "You'll probably hate men too, from time to time," she said. "At least mayonnaise you can avoid."

[19] This was the way Morgan taught. Not in instructions, but pronouncements. Everything was a lesson.

255

[20] "Lettuce," she announced later, pulling a head out of the plastic bag in front of us, "should be leafy, not slimy. And no black or brown edges. We use lettuce on everything: garnish, salads, burgers. A bad piece of lettuce can ruin your whole day."

[21] "Right," I said.

[22] "Chop it like this," she instructed, taking a few whacks with a knife before handing it to me. "Big chops, but not too big."

[23] I chopped. She watched. "Good," she said, reaching over to adjust my chops just a bit. I went on. "Very good."

[24] Morgan was this meticulous about everything. Preparing dressings was a **ritual**, every measurement carefully checked. Isabel, on the other hand, dumped it all in at once, knocked a spoon around, and came up with the same results, dipping in a finger and licking it to double-check.

[25] But Morgan had her own way.

[26] "Peel carrots away from you," she said, demonstrating, "and cut off the ends about a quarter inch each. When feeding them into the processor, pause about every five seconds. It gives a finer shred."

[27] I peeled, chopped, and stocked. I learned the perfect, **symmetrical** way to stack coffee cups and sugar packets, to fold rags at a right angle against flat surfaces, clean side up. Morgan kept the counter area spick-and-span, each element in its place. When she was nervous, she went around correcting things.

[28] "Take-out boxes on the *left*, cup lids on the *right*," she'd shout, slamming them around as she restored order to her universe. "And spoons are handle side *up*, Isabel."

[29] "Yeah, yeah," Isabel would say. When she was mad or just bored she purposely rearranged things just to see how long it took Morgan to find them. It was like a passive-aggressive treasure hunt.

[30] That first lunch, when Norman and I had stopped to pitch in, was a constant blur of people and noise and food. Everyone was screaming at each other, Isabel and Morgan running past with orders, Norman flipping burgers and yelling things to Bick, the other cook, who stayed stonily quiet and cool the entire time. I shoveled ice like my life depended on it, answered the phone and took orders although I knew almost nothing about the menu, and messed up the register so badly it stuck on $10,000.00 and beeped for fifteen minutes straight before Isabel, in a fit of rage, whacked it with a plastic water

256

pitcher. It was Us against Them, clearly, and for once I was part of Us. I didn't really know what I was doing; I had to go on faith. So I just handed out my drinks and grabbed the phone when it screamed, wrapping the cord around my wrist and stabbing the pen Morgan had tossed me in my hair, the same way Isabel wore hers, and fought on.

[31] "Last Chance," I'd shout over the din. "Can I help you?"

[32] And now, I was doing it every day.

[33] At first, just walking up to a table full of strangers had scared me to death. I couldn't even make eye contact, stuttering through the basic questions Morgan had taught me—*What would you like to drink? Have you decided? How would you like that cooked? Fries or hush puppies?*—my hand literally shaking as it moved across my order pad. It made me nervous to stand there so exposed, all of those people *looking* at me.

[34] But then, on about my third table, I finally got the nerve to glance up and realized that, basically, they *weren't*. For the most part, they were flipping through the menu, **extracting** Sweet'N Low packets from their toddler's grip, or so lost in their own conversation that I didn't even register: twenty minutes later they'd be flagging Isabel down, sure *she* was the one with their check. They didn't know or care about me. To them, I was just a waitress, a girl with an apron and a tea pitcher; they didn't even seem to notice my lip ring. And that was fine with me.

Connect to the Author

Sarah Dessen drew from her own experiences as a waitress to write *Keeping the Moon*. Dessen, who was born in 1970, worked as a waitress during college. Though she graduated with top honors, she continued to wait tables rather than find a corporate job. It gave her the time she needed to write. It also gave her a lot of material. For example, when a woman slapped Dessen's hand as she tried to remove her empty plate, Dessen immortalized her in a book as a bitter, nasty character. "I've learned that writing well can be the best revenge," Dessen says. Two of Dessen's novels were adapted into the 2003 movie *How to Deal*. In addition to writing novels, Dessen now teaches at her alma mater, UNC Chapel Hill.

Sarah Dessen

257

Comprehension and Vocabulary
Before Reading

1. In this Expedition, we're exploring the meaning of work in our lives. As we read, we're discovering that the work we do can become an expression of who we are—whether we're fighting for farm worker rights or serving food to customers.

2. The last text we read described a type of worker and his family. What was this job? (migrant work—picking crops) Before that, we read about a woman who has devoted her life to helping a particular group of people. Who is the woman, and what is her cause? (Dolores Huerta; her cause is improving conditions for farm workers)

3. Both texts that we've read so far in this Expedition focus on one aspect of feeding people: harvesting the fruit and vegetables we eat. Do you think that reading about the lives of Dolores Huerta and Juan Medina might affect how you feel the next time you eat an apple or a tomato? How so? (Possible responses: I might think about the hard work that goes into harvesting fruits and vegetables; I might picture Juan Medina picking the apple.)

4. In our next readings, we'll meet two young women who are also in the business of feeding people: both work at restaurants. Can you picture yourself waiting on customers at a restaurant? What do you think you'd enjoy about the work? What would you *not* enjoy about it? (Responses will vary.)

Introduce Vocabulary

5. We will read some new words in this and the next lesson's texts.
   - Write the vocabulary words on the board. Include Challenge Words to meet the needs of students who are advancing.
   - Read the words to students.

   - Call on individuals to read the words as you point to them.
   - Provide correction and feedback as needed.

   ▶ Have students write the words in the Vocabulary Log.

6. Tell students that knowing the meanings of these words will help them better understand the article.

   For each word:
   - Read the word with its definition and the sentence that follows.
   - Write the sentences on the board.
   - Call on students to use their own words to give the meaning and some examples of each vocabulary word.
   - For the Word Building Challenge Word, have students identify the base word (scribe), then guide them in determining how the base word can help them figure out the meaning of the larger words.

Vocabulary

sanitize *to clean thoroughly*
Restaurant employees must *sanitize* their hands often.

ritual *a set way of doing something*
Some workers use a certain *ritual* for completing their tasks.

symmetrical *each part having the same form or shape*
The plates were arranged in *symmetrical* stacks.

extract *to pull out or draw out*
The mother had to *extract* the toy from her toddler's grip.

Challenge Words

Word Building

transcribe *scribe, scribble, script, prescription, postscript*

Multiple Meaning

register *a machine that adds prices, records sales, and stores money*
To work in a clothing store, you must learn how to use a *register*.
to sign up for something, such as a class
If you want to *register* for karate camp, please fill out this form.

Introduce Interviews

7. Have students turn to Anthology page 251. Read the title and the introductory paragraph aloud.

- **What was the first step in creating the book *Gig*?** (Interviewers asked people about their jobs and taped their answers.)
- **Have you ever interviewed someone** **or been interviewed? If so, briefly tell how an interview works.** (Possible response: I wrote down questions to ask another person. When I asked the questions, I wrote down the person's answers.)

8. Write the following on the board:

Q: What has been your favorite job?

A: Washing elephants at a zoo

Have you ever seen this format for an interview? It's common in magazines and on Web sites. What does *Q* stand for? (question) **What does *A* stand for?** (answer) **This is called the question-and-answer, or *Q-and-A*, format.**

9. After the interviews were completed, what were the next steps in creating *Gig*? (The interviews were transcribed, cut down to create essays, and put together in a book.) Write the word *transcribe* on the board. **Who can guess the meaning of *transcribe* by looking at the parts of the word?** Allow time for student responses. *Transcribe* **means "to write out or type out." First, the editors wrote out what was said in each recorded interview— possibly in Q-and-A format. Then they shaped each interview into an essay.**

Review First-Person Narratives

10. Direct students' attention to the first paragraph of the essay, and read it aloud.

- **From whose point of view is this essay written?** (the worker's—Kysha Lewin)
- **What words in this paragraph are clues to the point of view?** (I, my)
- **What do we call this point of view?** (first person)

11. Have students scan the essay. **How is the format of this text different from the Q-and-A format on the board?** (It uses paragraphs instead of questions and answers that begin with *Q* and *A*; the questions aren't shown.) **All the words in the essay belong to Kysha Lewin. It's her story, told in her own words.**

Reading for Understanding   *Reading*

> **Places and Names to Look For:**
> • Kysha Lewin
> • Red Bank Regional High School
> • Little Silver, New Jersey

1. **As you read this essay, you may come across some unfamiliar places and names.**
   - Write the words on the board.
   - Point to each word as you read the following:

   In this essay, you will hear from *Kysha Lewin*, who attends *Red Bank Regional High School* and works at a McDonald's restaurant in *Little Silver, New Jersey*. When Kysha turned 15 years old, she decided to go to work to help her mother pay the bills. Kysha describes her early days on the job and tells why she enjoys her work.
   - Call on individuals to read the words.

2. **As we read this essay, try to get a feel for the "voice" behind it. Notice the things that matter to Kysha. Are they the same things that matter to you? Be alert for places in the essay where you find yourself thinking, "Yeah, I know how that feels." or "I feel differently about that."**

3. **Fluency** Read aloud the first two paragraphs as students follow along in their books. Then have partners read paragraphs 3 through 12, as well as the Connect to the Author feature, taking turns reading each paragraph. If necessary, review the following fluency correction procedure with students to ensure accuracy: **Offer help when your partner comes to an unfamiliar word or makes a reading error. Pause, then say, "That word is _____. Let's read it again."** As students read, monitor for reading rate, accuracy, and expression.

4. When students have completed their reading, check for literal comprehension of the text by asking these questions: KNOWLEDGE
   - *Paragraph 2:* **What is Kysha's job?** (She works at McDonald's.)
   - *Paragraph 3:* **What part of the job was difficult for Kysha at first?** (learning to use the cash register while taking people's orders)
   - *Paragraphs 4, 5, and 6:* **What are some of the rules Kysha has to follow at McDonald's?** (Possible responses: making sure you're always busy; keeping balloons in the lobby; sweeping and mopping every hour; washing your hands; being on time; stocking; cleaning up and helping others; having to be 16 to make fries)
   - *Paragraph 7:* **What does Kysha dislike about her job?** (dealing with some of the customers who have attitudes or try to get food for free)
   - *Paragraphs 8 and 9:* **How much does Kysha work?** (about 20 hours a week) **What does she do with her money?** (gives half of it to her mother to help with family expenses)
   - *Paragraph 10:* **What does Kysha like about her job?** (She likes her coworkers and she gets attention from boys.)
   - *Paragraph 12:* **What plans does Kysha have for her future?** (She would like to work with hair or clothes, or in a hospital, or with children.)

Checking for Comprehension *After Reading*

1. Direct students' attention to the first paragraph of the essay, and read the first four sentences aloud. **These sentences—especially the fourth one—sound like spoken language. Which part of the fourth sentence especially sounds like spoken language?** (Possible response: *. . . because it's like only my mom, you know?*)

2. Arrange students with partners, and assign each pair one paragraph from the essay, beginning with paragraph 2. Then have them do the following:
   • Find one phrase or expression in the paragraph that sounds like spoken language.
   • Compose a question that Kysha seems to be answering in the paragraph—one that may have been used in the original Q-and-A format.

3. When all students are finished, have partners read their question aloud, summarize how Kysha answers it in the paragraph, and then identify a word or phrase that sounds spoken. Move sequentially through the essay.

Connect to the Author

Direct students' attention to the Connect to the Author feature on Anthology page 254, and read the feature aloud. Explain that *diligence* means "dedication and effort." Then discuss these questions with the class:
• **Would you enjoy helping to create a book such as *Gig*? Why?**
• **Which part of this job would you most enjoy—writing interview questions, asking the questions, transcribing the interview, or shaping the transcribed interviews into essays? Why?**
• **The editors of *Gig* decided to stay behind the scenes and let the workers speak for themselves in the book. Do you think the decision to produce first-person texts was a good idea? Why?**
• **After reading the essay about Kysha Lewin, would you want to read the rest of the book *Gig*? Why?**

Connect to Careers

Use the following activity to help students examine jobs as food preparation workers.

- Take a poll of types of food service jobs students would prefer to do. Call on individuals to explain their preferences.
- Point out that many young people work as food preparation workers, part time or full time. These jobs are often available because of the frequent turnover. Young people experience conflicts with school schedules, transfer to higher-paying jobs, or quit for personal reasons.
- Explain that food preparation workers help prepare a variety of foods for chefs and cooks in various types of food service establishments. Point out that duties of a food preparation worker might include:
  – getting ingredients ready for a chef or cook
  – slicing vegetables
  – washing or peeling foods
  – measuring ingredients
  – cleaning the work areas
- Have students brainstorm skills that might be required of food preparation workers. List these on the board. (Possible responses: ability to listen well and follow directions, cooperating with others, working well under pressure)
- Distribute one blank "sticky note" to each student. Ask students to write the name of a well-known local restaurant or fast-food establishment on their note. Then, without showing the note to others, have students place the note on the back of another student. Tell students that they are food preparation workers at the restaurant written on their back.
- Have students circulate around the room and try to guess which restaurant they work for, based on other students' comments.

To increase difficulty: Have students contact managers of local food establishments to learn about the duties and wages of food preparation workers there.

Careers

Lesson 4

Anthology Selection

Language Arts

from Gig, Americans Talk About Their Jobs

To create the book Gig, interviewers sat down with several dozen Americans and asked them about their jobs. They taped the interviews, transcribed them, and then cut them down to create personal essays. In this essay, Kysha Lewin describes her job at McDonald's.

251

McDonald's Crew Member Kysha Lewin

¹I'm 16 and a half. I go to Red Bank Regional High School in Little Silver, New Jersey. I'm in tenth grade. Last year I decided I needed a job because it's like only my mom, you know? She's trying to take care of the bills, and it's hard for her. So I don't get allowance, and I'm still a child, I want to have fun, to go out, not just sit on the porch crying. So when I turned fifteen, I decided that I wanted to work. I heard that McDonald's would hire you at fifteen and I came and talked to the managers.

²They asked what kind of things you do—do you communicate with people well? Are you good at talking to them, understanding what they're saying? You know? They asked me do I like kids because they wanted me to do birthday parties for little kids. I'm like the hostess sometimes. And I love kids. And I guess they liked me, because they hired me.

³It was kind of difficult at first. I had to get to know the register, to listen and concentrate on what the person's ordering and then find the buttons on the board—it took me like two days or so to really get to understand it. But everybody was very relaxed, kinda like, "It's just gonna take you some time to get used to it." They were very patient with me, even the customers were patient. And now it's a breeze. I just pick up stuff easily. I'm a good listener, a person that loves to follow directions.

⁴The only real thing with this job is you have to make sure you're always busy. Because McDonald's is always busy. Make sure everything is stocked, cleaned—if you don't have a customer to serve, maybe somebody else has a customer, try to help them out, back them up, get the food, you know? Look at the screen on their register and see what food they don't already have. Go get it. Work together.

⁵They have a lot of rules, but it's not like rule crazy. . . . It's really pretty straightforward, like with the balloon situation—we just always have to make sure there's balloons in the lobby 'cause, you know, we want to make the kids happy. And we have to sweep and mop every hour. And we have this thing, it's like a timer, and when it goes off, everybody in the place has to go and **sanitize** their hands. There's like a liquid that you rub on that dries off real quick. You have to make sure you go do that or you get in trouble.

252

⁶The other rules are basically you have to be on time, you have to stock, clean up, help out. They also have a rule for fries. You have to be sixteen to make fries. If you're fifteen you can only stuff 'em, you can't pick 'em up outta the fryer. I think it's a dumb rule—I mean, what are we supposed to do if it gets busy and there's nobody at the fries but you and you're fifteen? Sit and wait? Then the customer gets mad. Dumb rule, but whatever. Now I'm sixteen, so I make fries sometimes. I just started doing that. . . .

⁷Some of the customers can be friendly, some can just have an attitude, and some try to make you a fool. I've seen it many a time. Like, for instance, I was working the drive-through and the guy said he was missing his fries, right? So I gave him a fry. He came back into McDonald's and told the manager that he was missing his fries. He was trying to just get another fry for free. I went and told the manager. I don't know why they think they can get over like that. These people are crazy. They say the customer is always right, but personally, me, I don't let 'em get away with that. It makes me mad. I mean, it's costing the boss money and if he loses money then we lose money because we lose our hours and I can't have that.

⁸I work about twenty hours a week, after school and weekends. When I turned sixteen they wanted me to take more hours but my mom didn't want me to mess up my school. So I just stayed around twenty. With schoolwork, I guess it's a lot. But I got God in my life, I have a lot of faith, I'm not tired. I'm young and have a lot of energy.

⁹I make five-fifteen an hour and I give my mother about half of my check because it helps. I mean, I live with my eleven-year-old brother, my four-year-old sister, and my eight-month-old baby sister and we get along real well, but my mother works hard. I see how hard. . . .

¹⁰I got a lot of friends here. They're real cool to talk to, chill with, go out with. There's turnover—some people aren't used to working and they get lazy or they don't come to work and get fired, or if they don't obey the rules they have to go—but still, the majority of my friends work here. And cute boys come through the drive-through and flirt. Like you catch their eye or whatever and they ask you for your phone number. [Laughs] I don't ever give out my number. I ask them for theirs, and I decide if I want to call them or not. I'm not giving my number 'cause eehhhhh, you know, some people

253

like to play on the phone and some boys are just disgusting. But it's nice sometimes. It makes me happy.

¹¹I know work won't be fun my whole life. 'Cause work is not always about fun and games. There comes a time when you have to be serious about what you're doing, you know? . . .

¹²But I'll always be grateful to McDonald's, you know? The majority of people I know first started here or some other kind of fast-food place before they got to a good job, a better job. I'd like to do something with hair or maybe clothes. Or I want to get a job working in the hospital—in the nursery with the little babies. I love little kids. I can't wait till I get older so I can have kids. I adore my sisters and my brothers, spoil them. So I'd like the hospital. But whatever happens, a year from now, I'm gonna have a better job. I have a lot of confidence in myself. There's nothing I can't do. I'm fine.

Connect to the Author

About 40 interviewers contributed to *Gig*. One of the interviewers was John Bowe, who also is an editor of the book. Bowe traveled around the country talking to a wide variety of people, including a carnival worker in Appalachia, a supermodel between flights at an airport, and truck drivers at a truck stop in Wyoming. The editors of the book wanted Americans to speak for themselves. "Our goal was to take accurate snapshots, person by person, of work as it is today in this country," writes Marisa Bowe, John's sister, another of the book's editors. "We were very moved by the wholehearted diligence that people bring to their work."

254

705

from

Keeping the Moon

by Sarah Dessen

Fifteen-year-old Colie Sparks is a loner. When her glamorous, outgoing mother leaves for Europe, Colie is forced to spend the summer with her oddball aunt Mira in the seaside town of Colby, South Carolina. There, Colie finds a job at the Last Chance Café. Her coworkers, Morgan and Isabel, teach her the ropes.

¹³"**M**ayonnaise," Morgan said, "is a lot like men."

¹⁴It was nine-thirty in the morning on my first day of work, but I'd been up since six. I kept thinking Morgan would forget me or change her mind but at nine-fifteen she pulled up in front of Mira's steps and beeped her horn, just as we'd planned.

¹⁵The restaurant was empty except for us and the radio, tuned to an oldies station. "Twisting the Night Away" was playing, and we were making salad dressing, both of us up to our elbows in thick, smelly mayonnaise.

¹⁶"It can," she went on, plopping another scoop into the bowl, "make everything much better, adding flavor and ease to your life. Or, it can just be sticky and gross and make you nauseous."

¹⁷I smiled, stirring my mayonnaise while I considered this. "I hate mayonnaise."

¹⁸"You'll probably hate men too, from time to time," she said. "At least mayonnaise you can avoid."

¹⁹This was the way Morgan taught. Not in instructions, but pronouncements. Everything was a lesson.

255

²⁰"Lettuce," she announced later, pulling a head out of the plastic bag in front of us, "should be leafy, not slimy. And no black or brown edges. We use lettuce on everything: garnish, salads, burgers. A bad piece of lettuce can ruin your whole day."

²¹"Right," I said.

²²"Chop it like this," she instructed, taking a few whacks with a knife before handing it to me. "Big chops, but not too big."

²³I chopped. She watched. "Good," she said, reaching over to adjust my chops just a bit. I went on. "Very good."

²⁴Morgan was this meticulous about everything. Preparing dressings was a **ritual**, every measurement carefully checked. Isabel, on the other hand, dumped it all in at once, knocked a spoon around, and came up with the same results, dipping in a finger and licking it to double-check.

²⁵But Morgan had her own way.

²⁶"Peel carrots away from you," she said, demonstrating, "and cut off the ends about a quarter inch each. When feeding them into the processor, pause about every five seconds. It gives a finer shred."

²⁷I peeled, chopped, and stocked. I learned the perfect, **symmetrical** way to stack coffee cups and sugar packets, to fold rags at a right angle against flat surfaces, clean side up. Morgan kept the counter area spick-and-span, each element in its place. When she was nervous, she went around correcting things.

²⁸"Take-out boxes on the *left*, cup lids on the *right*," she'd shout, slamming them around as she restored order to her universe. "And spoons are handle side *up*, Isabel."

²⁹"Yeah, yeah," Isabel would say. When she was mad or just bored she purposely rearranged things just to see how long it took Morgan to find them. It was like a passive-aggressive treasure hunt.

³⁰That first lunch, when Norman and I had stopped to pitch in, was a constant blur of people and noise and food. Everyone was screaming at each other, Isabel and Morgan running past with orders, Norman flipping burgers and yelling things to Bick, the other cook, who stayed stonily quiet and cool the entire time. I shoveled ice like my life depended on it, answered the phone and took orders although I knew almost nothing about the menu, and messed up the register so badly it stuck on $10,000.00 and beeped for fifteen minutes straight before Isabel, in a fit of rage, whacked it with a plastic water

256

pitcher. It was Us against Them, clearly, and for once I was part of Us. I didn't really know what I was doing; I had to go on faith. So I just handed out my drinks and grabbed the phone when it screamed, wrapping the cord around my wrist and stabbing the pen Morgan had tossed me in my hair, the same way Isabel wore hers, and fought on.

³¹"Last Chance," I'd shout over the din. "Can I help you?"

³²And now, I was doing it every day.

³³At first, just walking up to a table full of strangers had scared me to death. I couldn't even make eye contact, stuttering through the basic questions Morgan had taught me—*What would you like to drink? Have you decided? How would you like that cooked? Fries or hush puppies?*—my hand literally shaking as it moved across my order pad. It made me nervous to stand there so exposed, all of those people *looking* at me.

³⁴But then, on about my third table, I finally got the nerve to glance up and realized that, basically, they *weren't*. For the most part, they were flipping through the menu, **extracting** Sweet'N Low packets from their toddler's grip, or so lost in their own conversation that I didn't even register: twenty minutes later they'd be flagging Isabel down, sure *she* was the one with their check. They didn't know or care about me. To them, I was just a waitress, a girl with an apron and a tea pitcher; they didn't even seem to notice my lip ring. And that was fine with me.

Connect to the Author

Sarah Dessen

Sarah Dessen drew from her own experiences as a waitress to write *Keeping the Moon*. Dessen, who was born in 1970, worked as a waitress during college. Though she graduated with top honors, she continued to wait tables rather than find a corporate job. It gave her the time she needed to write. It also gave her a lot of material. For example, when a woman slapped Dessen's hand as she tried to remove her empty plate, Dessen immortalized her in a book as a bitter, nasty character. "I've learned that writing well can be the best revenge," Dessen says. Two of Dessen's novels were adapted into the 2003 movie *How to Deal*. In addition to writing novels, Dessen now teaches at her alma mater, UNC Chapel Hill.

257

Comprehension and Vocabulary *Before Reading*

1. **In Lesson 3, we read an essay based on an interview with a teenager named Kysha Lewin.**

- **How would you describe Kysha's personality, based on the essay?** (Possible responses: She is hardworking, bright, cheerful, thoughtful, and responsible.)
- **Which of Kysha's traits most impressed you? Why?** (Responses will vary.)
- **What do you think Kysha means when she says, "I know work won't be fun my whole life"?** (Possible response: As she takes on jobs with more responsibility, there won't be as much time to have fun with friends at work.) **Do you agree with her statement? Why?** (Responses will vary.)

2. **For Kysha, the job was hard at first because there was so much to learn. But it soon became "a breeze" for her. The teenager we will read about next—Colie Sparks—also has a lot to learn in her first days at the Last Chance Café.**

Vocabulary Review

3. Arrange students in pairs, and have them turn to Student Book page 188. Ask them to read the vocabulary words listed in the box and tell what each word means.

4. Display Transparency 11. Write the word *sanitize* in the center oval. **Let's map this word by thinking of examples and non-examples, by telling what the word looks like, and by telling what it means.**

- **One example of *sanitize* would be washing your hands in hot water, to kill the germs. What is another example of *sanitize*?** Write students' responses in the Examples box.
- **Now let's think of some non-examples of *sanitize*. One non-example would be using a**

dirty washcloth to wipe the kitchen counter. **What are some other non-examples?** Record students' suggestions in the Non-Examples box.

- **Let's move on to what the word looks like. To me, it looks like the word *sane*. The word *sane* is related to the word *sanitize* in a way. For me to stay *sane*, I have to keep my house clean. If I don't *sanitize* the bathroom once a week, I feel like I might go crazy.**
- **Does the word *sanitize* look like any other words to you?** Record and discuss students' ideas.
- **Finally, let's write a meaning for the word. Based on our examples, non-examples, and related words, it seems to me that *sanitize* means "to make clean." Let's write this in the What It Means box.**

5. Have students work with a partner to complete the Student Book activity using another word of their choice. When all students are finished, review their responses as a class.

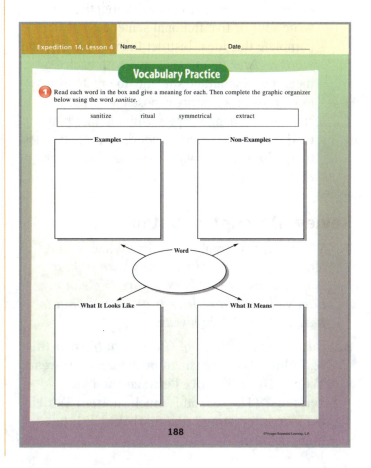

6. Challenge Words Use the following activities to review the Challenge Words with students.

Write the following on the board: *From the word <u>scribe</u>, we can make other words such as _____.*

- Call on students to complete the sentence, and write their responses on the board.

- **What does *scribe* mean?** (someone who writes)

- Ask students how knowing the base word helps them figure out the meaning of each word.

▶ Have students record these words and their possible meanings in the Vocabulary Log.

- On the board, write *register*, and ask students to give two different meanings for this word. (1. a machine that adds prices, records sales, and stores money; 2. to sign up for something, such as a class) Write the meanings on the board. Then write the following sentence on the board: *I decided that it was time to start my career.* Have partners work together to write four or five fictional sentences to complete this idea. Instruct them to include the word *register* two times, once with each meaning. Encourage students to create as humorous as scenario as possible. Then have students exchange papers with another pair, read the sentences, and underline context clues that help them know how *register* is used in each instance.

Review Descriptive Details

7. Write this paragraph on the board and read it aloud: *I got a job. The job was hard at first. Now it's easy. I stay busy. I have to clean my hands often. I have friends at work. I plan to have a better job in a year.*

8. Suppose the editors of *Gig* had published this text about Kysha instead of the essay we read. What's the difference between the two versions? (The second is much shorter.) **Which is more interesting?** (the first) **Why?** (It has more details.)

9. You already know that descriptive details make writing more interesting. Why is this so? (They help you picture a scene or an action.) Write *concrete details*, *sensory details*, and *figurative language* on the board, each on a separate line.

SKILL ✓

- **What are concrete details?** (specific, vivid details) Reread the sentence *The job was hard at first.* **What concrete details would make this sentence more interesting?** (Possible response: I had trouble working the register and listening to customers at the same time.)

- **What are sensory details?** (details that appeal to one or more of the five senses: hearing, taste, touch, smell, or sight) Reread the sentence *I have to clean my hands often.* **What sensory details would make this sentence more interesting?** (Possible response: I rub a minty-smelling, green, slippery liquid on my hands.)

- **What is figurative language?** (language that tells what something seems like) Reread the sentence *Now it's easy.* **What figurative language would make this sentence more interesting?** (Possible response: Now it's a breeze.)

10. Since we've been reading about a fast-food restaurant, let's consider the hamburger: how are descriptive details in writing like lettuce, tomatoes, pickles, and cheese on a burger? (They fill out the writing and make it more enjoyable.) **We're about to read a story about another person's job in a restaurant. As we read, let's pay attention to the kinds of details she uses to describe her experiences.**

Reading for Understanding

Reading

> **Names to Look For:**
> - Colie Sparks
> - Morgan
> - Mira
> - "Twisting the Night Away"
> - Isabel
> - Norman
> - Bick

1. **As you read this story from *Keeping the Moon*, you may come across some unfamiliar names.**
   - Write the words on the board.
   - Point to each word as you read the following:

   In this story, you will read about a teenager named *Colie Sparks* who gets a job at the Last Chance Café, while she spends the summer with her aunt *Mira*. On her first day at work, coworkers *Morgan* and *Isabel* teach her how to prepare the food, while a 1960s song called *"Twisting the Night Away"* plays on the radio. Cooks *Norman* and *Bick* are also part of the frenzied action at the restaurant.
   - Call on individuals to read the words.

2. Have students turn to Anthology page 255. **Take a brief glance at the text, and tell me whether you think it is narrative or expository.** (narrative) **Why?** (It seems to tell a story rather than give information.) **Would you say that it is a fictional, or made-up, story, or a real-life text?** (fictional) **What makes you think so?** (The short paragraphs and use of quotations are often found in fiction.)

3. Read the introductory text aloud. Have students identify examples of concrete details and figurative language in the introduction. (Possible responses: concrete detail—*glamorous, outgoing mother*; figurative language—*teach her the ropes*)

4. Read the first two paragraphs aloud. **What words tell you that this story is in the first person?** (my, I'd, I, me)

5. **Fluency** Have partners read paragraphs 15 through 34 and the Connect to the Author feature, taking turns reading each paragraph. If necessary, review the following fluency correction procedure with students to ensure accuracy: **Offer help when your partner comes to an unfamiliar word or makes a reading error. Pause, then say, "That word is _____. Let's read it again."** As students read, monitor for reading rate, accuracy, and expression.

6. When students have finished their reading, check literal comprehension of the text by asking these questions: **KNOWLEDGE**
   - *Introductory Paragraph:* **Why is Colie spending the summer with her aunt?** (Her mother is traveling in Europe.)
   - *Paragraph 24:* **How are Morgan and Isabel different?** (Morgan does everything very carefully, while Isabel does things in a more random manner.)
   - *Paragraph 30:* **How does Colie view the situation at the Last Chance Café?** (She sees it as an "Us vs. Them" situation.)
   - *Paragraphs 33 and 34:* **At first, what makes Colie nervous?** (being watched by all of the customers) **What does Colie soon realize?** (that none of them are really seeing her at all)

English Language Learners

Responding to Informational and Literary Texts

English language learners often need structure to communicate their responses to any text.

Use the following activity to encourage written and oral responses to informational or literary selections.

- Give each student a form such as the one below.

  The thing I liked best about today's reading is _____.
  I would change the title to _____.
  My favorite part was _____.
  One thing I learned from today's reading is _____.
  In my opinion, _____ is the most important vocabulary word in today's lesson because _____.
  For **informational texts**, you may want to include additional prompts such as: *An important piece of information is _____ because _____.* or *I would like to know more about _____.*
  For **literary texts**, you may want to include additional prompts such as: *My favorite character was _____.* or *I might change the ending by _____.*

- Have each student write an ending for the first item on the form. Then have students share and discuss their responses.

- Have students continue responding and sharing for each remaining item on the form.

ELL

Checking for Comprehension   *After Reading*

1. When all students are finished, have them turn to Student Book page 189. Read the instructions aloud. Have students work with their partners to complete each "menu item" with examples from the story. Monitor students as they work, providing correction and feedback as needed. When partners are finished, review their responses as a class.

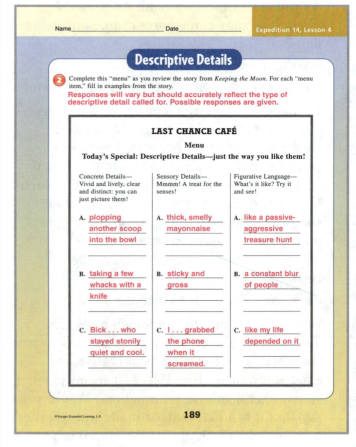

2. Use the following questions to help students make connections between the work experiences of Kysha and Colie.

- **How are Kysha and Colie alike?** SYNTHESIS (Both are teenagers working in restaurants; both find their work hard at first.) **How are their situations different?** (Kysha is working to help her mom; Colie appears to be working to pass the time.)

- **What are some differences between the teens' work environments?** SYNTHESIS (Possible responses: Kysha's is more ordered and structured; Colie's seems louder and less organized.)
- **Which work environment would you prefer? Why?** EVALUATION (Responses will vary.)
- **How do the girls' coworkers make their jobs easier or harder?** ANALYSIS (Kysha's coworkers are patient and relaxed; Colie's are helpful but some yell at one another and add to her nervousness.)
- **What is one question you would like to ask Kysha? Why?** ANALYSIS (Responses will vary.)
- **What is one piece of advice you'd like to give Colie? Why?** APPLICATION (Responses will vary.)

3. **Challenge Question Which text—the essay about Kysha Lewin or the story from *Keeping the Moon*—gives you a better sense of the satisfactions and challenges of work? Why?** EVALUATION (Possible responses: the essay, because it balanced the pluses and minuses; the story, because it made the work environment seem more real.)

Reading Response

Have students turn to Student Book page 190. Read the instructions aloud. Then have students look back at the essay and the story to help them formulate an answer to this question:

 Why have I included the stories of these two teenagers in my book?

Have students complete their writing independently. When all students are finished, call on individuals to read their paragraphs aloud.

Expedition 14, Lesson 4   Name_____ Date_____

Reading Response

3 You have put together a collection of stories about teenagers who work in restaurants. You want to send a description of your book to a publisher. You want to tell who you have included in your book, and why. Both Kysha Lewin and Colie Sparks are in your book. Use information from the essay and story to answer this question:

Why have I included the stories of these two teenagers in my book?

I chose to include the story of Kysha Lewin in my book because _____

Kysha is remarkable because she _____

Her experiences in her first job are interesting because _____

I also chose to include a story about a girl named Colie Sparks. Her story is important because _____

Even though Colie's story is made up, some parts are like real life, such as _____

Teenagers will enjoy reading about Colie because _____

She also _____

190   ©Voyager Expanded Learning, L.P.

Passport Reading Journeys Library

Building **Fluency**

1. Place students in pairs according to reading level to build fluency. When pairing students, be sure that one student is a stronger reader (Student A) than the other student (Student B). However, do not reveal that stronger readers are paired with weaker readers. See *Passport Reading Journeys* Library Teacher's Guide for grouping guidelines.

2. Have students quickly choose reading material from the *Passport Reading Journeys* Library or another approved selection that is at the reading level of Student B. If students have not finished the previously chosen selection, they may continue reading from that selection. See *Passport Reading Journeys* Library Teacher's Guide for material selection guidelines.

3. Tell students that Student A will read one paragraph, and Student B will reread that same paragraph.

4. Have students follow this routine until the end of class.

5. If necessary, review the following practices to enhance fluency:
   • Rate and accuracy of reading
   • Expression during reading
   • Correction procedures

Library *Highlights*

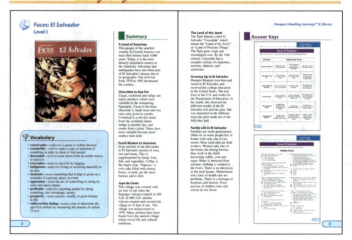

Vocabulary Connections

Vocabulary words are listed in the Teacher's Guide for each magazine or book. These words are content-related or used frequently in the reading material. The selected words can be the basis for independent or small-group vocabulary discussions and activities.

Student Opportunities

A summary of each book or magazine in the Library is included in the *Passport Reading Journeys* Library Teacher's Guide. This summary can be shared with students to help them decide which book or magazine to read.

Strategic Online Learning Opportunities®

Session 1   http://solo.voyagerlearning.com

Students read a passage about César Chavez and his work for civil rights for migrant farm workers.

Content Connection
Social Studies

César Chavez: His Fight for the Farm Workers *by Barbara Bloom*

Lexile Levels
Passage B 880L
Passage C 950L

Assessment
- Metacognition
- Content
- Vocabulary
- Main Idea
- Summary

Based on their assessment scores, students automatically are assigned either the Skills Practice for reinforcement or the Independent Practice and Extension Opportunities.

SKILLS PRACTICE

Vocabulary Strategies
- Context
- Word Parts: Prefixes and Suffixes
- Word Parts: Compound Words

Dictionary Skills

Main Idea Strategy: W–I–N
- Identifying the Most Important *Who* or *What*
- Identifying the Most Important *Information*
- Stating the Main Idea in a Small *Number* of Words

Questioning

Writing
- Writing a Summary Statement

INDEPENDENT PRACTICE

Vocabulary Strategies

Writing
- Writing a Summary Statement

EXTENSION OPPORTUNITIES
- Online Books
- Book Cart
- Review of Previous Passages

Advanced Word Study

Multisyllabic Words

1. **Remember, sometimes it's easier to read parts of a longer word before reading the entire word. One way is to use what we know about open and closed syllables.** Write the word *momentum* on the board. Underline the word part *mo*. **What is this word part?** (mo) **What kind of syllable is this word part?** (open) **How do we know?** (It has one long vowel sound with no consonants following it, or closing it in.) **What is the next part?** (men) **What kind of syllable is this word part?** (closed) **How do we know?** (It has one short vowel sound followed by one or more consonants.) **Read the rest of the word.** (tum) **What is the word?** (momentum) *Momentum* **means "energy or force."**

   Another way to read longer words is to use what we know about prefixes and suffixes. Write the word *indelible* on the board. Underline the prefix *in-*. **What is this prefix?** (in-) **What is the next part?** (del) Underline *-ible*. **What is the suffix?** (-ible) **What is the word?** (indelible) **The word** *indelible* **means "unable to remove."**

2. Have students turn to Student Book page E14, Lesson 6. Direct students to line 1. **What is the first word part?** (or) **What is the next word part?** (gan) **What is the next part?** (i) **What is the next part?** (za) **What is the suffix?** (-tion) **What is the word?** (organizations) **One meaning for** *organizations* **is "the act of organizing or arranging."** Repeat with the remaining words. Call on individuals to read the words in random order. Ask students to tell the meanings of the words.

3. Direct students to lines 2 and 3. Have them read the words. Then call on individuals to read the words in a different order. Ask students to tell the meanings of the words.

   #### ▼ To Correct
   For Multisyllabic Words: **What is the first word part? What is the next part? What is the word?** If students do not know the meaning of the word, review the word and/or word parts to determine the meaning of the word.

For Sounds in Words: Say the correct sound(s), then ask students to repeat the sound(s). Have them read the word again with the correct sound(s). If students do not know the meaning of the word, review the word and/or word parts to determine the meaning of the word.

1.	organizations	loneliness	traveling	confident
2.	qualifying	accomplished	substandard	national
3.	championship	positions	rookie	remaining

Sight Words

1. Direct students to line 1. Have them point to the first word. **This word is** *fuel*. **Read the word.** (fuel) **This is not a regular word. Let's read the word again.** (fuel) **Let's spell the word.** (f-u-e-l) **What is the word?** (fuel) Repeat with the remaining words. Then have students read the words. Ask students to tell the meanings of the words.

2. Direct students to lines 2 and 3. **Let's read these words.** Remind students that the rows of words consist of regular and irregular words. Point to the first word. **What is the word?** (accident) Repeat with the remaining words. Call on individuals to read the words in a different order. Ask students to tell the meanings of the words.

   #### ▼ To Correct
   For Regular Words: Say the sound(s) in the word, then ask students to repeat the sound(s). Have them read the word again with the correct sound(s). If students do not know the meaning of the word, review the word and/or word part to determine the meaning of the word.

   For Irregular Words: Immediately say the correct word. Then have students read the word, spell it, and read it again. If students do not know the meaning of the word, review the word.

1.	fuel I	characteristic I	league I	fourth I
2.	accident I	obey I	mayonnaise I	instance I
3.	judgment I	potential R	ritual I	concussion I

Anthology Selection

Social Studies

IndyCar® Rookie of the Year Danica Patrick races a go-cart in Union Square Park in New York City.

The Fast Track

[1]Race car driver Danica Patrick got her start almost by accident.

[2]When Danica was 10 years old, in Roscoe, Illinois, her sister Brooke wanted to race go-carts. Danica decided to give it a try too. While her sister soon lost interest, Danica was hooked. She found the thrill of racing to be **irresistible**. Within three months of taking up the sport, she broke the go-cart track record. Two years later, she was the national go-cart champion.

[3]By the time she was 16 years old, Danica had won three go-cart championships and was ready for racing bigger, faster cars against other top

258

young drivers. That meant moving to England and being **displaced** from her home and family. But the experience was worth the loneliness. "Going from [go-carting] to racing in England forced me to grow up very quickly," Danica says. "I had to learn to handle all kinds of situations." She continued her success, finishing second in the Formula Ford Festival in 2000. It was the best finish ever by an American.

[4]Former championship racer Bobby Rahal saw something special in the 5-foot 2-inch, 100-pound Danica. "She has desire, good judgment, and composure under pressure," Rahal says. "And she has that thing that only champions have, that chip on the shoulder that says, 'You don't think I can do it. Come out and take a shot at me.'" She also has another characteristic that is important to champions: confidence. "If I'm doing something, it's because I feel I can beat everyone; I feel like I can win," she says with **assurance**.

[5]Danica spent a couple of years driving cars in practice leagues, finishing in the top three several times. In 2004, she finished in third place in the overall championship standings. Rahal decided she was ready for big-time racing in 2005.

[6]Danica suffered a concussion when she crashed in her first big-time race in 2005, but she recovered in time for the next race. She improved with each race, even leading a race in Japan for 32 laps before finishing fourth.

[7]Next up for Danica was the biggest race in America, the Indianapolis 500. She stunned the racing world by posting the fastest speed during qualifying runs before the race. These qualifying runs decide the order in which drivers will line up at the start of the race. Danica qualified for the fourth position, the best ever by a woman driver at the Indy 500. She raced well, becoming the first woman ever to lead in that race. She might have won if she had not been forced to slow down near the end of the race to avoid running out of fuel. Still, her fourth-place finish was the best ever by a woman at the Indy 500.

[8]Danica finished her rookie season the same way she started it, with a crash. Despite this substandard finish, Danica had much to be proud of about her first year of big-time racing. She finished 12th in the overall standings and was named the Rookie of the Year. "I wanted more at the end, but I can walk away knowing that I accomplished many of the goals I set before the season," Danica says. "Now I have a year of IRL racing under me and we'll be ready for a good 2006 season."

259

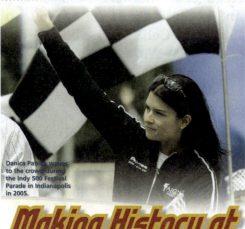

Danica Patrick waves to the crowd during the Indy 500 Festival Parade in Indianapolis in 2005.

Making History at Indianapolis

[9]The 89th Indianapolis 500 was filled with firsts for Danica Patrick. It was the first time she had raced at the Indy 500. In fact, the 500-mile race marked the first time that she had raced more than 300 miles. Then, early in the race, Danica became the first woman ever to lead the Indy 500.

[10]Four was another important number for Danica in the May 29, 2005, race. She was the fourth woman ever to drive in the race. During qualifying runs before the race, she earned the right to start in the fourth position. And

260

after three hours and 500 miles of racing, she finished in fourth place. Her starting and finishing positions were the best ever by a woman in the history of the race.

[11]The Indy 500 is one of the biggest car races of the year. Drivers race around an oval track for 200 laps while some 300,000 fans scream in the stands. Finishing first in this race can do wonders for a driver's **revenue**. The winner earns $1.5 million. The potential for a big payday drew some of the best drivers in the world, and Danica was out to prove that she belonged among them. She posted the fastest speed of all the drivers during the qualifying runs before the race, causing many to **speculate** that she might win the prestigious event. Danica was confident going into the race. "I think I have a great chance of winning this race," she said.

[12]She almost did, but a couple of what she called "rookie mistakes" cost her dearly. In the 52nd lap of the race, Danica briefly took the lead. About halfway through the race, she was still hanging on to fourth place. Then she pulled off the track to get some fuel. As she hit the gas pedal to get back on the track, the car's engine stalled. That error dropped her back into 16th place. But Danica was **persistent**; she patiently worked her way back to seventh place before making another costly error. She spun out and bashed into another car, damaging the front of her car.

[13]But Danica stayed calm and pulled her car off the track. Her team replaced the broken parts, and she was back on the track in 60 seconds. The accident cost her only two positions, dropping her to ninth place with 41 laps remaining. But time was running out. Danica would have to take a risk if she had any chance of winning.

[14]When the eight cars ahead of her pulled off the track for a final refueling in the 172nd lap, Danica decided to keep driving, hoping that she would have enough fuel to finish the race. If she was right, she would win. If she was wrong, she would lose.

[15]While the other drivers refueled, Danica zipped back into the lead. She held the lead for 12 laps, averaging 225 miles per hour. But she could not lengthen her lead, and her fuel was getting dangerously low. She lost the lead briefly on the 186th lap, but then charged back in front. But her lack of fuel forced her to slow down or risk not finishing the race.

[16]"I was disappointed because I had a chance to win the Indianapolis 500," she said. "But when I dropped back into second place, I told myself I wasn't going to be mad. I accomplished a lot." And most racing fans would agree with her.

261

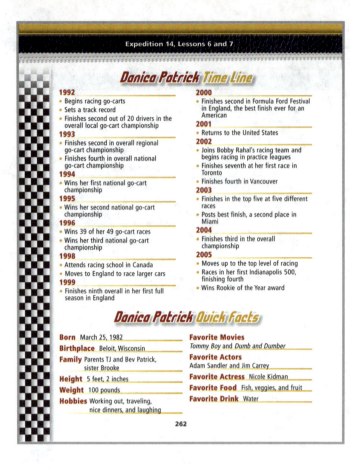

Expedition 14, Lessons 6 and 7

Danica Patrick Time Line

1992
- Begins racing go-carts
- Sets a track record
- Finishes second out of 20 drivers in the overall local go-cart championship

1993
- Finishes second in overall regional go-cart championship
- Finishes fourth in overall national go-cart championship

1994
- Wins her first national go-cart championship

1995
- Wins her second national go-cart championship

1996
- Wins 39 of her 49 go-cart races
- Wins her third national go-cart championship

1998
- Attends racing school in Canada
- Moves to England to race larger cars

1999
- Finishes ninth overall in her first full season in England

2000
- Finishes second in Formula Ford Festival in England, the best finish ever for an American

2001
- Returns to the United States

2002
- Joins Bobby Rahal's racing team and begins racing in practice leagues
- Finishes seventh at her first race in Toronto
- Finishes fourth in Vancouver

2003
- Finishes in the top five at five different races
- Posts best finish, a second place in Miami

2004
- Finishes third in the overall championship

2005
- Moves up to the top level of racing
- Races in her first Indianapolis 500, finishing fourth
- Wins Rookie of the Year award

Danica Patrick Quick Facts

Born March 25, 1982

Birthplace Beloit, Wisconsin

Family Parents TJ and Bev Patrick, sister Brooke

Height 5 feet, 2 inches

Weight 100 pounds

Hobbies Working out, traveling, nice dinners, and laughing

Favorite Movies
Tommy Boy and *Dumb and Dumber*

Favorite Actors
Adam Sandler and Jim Carrey

Favorite Actress Nicole Kidman

Favorite Food Fish, veggies, and fruit

Favorite Drink Water

262

Comprehension and Vocabulary *Before Reading*

1. Review the topic "what we do matters" by using the questions from Anthology page 245 and DVD 14.1 to activate prior knowledge. After showing DVD 14.1, call on individuals to read the questions. Have students discuss their responses using information from the DVD and the Lessons 1–4 texts.

2. **In this Expedition, we've been reading texts about the work people do—both for a living and to change lives.**

   • **In Lessons 1 and 2, we read texts related to the work of farm workers. What is this work like?** (Possible responses: It is difficult and the conditions are harsh; workers live in shacks and are paid little.)

   • **How has Dolores Huerta worked to improve farm workers' lives?** (She has led strikes and boycotts for better conditions; she helped found an organization to protect farm workers' rights.)

   • **In Lessons 3 and 4, we read texts about two teenagers. Who were these young women, and what did they have in common?** (Kysha Lewin and Colie Sparks; both worked in restaurants) **What challenges did both teens face?** (getting used to the procedures at the restaurants; having to work quickly)

3. **Next, we'll read articles that tell about a remarkable young woman.** Have students turn to Anthology pages 258 and 260 and preview the articles.

   • **Who are these articles about?** (Danica Patrick)

   • **At what does she excel?** (race car driving)

   Danica's achievements are not only amazing for a woman, they're amazing for anyone. Find out why when you read the articles.

Building Background Knowledge

Extend students' knowledge about the topic by sharing the following:

- The sport of automobile racing began in France, not long after the first gasoline-powered cars were developed in the late 1800s.
- The first Indianapolis 500 race was held in 1911, and the first woman to qualify for the race was Janet Guthrie in 1977.
- One Indy 500 tradition is for the winner to drink a bottle of milk just after the race. Years ago, milk companies sponsored the races and handed out bottles of milk to winners to promote their product.

Social Studies

Introduce Vocabulary

Vocabulary

Review Words

irresistible	*impossible to say no to*
displace	*to remove from a usual or common place*
assurance	*a feeling of certainty; confidence*
revenue	*money that is made; income*
speculate	*to make a guess*
persistent	*continuing with purpose*

Challenge Words

Word Meaning

composure	*calmness, especially in a difficult or stressful situation*
	The bride was able to keep her *composure* even though the groom was 30 minutes late.
concussion	*an injury to the brain*
	Mia fell off the monkey bars headfirst, which resulted in a mild *concussion*.

4. **Our next texts contain words with meanings we have already learned. We will review these words within the texts we are reading.**

5. Write each Review Word on the board. Then ask students to locate the word in one of the articles. Instruct them to read aloud the sentence containing the word, as well as any other sentences that provide context.

   - **What can you tell me about the word?**
   - Ask other questions that allow students to explore the word's meaning. (For example: **Does the word *speculate* mean the same as *know*? What is the opposite of *assurance*?**)

6. Ask students to respond to the following questions. Provide correction and feedback as necessary.

   - **What is a sport or other activity that you find *irresistible*? Why?**
   - **If you awoke one morning and found yourself *displaced*, where would you *least* want to be? Why?**
   - **What is a task that you can do with *assurance*? What is something you cannot yet do with *assurance*?**
   - **How could you turn your cooking skill into a source of *revenue*?**
   - **What is something most people can only *speculate* about? Why is that?**
   - **How can being *persistent* help you reach a goal, such as becoming a musician?**

7. Work with students to write a definition for each word on the board.

8. Include the Challenge Words to meet the needs of students who are advancing.

Extending Vocabulary

Affix Review

- Write *sub-* on the board. Ask students to tell the meaning of this prefix. (under or below)

- Have students scan paragraph 8 to find a word that contains the prefix *sub-*. (substandard) Write this word on the board. **How does the prefix help you figure out the meaning of the word?** (*Sub-* means "under" or "below," so *substandard* must mean "below standard.")
▶ Have students write this word and its meaning in the Vocabulary Log.

- **What other words do you know that contain the prefix *sub-*?** (Possible words: submarine, substructure, subnormal, submerge) Ask students to use the meaning of *sub-* to tell the meanings of the words.
▶ Have students write these additional words and their meanings in the Vocabulary Log.

Review Compare and Contrast

9. **We are going to compare and contrast the texts we will read in Lessons 6 and 7.**
   - **What does it mean to compare two or more things?** (to tell how they are similar)
   - **What does it mean to contrast two or more things?** (to tell how they are different)

10. Draw a Venn diagram on the board, and label the outer sections *Auto Racing* and *Bicycle Racing*. Work with students to generate similarities and differences between the two sports, and write these in the diagram. (Possible responses: similarities—Both involve using a wheeled vehicle; both can be dangerous; goal of both is to be the fastest. differences—Auto racers use fuel-powered machines, cyclists use leg-powered devices; auto racers race at faster speeds than do bicycle racers.)

11. **As we compare and contrast the articles about Danica Patrick, we'll follow a similar process. We'll look for ways in which they are alike, and ways in which they are different.**

Reading for Understanding

Reading

Places and Names to Look For:
- Roscoe, Illinois
- Brooke
- England
- Formula Ford Festival
- Bobby Rahal
- IRL
- Indianapolis 500/Indy 500
- Rookie of the Year

1. **As you read "The Fast Track," you may come across some unfamiliar places and names.**
   - Write the words on the board.
   - Point to each word as you read the following:

   This article will tell how Danica Patrick's interest in auto racing began when she and her sister, *Brooke*, first raced go-carts in *Roscoe, Illinois*. It will describe how Danica trained in *England*, later winning second place in the *Formula Ford Festival* there. The text will describe how champion racer *Bobby Rahal* helped Danica set her sights on the biggest race in America, the *Indianapolis 500*, also know as the *Indy 500*. It will also sum up her first year as a professional in the *IRL*—Indy Racing League—including being named *Rookie of the Year*.
   - Call on individuals to read the words.

2. Have students turn to Anthology page 258 and invite them to look at the format of the text—its title, its first line, and the way the pages are laid out.
   - **What kind of text is this?** (an expository text)
   - **How can you tell?** (It gives information.)

3. **Fluency** Read the first paragraph aloud while students follow along in their books. Then have students read the remainder of the article in small groups. If necessary, review the following fluency goal with students: **As you read aloud, use expression and combine words in phrases in a way that sounds like speech. This will show that you understand what you are reading.**

4. When students have finished their reading, check for literal comprehension by asking the following questions: **KNOWLEDGE**
   - *Paragraphs 2 and 3:* **What had Danica Patrick achieved by the time she was 16 years old?** (She had broken the go-cart track record, and had won three go-cart championships.) **Why did she move to England?** (to train as a race car driver)
   - *Paragraph 4:* **According to former racer Bobby Rahal, what qualities do many champions have?** (desire, good judgment, composure, and confidence)
   - *Paragraph 7:* **Briefly describe Danica's performance in the 2005 Indianapolis 500.** (She had the fastest qualifying time and started in fourth position. She led the race for part of the time but had to slow down toward the end to avoid running out of gas. She finished fourth.)

Checking for Comprehension *After Reading*

1. Have students apply what they understood from the text by asking the following questions:

    - **Tell me three important personality traits that have contributed to Danica's success as an auto racer.** ANALYSIS (Possible responses: the ability to perform under pressure; confidence; good judgment)

    - **Which personality trait of Danica is most like one of your traits? How is this trait useful to you?** APPLICATION (Responses will vary.)

2. **Challenge Question** **What is a question you would like to ask Danica if you could interview her?** ANALYSIS (Responses will vary.)

Connect to the Author

Have students discuss these questions with partners or small groups:

- **According to the writer of this article, what is one way that Danica and her sister are alike? What is one way in which they're different?** (alike—Both were interested in go-cart racing as young girls. different—Danica's sister lost interest in go-carts, but Danica fell in love with racing.)

- **Did the writer's use of quotations in the article make the text seem more, or less, interesting to you?** (Possible responses: more interesting, because they made Danica and Bobby Rahal seem more real; less interesting, because I just wanted to read facts, not opinions)

- **In your opinion, how well did the writer tell Danica's story?** (Responses will vary.) **What, if any, words, terms, or facts are still unclear from the text? What is one way you can find out their meanings?** (Responses will vary.)

Lesson 7

Anthology Selection

Social Studies

IndyCar® Rookie of the Year Danica Patrick races a go-cart in Union Square Park in New York City.

The Fast Track

[1] Race car driver Danica Patrick got her start almost by accident.
[2] When Danica was 10 years old, in Roscoe, Illinois, her sister Brooke wanted to race go-carts. Danica decided to give it a try too. While her sister soon lost interest, Danica was hooked. She found the thrill of racing to be **irresistible**. Within three months of taking up the sport, she broke the go-cart track record. Two years later, she was the national go-cart champion.
[3] By the time she was 16 years old, Danica had won three go-cart championships and was ready for racing bigger, faster cars against other top

258

young drivers. That meant moving to England and being **displaced** from her home and family. But the experience was worth the loneliness. "Going from [go-carting] to racing in England forced me to grow up very quickly," Danica says. "I had to learn to handle all kinds of situations." She continued her success, finishing second in the Formula Ford Festival in 2000. It was the best finish ever by an American.

[4] Former championship racer Bobby Rahal saw something special in the 5-foot 2-inch, 100-pound Danica. "She has desire, good judgment, and composure under pressure," Rahal says. "And she has that thing that only champions have, that chip on the shoulder that says, 'You don't think I can do it. Come out and take a shot at me.'" She also has another characteristic that is important to champions: confidence. "If I'm doing something, it's because I feel I can beat everyone; I feel like I can win," she says with **assurance**.

[5] Danica spent a couple of years driving cars in practice leagues, finishing in the top three several times. In 2004, she finished in third place in the overall championship standings. Rahal decided she was ready for big-time racing in 2005.

[6] Danica suffered a concussion when she crashed in her first big-time race in 2005, but she recovered in time for the next race. She improved with each race, even leading a race in Japan for 32 laps before finishing fourth.

[7] Next up for Danica was the biggest race in America, the Indianapolis 500. She stunned the racing world by posting the fastest speed during qualifying runs before the race. These qualifying runs decide the order in which drivers will line up at the start of the race. Danica qualified for the fourth position, the best ever by a woman driver at the Indy 500. She raced well, becoming the first woman ever to lead in that race. She might have won if she had not been forced to slow down near the end of the race to avoid running out of fuel. Still, her fourth-place finish was the best ever by a woman at the Indy 500.

[8] Danica finished her rookie season the same way she started it, with a crash. Despite this substandard finish, Danica had much to be proud of about her first year of big-time racing. She finished 12th in the overall standings and was named the Rookie of the Year. "I wanted more at the end, but I can walk away knowing that I accomplished many of the goals I set before the season," Danica says. "Now I have a year of IRL racing under me and we'll be ready for a good 2006 season."

259

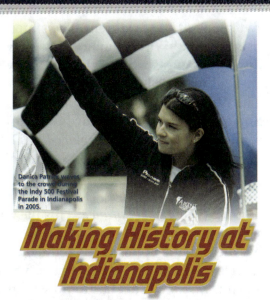

Danica Patrick waves to the crowd during the Indy 500 Festival Parade in Indianapolis in 2005.

Making History at Indianapolis

[9] The 89th Indianapolis 500 was filled with firsts for Danica Patrick. It was the first time she had raced at the Indy 500. In fact, the 500-mile race marked the first time that she had raced more than 300 miles. Then, early in the race, Danica became the first woman ever to lead the Indy 500.

[10] Four was another important number for Danica in the May 29, 2005, race. She was the fourth woman ever to drive in the race. During qualifying runs before the race, she earned the right to start in the fourth position. And

260

after three hours and 500 miles of racing, she finished in fourth place. Her starting and finishing positions were the best ever by a woman in the history of the race.

[11] The Indy 500 is one of the biggest car races of the year. Drivers race around an oval track for 200 laps while some 300,000 fans scream in the stands. Finishing first in this race can do wonders for a driver's **revenue**. The winner earns $1.5 million. The potential for a big payday drew some of the best drivers in the world, and Danica was out to prove that she belonged among them. She posted the fastest speed of all the drivers during the qualifying runs before the race, causing many to **speculate** that she might win the prestigious event. Danica was confident going into the race. "I think I have a great chance of winning this race," she said.

[12] She almost did, but a couple of what she called "rookie mistakes" cost her dearly. In the 52nd lap of the race, Danica briefly took the lead. About halfway through the race, she was still hanging on to fourth place. Then she pulled off the track to get some fuel. As she hit the gas pedal to get back on the track, the car's engine stalled. That error dropped her back into 16th place. But Danica was **persistent**; she patiently worked her way back to seventh place before making another costly error. She spun out and bashed into another car, damaging the front of her car.

[13] But Danica stayed calm and pulled her car off the track. Her team replaced the broken parts, and she was back on the track in 60 seconds. The accident cost her only two positions, dropping her to ninth place with 41 laps remaining. But time was running out. Danica would have to take a risk if she had any chance of winning.

[14] When the eight cars ahead of her pulled off the track for a final refueling in the 172nd lap, Danica decided to keep driving, hoping that she would have enough fuel to finish the race. If she was right, she would win. If she was wrong, she would lose.

[15] While the other drivers refueled, Danica zipped back into the lead. She held the lead for 12 laps, averaging 225 miles per hour. But she could not lengthen her lead, and her fuel was getting dangerously low. She lost the lead briefly on the 186th lap, but then charged back in front. But her lack of fuel forced her to slow down or risk not finishing the race.

[16] "I was disappointed because I had a chance to win the Indianapolis 500," she said. "But when I dropped back into second place, I told myself I wasn't going to be mad. I accomplished a lot." And most racing fans would agree with her.

261

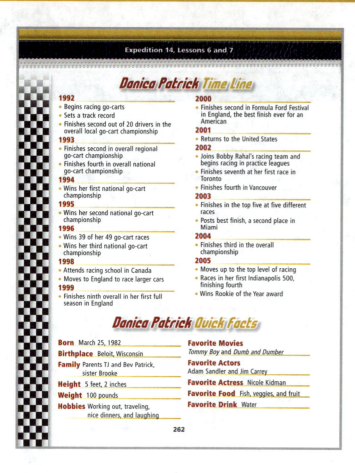

Danica Patrick *Time Line*

1992
- Begins racing go-carts
- Sets a track record
- Finishes second out of 20 drivers in the overall local go-cart championship

1993
- Finishes second in overall regional go-cart championship
- Finishes fourth in overall national go-cart championship

1994
- Wins her first national go-cart championship

1995
- Wins her second national go-cart championship

1996
- Wins 39 of her 49 go-cart races
- Wins her third national go-cart championship

1998
- Attends racing school in Canada
- Moves to England to race larger cars

1999
- Finishes ninth overall in her first full season in England

2000
- Finishes second in Formula Ford Festival in England, the best finish ever for an American

2001
- Returns to the United States

2002
- Joins Bobby Rahal's racing team and begins racing in practice leagues
- Finishes seventh at her first race in Toronto
- Finishes fourth in Vancouver

2003
- Finishes in the top five at five different races
- Posts best finish, a second place in Miami

2004
- Finishes third in the overall championship

2005
- Moves up to the top level of racing
- Races in her first Indianapolis 500, finishing fourth
- Wins Rookie of the Year award

Danica Patrick *Quick Facts*

Born March 25, 1982

Birthplace Beloit, Wisconsin

Family Parents TJ and Bev Patrick, sister Brooke

Height 5 feet, 2 inches

Weight 100 pounds

Hobbies Working out, traveling, nice dinners, and laughing

Favorite Movies *Tommy Boy* and *Dumb and Dumber*

Favorite Actors Adam Sandler and Jim Carrey

Favorite Actress Nicole Kidman

Favorite Food Fish, veggies, and fruit

Favorite Drink Water

262

Comprehension and Vocabulary   *Before Reading*

1. **In Lesson 6, we read "The Fast Track."**
    - **What is an important point the article makes?** (Possible response: Danica has exceptional talent as an auto racer.)
    - **What is one personality trait the article highlights?** (Possible responses: her confidence, her determination)
    - **Which trait do you think is most responsible for her success?** (Possible response: her determination)

2. **Our next article, "Making History at Indianapolis," takes us inside the car with Danica during the 2005 Indy 500. Be sure to fasten your seatbelts.**

Vocabulary Review

3. Arrange students with partners, and have them turn to Student Book page 191. Read the vocabulary words aloud. Call on individuals to tell what each word means. Then read the instructions aloud.

4. **Let's look at the first item. The statement we overhear is: "With so many good drivers, it's anybody's guess who might win today's race." Now let's look at the words in the box. The first two are *irresistible* and *displaced*. Something *irresistible* is hard to ignore; someone or something *displaced* has been taken out of its usual place. Neither of these words seems to have anything to do with a prediction about a race. Let's keep looking. The next word is *assurance*. This has to do with confidence. But the statement we overhear is the opposite of confidence—it's not clear *who* might win the race. The next word is *revenue*. This has to do with money. The winner of the race might win money, but the statement isn't about money, it's about the winner. Moving on to the next word, *speculate*, we recall that the word means "to**

make a guess." The statement is about how hard it is to *guess* who might win. So *speculate* may be the right answer. Just to be sure, though, let's check the last word: *persistent*. This word relates to keeping on, with a sense of purpose. Nothing in the statement seems to relate to this. So, *speculate* must be the answer. Let's write it on the line.

5. Have partners complete the remaining items. When all partners are finished, call on students to report their responses and to explain their thinking.

6. **Challenge Words** Write the words *composure* and *concussion* on the board, along with the following items. Have students complete the items along with those in the Student Book.

   • *"No matter what terrible thing happens out there on the track, you have to stay calm and collected."* (composure)

   • *"You have to think fast and drive smart— otherwise, you might end up in the hospital with a head injury."* (concussion)

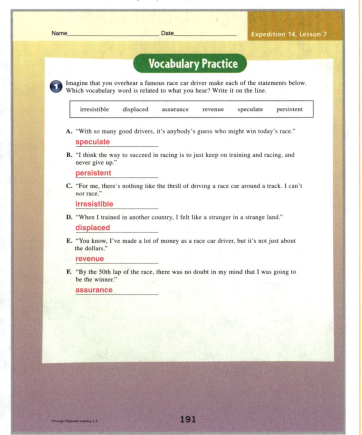

Extending Vocabulary

Affix Review

• Write *-en* on the board. Ask students to tell the meaning of this suffix. (to make)

• Write the word *lengthen* on the board. **You will encounter this word in today's text. How does the suffix *-en* help you figure out the meaning of *lengthen*?** (*-En* means "to make," so *lengthen* must mean "to make longer.")

▶ Have students write this word and its meaning in the Vocabulary Log.

• **What other words do you know that contain the suffix *-en*?** (Possible words: awaken, strengthen, weaken, fasten) Ask students to use the meaning of *-en* to tell the meanings of the words.

▶ Have students write these additional words and their meanings in the Vocabulary Log.

• Explain that there are other meanings of *-en*. Write the words *written* and *forgotten* on the board. Underline *en* in each. **Sometimes these letters appear at the end of a verb, but do not mean "to make." In words such as these, *-en* is an ending used to show past tense, like the ending *-ed*.** Point to *written*. **You could not say that *written* means "to make write." That doesn't make sense.** Point to *forgotten*. **Nor could you say "to make forget."**

• Write *eaten* and *sharpen* on the board. **In which word is *-en* a suffix meaning "to make"? In which word is it a past-tense ending? How do you know?** (*-En* is a suffix meaning "to make" in *sharpen*, because it makes sense to say "to make sharp." It is a past-tense ending in *eaten*, because it doesn't make sense to say "to make eat.")

Reading for Understanding
Reading

1. Have students turn to Anthology page 260 and preview the text by looking at the format.
   - **How is this article similar to "The Fast Track"?** (They are both about Danica Patrick.)
   - **What features, or parts, does this text have that "The Fast Track" doesn't have?** (a time line and a chart)
   - **What do you predict the article will be about?** (It will tell about Danica Patrick's experiences in the 2005 Indianapolis 500.)
   - Have students turn to Anthology page 262 and preview the time line. **What do you think this time line will provide a summary of?** (important events in Danica's racing career)
   - **What information does the chart appear to contain?** (facts about Danica's personal life)

2. **Fluency** Read the first paragraph of the article aloud while students follow along in their books. Then have students read the remainder of the article, the time line, and the chart in small groups. If necessary, review the following fluency goal with students to increase reading rate: **As you become more familiar with the text, try to increase the speed with which you read.**

3. When students have finished their reading, check for literal comprehension by asking the following questions: **KNOWLEDGE**
   - *Paragraph 10:* **What record did Danica set in the 2005 Indy 500?** (Her starting and finishing positions were the best ever by a woman in the race.)
   - *Paragraph 12:* **What two "rookie mistakes" cost Danica the lead?** (hitting the gas pedal too hard after refueling; spinning out and hitting another car)
   - *Paragraph 14:* **What risk did Danica take late in the race?** (She chose to keep driving rather than refueling, in the hopes that she could finish on the gas she had.)
   - *Time Line:* **In what year did Danica win her first go-cart championship?** (1994)
   - *Time Line:* **What did Danica do in 2001?** (returned to the United States from England)
   - *Time Line:* **In what year did she finish in the top five in five different races?** (2003)
   - *Quick Facts:* **Where was Danica born?** (Beloit, Wisconsin)
   - *Quick Facts:* **In what year was she born?** (1982)

Checking for Comprehension *After Reading*

SKILL ✓

1. Have students apply what they understood from the text by asking the following questions:

   - **This text tells about Danica's experiences in the 2005 Indy 500. Is it written from Danica's point of view, or from the writer's point of view?** (writer's point of view) **What kind of text is it, then?** ANALYSIS (a biography)

   - **What are the *firsts* that Danica achieved in this race?** COMPREHENSION (her first Indy 500, first time she had raced more than 300 miles, first woman to lead the race) **What *first* seems most impressive to you? Why?** (Responses will vary.)

   - **If you had been a sports reporter at the race, tell me the *first* question you would've asked her after this race.** APPLICATION (Responses will vary.)

   - Read aloud the last paragraph of the article.

   - **How would you describe Danica's attitude toward her performance in the race?** EVALUATION (Possible responses: upbeat, positive, hopeful, realistic) **Do you think you would have felt the same way? Why?** APPLICATION (Responses will vary.)

2. **Challenge Questions If you were at a restaurant with Danica, which of these would she most likely order—a hamburger with fries, or grilled trout with broccoli? Why?** COMPREHENSION (trout with broccoli, because her favorite foods are fish and veggies) **How do you think these food choices are related to Danica's accomplishments?** SYNTHESIS (Possible response: They show that she takes care of herself; they keep her healthy and energetic, so that she can pursue her goals.)

3. Have students turn to Student Book page 192. Read the instructions aloud. Then have students work with a partner to fill in the chart. Monitor students as they work, providing correction and feedback as needed. When students are finished, review their responses as a class.

Expedition 14, Lesson 7   Name_____ Date_____

Comparing and Contrasting Texts

2 Complete the chart below to show how the two texts about Danica Patrick are similar and different.

	"The Fast Track"	"Making History at Indianapolis"
What kind of text is it?	expository article	expository article/time line/chart
What or who is it about?	Danica Patrick	Danica Patrick
What is the main idea?	Possible response: Danica loved racing as a young girl; she trained hard and had a great rookie year.	Possible response: Danica had a great race at the 2005 Indy 500.
What time period is covered in the text?	from the time she was 10 years old to 2005	text—May 29, 2005; time line—1992–2005
What did you most enjoy about this text?	Responses will vary.	Responses will vary.

192   ©Voyager Expanded Learning, L.P.

Provide English language learners support in using concrete and sensory details to build mental images of what they read. As students read selections with a partner, have them stop after specific paragraphs or after every two or three paragraphs and do the following:

• Write key concrete and sensory details from the text. For example: *Drivers race around an oval track for 200 laps while 300,000 fans scream in the stands.*

• Use the details to draw a picture of the scene.

• Write a description of the scene.

• Describe the scene aloud to one another.

• Reread the paragraph.

For a complete model of this strategy, see Expedition 12, Lesson 3.

Reading Response

Have students turn to Student Book page 193. Read the instructions aloud. Then have students work independently to write a response to these questions:

 What is remarkable about Danica Patrick? What lessons can teenagers learn from her success?

When students are finished, call on them to read their responses aloud.

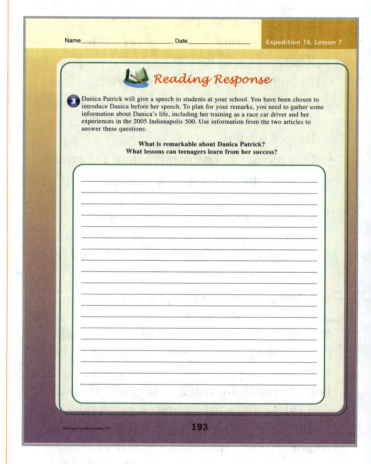

Passport Reading Journeys Library

Building Fluency

1. Place students in pairs according to reading level to build fluency. When pairing students, be sure that one student is a stronger reader (Student A) than the other student (Student B). However, do not reveal that stronger readers are paired with weaker readers. See *Passport Reading Journeys* Library Teacher's Guide for grouping guidelines.

2. Have students quickly choose reading material from the *Passport Reading Journeys* Library or another approved selection that is at the reading level of Student B. If students have not finished the previously chosen selection, they may continue reading from that selection. See *Passport Reading Journeys* Library Teacher's Guide for material selection guidelines.

3. Tell students that Student A will read one paragraph, and Student B will reread that same paragraph.

4. Have students follow this routine until the end of class.

5. If necessary, review the following practices to enhance fluency:
   • Rate and accuracy of reading
   • Expression during reading
   • Correction procedures

Library *Highlights*

Reading Independently

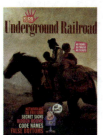

Level II

Students who enjoy learning about the history of the United States may enjoy *Kids Discover: Underground Railroad*, which explains reasons people secretly fled to the North.

Level III

Students might also enjoy reading *Kids Discover: Immigration*, which offers explanations for why people left their homelands for a new life in the United States.

Lesson 8

Advanced Word Study

Spelling

1. Direct students to Student Book page E14, Lesson 8. **We use the sounds we know and hear in a word to spell the word.** *Sub-* **is a prefix. Remember, a prefix is a word part that occurs at the beginning of a word.** *-En* **is a suffix. Remember, a suffix is a word part that occurs at the end of a word. Prefixes and suffixes often help us understand the meaning of a word. Let's spell words with this prefix and suffix. The first word is** *tighten.* **Say the word parts in the word** *tighten.* (tight, en) **What is the first word part?** (tight) **What are the sounds in** *tight*? (/t/ /ī/ /t/) **Write those sounds. What is the suffix?** (-en) **What are the sounds in** *-en*? (/e/ /n/) **Write those sounds.** Repeat with *weaken, spoken, sublime, subtract,* and *subside.*

2. Write the words on the board as students check and correct their words. Have them read the list of words.

1.	tighten	4.	sublime
2.	weaken	5.	subtract
3.	spoken	6.	subside

Sight Words

1. Direct students to line 1. Have them point to the first word. **This word is** *barrier.* **Read the word.** (barrier) **This is not a regular word. Let's read the word again.** (barrier) **Let's spell the word.** (b-a-r-r-i-e-r) **What is the word?** (barrier) Repeat with the remaining words. Then have students read the words. Ask students to tell the meanings of the words.

2. Direct students to lines 2 and 3. **Let's read these words.** Remind students that the rows of words consist of regular and irregular words. Point to the first word. **What is the word?** (refueled) Repeat with the remaining words. Call on individuals to read the words in a different order. Ask students to tell the meanings of the words.

▼ To Correct
For Regular Words: Say the sound(s) in the word, then ask students to repeat the sound(s). Have them read the word again with the correct sound(s). If students do not know the meaning of the word, review the word and/or word part to determine the meaning of the word.

For Irregular Words: Immediately say the correct word. Then have students read the word, spell it, and read it again. If students do not know the meaning of the word, review the word.

1. barrier I	priority I	genius I	agency I
2. refueled I	foreign I	height I	candidate R
3. league I	fourth I	characteristic I	lawyer R

Building to Fluency

1. Direct students to the phrases in the Student Book. Have them read through each phrase for accuracy. Then have students reread the phrases to increase their accuracy and fluency so that the phrases sound like natural speech.

2. Direct students to the Anthology article to locate the sentences containing the phrases. Have them read the sentences in the article accurately and fluently. Remind students to read in a way that sounds like natural speech.

▼ To Correct
Immediately say the correct word. Have students reread the word, then read the phrase or sentence again.

1. . . . a beacon of freedom and opportunity . . . *paragraph 3*
2. . . . hold these truths to be self-evident . . . *paragraph 9*
3. . . . having to compete with their own children for jobs . . . *paragraph 12*

Anthology Selection

OUT OF MANY, ONE

U.S. Senator Barack Obama delivers the keynote address at the Democratic National Convention in 2004.

In 2004, Barack Obama, a state senator from Illinois, ran as a candidate for the United States Senate. About four months before the election, Obama was invited to give the keynote speech to the Democratic National Convention. The following is an excerpt from that speech.

263

---

¹On behalf of the great state of Illinois, crossroads of a nation, Land of Lincoln, let me express my deepest gratitude for the privilege of addressing this convention.

²Tonight is a particular honor for me because, let's face it, my presence on this stage is pretty unlikely. My father was a foreign student, born and raised in a small village in Kenya. He grew up herding goats, went to school in a tin-roof shack. His father—my grandfather—was a cook, a domestic servant to the British.

³But my grandfather had larger dreams for his son. Through hard work and perseverance my father got a scholarship to study in a magical place, America, that shown as a beacon of freedom and opportunity to so many who had come before.

⁴While studying here, my father met my mother. She was born in a town on the other side of the world, in Kansas. Her father worked on oil rigs and farms through most of the Depression. The day after Pearl Harbor my grandfather signed up for duty; joined Patton's army, marched across Europe. Back home, my grandmother raised a baby and went to work on a bomber assembly line. After the war, they studied on the G.I. Bill, bought a house through FHA and later moved west, all the way to Hawaii, in search of opportunity.

⁵And they, too, had big dreams for their daughter. A common dream, born of two continents.

⁶My parents shared not only an improbable love, they shared an abiding faith in the possibilities of this nation. They would give me an African name, Barack, or "blessed," believing that in a **tolerant** America, your name is no barrier to success. They imagined me going to the best schools in the land, even though they weren't rich, because in a generous America you don't have to be rich to achieve your potential.

⁷They're both passed away now. And yet, I know that on this night, they look down on me with great pride.

⁸And I stand here today, grateful for the diversity of my heritage, aware that my parents' dreams live on in my two precious daughters. I stand here knowing that my story is part of the larger American story, that I owe a debt to all of those who came before me, and that, in no other country on Earth, is my story even possible.

264

---

⁹Tonight, we gather to **affirm** the greatness of our nation—not because of the height of our skyscrapers, or the power of our military, or the size of our economy. Our pride is based on a very simple premise, summed up in a declaration made over two hundred years ago: "We hold these truths to be self-evident, that all men are created equal, that they are **endowed** by their Creator with certain inalienable rights, that among these are life, liberty and the pursuit of happiness."

¹⁰That is the true genius of America—a faith in simple dreams, an insistence on small miracles; that we can tuck in our children at night and know that they are fed and clothed and safe from harm; that we can say what we think, write what we think, without hearing a sudden knock on the door; that we can have an idea and start our own business without paying a bribe; that we can participate in the political process without fear of retribution; and that our votes will be counted—at least, most of the time.

¹¹This year, in this election, we are called to reaffirm our values and our commitments, to hold them against a hard reality and see how we are measuring up to the legacy of our forbearers and the promise of future generations.

¹²And fellow Americans, Democrats, Republicans, Independents, I say to you, tonight: We have more work to do—more work to do for the workers I met in Galesburg, Illinois, who are losing their union jobs at the Maytag plant that's moving to Mexico, and now they're having to compete with their own children for jobs that pay 7 bucks an hour; more to do for the father I met who was losing his job and choking back the tears, wondering how he would pay $4,500 a month for the drugs his son needs, without the health benefits that he counted on; more to do for the young woman in East St. Louis, and thousands more like her, who has the grades, has the drive, has the will, but doesn't have the money to go to college.

¹³Now, don't get me wrong, the people I meet—in small towns and big cities and diners and office parks—they don't expect government to solve all of their problems. They know they have to work hard to get ahead—and they want to.

¹⁴Go into the collar counties around Chicago, and people will tell you they don't want their tax money wasted by a welfare agency or by the Pentagon.

265

---

¹⁵Go into any inner-city neighborhood, and folks will tell you that government alone can't teach our kids to learn; they know that parents have to teach, that children can't achieve unless we raise their expectations and turn off the television sets and eradicate the **slander** that says a black youth with a book is acting white. They know those things.

¹⁶People don't expect government to solve all their problems. But they sense, deep in their bones, that with just a slight change in **priorities**, we can make sure that every child in America has a decent shot at life, and that the doors of opportunity remain open to all. They know we can do better. And they want that choice. . . .

¹⁷Alongside our famous individualism, there's another ingredient in the American saga, a belief that we are all connected as one people.

¹⁸If there is a child on the south side of Chicago who can't read, that matters to me, even if it's not my child. If there is a senior citizen somewhere who can't pay for his or her prescription drugs, and having to choose between medicine and the rent, that makes my life poorer, even if it's not my grandparent. If there's an Arab American family being rounded up without benefit of an attorney or due process, that threatens my civil liberties.

¹⁹It is that fundamental belief—I am my brothers' keeper, I am my sisters' keeper—that makes this country work. It's what allows us to pursue our individual dreams and yet still come together as one American family.

²⁰"E pluribus unum:" Out of many, one.

Connect to the Author

Barack Obama was elected to the United States Senate in November 2004, less than four months after he gave this speech. Obama was born in 1961 in Hawaii. He graduated from Columbia University and then earned his law degree from Harvard, where he was the first African American to serve as editor of the *Harvard Law Review*. He worked as a civil rights lawyer, was elected to the Illinois State Senate, and then to the U.S. Senate. Obama is currently the only African American in the U.S. Senate.

Barack Obama

266

729

Comprehension and Vocabulary   *Before Reading*

1. Write these statements on the board:

   A. *One person working for justice cannot make a difference in people's lives.*

   B. *Migrant workers live and work under good conditions.*

   C. *Teenagers are too young to work in restaurants.*

   D. *Women lack the skills to be race car drivers.*

2. Have students list the letters *A–D* on a sheet of paper. **I will read aloud each statement on the board. Write "agree" or "disagree" next to the corresponding letter on your paper.**

3. After students respond to the statements, call on individuals to explain their responses. Expand the discussion by asking questions such as these:

   • **What can inspire someone to work for justice?** (Possible response: seeing barefoot and hungry children)

   • **Why do you disagree with statement *B*?** (Possible response: The account of Juan Medina's life describes hardships for migrants.)

   • **Why do many restaurants hire teens?** (Possible response: Teens are eager to learn and have a lot of energy.)

   • **What are two skills that make Danica a winner?** (Possible response: confidence and composure under pressure)

4. Write this statement on the board: *The son of a man raised in a small African village cannot become a U.S. senator.* **Do you agree or disagree? Why? Do you remember our discussion of how the work you do can reflect who you are? In the next text, you'll see that what you do can also reflect who your parents and grandparents are.**

Introduce Vocabulary

5. **We will read some new words in our next text, "Out of Many, One."**

   • Write the vocabulary words on the board. Include Challenge Words to meet the needs of students who are advancing.

   • Read the words to students.

   • Call on individuals to read the words as you point to them.

   • Provide correction and feedback as needed.

   ▶ Have students write the words in the Vocabulary Log.

6. Tell students that knowing the meanings of these words will help them better understand the article.

   For each word:

   • Read the word with its definition and the sentence that follows.

   • Write the sentences on the board.

   • Call on students to use their own words to give the meaning and some examples of each vocabulary word.

Vocabulary

tolerant	*allowing to exist; not wanting to limit*
	In a *tolerant* country, your name is not a barrier to success.
affirm	*to state that something is true*
	I want to *affirm* the greatness of this nation.
endow	*to provide or furnish*
	Parents can *endow* their children with pride in their heritage.
slander	*a critical and usually false statement*
	Let's do away with the *slander* that certain people do not have equal rights.
priority	*something given special attention; a main focus*
	One *priority* of a nation should be to educate all its children.

Challenge Words

Word Meaning

perseverance	*continuing with something even though it is difficult*
	You need *perseverance* as well as physical strength to run a marathon.
premise	*the starting point in a line of thinking*
	Based on the *premise* that all teenagers sleep late, we decided to hold the graduation party in the afternoon instead of the morning.

Review Persuasion

7. Have students recall Dolores Huerta's editorial, in which she urges women to get involved in solving some of the nation's problems. **What type of writing is the editorial?** (persuasive)

- **What is the purpose of persuasive writing?** (to convince readers to take a certain action or accept a certain way of thinking)

- **We've seen that persuasion can come in forms other than editorials, such as in advertisements and magazine articles. What are some ways you've practiced the art of persuasion?** (Possible responses: letters, e-mails, oral arguments)

8. Have students turn to Anthology page 263. **The text we'll read in this lesson uses persuasion.** Read aloud the introduction. **What is the form of this text?** (a speech) **What elements of persuasion would you expect to find in this speech?** (opinion statement, supporting reasons and details, counterargument, and conclusion)

9. **Speeches can have purposes other than persuasion. Think of speeches you've heard or read that were not meant to persuade. What were their purposes?** (Possible responses: to accept an award, to inform, to compare or describe, to entertain)

10. **As we read this speech, let's look for the elements of persuasion. Let's also pay attention to the effects of the speaker's words on us. Keep track of what goes on in your heart and your head as you read and listen. Remember that persuasion can target our emotions—or feelings—or our powers of logic—or reasoning—or both.**

Reading for Understanding

Reading

Places and Names to Look For:
- Barack Obama
- Patton
- Republicans
- Maytag
- Kenya
- Democrats
- Galesburg, Illinois
- East St. Louis

1. **As you read "Out of Many, One," you may come across some unfamiliar places and names.**
   - Write the words on the board.
   - Point to each word as you read the following:

   Our text is a speech given to *Democrats*, but meant for *Republicans* and all Americans as well. In it, Senator *Barack Obama* describes his diverse heritage. He tells of how his father came to America from *Kenya*, a country in Africa, in search of opportunity and of how, after the Pearl Harbor attack, his mother's father fought in General George *Patton's* army and later moved to Hawaii, where Obama was born. In the speech, Obama also urges Americans to renew their commitment to their common values. He highlights some of the nation's problems, using examples such as the workers at a *Maytag* plant in *Galesburg, Illinois*, who have lost jobs, and a young woman in *East St. Louis* who wants to go to college but lacks the money.
   - Call on individuals to read the words.

2. Read the first two paragraphs of the speech aloud, while students follow along in their books. Then have students read the remainder of the article with a partner. If necessary, review fluency goals with students and monitor for reading rate, accuracy, and expression.

3. When students have completed their reading, check for literal comprehension by asking the following questions: **KNOWLEDGE**
   - *Paragraph 2:* **Why did Obama think it unlikely that he would be giving a speech at this convention?** (His father grew up herding goats in Kenya, and his grandfather was a domestic servant.)
   - *Paragraph 3:* **How was Obama's father able to come to America?** (He got a scholarship to study in America.)
   - *Paragraph 4:* **Where did his mother grow up?** (Kansas)
   - *Paragraph 6:* **What does the name "Barack" mean?** ("blessed")
   - *Paragraph 9:* **On what idea does Obama say the greatness of our nation is based?** (the idea that all people are created equal and have certain basic rights)
   - *Paragraph 12:* **What main message does Obama want to give in this speech?** (That this country is great, but that we have more work to do.)
   - *Paragraph 20:* **What does the Latin phrase "E pluribus unum" mean?** ("Out of many, one.")
   - *Connect to the Author:* **What jobs did Obama hold before becoming a U.S. Senator?** (He worked as a civil rights lawyer and served on the Illinois State Senate.)

4. Have students reread the speech independently. Encourage students to monitor their own comprehension of the text by pausing occasionally to ask themselves *Am I understanding what I'm reading?* Tell students that when they do not understand what they are reading, they should reread that portion of the text.

732

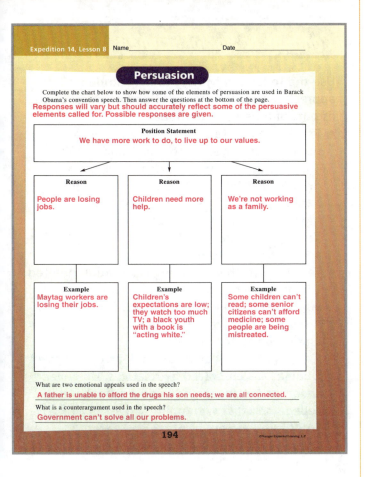

Expedition 14, Lesson 8   Name_____ Date_____

Persuasion

Complete the chart below to show how some of the elements of persuasion are used in Barack Obama's convention speech. Then answer the questions at the bottom of the page.
Responses will vary but should accurately reflect some of the persuasive elements called for. Possible responses are given.

Position Statement
We have more work to do, to live up to our values.

Reason	Reason	Reason
People are losing jobs.	Children need more help.	We're not working as a family.

Example	Example	Example
Maytag workers are losing their jobs.	Children's expectations are low; they watch too much TV; a black youth with a book is "acting white."	Some children can't read; some senior citizens can't afford medicine; some people are being mistreated.

What are two emotional appeals used in the speech?
A father is unable to afford the drugs his son needs; we are all connected.

What is a counterargument used in the speech?
Government can't solve all our problems.

194

Checking for Comprehension   *After Reading*

1. Have students return to Anthology page 263 and turn to Student Book page 194. Read the instructions aloud. Then have students work in pairs to fill in the chart as they take turns rereading paragraphs in the speech. When all students are finished, review their responses as a class.

2. Have students apply what they understood from the text by asking the following questions:

- **What does Obama believe is the source of America's greatness?** KNOWLEDGE (that "all men are created equal" and have certain rights) **Do you agree with him? Why or why not?** EVALUATION (Responses will vary.)

- **In the first part of the speech, Obama tells the story of his heritage. Why do you think he included this biographical information?** ANALYSIS (Possible response: to illustrate how people can come from humble beginnings in a poor country and succeed in America) **Does this information make his message more credible, or trustworthy, or less so? Why?** EVALUATION (Possible response: more credible, because we see how his family has passed on their belief that we can make our dreams come true)

- **What are two *why* questions that are answered in the speech?** ANALYSIS Write students' questions on the board. Call on other students to answer them.

- **Part of Obama's overall opinion statement is the belief in America's greatness. How is this belief related to his personal story?** (His personal story shows that there is much opportunity in America, even for immigrants.)

- **How would Dolores Huerta, Juan Medina and his family, and Danica Patrick likely react to Obama's speech?** SYNTHESIS (Possible response: They would all agree that everyone deserves an equal opportunity.)

733

3. **Challenge Question** According to Obama, what two ingredients make up "the American saga," or story? KNOWLEDGE (our individuality and our connection as people) In your opinion, which of these ingredients is more important? Why? EVALUATION (Responses will vary.)

Connect to Social Studies

Use the following activity to help students appreciate the importance of geographical place as part of a person's heritage.

- Explain that Barack Obama visited his father's homeland, Kenya, for the first time in 1987. There, Obama learned about the lives of his grandfather and father, neither of whom he had known very well. He visited Kenya again in the early 1990s to introduce his wife to his Kenyan relatives. In 2006, Obama returned for a third time to Kenya.

- Tell students that a rousing celebration greeted Obama in Kenya on his most recent trip, his first visit since being elected to the U.S. Senate. Crowds spilled into the streets, singing to him and cheering for him. Why do you think Kenyans gave Obama such a hearty welcome?

- Obama was embraced by relatives. He gave speeches to students in middle school and in college and met with political leaders of Kenya. "All of you are my brothers and sisters," Obama told the crowds in one of the poorest areas.

- Have students explore how they might feel about visiting an ancestor's homeland as Barack Obama did. Ask them to do the following:
  – Imagine that one or both of your parents grew up in a country other than the one in which you grew up. Like Barack Obama, you decide to visit your parent's homeland.
  – Write a journal entry in which you describe your feelings about seeing your parent's home country and meeting some of your relatives for the first time.

- Call on individuals to share their journal entries.

To increase difficulty: Have students work as a group to gather information about Kenya and prepare a report for the class.

Social Studies

Lesson 9

Anthology Selection

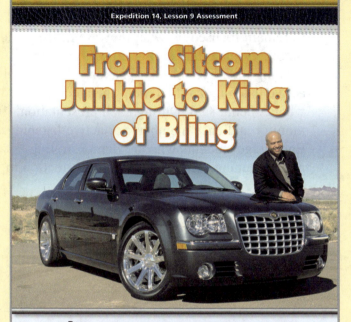

From Sitcom Junkie to King of Bling

[1]Ralph hated college and dropped out before the end of his first semester. With no real plan for his life, he spent his days in front of the television in his parents' basement. For a while he got by on a steady diet of granola and reruns of the *The Dukes of Hazzard*. This is not your typical picture of a success in the making. But that's exactly what Ralph Gilles was. Within a few years, he would become one of the hottest young car designers in America.

267

[2]So what inspired a sitcom junkie to climb out of the basement and all the way to the top of the corporate ladder? For starters, his older brother Max lit a fire under him. Max had watched Ralph make incredible sketches of cars ever since they were kids. He hated seeing all that talent go to waste.

[3]Everyone around Ralph recognized that he had a gift. When he was just 14 years old, his aunt sent a letter to the chairman of Chrysler. "My nephew sketches cars. You guys should hire him!" she wrote. A designer at Chrysler sent her a reply suggesting that Ralph go to a design school such as the Center for Creative Studies in Detroit.

[4]Max remembered that designer's advice and got his brother an application to the school. That was just the nudge that Ralph needed. He decided to go for it, but it wasn't easy to meet the deadline for enrollment. He had just one week to create 10 sketches and turn in his paperwork! Ralph worked night and day. He just barely made the deadline.

[5]Submitting that application was the first step in Ralph's turnaround. The next thing he knew, he got an acceptance letter in the mail! Then it was up to Ralph. This time around, he thrived at school. During his years at design school, he worked hard doing what he loved—designing cars! After he graduated, several companies offered him a job. One of them was Chrysler. There was no place in the world he would rather work! Chrysler made the Dodge Charger, like the one named "General Lee" in *The Dukes of Hazzard* TV show Ralph loved so much. Chrysler also made the powerful Viper, Ralph's favorite "bad-boy" muscle car. As soon as Chrysler made an offer, Ralph took the job.

[6]At first, the job had nothing to do with creating showy body designs for muscle cars. In fact, his first assignment was to design a speedometer needle. It certainly wasn't glamorous work. But Ralph was paid well, and he felt like a success. During this time, he bought his mother a PT Cruiser and started buying and customizing race cars for fun.

[7]While working on interiors, Ralph put his best foot forward. He showed a rare talent for designing and sketching both the interiors and exteriors of cars. At the same time, he showed he was passionate about good design. He argued for features and materials that would improve the image of Chrysler cars. Soon, "higher-ups" noticed Ralph's great instincts for what made a

268

car look bold, aggressive, and downright cool. After just a few years at the company, Ralph was named design director of one of Chrysler's seven design teams.

[8]That's how Ralph Gilles got the dream job he has today. He guides a team of 30 designers to come up with fresh, new designs customers will love. Gilles starts by finding what works in his designers' sketches and ideas. Then he discusses changes and possibilities with his team. Finally, he gives suggestions for improvements and sends the team back to make new drawings and models.

[9]Gilles tries to capture the appeal American cars used to have. He loves the cars of the past that were showy and bold. "It's bringing back what's good about American cars," Gilles says. "American cars have to be about not just a great car, but also a great-looking car, and an artful car—a car that says more about transportation than simply getting from point A to point B."

[10]One look at the new Chrysler 300 makes it easy to see what Gilles considers "great-looking" and "artful." It was named 2004 Car of the Year in most car magazines and is as popular with the young, hip crowd as it is with the CEO set. The 300 is a luxury sedan with a long hood and low roof. Its big rounded fenders and deep body give it a "muscular" look. But its real personality is in the broad grillwork across the front of the car. It makes the car seem to bare its teeth and growl.

[11]That fierce grillwork is a strong feature of the new Dodge Charger that Gilles's team designed too. The Charger is an updated version of the *Dukes of Hazzard* muscle car. The new model is tamer, but Gilles made sure it captured the same in-your-face personality of the old Charger. "In the company, a lot of people did comment, 'Wow, this car looks like it's angry!'" he says, obviously pleased at the effect.

[12]So far, it seems that the public loves what Gilles loves. His designs have won over 30 awards, and *Time Magazine* named him the "King of Bling." The new models he has worked on are selling well and boosting Chrysler's sales. In one year the company went from over $600 million in losses to almost $2 billion in profits! That is a near-miracle at a time when American car makers are in a sales slump.

[13]Glowing reviews and strong sales give Gilles confidence that he'll get

269

to keep on doing what he loves. "I'm one of the few people who can say I pinch myself every day, because this is exactly what I wanted," says Gilles. "The first 10 years have been pretty, pretty cool."

[14]So what does the future hold for this young trendsetter? "I really see myself with this company, and I really have no desire at all to look elsewhere," says Gilles.

[15]That's not surprising to hear from a man who has found a job where dreams come true!

Design Achievements in Gilles's Career

Assignment	Model
Interior design	Jeep Liberty
	Viper SRT-10
Overall design	Dodge M80
	Dodge Magnum
	Chrysler 300
	Dodge Charger

270

Expedition Review

1. Write the following names on the board: *Dolores Huerta, Juan Medina, Kysha Lewin, Colie Sparks, Danica Patrick, Barack Obama.* One by one, ask students briefly to tell what they learned about each in this Expedition.

   - **What qualities do all of these people share?** (hard work, determination)
   - **Which person do you think faced the greatest challenges in the struggle to succeed? Why?** (Responses will vary.)
   - **Which person do you admire the most? Why?** (Responses will vary.) **Which person are you most like? In what ways?** (Responses will vary.)
   - **Which person was the subject of a first-person fictional narrative?** (Colie Sparks) **Which was the subject of an interview?** (Kysha Lewin) **Which person is referred to in this descriptive detail that uses figurative language: She has that** *chip on the shoulder* **that says, "You don't think I can do it"?** (Danica Patrick)

2. Arrange students in groups, and assign each group a person listed on the board. Have students return to the text(s) about their subject and locate one quotation that shows something important about that person. (The quotation should be spoken by the actual person.) Then have students work together to write a sentence or two explaining what the quotation shows. Instruct students to use one or more of the following words in their sentences: *falter, migrant, assurance, persistent, tolerant, affirm, priority.*

3. **Challenge Words** If students have learned the Challenge Words, instruct them to include at least one of those words in their sentences, as well.

4. **Listening and Speaking** When all groups finish, have a representative from each read aloud the group's quotation and sentences. Encourage audience members to stay alert and to remain focused on what they are hearing and seeing. Explain that sitting up straight and keeping their eyes on the speaker is considered active listening and will help them comprehend what is being said. During each presentation, monitor audience members for active listening. Encourage students who are demonstrating good listening skills, and provide correction to others as needed.

5. After each group's sentences are read, call on other individuals to identify and give a meaning for the vocabulary word they heard.

Assessment

1. Have students turn to Student Book page 195. Then have them turn to Anthology page 267. Explain to students that they will read "From Sitcom Junkie to King of Bling" before they answer the questions on the Student Book page.

2. Read aloud the Tips for Success and assessment instructions. Then have students complete the assessment independently.

Reteaching Guidelines

Comprehension

If students incorrectly answer more than 2 out of 11 questions on the Comprehension Assessment, refer to the Reteach lesson on page 740a. Using the Comprehension section, reteach the skills, guide students in completing the practice activity, and reassess comprehension.

Vocabulary

If more than 20 percent of the students miss certain vocabulary items, reteach and practice those words using the Vocabulary section of the Reteach lesson on page 740c.

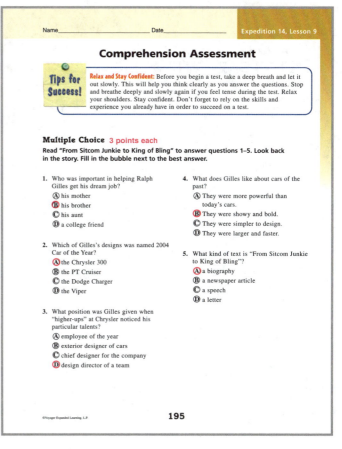

Name_____ Date_____   Expedition 14, Lesson 9

Comprehension Assessment

Tips for Success! **Relax and Stay Confident:** Before you begin a test, take a deep breath and let it out slowly. This will help you think clearly as you answer the questions. Stop and breathe deeply and slowly again if you feel tense during the test. Relax your shoulders. Stay confident. Don't forget to rely on the skills and experience you already have in order to succeed on a test.

Multiple Choice 3 points each
Read "From Sitcom Junkie to King of Bling" to answer questions 1–5. Look back in the story. Fill in the bubble next to the best answer.

1. Who was important in helping Ralph Gilles get his dream job?
   Ⓐ his mother
   Ⓑ his brother
   Ⓒ his aunt
   Ⓓ a college friend

2. Which of Gilles's designs was named 2004 Car of the Year?
   Ⓐ the Chrysler 300
   Ⓑ the PT Cruiser
   Ⓒ the Dodge Charger
   Ⓓ the Viper

3. What position was Gilles given when "higher-ups" at Chrysler noticed his particular talents?
   Ⓐ employee of the year
   Ⓑ exterior designer of cars
   Ⓒ chief designer for the company
   Ⓓ design director of a team

4. What does Gilles like about cars of the past?
   Ⓐ They were more powerful than today's cars.
   Ⓑ They were showy and bold.
   Ⓒ They were simpler to design.
   Ⓓ They were larger and faster.

5. What kind of text is "From Sitcom Junkie to King of Bling"?
   Ⓐ a biography
   Ⓑ a newspaper article
   Ⓒ a speech
   Ⓓ a letter

©Voyager Expanded Learning, L.P.   **195**

Expedition 14, Lesson 9   Name_____   Date_____

Short Response 4 points each
Read "From Sitcom Junkie to King of Bling" to answer questions 6–10. Look back in the story. Then write your answer on the line(s).

6. Explain the meaning of the title of this text: "From Sitcom Junkie to King of Bling."
   Before Gilles got into design school, he was a college dropout who spent his days watching an old sitcom, *The Dukes of Hazzard*. After he went to work for Chrysler and won awards for his flashy designs, *Time* magazine named him the "King of Bling."

7. Even though Gilles's early work at Chrysler wasn't glamorous, what two things encouraged him to keep working at the company?
   a. He was paid well.
   b. He felt like a success.

8. What are the three main steps that Gilles takes when working with his team to design a new car? Describe these in the order in which they occur.
   First step: He finds out what works in his designers' sketches.

   Second step: He discusses changes and possibilities with the team.

   Third step: He gives suggestions for improvements and has the team make new drawings and models.

9. Why is Gilles confident that he'll continue doing what he loves? List two reasons.
   Reason 1: He gets glowing reviews and awards.
   Reason 2: The cars he designs are selling well.

10. Based on the chart, name one car that Gilles has designed the interior for and one that he has designed overall.
    Interior: Possible responses: Jeep Liberty, Viper SRT–10
    Overall: Possible responses: Dodge M80, Dodge Magnum, Chrysler 300, Dodge Charger

196   ©Voyager Expanded Learning, L.P.

Name_____ Date_____   Expedition 14, Lesson 9

Extended Response 20 points

Read "From Sitcom Junkie to King of Bling" to plan your answer to question 11. Look back in the story. Use the information you find to complete the chart.

11. Imagine that you work for an automobile company. You are writing a letter to the company president to persuade her to hire Ralph Gilles. In your letter you write this opinion statement: *We should hire Ralph Gilles away from Chrysler.* Now you want to write supporting reasons in your letter. You have brainstormed several possible ideas. What is a reason to hire him related to each idea? **Possible responses are given.**

Idea Starters	Reasons to Hire
As a kid . . .	Even as a young boy, he was good at sketching cars.
In design school . . .	He did so well in school that several companies offered him a job.
Good instincts . . .	He has good instincts for what makes a car look bold and cool.
Success at Chrysler . . .	He has won more than 30 awards; his cars sell well.

©Voyager Expanded Learning, L.P.

197

Name_____ Date_____   Expedition 14, Lesson 9

21. We need to erase the <u>slander</u> that says a black youth with a book is "acting white." What does the word *slander* mean?
   - Ⓐ a critical and false statement
   - Ⓑ a statement that is repeated
   - Ⓒ a statement that is widely believed
   - Ⓓ a statement made as a joke

22. Juan nodded toward a <u>sliver</u> of sun peeking above the hillside. What does the word *sliver* mean?
   - Ⓐ a silver ray
   - Ⓑ a thin slice
   - Ⓒ a hidden object
   - Ⓓ a beam of light

23. I learned the perfect, <u>symmetrical</u> way to stack coffee cups and sugar packets. What does the word *symmetrical* mean?
   - Ⓐ requiring little effort
   - Ⓑ having the same form
   - Ⓒ taking little time
   - Ⓓ taking the least amount of space

24. In a <u>tolerant</u> America, your name is no barrier to success. What does the word *tolerant* mean?
   - Ⓐ caring
   - Ⓑ hard-working
   - Ⓒ accepting
   - Ⓓ free

25. Workers and their families <u>trek</u> northward as the days grow warmer. What does the word *trek* mean?
   - Ⓐ look
   - Ⓑ dream
   - Ⓒ hope
   - Ⓓ travel

26. At first, a table full of customers would <u>frighten</u> Colie. What does the word *frighten* mean?
   - Ⓐ make scared
   - Ⓑ confuse
   - Ⓒ make welcome
   - Ⓓ tease

©Voyager Expanded Learning, L.P.

199

Expedition 14, Lesson 9   Name_____ Date_____

Vocabulary Assessment 3 points each

For questions 12–26, read each sentence. Fill in the bubble next to the correct meaning for the underlined word.

12. Tonight we gather to <u>affirm</u> the greatness of our nation. What does the word *affirm* mean?
   - Ⓐ try to define
   - Ⓑ make better
   - Ⓒ state that something is true
   - Ⓓ give thanks for

13. Huerta organized a <u>boycott</u> against certain grape growers. What does the word *boycott* mean?
   - Ⓐ a violent demonstration
   - Ⓑ the refusal to buy something
   - Ⓒ a newspaper editorial
   - Ⓓ a type of announcement

14. Does the Constitution <u>endow</u> all citizens with certain rights? What does the word *endow* mean?
   - Ⓐ prevent
   - Ⓑ protect
   - Ⓒ provide
   - Ⓓ promote

15. She saw the father <u>extract</u> the toy from his child's grip. What does the word *extract* mean?
   - Ⓐ to play with
   - Ⓑ to pull out
   - Ⓒ to give to
   - Ⓓ to ask for

16. Dolores's marriage began to <u>falter</u>. What does the word *falter* mean?
   - Ⓐ fall apart
   - Ⓑ grow stronger
   - Ⓒ give up
   - Ⓓ find fault

17. Juan Medina is a <u>migrant</u> who was born in Mexico. What does the word *migrant* mean?
   - Ⓐ someone who moves often
   - Ⓑ someone not from the United States
   - Ⓒ someone who grows crops
   - Ⓓ someone who supports a cause

18. One <u>priority</u> should be to teach all children to read. What does the word *priority* mean?
   - Ⓐ way of performing a task
   - Ⓑ main focus
   - Ⓒ idea
   - Ⓓ problem

19. Preparing dressings was a <u>ritual</u>. What does the word *ritual* mean?
   - Ⓐ a difficult task
   - Ⓑ the first step in a series
   - Ⓒ a set way of doing things
   - Ⓓ a requirement

20. All employees have to <u>sanitize</u> their hands. What does the word *sanitize* mean?
   - Ⓐ wipe
   - Ⓑ clean
   - Ⓒ cover
   - Ⓓ use

198   ©Voyager Expanded Learning, L.P.

Expedition Wrap-Up

1. After students have completed the assessment, bring them together to discuss the probing questions as a way to provide closure for Expedition 14. Briefly discuss each of the Expedition texts. Then watch DVD 14.2 together as a class. Have students turn to Anthology page 245. Ask students to summarize the response to each probing question that was given on the DVD.

2. Conclude the Expedition by reviewing with students some of the jobs and causes they read about in this Expedition. Then ask them to brainstorm a list of jobs they would like to have and causes they would like to work for. Discuss with students where they could find out more about these jobs and causes. Have students record and save these ideas as possible future research topics.

Strategic Online Learning Opportunities®

Students read a passage about Mary Bethune and her work in making education available for African American children and adults.

Content Connection

Social Studies

$1.50 and a Dream
by Toni A. Watson

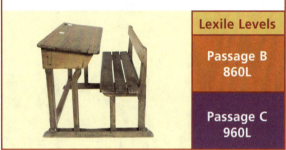

Lexile Levels
Passage B 860L
Passage C 960L

Assessment

- Metacognition
- Content
- Vocabulary
- Main Idea
- Summary

SKILL ✓

Based on their assessment scores, students automatically are assigned either the Skills Practice for reinforcement or the Independent Practice and Extension Opportunities.

SKILLS PRACTICE

Vocabulary Strategies
- Context
- Word Parts: Prefixes and Suffixes
- Word Parts: Compound Words

Dictionary Skills

Main Idea Strategy: W–I–N
- Identifying the Most Important *Who* or *What*
- Identifying the Most Important *Information*
- Stating the Main Idea in a Small *Number* of Words

Questioning

Writing
- Responding to Texts
- Writing a Summary Statement

INDEPENDENT PRACTICE

Vocabulary Strategies

Writing
- Writing a Summary Statement
- Responding to Texts

EXTENSION OPPORTUNITIES

- Online Books
- Book Cart
- Review of Previous Passages

Reteach

■ Comprehension

┌───┐
Reteach Skills

✔ Biography — Lesson 1

✔ Autobiography — Lesson 1

✔ Direct Quotations — Lesson 4
└───┘

Before Reading

Biography and Autobiography

1. **In this Expedition, we learned about a kind of narrative called a *biography*. The word part *bio-* means "life." What kind of story does a biography tell?** (a story about someone's life)

2. Write these titles on the board: *All About Callie the Cowgirl*, by U. Bet; *My Life as a Cowgirl*, by Callie Corral.

3. **Remember that a biography tells the story of someone *else's* life. The author and the subject of the biography are two different people. Which of these is the title of a biography?** (the first) **How can you tell?** (It is about Callie the Cowgirl, but it is written by U. Bet.)

4. **We also learned about a narrative called an *autobiography*. The word part *auto-* means "self." What kind of story does an autobiography tell?** (a story about oneself) **Which title on the board is the title of an autobiography?** (the second) **How can you tell?** (It is written by Callie and tells about Callie's own life.)

5. **Autobiographies are *first-person narratives*. First-person narratives are told from the writer's point of view. They use the words *I*, *me*, *we*, and *our*.** Write the following sentences on the board:
   - *I was born to Ida and Irwin Corral in the year 1845.*
   - *Callie Corral was the daughter of Ida and Irwin Corral.*

Have students tell which sentence is from a biography and which is from a first-person narrative. Ask them to explain their thinking.

6. If students have difficulty answering questions, model how to distinguish biography from autobiography using the instructional frameworks in Lesson 1.

Reading for Understanding

1. Have students turn to Anthology page 267. **As we read this text, let's think about whether it is a biography or or whether it is told from first-person point of view.**

2. Read aloud the first paragraph, then have students read the remainder of the text aloud with you.

After Reading

Direct Quotations

1. **Is the text we just read a biography or an autobiography?** (a biography) **How do you know?** (It tells about Ralph Gilles's life, but it is not written by Gilles.)

2. **Someone other than Ralph Gilles wrote this text. However, the writer included some of Gilles's own words.** Direct students' attention to paragraph 9, and point out the quotation marks around Gilles's words in the second sentence. **In a biography, the words that appear inside quotation marks are *direct quotations*, or words that someone other than the author actually said in real life. A writer uses direct quotations to add interest to the text, or to help illustrate a certain point.**

3. Distribute copies of Reteach page 27, and draw a two-column chart on the board. Read the instructions aloud. Guide students to complete the chart as you fill in the chart on the board.

4. Have students compare and contrast each detail listed in the chart with the quotation that illustrates it. **Which is more interesting or memorable? Why? What strong words or vivid images stand out in the quotation?**

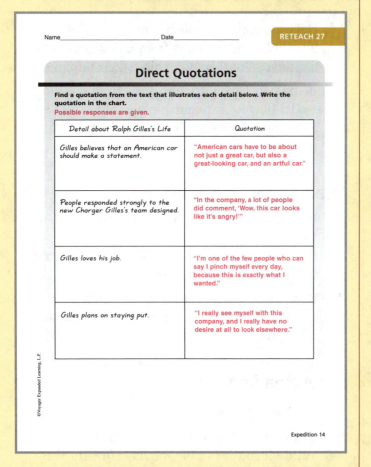

Checking for Comprehension

1. Distribute copies of Reteach page 28. Then have students turn to the text on Anthology page 267. Explain to students that they will read this text before answering the questions on Reteach page 28.

2. Read aloud the Keys to Comprehension section and the assessment instructions. Then have students complete the assessment independently.

3. Review the correct answers and discuss any questions that students answered incorrectly.

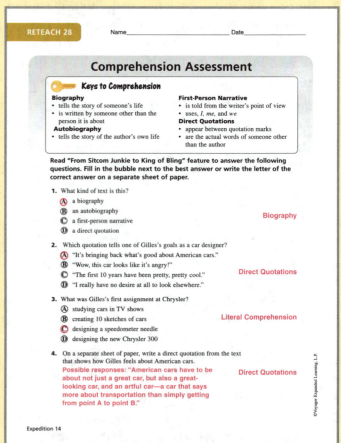

Extra Support

Biography and Autobiography

If students need additional support, write the following titles on strips of paper: *The Life of Teensy Tall, How I Became a Dog Food Chef, Dr. Dungeon: The Dark Years,* and *My Life as a Mystery Shopper.* Have students tell whether each is the title of a biography or an autobiography, and why. Then have students write their own made-up titles on sentence strips, exchange strips with a partner, and tell what kind of text the title indicates.

■ Vocabulary

1. Write on the board the specific words that students have missed. Then provide two or three categories into which these words might be sorted (such as *Thing*, *Action Word*, and *Describing Word*; or *Related to Success* and *Not Related to Success*). Alternatively, guide students to come up with categories of their own. Write the categories on the board in a table such as this one, and assist students in sorting the words. Then discuss why students categorized words the way they did.

Category 1:	Category 2:	Category 3:

2. When students have completed the graphic organizer, check comprehension by having them write in their own words the meaning of each vocabulary word.

■ Research Process

Teach and Model

1. You have written several kinds of expository texts so far. You have written a compare-and-contrast text, a persuasive text, a cause-and-effect text, and others. The ideas for these texts came from your own knowledge and experience. In fact, every piece of good writing starts in the writer's mind. However, you will sometimes find that you have to look elsewhere for information. You might need to find answers to questions you have about a topic. Or you might need to find facts and details that support what you already know. When you look elsewhere for information—for example, in books or on the Internet—you are doing *research*. In this lesson, we will learn how to begin the research process.

2. Let's say you come across an unusual sporting event on TV. It looks a little bit like polo, a game played on horseback that you have seen before, but not exactly. You hear the announcer say the name of the sport, which you don't recognize, and also *Argentina*, which you know is a country in South America. You like learning about unusual games, so you decide to research the sports of Argentina. The next morning, you jump on your bike and ride to the library.

Sample Sources

1. Once you arrive at the library, you're not sure where to begin looking. Then you remember that the library recently purchased a brand-new set of encyclopedias. You also know that encyclopedias include information on just about every topic. You head to the encyclopedia table. You look at the letters on the spines of the volumes. You start to choose volume *S* for *Sports*, but then decide the article on sports might be too general. It probably won't include information on sports played in the country of Argentina. You decide to look in volume *A* for *Argentina* instead. Distribute Writing pages 49 and 50 to students.

Name_____ Date_____

WRITING 49

ENCYCLOPEDIA

ARGENTINA

Argentina is the second-largest country of South America. It is located in the southern tip of the continent, stretching north to south alongside its neighbor, Chile. Argentina is made up of a wide variety of landforms, climates, and peoples.

GOVERNMENT

Argentina has a federal government consisting of three branches. The executive branch is made up of a president and a vice president, who are elected every four years. The legislative branch consists of the National Congress, which has two houses, the Chamber of Deputies and the Senate. Its judicial branch consists of a supreme court and a federal court system.

CULTURE

Argentineans enjoy a wide array of fine arts and leisure activities, including music, dance, and sports. It is also well-known for its delicious foods, many of which are grown or produced in the country. Argentina is home to many writers and artists, and has one of the strongest movie-making industries in Latin America.

Music. Argentinean music is closely tied to a variety of dances. The most well-known of these is the tango. Folk music such as chacacera, zamba, and milonga are also popular forms of Argentinean music. These forms combine Spanish music, inherited from early settlers from Spain, and native Indian music. The guitar is one of the most common instruments in Argentinean music.

Food. Argentinean cuisine is a mixture of European and native Indian flavors and dishes. Many Argentinean dishes contain beef or other meat, along with regionally grown vegetables and grains. Carbonada, a beef stew with rice, potatoes, corn, squash, apples, and pears, is a typical Argentinean dish. The empanada, a fried or baked dumpling filled with meats and vegetables, is another traditional Argentinean favorite.

Sports. The people of Argentina love sports, soccer or fútbol in particular. The Argentinean national soccer team has won two World Cups and has come in second place twice. Native Argentinean sports include a game called pato, which is played on horseback.

©Voyager Expanded Learning, L.P.

63

Expedition 14

2. You open volume *A*. Its entries are arranged alphabetically. You find this article on Argentina in between articles on the Arctic and Aristotle. You start reading at the beginning of the entry. Read the introductory paragraph aloud. This introduction gives a general overview of the country, but it doesn't mention sports. So you begin to preview the text. When you scan it, you see that it is has headings such as *Government* and *Culture*. You also see a photo of a soccer match. That seems directly related to the topic of sports, so you decide there is probably information about sports on one of these pages. You look more closely at the headings. You notice that the section titled *Culture* has other boldfaced headings in it. One is *Music*. Another is *Food*. Then you see *Sports*. You have found just what you are looking for!

Name_____ Date_____

ENCYCLOPEDIA

Fig.-3: Argentineans enjoy participating in team sports.

ARGENTINA *continued*

ECONOMY
Traditionally, Argentina's economy is based on agriculture, although in the years following World War II its government encouraged industrialization.

Agriculture. In spite of the growth of manufacturing in the late 1900s, agriculture remains a vital part of Argentina's economy. Corn, soybeans, and wheat are its major crops, and grapes and other fruits are grown in the foothills of the Andes mountains.

Manufacturing. Most of Argentina's manufacturing occurs in and around the cities of Buenos Aires, Córdoba, and Rosario. Major industries include

64

Expedition 14

Evaluating Sources

1. **When you are researching a topic, you have to decide whether you can trust a source before you use its information. In other words, you have to evaluate its credibility. This is especially true of sources on the Internet. They all tend to look alike—but this does not mean that they all contain true and accurate information. For example, some Web sites want you to buy something, so they might exaggerate information or tell half-truths. Other Web sites—such as those connected to schools or nonprofit organizations—usually have a more trustworthy purpose. Their main goal is to provide people with accurate, helpful information.** On the board, write *www.utexas.edu* and *www.redcross.org*. Circle the domains *.edu* and *.org*. **These endings help you to know which sites are trustworthy. *Edu* tells you that the Web site is attached to a school, and *org* tells you that it is attached to an organization. These are the kinds of Web sites you want to find and use when you are researching a topic.**

2. Distribute Writing page 52 to students. **This checklist includes some of the things that make a source trustworthy.** Call on a student to read the qualities of a credible source in the first column. **Let's look more closely at what each of these means by returning to the encyclopedia entry on Argentina.**

3. Have students return to the sample entry on Writing pages 49 and 50. Guide students to use the questions on the checklist to evaluate the credibility of the source. Have them place a checkmark next to each question they answer *yes*.

4. **Based on this checklist, is the encyclopedia entry a credible source? Why?** (Yes, because it relates to my topic, its main purpose is to inform, it is current, and it is well-known for its correct facts.)

---

3. Read the subsection on sports aloud. Then ask a student to summarize the information. **This gives you a good start—it even mentions a game played on horseback. But the information isn't as detailed as you had hoped. You bookmark the article and leave it on your table. Then you decide to search the Internet. You find an available computer and locate the search window on the home page. In the search window, you type the key words *Argentina* and *sports*. The search engine gives you several Web sites to choose from. You click on the first one.**

4. Distribute Writing page 51. **This is the Web site you have chosen. You skim the page.** Read the title and the headings aloud. **This page seems to include a lot more information than the encyclopedia did. You print the page out and return to your table.**

the Thrill of Sports — Argentina

SPORTS

Futbol
As in other Latin American countries, soccer, or *fútbol*, ranks as the most popular sport. This sport is played by two opposing teams who attempt to kick the ball down a field and into a goal. The game of soccer was first introduced to Argentina in the late 1800s by British soldiers. Today, two of the most popular Argentinean soccer teams are the Boca Juniors and the River Plate. These dreams draw huge crowds to the soccer stadiums of Buenos Aires each weekend.

Pato
Pato is a uniquely Argentinean sport. It was first played by the Gauchos, early cowboys who wandered the plains of Argentina during the 1600s and 1700s. *Pato* is the Spanish word for "duck." Originally, the game was played by two teams on horseback who battled over a duck in a leather pouch with two handles. Players on opposite teams would grab the handles of the pouch and pull until the one of the players let go. Today, a leather ball with handles is used in place of the unlucky duck.

Tennis
Wealthy British immigrants first brought the game of tennis to Argentina in the 1800s. This sport was reserved for the upper classes until Argentinean Guillermo Vilas became a world tennis champion in the 1970s. Since then, tennis has grown wildly popular among young Argentineans. In the late 1980s and early 1990s, Gabriela Sabatini was a top-ranked female player, followed by Paola Suárez in the early 2000s.

Source: Colombo, Clara. Sports in Argentina. Buenos Aires: Poco Publications, 2007.

If you like sports and a rowdy crowd, Argentina has the stadium for you.

About Argentina
Argentina is the second-largest country of South America. It is located in the southern tip of the continent, stretching north to south alongside its neighbor, Chile. Argentina is made up of a wide variety of landforms, climates, and peoples.

HOME / TRAVEL / LODGING / TRANSPORTATION / ATTRACTIONS

Expedition 14

Research Process

Credibilty Checklist

✔ A Credible Source Is . . .	Questions to Ask Yourself
Relevant	• Does this source relate to my general topic? • Does this source contain information about my specific topic?
Objective	• Is the author's main purpose to inform? • Is the author's main purpose to make money?
Current	• Was this source printed, posted, or updated within the last several years?
Accurate	• Is the source well-known for its correct facts? • If not, does the source tell where its information came from?

Expedition 14

5. Distribute clean copies of the checklist to students, and redirect their attention to Writing page 51. Then have students work in pairs to evaluate the credibility of the Web site. Before they begin, point out that the Web site seems to have two purposes, or motives: giving information about Argentinean sports, as well as persuading the reader to visit Argentina. The second motive may make the Web site biased, or intent on making something sound better than it is. However, because the source of the information is listed at the bottom of the page, you can be reasonably sure the information is credible.

6. Based on this checklist, is the Web page a credible source? Why? (Yes; it relates to my topic, one of its purposes is to inform, it is current, and it tells where its facts came from.)

Guided Practice

1. Now that you've decided that both of your sources are credible, it is time to dive into them to find the information you need. Once you find this information, you will take notes on it so that you can recall it later on. Distribute Writing page 53, and draw the outline for Source 1 on the board. Have students write *Argentina* in the topic box. **When you are researching a specific topic, it is good to come up with some questions that will guide you. Here are some good questions to use when researching the foods of a certain country.** Read the questions aloud.

Name_____ Date_____ **WRITING 53**

Finding Sources and Taking Notes

Use the graphic organizer to find sources and take notes on your topic.
Use an extra sheet of paper, if needed.

TOPIC

My research topic is sports in the country of _____

SOURCE 1

My first source is: _____

What are some popular sports in this country?

I.   First sport: _____
    A. How is it played? _____
    B. How or where did it get started? _____
    C. Who are some famous players or teams? _____

II. Second sport: _____
    A. How is it played? _____
    B. How or where did it get started? _____
    C. Who are some famous players or teams? _____

III. Third sport: _____
    A. How is it played? _____
    B. How or where did it get started? _____
    C. Who are some famous players or teams? _____

Additional Information
_____

Expedition 14

WRITING 54 Name_____ Date_____

Finding Sources and Taking Notes

SOURCE 2

My second source is: _____

What are some popular sports in this country?

I.   First sport: _____
    A. How is it played? _____
    B. How or where did it get started? _____
    C. Who are some famous players or teams? _____

II. Second sport: _____
    A. How is it played? _____
    B. How or where did it get started? _____
    C. Who are some famous players or teams? _____

III. Third sport: _____
    A. How is it played? _____
    B. How or where did it get started? _____
    C. Who are some famous players or teams? _____

Additional Information
_____

Expedition 14

---

2. **Let's start with the encyclopedia entry. Where did we first locate information about some sports that are played in Argentina?** (under the Culture heading, in the Sports section) Reread the first two sentences aloud. **We just learned that one popular sport in Argentina is soccer, or *fútbol*.** Write this next to item *I* on the outline and have students do the same. Read the first question under section I aloud. **Did we learn the answer to this question?** (no) **Let's keep reading.** Finish reading the section aloud. **What do these sentences tell us about?** (pato) Have students write this next write this next to item II. Continue reading, then have students write an answer to the first question under section II.

3. **There are still quite a few blanks in our outline. This source gave us some information, but not enough. Let's read the Web page to see what we can find there.** Redirect students' attention to the Web page on Writing page 51. Distribute Writing page 54 to students, and write a second outline on the board.

4. Read the section on Fútbol aloud, and have students identify and write information in the first part of the outline.

5. Have students work in small groups or in pairs to complete the outline using information from the remaining two sections on the Web page. Monitor and guide students as they work. When all students are finished, have them share what they wrote with the class. Write students' responses on the board.

Independent Practice

1. Take students to the library. Distribute two clean copies of Writing page 52 and one clean copy of Writing pages 53 and 54 to students. **Now it is your turn to do your own research. Later, we will turn the information we find into a research report. Now, though, your job is simply to gather information.**

2. **The first step is to choose a country whose sports you would like to learn more about.** If possible, display a world map, provide a list of major world countries, or provide books on world sports for students to look through. When they are ready, have students write their country of choice in the topic box.

3. **The next step is to find credible, relevant sources. For this research report, I'd like you to find information from two kinds of sources: an encyclopedia article, and a Web page of your choice.** Have some students begin working online, while others use the encyclopedias. Remind students to write the specific name of their source on the top line of each source box. For the Web page, have students copy the Web address from the address window, along with any other sources mentioned on the page. For the encyclopedia, have them copy the full title of the encyclopedia from the title page, as well as the publisher and the date of publication from the copyright page. Guide students to evaluate each source using one of the checklists you provided.

4. **Once you have found a credible source, the next step is to skim it, read the relevant portions, and write down important information related to your topic in your own words.** Have students take notes by filling in the outlines on Writing pages 53 and 54. Encourage students to use their own words, rather than copying the information verbatim from the source. Explain that using someone else's exact words is called plagiarism, which is a serious ethical violation.

5. Help students locate information as needed. If a third source is required, have students write another outline on a separate sheet of paper. Encourage students to write down additional interesting information they find in the box on Writing page 54.

6. After students have taken notes from at least two sources, ask them to share one or two interesting pieces of information they discovered with the class. Next, guide them to compare and contrast the two sources they found. Use the following questions:
   - What information did one source include that the other did not?
   - Did either source include helpful features such as maps, diagrams, or photos? How did these features aid your understanding of the topic?
   - Which source did you find most credible? Most interesting? Most informative? Why?

7. Close the lesson by telling students that in the next writing lesson, they will pull all of their information together in the form of a research report. Collect all of students' papers and save them for use in the next lesson.

Writing and Technology

When online or CD-ROM encyclopedias are available, allow students to use these, as well. Guide them to navigate the software or the Web site by choosing appropriate key words and by selecting links that will take them to the information they are looking for. Finally, help students print out relevant portions of the entry to use as they take notes.

Expedition

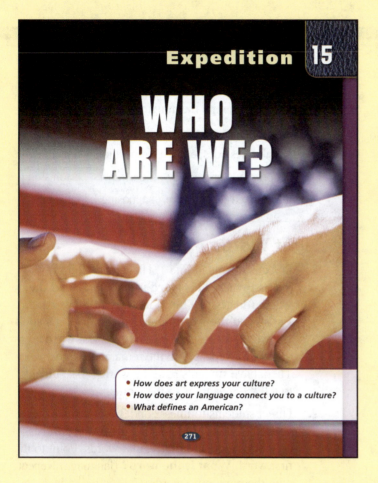

Expedition 15

WHO ARE WE?

- How does art express your culture?
- How does your language connect you to a culture?
- What defines an American?

271

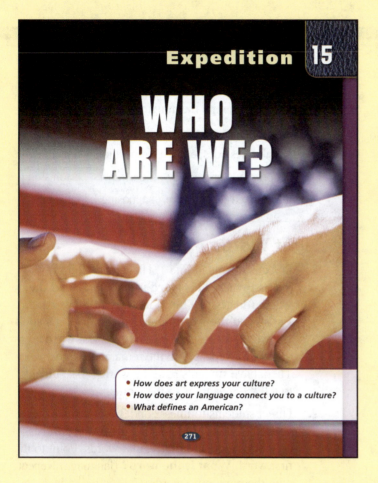
DVD 15.1, 15.2

In this Expedition, the DVD segments illustrate the many things that go into defining a person's cultural identity, both individually and as an American. They investigate how all sorts of influences—from languages to artistic expression—lead individuals to answer the question, "Who Are We?"

Strategic Online Learning Opportunities®

Students access the Web site http://solo.voyagerlearning.com for an interactive SOLO® session. In each session, students apply previously taught strategic skills to new readings on the student's appropriate Lexile® level. Consult the *Passport Reading Journeys*™ SOLO User Guide for a comprehensive overview of this component.

Passport Reading Journeys Library

Students may select reading materials from the *Passport Reading Journeys* Library. Partner and independent reading opportunities allow students to read authentic text on their Lexile level to build fluency. Teacher resources are provided in the *Passport Reading Journeys* Library Teacher's Guide.

In This Expedition

READINGS

Lessons 1 and 2
from Learning English: My New Found Land, by Julia Alvarez
How I Learned English, by Gregory Djanikian

Lessons 3 and 4
I Hear America Singing, by Walt Whitman
I, Too, by Langston Hughes

Lessons 6 and 7
Graffiti Is a Crime!
Turn Vandals into Artists

Lesson 8
Phizzog, by Carl Sandburg
In the Beauty Zone with Image Zone

Lesson 9 Assessment
Immigrants in America: Wheatsville Sounds Off

SKILLS

CPR Vocabulary Strategy Review
- Context, Word Parts, Resources

Narrative and Expository Texts Review
- Autobiography
- Poetry
- Description
- Persuasion
- Problem/Solution

Advanced Word Study

Multisyllabic Words

1. **Remember, sometimes it's easier to read parts of a longer word before reading the entire word. One way is to use what we know about open and closed syllables.** Write the word *rivalry* on the board. Underline the word part *ri*. **What is the first word part?** (ri) **What kind of syllable is this word part?** (open) **How do we know?** (It has one long vowel sound with no consonants following it, or closing it in.) Underline *val*. **What is the next word part?** (val) **Read the rest of the word.** (ry) **What is the word?** (rivalry) *Rivalry* means "competing for the same thing."

   Another way to read longer words is to use what we know about prefixes and suffixes. Write the word *untreatable* on the board. Underline the prefix *un-*. **What is this prefix?** (un-) **What is the next part?** (treat) Underline the suffix *-able*. **What is this suffix?** (-able) **What is the word?** (untreatable) **The word** *untreatable* means "not treatable or curable."

2. Have students turn to page E15, Lesson 1 in the back of the Student Book. Direct students to line 1. **What is the first word part?** (poss) **What is the next part?** (ib) **What is the next part?** (il) **What is the next part?** (it) **What is the suffix?** (-ies) **What is the word?** (possibilities) **The word** *possibilities* **means "options or chances."** Repeat with the remaining words. Call on individuals to read the words in random order. Ask students to tell the meanings of the words.

3. Direct students to lines 2 and 3. Have them read the words. Then, call on individuals to read the words in a different order. Ask students to tell the meanings of the words.

   #### ▼ To Correct
   For Multisyllabic Words: **What is the first word part? What is the next part? What is the word?** If students do not know the meaning of the word, review the word and/or word parts to determine the meaning of the word.

   For Sounds in Words: Say the correct sound(s), then ask students to repeat the sound(s).

Have them read the word again with the correct sound(s). If students do not know the meaning of the word, review the word and/or word parts to determine the meaning of the word.

1. possibilities	desperation	prepositional	unnatural
2. deportations	incredibly	skyscrapers	astonishing
3. immigrated	expressive	supposing	interminably

Sight Words

1. Direct students to line 1. Have them point to the first word. **This word is** *diagram*. **Read the word.** (diagram) **This is not a regular word. Let's read the word again.** (diagram) **Let's spell the word.** (d-i-a-g-r-a-m) **What is the word?** (diagram) Repeat with the remaining words. Then, have students read the words. Ask students to tell the meanings of the words.

2. Direct students to lines 2 and 3. **Let's read these words.** Remind students that the rows of words consist of regular and irregular words. Point to the first word. **What is the word?** (language) Repeat with the remaining words. Call on individuals to read the words in a different order. Ask students to tell the meanings of the words.

   #### ▼ To Correct
   For Regular Words: Say the sound(s) in the word, then ask students to repeat the sound(s). Have them read the word again with the correct sound(s). If students do not know the meaning of the word, review the word and/or word part to determine the meaning of the word.

   For Irregular Words: Immediately say the correct word. Then have students read the word, spell it, and read it again. If students do not know the meaning of the word, review the word.

1. diagram I	anxiety I	accentuate I	fluent I
2. language I	nurture I	barrier I	priority R
3. genius I	turbulent I	agency I	writhing R

Anthology Selection

from

LEARNING ENGLISH: MY NEW FOUND LAND

by Julia Alvarez

In this essay, the author describes the uneasiness and disorientation she felt when she first arrived in New York, unable to speak English. She explains how she quickly learned more and more, and she captures the feeling of triumph she felt when at last she mastered the new language.

272

---

[1]When I was 10, we immigrated to New York. How astonishing, a country where everyone spoke English! These people must be smarter, I thought. Maids, waiters, taxi drivers, doormen, bums on the street, garbagemen, all spoke this difficult language. It took some time before I understood that Americans were not necessarily a smarter, superior race. It was as natural for them to learn their mother tongue as it was for a little Dominican baby to learn Spanish. . . .

[2]Soon it wasn't so strange that everyone was speaking in English instead of Spanish. I learned not to hear it as English, but as sense. I no longer strained to understand; I understood. I relaxed in this second language. Only when someone with a heavy Southern or British accent spoke in a movie or when the priest **droned** his sermon—only then did I experience that little catch of anxiety. I worried that I would not be able to "keep up" with the voice speaking in this second language. I would be like those people from the Bible we had studied in religion class, at the foot of an enormous tower that looked just like the skyscrapers all around me. They had been punished for their pride by being made to speak some slightly different version of the same language so that they didn't understand what anyone was saying.

[3]But at the foot of those towering New York skyscrapers, I began to understand more and more—not less and less—English. In sixth grade, I had one of the first of a lucky line of great teachers who began to **nurture** a love of the language, a love that had been there since childhood of listening closely to words. Sister Bernadette did not make our class **interminably** diagram sentences from a workbook or learn a catechism of grammar rules. Instead, she asked us to write little stories imagining we were snowflakes, birds, pianos, a stone in the pavement, a star in the sky. What would it feel like to be a flower with roots in the ground? If the clouds could talk, what would they say? She had an expressive, dreamy look that was accentuated by her face being framed in a wimple. Supposing, just supposing . . . My mind would take off, soaring into possibilities: a flower with roots, a star in the sky, a cloud full of sad, sad tears, a piano crying out each time its back was tapped, music only to our ears.

[4]Sister Bernadette stood at the chalkboard. Her chalk was always snapping in two because she wrote with so much energy, her whole habit shaking with the swing of her arm, her hand tap tap tapping on the board. "Here's a simple sentence: *The snow fell.*" Sister Bernadette pointed with

catechism: instruction in Christianity

wimple: woman's head covering

habit: dark gown worn by nuns

273

---

her chalk, her eyebrows lifted, her wimple poked up. "But watch what happens if we put an adverb at the beginning and a prepositional phrase at the end: *Gently the snow fell on the bare hills.*"

[5]I thought about the snow. I saw how it might fall on the hills, tapping lightly on the bare branches of trees. Softly it would fall on the cold, cold fields. On toys children had left out in the cold, and on cars and on little birds and on people out late walking on the streets. Sister Bernadette filled the chalkboard with snowy print, on and on, handling and shaping and moving language, scribbling all over the board until English, those little bricks of meaning, those little fixed units and counters, became a charged, fluid mass that carried me in its great fluent waves, rolling and moving onward, to **deposit** me on the shores of the only homeland. I was no longer a foreigner with no ground to stand on. I had landed in language.

[6]I had come into my English.

Connect to the Author

Though she was born in New York City in 1950, Julia Alvarez spent her first 10 years in the Dominican Republic. This country occupies two-thirds of an island in the Caribbean Sea. It has had a turbulent history. During Alvarez's childhood, an oppressive dictator ruled the island. Alvarez and her family had to flee in 1960 when authorities discovered her father's part in a plot to overthrow the dictator. Much of Alvarez's writing deals with the Dominican Republic and the people who live there. She draws from her experiences and the history of the island. She also writes about herself and her own feelings. "I think of myself at 10 years old, newly arrived in this country, feeling out of place, feeling that I would never belong in this world of United States of Americans who were so different from me," Alvarez once said. "Back home in the Dominican Republic, I had been an active, lively child, a bad student full of fun with plentiful friends. In New York City I was suddenly thrown back on myself . . . I found myself turning more and more to writing as the one place where I felt I belonged and could make sense of myself, my life, all that was happening to me."

Julia Alvarez

274

How I ★ ★ ★ Learned ★ ★ ★ English

by Gregory Djanikian

The boy in this poem has just arrived in the United States. In spite of his limited English, or perhaps because of it, the boy experiences a moment of acceptance in his new country.

[7]It was an empty lot
Ringed by elms and fir and honeysuckle.
Bill Corson was pitching in his buckskin jacket,
Chuck Keller, fat even as a boy, was on first,
His T-shirt riding up over his gut,
Ron O'Neill, Jim, Dennis, were talking it up
In the field, a blue sky above them
Tipped with cirrus.

cirrus: thin, wispy clouds

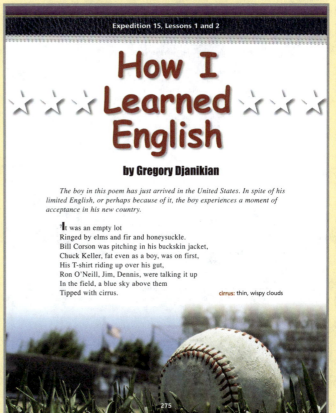

275

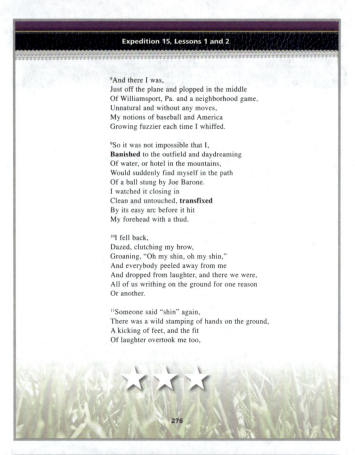

[8]And there I was,
Just off the plane and plopped in the middle
Of Williamsport, Pa. and a neighborhood game,
Unnatural and without any moves,
My notions of baseball and America
Growing fuzzier each time I whiffed.

[9]So it was not impossible that I,
Banished to the outfield and daydreaming
Of water, or hotel in the mountains,
Would suddenly find myself in the path
Of a ball stung by Joe Barone.
I watched it closing in
Clean and untouched, **transfixed**
By its easy arc before it hit
My forehead with a thud.

[10]I fell back,
Dazed, clutching my brow,
Groaning, "Oh my shin, oh my shin,"
And everybody peeled away from me
And dropped from laughter, and there we were,
All of us writhing on the ground for one reason
Or another.

[11]Someone said "shin" again,
There was a wild stamping of hands on the ground,
A kicking of feet, and the fit
Of laughter overtook me too,

276

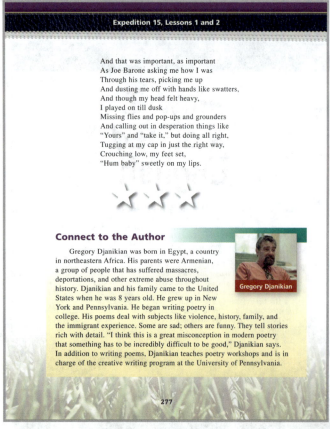

And that was important, as important
As Joe Barone asking me how I was
Through his tears, picking me up
And dusting me off with hands like swatters,
And though my head felt heavy,
I played on till dusk
Missing flies and pop-ups and grounders
And calling out in desperation things like
"Yours" and "take it," but doing all right,
Tugging at my cap in just the right way,
Crouching low, my feet set,
"Hum baby" sweetly on my lips.

Connect to the Author

Gregory Djanikian was born in Egypt, a country in northeastern Africa. His parents were Armenian, a group of people that has suffered massacres, deportations, and other extreme abuse throughout history. Djanikian and his family came to the United States when he was 8 years old. He grew up in New York and Pennsylvania. He began writing poetry in college. His poems deal with subjects like violence, history, family, and the immigrant experience. Some are sad; others are funny. They tell stories rich with detail. "I think this is a great misconception in modern poetry that something has to be incredibly difficult to be good," Djanikian says. In addition to writing poems, Djanikian teaches poetry workshops and is in charge of the creative writing program at the University of Pennsylvania.

Gregory Djanikian

277

Comprehension and Vocabulary   *Before Reading*

Introduce the Expedition

1. Display Transparency 12, and give each student a copy of it. In the center oval, write *Who Am I?* In the outer ovals, write *At Home, At My School, In My Neighborhood, In My Culture.* **Think about the roles you play at home and the way your family sees you. What words explain who you are to those who live in your home?** Guide the discussion to help students come up with labels for their roles such as son, daughter, brother, sister, entertainer, babysitter, pet trainer, homework tutor, and so on. Have students write in each of the ovals words that name who they are in that setting. Then suggest students label blank ovals for other settings in their life such as *On My Soccer Team, At My Church,* or *At the Skateboard Park.*

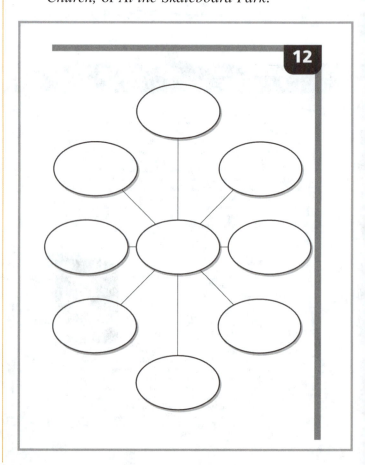

2. Call on several individuals to read aloud the entries in their identity web. Then ask these students how well they think their list of roles captures the essence of who they *really* are, and why. **Think about the words you might write in an oval entitled** ***On My Own.***

3. **Everyone is unique. We each have a certain identity that is unlike any other person's in the world—or even in history. This uniqueness is impossible to explain fully. We can list things that help make up our identity. We can name our family members and describe our different qualities, goals, and beliefs. Somehow, who we are is much more than a collection of our parts. Thinking about who we really are—solving the mystery of our unique identity—is the work of a lifetime.**

4. **In the last Expedition, we talked about the idea that what we do matters, and we learned about people who have done important work in the world. The work we do is an important part of our identity. Where we come from, our place in the culture around us, what holds us back or motivates us, how we treat others, and how we express ourselves are also important aspects of identity. In this Expedition, we will view identity from some of these different angles.**

5. Have students turn to Anthology page 271. Read the title of the Expedition. Then call on individuals to read aloud each probing question.

- **How does art express your culture?**
- **How does your language connect you to a culture?**
- **What defines an American?**

6. Tell students that they will return to these questions as they learn more about identity. Show DVD 15.1.

7. After students view the video, have them summarize its main points and recall supporting details. If necessary, prompt students with questions such as the following:
- **What main message were the people in this video trying to communicate?**
- **What did they have to say about _____?**
- **What parts of the video helped illustrate or support this idea?**

Introduce Vocabulary

8. **We will read some new words in today's and the next lesson's texts.**
- Write the vocabulary words on the board. Include the Challenge Words to meet the needs of students who are advancing.
- Read the words to students.
- Call on individuals to read the words as you point to them.
- Provide correction and feedback as needed.
▶ Have students write the words in the Vocabulary Log.

9. Tell students that knowing the meanings of these words will help them better understand the article.

For each word:
- Read the word with its definition and the sentence that follows.
- Write the sentences on the board.
- Call on students to use their own words to give the meaning and some examples of each vocabulary word.
- For the Word Building Challenge Word, have students identify the base word (orient), then guide them in determining how the base can help them figure out the meaning of the larger words.

745

Vocabulary

drone	*to talk in a boring way*	
	I dread going to my uncle's house because I know he will *drone* on and on about politics.	
nurture	*to care for and help grow*	
	You have to *nurture* an orchid plant if you want it to bloom.	
interminably	*endlessly*	
	The children quarreled and whined *interminably*.	
deposit	*to put something in a certain place*	
	The mother bird will catch an insect and then *deposit* it right in the baby bird's mouth.	
banish	*to kick out or make stay away*	
	When the rebels took over, the old dictator was *banished* from the country.	
transfixed	*to be frozen in place by shock or surprise*	
	The girl stood *transfixed* while the rock star autographed her CD.	

Challenge Words

Word Building

disorientation *orient, oriented, orientation, disorient, disoriented, disorientation, reorient, reoriented, reorientation*

Word Meaning

accentuate *to make something more noticeable*
I like how these tiny pearls *accentuate* the shirt's pretty collar.

Review Vocabulary Strategies: CPR

10. **Remember that if you come across an unfamiliar word as you read, you can use one of the CPR strategies to figure out its meaning.** Write *C*, *P*, and *R* on the board, one under the other. **What strategy does each letter stand for?** (**C**ontext, **P**arts of a Word, **R**esource) Write these on the board.

11. Have students turn to Student Book page 200. **As we read the text, we will use this chart and the CPR strategies to determine the meanings of some unfamiliar words.**

Review Autobiography

12. Have students turn to Anthology page 272. **This lesson's text comes from a longer work called** *Learning English: My New Found Land*, **by Julia Alvarez.**

- Have students turn to the Connect to the Author feature on Anthology page 274. **What is a biography?** (the story of a person's life written by someone other than that person) Read the biography aloud as students follow along. Lead students to identify important facts and details about the author's life.

- **Where was Alvarez born?** (New York City)

- **Where did Alvarez live until she was 10 years old?** (in the Dominican Republic)

- **Why did Alvarez and her family have to leave the Dominican Republic?** (Authorities there found out her father was part of a plot to overthrow the Dominican dictator.)

- **What are important topics in Alvarez's writing?** (the people and history of the Dominican Republic as well as her life there; her life and feelings as a United States immigrant)

- **What led Alvarez to become a writer?** (Writing helped her make sense of her new life after leaving her Dominican home.)

13. Have students turn back to Anthology page 272, and read the title of the text and the introductory paragraph aloud.

- **What do the title and introduction tell about the kind of text this is, about the topic of the text, and about who is writing the piece?** (It is an essay about the author's feelings when she first arrived in New York. Alvarez herself is writing about the topic.)

14. Write *essay* on the board.

- **What is an essay?** (a short composition in which an author gives his or her perspective on a topic) **Essays always include the author's ideas and opinions about a topic, but they may also include facts that support the author's view. Essays may be serious, humorous, persuasive, or nostalgic in tone.**

15. Write *autobiography* on the board.

> **SKILL** ✓

- **How is this essay like an autobiography?** (An autobiography is the story of someone's life, told by that person. This essay tells about a part of someone's life story, told by that person.) **Though it doesn't tell the story of Alvarez's entire life, this essay is written in the style of an autobiography.**
- **What words are clues that a text is autobiographical?** (I, me, my, mine)
- **A few moments ago we read a short biography of Julia Alvarez. How was it different from an autobiography?** (It was written about Alvarez by someone else.)
- Remind students that biographies and autobiographies have elements of both narrative and expository writing.

Review Elements of Description

16. Use these questions to review descriptive writing with students.

> **SKILL** ✓

- **Why do authors use description in their writing?** (to bring a scene or a situation to life for their readers)
- **Why do you think authors of autobiographies, in particular, would use descriptive writing?** (Possible responses: to help readers understand what they actually experienced; to help readers see things from their point of view)
- **What are some elements of descriptive writing?** (concrete details, sensory details, strong words, figurative language) List these on the board.

17. Write the following paragraph on the board.

It was a toe-numbing, teeth-chattering day—the kind of day that would find Tina outdoors from dawn until dark. The little girl scooped up handfuls of soft, white powder and threw it skyward to watch it fall like confetti at a parade. Suddenly inspiration struck and she began scooping snow and packing it into her mittened hand. When the ball was the size of an orange, she tucked it into her coat pocket and slogged off through the snow in search of a victim.

Guide students to identify in the paragraph each of the descriptive elements listed on the board. Underline and label each as it is identified. (concrete detail: *scooping snow and packing it into her mittened hand; slogged off through the snow in search of a victim;* sensory detail: *toe-numbing, teeth-chattering day; soft, white powder; size of an orange;* strong words: *toe-numbing, teeth-chattering, skyward, mittened, slogged;* figurative language: *fall like confetti at a parade*)

18. Have students suggest weaker words the author could have used in place of some of the strong words. (Possible responses: *toe-numbing, teeth-chattering*—cold; *skyward*—up; *slogged*—walked)

19. Direct students' attention to the figurative language *to watch it fall like confetti at a parade*. **Figurative language is the opposite of literal language.**

- **What is literal language?** (language that says how something actually is, not how it seems)
- **If the writer had wanted to be *literal* rather than *figurative*, what might she have said instead?** (Possible response: watch the flakes fall to the ground)

20. **As we read the excerpt from *Learning English: My New Found Land*, let's think about the way things *seem* to Julia Alvarez, compared with the way they might really have been.**

Reading for Understanding

Reading

Places and Names to Look For:
- Dominican
- New York
- Sister Bernadette

1. **As you read this essay, you may come across some unfamiliar places and names.**
- Write the words on the board.
- Point to each word as you read the following:

In this essay, the author describes how she felt as a young *Dominican* girl in *New York*. She tells how difficult it was to learn English until she met a nun named *Sister Bernadette*. Sister Bernadette made the language easy by creating pictures with words, and she inspired a love of writing in her students.

- Call on individuals to read the words.

2. Read aloud the first two paragraphs as students follow along in their books. When you reach the end of the second paragraph, repeat the word *anxiety*. **Alvarez says that when people spoke with an accent or the priest gave his sermon, she felt a little *anxiety*. I'm not sure what the word *anxiety* means. Let's use the CPR strategies to figure it out.** Display Transparency 2, and have students turn to Student Book page 200. Write the word *anxiety* and *paragraph 2* in the Word row, and have students do the same.

- **Does *anxiety* have any word parts that can help us figure out its meaning?** (no)
- **Let's see if context can help us figure out the meaning.** Guide students to identify context ("I worried that I would not be able to keep up"; "I would be like those people from the Bible . . . They had been punished for their pride . . . they didn't understand what anyone was saying."). Work with students as they use this context to help them

---

Vocabulary Strategy: CPR

Use one of the CPR strategies to figure out the meaning of an unfamiliar word in the excerpt from *Learning English: My New Found Land.*

Responses will vary.

Word:

Context	Parts of a Word	Resource: dictionary

Meaning

Word:

Context	Parts of a Word	Resource: dictionary

Meaning

200   ©Voyager Expanded Learning, L.P.

---

state the meaning of *anxiety* in their own words (for example, "a feeling of worry"). Have them write this in the Meaning row on the chart.

- **As we finish reading the excerpt, look for another unfamiliar word. List it in the second chart, along with the paragraph in which it appears. Later on we'll use one or more of the CPR strategies to figure out its meaning.**

3. **Fluency** Have students read the remainder of the text and the Connect to the Author feature with a partner. Remind students to be on the lookout for an unfamiliar word and to record it in their Student Book. If necessary, review the following fluency goal with students to practice prosody: **As you read aloud, use expression and combine words in phrases in a way that sounds like speech. This will show that you understand what you are reading.**

4. When students are finished with their reading, check for literal comprehension by asking these questions: KNOWLEDGE

- *Paragraph 1:* **Who is this story mainly about?** (the author, Julia Alvarez) **How old was the author when the story takes place?** (10) **What important event happens in her life at this time?** (Her family immigrates to New York City.)

- *Paragraph 3:* **What kinds of assignments did Sister Bernadette give her class?** (She had them write little stories in which they imagined being something else, such as a flower or a cloud.) **Did Julia enjoy these assignments? Why?** (yes, because they sparked her imagination)

- *Paragraph 5:* **Where does Sister Bernadette help Julia "land"?** (in the English language)

- *Connect to the Author:* **Where did Alvarez spend the first 10 years of her life?** (in the Dominican Republic) **In the United States, why did the young Alvarez turn "more and more to writing"?** (It was the one place where she felt she belonged and could make sense of herself.)

ELL Provide English language learners support in using concrete and sensory details to build mental images of what they read. As students read selections with a partner, have them stop after specific paragraphs or after every two or three paragraphs and do the following:

- Write key concrete and sensory details from the text. For example: *I thought about the snow. I saw how it might fall on the hills, tapping lightly on the bare branches of trees. Softly it would fall on the cold, cold fields.* (paragraph 5)
- Use the details to draw a picture of the scene.
- Write a description of the scene.
- Describe the scene aloud to one another.
- Reread the paragraph.

For a complete model of this strategy, see Expedition 12, Lesson 3.

Checking for Comprehension *After Reading*

1. Direct students' attention to Student Book page 200. Have partners work together to apply the CPR strategy to figure out the meaning of the word they listed in the chart. Then call on students to identify the word, explain how they determined its meaning, and read the meaning aloud.

2. Have students apply what they understood from the text and assess their understanding of the narrative and expository elements of an autobiography by asking the following questions:

SKILL ✔

- **What is Julia's main problem in this story? What conflict does she face?** COMPREHENSION (Possible response: She feels confused and inferior to Americans because she doesn't know English. She is afraid she will be like the people in the Bible who could not understand the people around them.)

- **How is this conflict resolved?** COMPREHENSION (Possible response: Her teacher, Sister Bernadette, helps her learn English through beautiful descriptive language.)

- **How did learning English change Julia?** SYNTHESIS (Possible responses: She no longer felt like a foreigner. She felt at home with her new language.)

- **In what way is this essay a narrative text? In what way is it expository?** ANALYSIS (It is narrative because it tells a story with a beginning, a middle, and an end, and it is about a character who resolves a problem. It is expository because it is about real events and real people.)

3. **Challenge Question Alvarez shows us that we can be "foreigners" not only in places, but in languages and social situations, too. What experience in your own life has made you feel like a "foreigner"? How was this feeling resolved, or, based on Alvarez's essay, how might it be?** APPLICATION (Responses will vary.)

Connect to the Author

Have students discuss these questions with a partner or in small groups:

- **If you could meet with Alvarez, what questions would you like to ask her?**
- **Why would you ask those particular questions?**
- **What message about identity do you take from this story?**

Connect to Social Studies

Use the following activity to help students investigate Jim Crow laws.

- Write these "laws" on the board:
  - Students with last names that begin with *R* must attend separate schools from other students.
  - Students with brown hair cannot be friends with students with blond hair.
  - Students wearing jeans must sit at the back of the classroom.
  - Students wearing red cannot join in any school activities.
  - Students wearing watches cannot check out books from the library.
- Discuss these "laws" with students. Explain that between 1876 and 1965, the United States deprived blacks of their civil rights and segregated blacks and whites through practices and state laws known as Jim Crow laws, after a popular minstrel song that stereotyped African Americans. **When you read some of these laws today, they seem as outrageous as the laws on the board.**
- Read aloud these examples of Jim Crow laws:
  - White teachers will be imprisoned for teaching black students (Virginia).
  - Libraries must have a separate building with different books for blacks (Texas).
  - Textbooks issued to blacks students can never be issued to white students, and vice versa (Kentucky).
  - Bus stations must have separate waiting areas for blacks and whites (Alabama).
  - Marriage between blacks and whites is illegal (Arkansas).
- Tell students that the Civil Rights Movement of the 1950s and 1960s helped abolish these laws.
- Have groups illustrate a Jim Crow law through role-play. After students perform their role-play, lead a discussion of how acting in or viewing the role-plays made students feel.

To increase difficulty: Have students conduct research on racial segregation and discrimination in the U.S. between 1876 and 1965 and prepare a time line of major events.

Lesson 2

Page 272

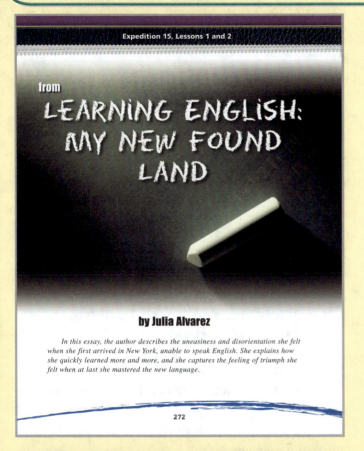

from

LEARNING ENGLISH: MY NEW FOUND LAND

by Julia Alvarez

In this essay, the author describes the uneasiness and disorientation she felt when she first arrived in New York, unable to speak English. She explains how she quickly learned more and more, and she captures the feeling of triumph she felt when at last she mastered the new language.

272

Page 273

¹When I was 10, we immigrated to New York. How astonishing, a country where everyone spoke English! These people must be smarter, I thought. Maids, waiters, taxi drivers, doormen, bums on the street, garbagemen, all spoke this difficult language. It took some time before I understood that Americans were not necessarily a smarter, superior race. It was as natural for them to learn their mother tongue as it was for a little Dominican baby to learn Spanish. . . .

²Soon it wasn't so strange that everyone was speaking in English instead of Spanish. I learned not to hear it as English, but as sense. I no longer strained to understand; I understood. I relaxed in this second language. Only when someone with a heavy Southern or British accent spoke in a movie or when the priest **droned** his sermon—only then did I experience that little catch of anxiety. I worried that I would not be able to "keep up" with the voice speaking in this second language. I would be like those people from the Bible we had studied in religion class, at the foot of an enormous tower that looked just like the skyscrapers all around me. They had been punished for their pride by being made to speak some slightly different version of the same language so that they didn't understand what anyone was saying.

³But at the foot of those towering New York skyscrapers, I began to understand more and more—not less and less—English. In sixth grade, I had one of the first of a lucky line of great teachers who began to **nurture** a love of the language, a love that had been there since childhood of listening closely to words. Sister Bernadette did not make our class **interminably** diagram sentences from a workbook or learn a catechism of grammar rules. Instead, she asked us to write little stories imagining we were snowflakes, birds, pianos, a stone in the pavement, a star in the sky. What would it feel like to be a flower with roots in the ground? If the clouds could talk, what would they say? She had an expressive, dreamy look that was accentuated by her face being framed in a wimple. Supposing, just supposing . . . My mind would take off, soaring into possibilities: a flower with roots, a star in the sky, a cloud full of sad, sad tears, a piano crying out each time its back was tapped, music only to our ears.

⁴Sister Bernadette stood at the chalkboard. Her chalk was always snapping in two because she wrote with so much energy, her whole habit shaking with the swing of her arm, her hand tap tap tapping on the board. "Here's a simple sentence: *The snow fell.*" Sister Bernadette pointed with

catechism: instruction in Christianity

wimple: woman's head covering

habit: dark gown worn by nuns

273

Page 274

her chalk, her eyebrows lifted, her wimple poked up. "But watch what happens if we put an adverb at the beginning and a prepositional phrase at the end: *Gently the snow fell on the bare hills.*"

⁵I thought about the snow. I saw how it might fall on the hills, tapping lightly on the bare branches of trees. Softly it would fall on the cold, cold fields. On toys children had left out in the cold, and on cars and on little birds and on people out late walking on the streets. Sister Bernadette filled the chalkboard with snowy print, on and on, handling and shaping and moving language, scribbling all over the board until English, those little bricks of meaning, those little fixed units and counters, became a charged, fluid mass that carried me in its great fluent waves, rolling and moving onward, to **deposit** me on the shores of the only homeland. I was no longer a foreigner with no ground to stand on. I had landed in language.

⁶I had come into my English.

Connect to the Author

Julia Alvarez

Though she was born in New York City in 1950, Julia Alvarez spent her first 10 years in the Dominican Republic. This country occupies two-thirds of an island in the Caribbean Sea. It has had a turbulent history. During Alvarez's childhood, an oppressive dictator ruled the island. Alvarez and her family had to flee in 1960 when authorities discovered her father's part in a plot to overthrow the dictator. Much of Alvarez's writing deals with the Dominican Republic and the people who live there. She draws from her experiences and the history of the island. She also writes about herself and her own feelings. "I think of myself at 10 years old, newly arrived in this country, feeling out of place, feeling that I would never belong in this world of United States of Americans who were so different from me," Alvarez once said. "Back home in the Dominican Republic, I had been an active, lively child, a bad student full of fun with plentiful friends. In New York City I was suddenly thrown back on myself . . . I found myself turning more and more to writing as the one place where I felt I belonged and could make sense of myself, my life, all that was happening to me."

274

Page 275

How I ✦✦✦ Learned ✦✦✦ English

by Gregory Djanikian

The boy in this poem has just arrived in the United States. In spite of his limited English, or perhaps because of it, the boy experiences a moment of acceptance in his new country.

⁷It was an empty lot
Ringed by elms and fir and honeysuckle.
Bill Corson was pitching in his buckskin jacket,
Chuck Keller, fat even as a boy, was on first,
His T-shirt riding up over his gut,
Ron O'Neill, Jim, Dennis, were talking it up
In the field, a blue sky above them
Tipped with cirrus.

cirrus: thin, wispy clouds

275

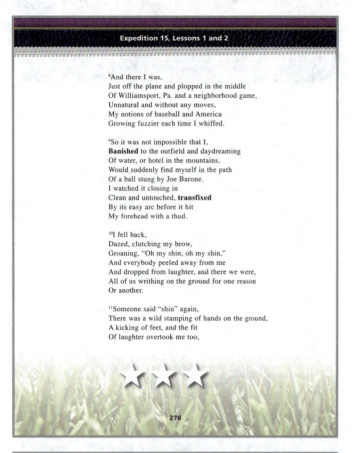

Expedition 15, Lessons 1 and 2

⁸And there I was,
Just off the plane and plopped in the middle
Of Williamsport, Pa. and a neighborhood game,
Unnatural and without any moves,
My notions of baseball and America
Growing fuzzier each time I whiffed.

⁹So it was not impossible that I,
Banished to the outfield and daydreaming
Of water, or hotel in the mountains,
Would suddenly find myself in the path
Of a ball stung by Joe Barone.
I watched it closing in
Clean and untouched, **transfixed**
By its easy arc before it hit
My forehead with a thud.

¹⁰I fell back,
Dazed, clutching my brow,
Groaning, "Oh my shin, oh my shin,"
And everybody peeled away from me
And dropped from laughter, and there we were,
All of us writhing on the ground for one reason
Or another.

¹¹Someone said "shin" again,
There was a wild stamping of hands on the ground,
A kicking of feet, and the fit
Of laughter overtook me too,

276

Expedition 15, Lessons 1 and 2

And that was important, as important
As Joe Barone asking me how I was
Through his tears, picking me up
And dusting me off with hands like swatters,
And though my head felt heavy,
I played on till dusk
Missing flies and pop-ups and grounders
And calling out in desperation things like
"Yours" and "take it," but doing all right,
Tugging at my cap in just the right way,
Crouching low, my feet set,
"Hum baby" sweetly on my lips.

Connect to the Author

Gregory Djanikian was born in Egypt, a country in northeastern Africa. His parents were Armenian, a group of people that has suffered massacres, deportations, and other extreme abuse throughout history. Djanikian and his family came to the United States when he was 8 years old. He grew up in New York and Pennsylvania. He began writing poetry in college. His poems deal with subjects like violence, history, family, and the immigrant experience. Some are sad; others are funny. They tell stories rich with detail. "I think this is a great misconception in modern poetry that something has to be incredibly difficult to be good," Djanikian says. In addition to writing poems, Djanikian teaches poetry workshops and is in charge of the creative writing program at the University of Pennsylvania.

Gregory Djanikian

277

Comprehension and Vocabulary *Before Reading*

1. **In Lesson 1, we read an excerpt from an autobiographical essay.**
   - **What makes this writing autobiographical?** (It is a story about the author's life, told by the author.)
   - **What is the story about?** (the author's childhood experience as an immigrant learning English)
   - **How did Sister Bernadette change the way Julia viewed English?** (She helped her see how beautiful it could be instead of how difficult it was.)
   - **When Alvarez compares English to "little bricks" and "a fluid mass with great fluent waves," she is using figurative language. What is figurative language?** (It says how something seems, rather than how it really is.)

2. **This lesson's reading will give us a look at the experience of another young immigrant in America.**

Vocabulary Review

3. Arrange students in pairs, and have them turn to Student Book page 201. Ask them to read the vocabulary words listed in the box. Call on students to tell what each word means and to use the word in a sentence.

4. **Let's take a closer look at the word *transfixed*.**
   - **What does the word *transfixed* mean?** (to be frozen in place by shock or surprise) **Let's write this in the first box.**
   - **What other, smaller word does the word *transfixed* contain?** (fix) Have students write this word in the second box. Then have someone provide a meaning for *fix*. (Possible response: to hold in place)

752

- **I know some other words that contain the word *fix*. For example: The word *fixate*, which can mean "to hold your attention on something,"** also contains the root *fix*. Write this word and definition in the first Related Word box, and have students do the same.

- Have pairs brainstorm other words that contain the word *fix*. (Possible responses: fixture, fixation, prefix, suffix, etc.) Have students choose two of these words and write them in the remaining Related Word boxes. Then have them use the CPR vocabulary strategy to determine meanings for the words. When all students are finished, call on individuals to share the words and meanings they recorded. **SKILL ✔**

- Have students complete sections 2 and 3 independently. Then review students' responses and drawings as a class.

5. **Challenge Words** Have students make a copy of the chart on the Student Book page and complete it for the word *disorientation*. Then have students use the CPR strategy to determine the meaning of the word *accentuate* (paragraph 3).

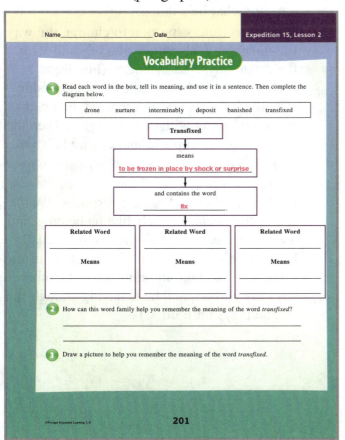

Reading for Understanding *Reading*

Places and Names to Look For:
- Bill Corson
- Ron O'Neill
- Dennis
- Chuck Keller
- Joe Barone
- Williamsport, PA

1. **As you read this text, you may come across some unfamiliar places and names.**
   - Write the words on the board.
   - Point to each word as you read the following:

   In this text, you will read about a young immigrant who has just arrived in *Williamsport, PA*, or Pennsylvania. He finds himself in a baseball game without knowing how to play the game or how to speak English. The other players on his team—*Bill Corson, Chuck Keller, Ron O'Neill*, Jim, and *Dennis*—send him to play outfield. When the batter, *Joe Barone*, gets a hit, the ball flies straight toward the new boy. What happens next opens the door for the young immigrant to begin finding his place in his new home.
   - Call on individuals to read the words.

2. Have students turn to Anthology page 275. **Look at the format of this text. What kind of text is it?** (a poem) **How do you know?** (It is written in lines and verses rather than paragraphs.)

3. Read the introductory text aloud. **What do you think "a moment of acceptance" means?** (a situation in which an outsider is made to feel he or she belongs) Tell students they will learn how that moment of acceptance comes about for the author.

4. Ask students to listen for setting details and the names of characters as you read the first verse aloud. Then have students read the remainder of the poem and the Connect to the Author feature independently. Encourage students to

monitor their own comprehension of the text by pausing occasionally to ask themselves *Am I understanding what I'm reading?* Tell students that when they do not understand what they are reading, they should reread that portion of the text. When all students are finished, read the entire poem aloud together.

5. Check literal comprehension of the poem by asking the following questions: KNOWLEDGE

   • *Paragraph 8:* **In what situation does the speaker find himself?** (He is in a new country and a new town, in the middle of a baseball game with kids he doesn't really know.)

   • *Paragraph 9:* **What surprises the speaker?** (He is daydreaming in the outfield when a fly ball soars toward him and hits him in the forehead.)

   • *Paragraph 10:* **What does the speaker call his forehead?** (his shin) **How do the other boys respond?** (They fall onto the ground in laughter.)

   • *Paragraph 11:* **What does the speaker do in response to the other boys' laughter?** (He starts laughing, too.) **Why is this "important"?** (because it helps him fit in)

   • *Connect to the Author:* **From where did Gregory Djanikian's family emigrate to the U.S.?** (Egypt) **What misconception, or wrong idea, does Djanikian say people have about poetry?** (that it has to be difficult to be good)

6. Have students apply what they understood from the text by asking questions such as the following:

   • **Why did the author write this poem?** ANALYSIS (Possible response: to share a memory of an immigrant's first experience in America)

   • **Djanikian chose to share this memory in the form of a poem rather than a short story. As an experiment, let's try telling the same events in story form.** SYNTHESIS (Retellings should include descriptions of the setting, characters, and events included in the poem.)

Reread the poem pausing after every few lines, and have students paraphrase that section. Record students' responses in paragraph form on the board. Read aloud the completed summary.

   • **Which is more powerful, the poet's version or our summary? Why?** EVALUATION (Possible response: the poet's, because it is told from his perspective and contains descriptive language)

   • **What are three sensory details the poet uses? Name the sense to which each one appeals.** ANALYSIS (Possible responses: "tipped with cirrus"—sight; "a ball stung by Joe Barone"—touch; "hit my forehead with a thud"—hearing; "writhing on the ground"—sight, touch; "wild stamping of hands on the ground"—sight, touch; "dusting me off with hands like swatters"—sight, touch)

   • **At the beginning of the poem, how does the boy telling the story see himself?** COMPREHENSION (Possible responses: He sees himself as "unnatural, without any moves." He feels like he doesn't fit in because he's not sure what he's doing.)

   • **What two things happen to change the way the narrator feels about playing ball with the other boys?** COMPREHENSION (Possible response: When he mistakenly hollers "shin" after the ball hits him in the head, he laughs at himself along with everyone else. Then the batter helps him up and makes sure he's OK.)

   • **How do you think his identity changes by the end of the poem? What clues make you think so?** SYNTHESIS (Possible response: By the end of the poem, he feels like he belongs and that he can learn both English and baseball. He says he's "doing all right," he starts using English words and imitating what the other boys say and do, and he is having enough fun that he plays until dusk.)

754

Checking for Comprehension *After Reading*

1. **The poem we read in this lesson contains the words** *I, me, my,* **and** *myself.* **What does this tell us?** (that the poem is written in first person) **Julia Alvarez's essay was also written in first person. What is another way these two texts are alike?** (They are both about young immigrants and how they learned English.)

2. **Let's compare these two texts further.** Have students turn to Anthology pages 272 and 275 and Student Book page 202. Read the Student Book instructions aloud.

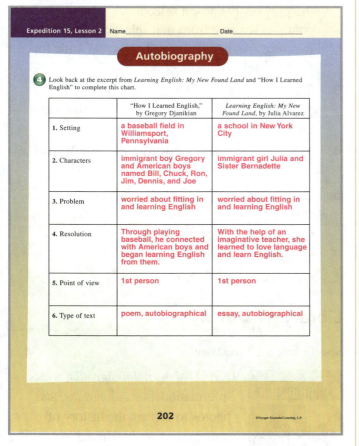

Expedition 15, Lesson 2   Name_____   Date_____

Autobiography

4 Look back at the excerpt from *Learning English: My New Found Land* and "How I Learned English" to complete this chart.

	"How I Learned English," by Gregory Djanikian	*Learning English: My New Found Land,* by Julia Alvarez
1. Setting	a baseball field in Williamsport, Pennsylvania	a school in New York City
2. Characters	immigrant boy Gregory and American boys named Bill, Chuck, Ron, Jim, Dennis, and Joe	immigrant girl Julia and Sister Bernadette
3. Problem	worried about fitting in and learning English	worried about fitting in and learning English
4. Resolution	Through playing baseball, he connected with American boys and began learning English from them.	With the help of an imaginative teacher, she learned to love language and learn English.
5. Point of view	1st person	1st person
6. Type of text	poem, autobiographical	essay, autobiographical

202   ©Voyager Expanded Learning, L.P.

3. **Let's look at the first element in the chart. What is the setting of "How I Learned English"?** (a baseball field in Williamsport, Pennsylvania) Have students record in the first column everything they know about the poem's setting. **Now let's identify the setting of Alvarez's story.** Have students turn to Anthology page 272 and quickly review the story to identify the setting of *Learning English: My New Found Land.* Have them list it on the chart.

4. Have partners work together to study both texts and complete the comparison chart. Monitor students' work, providing correction and feedback as needed.

5. When all students are finished, call on students to share responses with the entire class.

6. With students, compose comparison statements telling ways the two texts are similar and ways they are different.

Connect to the Author

Have students discuss these questions in pairs or small groups:

- **If you were to have a conversation with the poet, what is one "how" question you would ask him?** (Responses will vary.)

- **Djanikian says that he doesn't think something "has to be incredibly difficult to be good." Do you think the poem "How I Learned English" proves that? Why or why not?** (Possible responses: Yes, it is short and simple without big words, but it is a good story that everyone can relate to; No, I think it would be difficult to write a poem like this one.)

- **If you were going to read another poem by Djanikian, would you rather read one that is about the poet's life before he came to America or after? Why?** (Responses will vary.)

Reading Response

Have students turn to Student Book page 203. Read the instructions aloud. Then have them look back in the excerpt from *Learning English: My New Found Land* and "How I Learned English" to answer these questions:

 How do the new students feel as immigrants to the United States? What can help them adjust to their new home?

Students may work with partners or small groups. When students have completed their responses, call on individuals to read their sentences aloud.

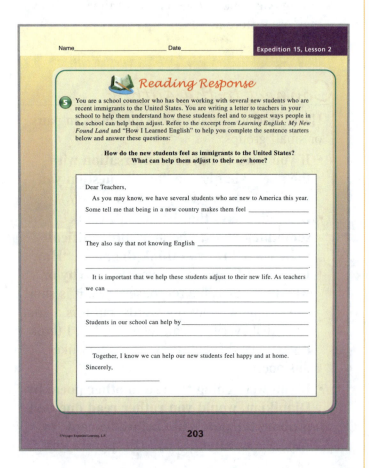

Name_____ Date_____   Expedition 15, Lesson 2

Reading Response

5 You are a school counselor who has been working with several new students who are recent immigrants to the United States. You are writing a letter to teachers in your school to help them understand how these students feel and to suggest ways people in the school can help them adjust. Refer to the excerpt from *Learning English: My New Found Land* and "How I Learned English" to help you complete the sentence starters below and answer these questions:

How do the new students feel as immigrants to the United States? What can help them adjust to their new home?

Dear Teachers,

As you may know, we have several students who are new to America this year. Some tell me that being in a new country makes them feel _____
_____.

They also say that not knowing English _____
_____.

It is important that we help these students adjust to their new life. As teachers we can _____
_____.

Students in our school can help by _____
_____.

Together, I know we can help our new students feel happy and at home.
Sincerely,
_____

203

Passport Reading Journeys Library

Building Fluency

1. Place students in pairs according to reading level to build fluency. When pairing students, be sure that one student is a stronger reader (Student A) than the other student (Student B). However, do not reveal that stronger readers are paired with weaker readers. See *Passport Reading Journeys* Library Teacher's Guide for grouping guidelines.

2. Have students quickly choose reading material from the *Passport Reading Journeys* Library or another approved selection that is at the reading level of Student B. If students have not finished the previously chosen selection, they may continue reading from that selection. See *Passport Reading Journeys* Library Teacher's Guide for material selection guidelines.

3. Tell students that Student A will read one paragraph, and Student B will reread that same paragraph.

4. Have students follow this routine until the end of class.

5. If necessary, review the following practices to enhance fluency:
   - Rate and accuracy of reading
   - Expression during reading
   - Correction procedures

Library Highlights

Spotlight on a Magazine

Level III

Kids Discover: Immigration uses informational text, diagrams, and photos to explain the history of immigration to the United States. The magazine presents interviews with seven children who have immigrated to the United States from around the world, showing the diverse expectations and motivations of people who move to this country.

Advanced Word Study

Multisyllabic Words

1. **Remember, sometimes it's easier to read parts of a longer word before reading the entire word. One way is to use what we know about open and closed syllables.** Write the word *digressing* on the board. Underline the word part *di*. **What is the first word part?** (di) **What kind of syllable is this word part?** (open) **How do we know?** (It has one long vowel sound with no consonants following it, or closing it in.) Underline *gress*. **What is the next word part?** (gress) **What kind of syllable is this word part?** (closed) **How do we know?** (It has one short vowel sound followed by one or more consonants.) **Read the rest of the word.** (-ing) **What is the word?** (digressing) *Digressing* **means "straying" or "getting off the subject."**

   Another way to read longer words is to use what we know about prefixes and suffixes. Write the word *dismissal* on the board. Underline the prefix *dis-*. **What is this prefix?** (dis-) **What is the next part?** (miss) Underline the suffix *-al*. **What is this suffix?** (-al) **What is the word?** (dismissal) **The word *dismissal* means "relating to someone being dismissed or removed from office."**

2. Have students turn to Student Book page E15, Lesson 3. Direct students to line 1. **What is the prefix?** (dis-) **What is the next part?** (crim) **What is the next part?** (in) **What is the next part?** (at[e]) **What is the suffix?** (-ed) **What is the word?** (discriminated) **The word *discriminated* means "not included in the group" or "singled out."** Repeat with the remaining words. Call on individuals to read the words in random order. Ask students to tell the meanings of the words.

3. Direct students to lines 2 and 3. Have them read the words. Then, call on individuals to read the words in a different order. Ask students to tell the meanings of the words.

   ▼ **To Correct**
   For Multisyllabic Words: **What is the first word part? What is the next part? What is the word?** If students do not know the meaning of the word, review the word and/or word parts to determine the meaning of the word.

For Sounds in Words: Say the correct sound(s), then ask students to repeat the sound(s). Have them read the word again with the correct sound(s). If students do not know the meaning of the word, review the word and/or word parts to determine the meaning of the word.

1.	discriminated	melodious	intermission	unexpected
2.	marvelous	committed	published	extraordinary
3.	delicious	considered	intellectual	contribution

Sight Words

1. Direct students to line 1. Have them point to the first word. **This word is *mechanics*. Read the word.** (mechanics) **This is not a regular word. Let's read the word again.** (mechanics) **Let's spell the word.** (m-e-c-h-a-n-i-c-s) **What is the word?** (mechanics) Repeat with the remaining words. Then, have students read the words. Ask students to tell the meanings of the words.

2. Direct students to lines 2 and 3. **Let's read these words.** Remind students that the rows of words consist of regular and irregular words. Point to the first word. **What is the word?** (measures) Repeat with the remaining words. Call on individuals to read the words in a different order. Ask students to tell the meanings of the words.

   ▼ **To Correct**
   For Regular Words: Say the sound(s) in the word, then ask students to repeat the sound(s). Have them read the word again with the correct sound(s). If students do not know the meaning of the word, review the word and/or word part to determine the meaning of the word.

   For Irregular Words: Immediately say the correct word. Then have students read the word, spell it, and read it again. If students do not know the meaning of the word, review the word.

1.	mechanics I	rhyme I	young I	varied I
2.	measures I	fluent I	wounded I	diagram I
3.	accentuate I	anxiety I	bigotry I	essayist R

Anthology Selection

Language Arts

I Hear America Singing

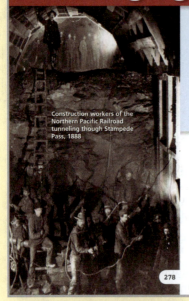

Construction workers of the Northern Pacific Railroad tunneling though Stampede Pass, 1888

In this poem, Walt Whitman describes the individual voices that make up America. The songs represent the literal music each working man and woman sings. They also stand for the work itself. Whitman tells how each person, each song, each kind of work, contributes to the chorus that is America.

by Walt Whitman

I hear America singing, the **varied** carols I hear,
Those of mechanics, each one singing his, as it should be, blithe and strong,
The carpenter singing his as he measures his **plank** or **beam**,
The **mason** singing his, as he makes ready for work, or leaves off work,

278

The boatman singing what belongs to him in his boat, the deckhand singing on the steamboat deck,
The shoemaker singing as he sits on his bench, the hatter singing as he stands,
The woodcutter's song, the ploughboy's on his way in the morning, or at noon **intermission** or at sundown,
The delicious singing of the mother, or of the young wife at work, or of the girl sewing or washing,
Each singing what belongs to him or her and to none else,
The day what belongs to the day, at night the party of young fellows, robust, friendly,
Singing with open mouths their strong **melodious** songs.

robust: strong and healthy

Connect to the Author

Walt Whitman is considered to be the "voice" of his age. Whitman was born in Long Island, New York, in 1819. By the age of 37, he had been fired as an editor and had failed in real estate. He showed little promise. So it was unexpected when in 1855 he came out with a self-published book of poems called *Leaves of Grass*. That book included the poem above. The poems were in a style no one had seen before. Whitman wrote poetry without meter or rhyme. Many readers found it quite unpoetic. But some, like poet and essayist Ralph Waldo Emerson, thought it was marvelous. He called it "the most extraordinary piece of wit and wisdom" America had produced. There were nine editions of the book in Whitman's lifetime. Whitman kept changing the poems—adding or rearranging lines, changing titles, adding or cutting entire poems. During the Civil War, Whitman wrote graphic and moving poems about the horrors he witnessed. In his spare time, he visited wounded soldiers. To cheer them up, he spent his small salary on little gifts for soldiers from both sides.

Through his poetry, Whitman became a symbol of the young nation. He wrote about the American experience. He championed the common person. Though he died in 1892, Whitman is still considered one of America's greatest poets.

Walt Whitman

279

I, Too

Langston Hughes, 1914

In this poem, Langston Hughes adds his voice to the chorus that makes up America. Hughes published this poem in 1925, at a time when African Americans were segregated and routinely discriminated against. It is a direct response to Whitman's romantic view of working-class America.

by Langston Hughes

¹I, too, sing America.

²I am the darker brother.
They send me to eat in the kitchen
When company comes,
But I laugh,
And eat well,
And grow strong.

³Tomorrow,
I'll sit at the table
When company comes.
Nobody'll dare
Say to me,
"Eat in the kitchen,"
Then.

280

⁴Besides,
They'll see how beautiful I am
And be ashamed—

⁵I, too, am America.

Connect to the Author

James Langston Hughes was one of the most important figures of the Harlem Renaissance of the 1920s. During this period, musicians, artists, and writers like Hughes gathered in New York City's vast ghetto of Harlem. They explored black life and culture in ways that had never been done. Hughes wrote in many different forms, including poetry, short stories, novels, plays, and essays. Like Walt Whitman, whom he counted as a major influence, Hughes focused on working-class people. But unlike Whitman, he focused on the African American experience. Hughes was born in Joplin, Missouri, in 1902. After high school, Hughes taught English in Mexico, where his father lived. He left after a year, and briefly attended college. Because he was black, he was assigned the worst dorm room. He experienced other forms of bigotry too. He found his professors boring and often skipped class to attend shows and lectures elsewhere. Hughes left college after his freshman year and signed on as a cabin boy on a ship. He got off the ship in the Netherlands and spent a poverty-stricken year in Europe. When he returned to the United States, he worked a series of low-wage jobs and wrote poetry. He began to be recognized for his work. Some black intellectuals criticized him for his images of lower-class life. But he remained committed to recording the truth as he saw it. "I didn't know the upper class Negroes well enough to write much about them. I knew only the people I had grown up with, and they weren't people whose shoes were always shined, who had been to Harvard, or who had heard of Bach. But they seemed to me good people too."

Langston Hughes

281

Comprehension and Vocabulary *Before Reading*

1. **In Lessons 1 and 2, we read two autobiographical works. What experience did both texts describe?** (coming to America and trying to learn English and fit in) **How was the identity of each person affected by the experience?** (Each felt uncomfortable because they were different. Each found a way to begin fitting in.)

2. **In this lesson's reading, "I Hear America Singing," we will get a different perspective on life in America. The poet, Walt Whitman, lived all his life in America in the 1800s. As we read, we will try to infer the author's opinion. We will also explore the images and descriptive language he uses to paint a picture of Americans.**

Introduce Vocabulary

3. **We will read some new words in this lesson and the next lesson's texts.**
   - Write the vocabulary words on the board. Include the Challenge Words to meet the needs of students who are advancing.
   - Read the words to students.
   - Call on individuals to read the words as you point to them.
   - Provide correction and feedback as needed.

   ▶ Have students write the words in the Vocabulary Log.

4. Tell students that knowing the meanings of these words will help them better understand the article.

   For each word:
   - Read the word with its definition and the sentence that follows.
   - Write the sentences on the board.
   - Call on students to use their own words to give the meaning and some examples of each vocabulary word.

Vocabulary

varied	*of many kinds*
	The *varied* plants in the yard all needed attention.
plank	*a long, flat board*
	A *plank* laid across the ditch served as a narrow bridge.
beam	*a long, sturdy piece of lumber that is very thick and is often used to support a roof*
	A large *beam* held the roof timbers in place.
mason	*a worker who builds with stone*
	A *mason* carefully laid the bricks to build the wall.
intermission	*a pause or break*
	The tired workers enjoyed an *intermission* for lunch.
melodious	*having a pleasant melody or musical sound*
	Melodious bird songs filled the air in the park.

Challenge Words

Word Meaning

blithe	*happy and carefree*
	Her *blithe*, outgoing personality makes her fun to be around.
graphic	*having pictures or illustrations*
	This *graphic* novel retells the story of Dr. Frankenstein using illustrations and captions.

Review Persuasion

5. **We have talked about persuasive writing in advertisements, speeches, and letters to the editor. Poetry can be persuasive, too. Poems often present a view that the author would like readers to adopt or consider. For example, a poem might express the author's feelings about political or social issues.**

SKILL ✔

- On the board, write:

  Call to the Frontier
  Go west, go west! Find what you seek:
  Rich soil, tall trees, and sparkling creeks.
  Where life is good and land is free.
  Go west! It's where you're meant to be.

- **This poem is about settling the West back in frontier days. What does the author hope the reader will do?** (move out west) **The author is trying to convince the reader to see the West the way he does.**

6. **The persuasive elements in a poem are not always as direct as in other kinds of texts, but they can be just as convincing. In persuasive texts, authors often state their position on an issue. What are those statements called?** (opinion statements) **Does the person who wrote "Call to the Frontier" come right out and state his opinion?** (no) **What opinion of the author can you infer from reading the poem?** (He believes life out west is better than in other places.)

- **A poem may directly state supporting reasons for an opinion, or it may use descriptive language and powerful images to paint a picture that supports the author's view. What tools does this author use to persuade the reader to agree with his opinion?** (supporting reasons, descriptive language) **What supporting reasons and persuasive pictures are included in this poem?** (The West offers rich soil, tall trees, sparkling creeks, a good life, and free land.)

- **What other elements do persuasive texts often include?** (counterarguments, supporting details, emotional appeals, quotations from experts, promises or guarantees) **Does this poem include any of these elements?** (Yes, the poem promises that you will find what you seek if you go west. It makes an emotional appeal by saying the West is where you belong.)

7. **Do you think this poem would have been convincing to people in frontier days? Why?** (Possible responses: Yes, people who couldn't afford land or who were unhappy with their life might be tempted by the idea of getting a new start for free; no, people would know that the promise is too good to be true and that life in the West could be hard.)

8. **In this lesson, we'll read a poem about life in America in the 1800s. As we read, we'll try to infer the author's opinion. We'll also think about whether the poem offers reasons or images to persuade us that the author's view is right.**

English Language Learners

Understanding Complex Sentence Structures

English language learners may have difficulty understanding sentences that have unusual or complex structures. It is important to discuss these sentences with students before they encounter them in the text. Use the following activity to support English language learners in this area.

- Write a complex sentence from the text on the board. For example: *I hear America singing, the varied carols I hear.*

- Some sentence structures can be confusing or difficult to understand. Sometimes the author has arranged the words in a way that is uncommon in everyday speech. In these cases, it is helpful to take some time to examine the sentence. Let's take a closer look at this sentence from our reading.

- Point to the sentence as you read it with students.

- The second half of this sentence is arranged in an unusual way. The poet switches the order of the subject, verb, and object. Instead of saying "I hear the varied carols," he says "The varied carols I hear."

- Underneath the sentence, write several other sentences with the same construction. These sentences should contain words and concepts with which students are already familiar. For example:

  I hear the dog barking; the barking dog I hear.

  I see the sun shining; the shining sun I see.

  I taste the cool ice cream; _____.

- Read the first two sentences aloud. Point out that the second half of each sentence contains the same elements, but that they are in a different order. Then have students complete the third sentence.

- Point to the sentence from the text. How could I rewrite the second half of this sentence to make it easier to understand? (I hear the varied carols.)

- Have partners take turns reading aloud the last line of the poem. Then have them rewrite the phrase in an order that makes it easier to understand. (singing their strong melodious songs with open mouths)

ELL

761

Reading for Understanding *Reading*

1. In this lesson's and the next lesson's texts, you will read poems expressing two different views of life in America.

2. Have students turn to Anthology page 278. Read aloud the title of the piece. **What kind of text is this?** (a poem) **What features show that it is a poem?** (It is written in lines rather than paragraphs.) **As we read this text, you will find that the rhythm of the words also shows that it is a poem.**

3. Read aloud the introductory paragraph. **As we read, watch for the word *songs* used both as a concrete detail—referring to songs that people actually sing—and as figurative language—a symbol for the work people do.** As necessary, review the meanings of concrete details and figurative language.

4. **Fluency** Read aloud the entire poem as students follow along in their books. Then have partners take turns reading the poem to each other. If necessary, review the following fluency correction procedure with students to ensure accuracy: **Offer help when your partner comes to an unfamiliar word or makes a reading error. Pause, then say, "That word is _____. Let's read it again."** As students read, monitor for reading rate, accuracy, and expression.

5. When students have completed their reading, check for literal comprehension of the text by asking these questions: **KNOWLEDGE**

   • **In this poem, what is the speaker listening to?** (the songs of the different workers in America)

   • **Name the workers whose songs he hears.** (the mechanics, the carpenter, the mason, the boatman, the shoemaker, the woodcutter, the mother, the young wife, the girl sewing or washing)

   • **What does the speaker say each singer is singing?** (what belongs to him or her, and no one else)

Checking for Comprehension *After Reading*

1. Have students apply what they understood from the text by asking the following questions:

   • **Look back at the first two lines. What does the author mean by "varied carols"?** (songs of many kinds) **How does Whitman describe the songs of mechanics?** **COMPREHENSION** (as blithe and strong)

   • **Reread the next two lines. How does the poet create mental pictures of the carpenter and the mason?** **ANALYSIS** (Possible response: He describes what they are doing as they sing—the carpenter measuring lumber and the mason getting ready for or finishing up the workday.)

   • Have students identify phrases that help them picture the workers in the poem. **ANALYSIS**

   • **Notice the words "what belongs to him" in the line about the boatman. It seems that the poet is saying that the worker feels ownership of something. What other words that show possession do you find in previous lines?** (*His* occurs in stanzas 2, 3, and 4.) **What does Whitman think these workers "own"?** **ANALYSIS** (Possible responses: They are masters of their craft; they are their own bosses; they are free to live and work as they please.)

   • **Look back at the lines about women.** (lines 8 and 9) **What sensory image does Whitman use here?** (delicious singing) *Delicious* **is an unexpected word for describing a song. Does the poet's word choice make the image stronger for you? Why?** (Responses will vary.) **Find phrases that show possession in these lines.** **ANALYSIS** (belongs to him or her, and to none else)

- Whitman ends his description of people singing as they work by saying, "The day what belongs to the day." How does the poem change after that statement? (He describes what happens at night when young fellows are finished working.) **How is this part of the poem like the rest of the poem?** ANALYSIS (The fellows out at night sing, just as the other people in the poem do.)

- Based on this poem, what is Whitman's opinion of Americans? SYNTHESIS (Possible responses: They are happy doing their chosen work; they enjoy doing their part to make a great nation; they feel like masters of their own destiny; they are strong, proud, and joyful.)

- How does Whitman persuade the reader to agree with him? SYNTHESIS (Possible responses: He uses the words *song* and *singing* repeatedly. He explains that people sing when they are happy and relaxed so it makes it seem that all the workers love what they are doing; using songs as a symbol of work suggests that people work to express who they are in a joyful way.)

2. **Challenge Questions** Do you agree with Whitman's opinion of Americans—that they are happy doing their chosen work, and that they are strong, proud, and joyful? Why or why not? EVALUATE (Responses will vary.) **What do you think your chosen work might be? What kind of work would make you sing a proud, joyful song?** APPLICATION (Responses will vary.)

Connect to the Author

Have students discuss these questions with a partner or in small groups:

- **People who knew Whitman were surprised by the success of his first book of poetry. Are you surprised that he became successful? Why?**

- **Early critics found Whitman's poetry to be "unpoetic"? Do you agree? Explain.**

- **What would you like to do that people wouldn't expect of you?**

Lesson 4

Anthology Selection

I Hear America Singing

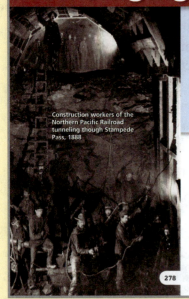

Construction workers of the Northern Pacific Railroad tunneling though Stampede Pass, 1888

In this poem, Walt Whitman describes the individual voices that make up America. The songs represent the literal music each working man and woman sings. They also stand for the work itself. Whitman tells how each person, each song, each kind of work, contributes to the chorus that is America.

by Walt Whitman

I hear America singing, the **varied** carols I hear,
Those of mechanics, each one
singing his, as it should be,
blithe and strong,
The carpenter singing his as
he measures his **plank** or
beam,
The **mason** singing his, as he
makes ready for work, or
leaves off work,

278

The boatman singing what belongs to him in his boat, the deckhand
singing on the steamboat deck,
The shoemaker singing as he sits on his bench, the hatter singing
as he stands,
The woodcutter's song, the ploughboy's on his way in the morning,
or at noon **intermission** or at sundown,
The delicious singing of the mother, or of the young wife at work, or
of the girl sewing or washing,
Each singing what belongs to him or her and to none else,
The day what belongs to the day, at night the party of young fellows,
robust, friendly,
Singing with open mouths their strong **melodious** songs.

robust: strong and healthy

Connect to the Author

Walt Whitman is considered to be the "voice" of his age. Whitman was born in Long Island, New York, in 1819. By the age of 37, he had been fired as an editor and had failed in real estate. He showed little promise. So it was unexpected when in 1855 he came out with a self-published book of poems called *Leaves of Grass.* That book included the poem above. The poems were in a style no one had seen before. Whitman wrote poetry without meter or rhyme. Many readers found it quite unpoetic. But some, like poet and essayist Ralph Waldo Emerson, thought it was marvelous. He called it "the most extraordinary piece of wit and wisdom" America had produced. There were nine editions of the book in Whitman's lifetime. Whitman kept changing the poems—adding or rearranging lines, changing titles, adding or cutting entire poems. During the Civil War, Whitman wrote graphic and moving poems about the horrors he witnessed. In his spare time, he visited wounded soldiers. To cheer them up, he spent his small salary on little gifts for soldiers from both sides.

Through his poetry, Whitman became a symbol of the young nation. He wrote about the American experience. He championed the common person. Though he died in 1892, Whitman is still considered one of America's greatest poets.

Walt Whitman

279

I, Too

Langston Hughes, 1914

In this poem, Langston Hughes adds his voice to the chorus that makes up America. Hughes published this poem in 1925, at a time when African Americans were segregated and routinely discriminated against. It is a direct response to Whitman's romantic view of working-class America.

by Langston Hughes

¹I, too, sing America.

²I am the darker brother.
They send me to eat in the kitchen
When company comes,
But I laugh,
And eat well,
And grow strong.

³Tomorrow,
I'll sit at the table
When company comes.
Nobody'll dare
Say to me,
"Eat in the kitchen,"
Then.

280

⁴Besides,
They'll see how beautiful I am
And be ashamed—

⁵I, too, am America.

Connect to the Author

James Langston Hughes was one of the most important figures of the Harlem Renaissance of the 1920s. During this period, musicians, artists, and writers like Hughes gathered in New York City's vast ghetto of Harlem. They explored black life and culture in ways that had never been done. Hughes wrote in many different forms, including poetry, short stories, novels, plays, and essays. Like Walt Whitman, whom he counted as a major influence, Hughes focused on working-class people. But unlike Whitman, he focused on the African American experience. Hughes was born in Joplin, Missouri, in 1902. After high school, Hughes taught English in Mexico, where his father lived. He left after a year, and briefly attended college. Because he was black, he was assigned the worst dorm room. He experienced other forms of bigotry too. He found his professors boring and often skipped class to attend shows and lectures elsewhere. Hughes left college after his freshman year and signed on as a cabin boy on a ship. He got off the ship in the Netherlands and spent a poverty-stricken year in Europe. When he returned to the United States, he worked a series of low-wage jobs and wrote poetry. He began to be recognized for his work. Some black intellectuals criticized him for his images of lower-class life. But he remained committed to recording the truth as he saw it. "I didn't know the upper class Negroes well enough to write much about them. I knew only the people I had grown up with, and they weren't people whose shoes were always shined, who had been to Harvard, or who had heard of Bach. But they seemed to me good people too."

Langston Hughes

281

Comprehension and Vocabulary *Before Reading*

1. **In Lesson 3, we read a poem by Walt Whitman.**
   - **What was the poem about?** (the working people of America)
   - **What opinion did Whitman present through his poem?** (that Americans are happy doing their chosen work and living as they choose)
   - **What tools did Whitman use to persuade readers to see America as he did?** (concrete and sensory details, strong words, figurative language and symbols) **Did he persuade you to think his view was right? Why or why not?** (Responses will vary.)

2. **In this lesson we will read a poem that was written in response to Whitman's poem. It gives another view of life in America. As we read, think about the author's purpose, his opinion, and the tools he uses to present his view. Then we will compare his view of American life to Whitman's.**

Vocabulary Review

3. Arrange students with partners, and have them turn to Student Book page 204. Read the instructions aloud. Call on individuals to read the vocabulary words listed in the box and to give a meaning for each word.

4. Read aloud the first item and model a response. **Let's start by looking at the first word in the box: *varied*. This means "of many kinds." A neighborhood with many kinds of houses wouldn't be boring. That could be why the speaker likes this neighborhood, so *varied* makes sense in the context of this sentence. The homes could be *varied* in color or in style or size. *Varied in color and style* is a good ending to this sentence. Let's write it down, and then underline *varied*.**

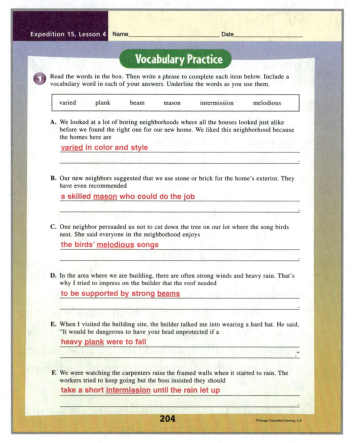

5. Have students work with their partner to discuss and complete the remaining sentences. When all partners are finished, call on students to share their responses. Provide correction and feedback as necessary.

6. **Challenge Words** Write the following items on the board, along with the words *blithe* and *graphic*. Have students complete the items along with those in the Student Book.
   - *When the storm finally passed and the sun came out, everybody cheered. For the rest of the work day, the builders were ____.* (Possible response: in a blithe mood)
   - *My cousin Jerell would have enjoyed seeing the house being built, but he lives far away. To show him how it happened, I might ____.* (Possible response: write him a graphic story that shows all the steps)

Review Poetry

7. In the last lesson we read a Walt Whitman poem about life in America. We talked about how and why the poet wrote the poem. [SKILL ✓]

- **A poet can write as a means of personal expression, to describe an idea or something in the world that he or she finds moving or interesting. How did Whitman use "I Hear America Singing" for personal expression?** (He used rich language to describe something that he found moving or interesting.)

- **A poet can also write to persuade readers to adopt or consider a certain view of things. In what way was Whitman's poem persuasive writing?** (It showed America as a happy place filled with skilled, hard-working Americans who do their part and like their life.)

8. As we read "I, Too" in this lesson, let's think about the poet's purpose in writing it and compare it to the poem we read in the last lesson.

Reading for Understanding *Reading*

1. Have students turn to Anthology page 280. Read the poem aloud as students follow along in their books. Encourage them to make notes about the poet's opinions, as well as similarities and differences they identify between this poem and Whitman's "I Hear America Singing."

2. When students have finished their reading, check literal comprehension of the text by asking these questions: **KNOWLEDGE**

- *Introductory Paragraph:* **In what year was this poem written?** (1925) **What was life like for African Americans at that time?** (They were segregated and discriminated against.)

- *Poem:* **Where does the speaker say he eats his meals when company comes now?** (in the kitchen)

- *Poem:* **Where does he say he will eat his meals when company comes tomorrow?** (at the table)

3. **Look back at the first four lines of the poem. Explain in your own words what Hughes is saying.** (Possible response: Because I am African American, I am not allowed to have the same respect and privileges as others.) **The next three lines explain how the author responds to this treatment. What do you think those lines mean?** (Possible response: Rather than be bitter, he lives in a way that makes him strong.)

4. **How do you think "growing strong" is related to the ideas in the third stanza?** (Possible response: Once he is strong, no one can stop him from sitting at the table.) **Do you think the author is talking for himself alone?** (Possible response: No, he is talking for all African Americans.) **What does sitting at the table represent?** (equal rights for African Americans)

5. **In the fourth stanza, Hughes says, "They'll see how beautiful I am." What change is he predicting?** (Possible responses: an end to prejudice; people learning to appreciate others in spite of differences) **What do you think Hughes is saying to Walt Whitman by choosing the title, the first line, and the last line that he did?** (Possible response: Mr. Whitman, you left my people out of your picture of America. We, too, are part of the American story.)

Checking for Comprehension *After Reading*

1. Have students turn to Anthology pages 278 and 280, and Student Book page 205. Read the instructions aloud, and help students brainstorm ways Whitman might complete the first statement. Have students work with a partner to complete the activity. Encourage students to revisit statements and images in the poems as they discuss the poets' views and decide how each would complete the statements. Monitor students' work, providing correction and feedback as necessary. When all students have completed the activity, invite partners to role-play the two poets, reading their responses as a conversation or debate.

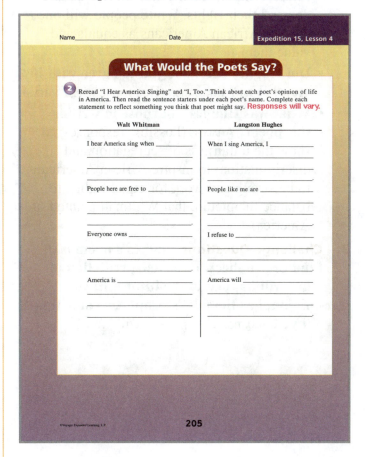

Name_____ Date_____ Expedition 15, Lesson 4

What Would the Poets Say?

Reread "I Hear America Singing" and "I, Too." Think about each poet's opinion of life in America. Then read the sentence starters under each poet's name. Complete each statement to reflect something you think that poet might say. **Responses will vary.**

Walt Whitman

I hear America sing when _____

People here are free to _____

Everyone owns _____

America is _____

Langston Hughes

When I sing America, I _____

People like me are _____

I refuse to _____

America will _____

205

2. Have students apply what they understood from the text by asking the following questions:

   - **How is Hughes's picture of America different from Whitman's?** SYNTHESIS (Possible response: He shows what America was like for African Americans who were not given the same rights as all the happy workers in Whitman's poem.)

   - **What does Hughes use as a symbol of respect and privilege?** COMPREHENSION (eating at the table when company comes)

   - **What statements in the poem predict political or social changes?** ("Tomorrow, I'll sit at the table"; "Nobody'll dare say to me, 'Eat in the kitchen'"; "They'll see how beautiful I am and be ashamed.") **What do these statements mean?** ANALYSIS (In the future, African Americans will rise up and demand their rights. White people will one day see African Americans as equals and value them.)

   - **Did Hughes persuade you to agree with his view? Why?** EVALUATION (Responses will vary.)

   - **What was Hughes's purpose in writing this poem?** ANALYSIS (Possible responses: to show the unfairness of segregation and discrimination; to inspire African Americans to be strong and work for equal rights; to balance the picture that Whitman painted of America)

3. **Challenge Questions** Hughes's poem is a kind of prophecy, or a wise prediction of what will happen in the future. In your opinion, has the poet's prophecy come true? Why? EVALUATION (Responses will vary.)

Connect to the Author

Have students discuss these questions with a partner or in small groups:

- **How was the work of Langston Hughes similar to and different from that of Walt Whitman?**

- **If you could have talked to Langston Hughes, what "how" question would you have asked him?**

- **If you were to address political issues in poetry as Hughes did, what issues would you write about?**

Reading Response

Have students turn to Student Book page 206. Read the instructions aloud. Then have students look back at the poems, think about their own views of America, and answer these questions:

 What do you question or agree with in each poem? How do you "sing" America?

Tell students that they may write their answer as a poem or in paragraph form. Remind them to use concrete details, sensory images, and strong words in their writing. Have students complete their writing independently. When all students are finished, call on individuals to read their response aloud.

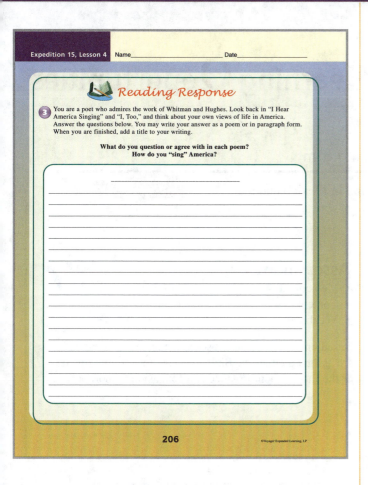

Expedition 15, Lesson 4   Name_____   Date_____

Reading Response

3 You are a poet who admires the work of Whitman and Hughes. Look back in "I Hear America Singing" and "I, Too," and think about your own views of life in America. Answer the questions below. You may write your answer as a poem or in paragraph form. When you are finished, add a title to your writing.

What do you question or agree with in each poem?
How do you "sing" America?

206   ©Voyager Expanded Learning, LP

Passport Reading Journeys Library

Building Fluency

1. Place students in pairs according to reading level to build fluency. When pairing students, be sure that one student is a stronger reader (Student A) than the other student (Student B). However, do not reveal that stronger readers are paired with weaker readers. See *Passport Reading Journeys* Library Teacher's Guide for grouping guidelines.

2. Have students quickly choose reading material from the *Passport Reading Journeys* Library or another approved selection that is at the reading level of Student B. If students have not finished the previously chosen selection, they may continue reading from that selection. See *Passport Reading Journeys* Library Teacher's Guide for material selection guidelines.

3. Tell students that Student A will read one paragraph, and Student B will reread that same paragraph.

4. Have students follow this routine until the end of class.

5. If necessary, review the following practices to enhance fluency:
   • Rate and accuracy of reading
   • Expression during reading
   • Correction procedures

Library Highlights

Spotlight on an Author

Level I

Adam Canfield of the Slash is about journalism in a school setting. Author Michael Winerip worked as an education reporter and columnist with the *New York Times*. In 2001, Winerip received the Pulitzer Prize for National Reporting while on staff at the *New York Times*.

Strategic Online Learning Opportunities®

Students read a passage about types of cultural art found in Mexico and the United States.

Content Connection

Fine Arts

Art that Celebrates Culture
by Elisabeth Archer

Lexile Levels
Passage B 940L
Passage C 1,000L

Assessment
- Metacognition
- Content
- Vocabulary
- Main Idea
- Summary

Based on their assessment scores, students automatically are assigned either the Skills Practice for reinforcement or the Independent Practice and Extension Opportunities.

SKILLS PRACTICE

Vocabulary Strategies
- Context
- Word Parts: Prefixes and Suffixes
- Word Parts: Compound Words

Dictionary Skills

Main Idea Strategy: W–I–N
- Identifying the Most Important *Who* or *What*
- Identifying the Most Important *Information*
- Stating the Main Idea in a Small *Number* of Words

Questioning

Writing
- Writing a Summary Statement

INDEPENDENT PRACTICE

Vocabulary Strategies

Writing
- Writing a Summary Statement

EXTENSION OPPORTUNITIES
- Online Books
- Book Cart
- Review of Previous Passages

Lesson 6

Advanced Word Study

Multisyllabic Words

1. **Remember, sometimes it's easier to read parts of a longer word before reading the entire word. One way is to use what we know about open and closed syllables.** Write the word *migration* on the board. Underline the word part *mi*. **What is the first word part?** (mi) **What kind of syllable is this word part?** (open) **How do we know?** (It has one long vowel sound with no consonants following it, or closing it in.) Underline *gra*. **What is the next word part?** (gra) **What kind of syllable is *gra*?** (open) **How do we know?** (It has one long vowel sound with no consonants following it, or closing it in.) **Read the rest of the word.** (-tion) **What is the word?** (migration) *Migration* means "the act of moving or relocating."

Another way to read longer words is to use what we know about prefixes and suffixes. Write the word *intrusion* on the board. Underline the prefix *in-*. **What is this prefix?** (in-) **What is the next part?** (tru) Underline the suffix *-sion*. **What is this suffix?** (-sion) **What is the word?** (intrusion) **The word *intrusion* means "the act of intruding or interrupting."**

2. Have students turn to Student Book page E15, Lesson 6. Direct students to line 1. **What is the prefix?** (de-) **What is the next part?** (lin) **What is the last part?** (quents) **What is the word?** (delinquents) **The word *delinquents* means "criminals or lawbreakers."** Repeat with the remaining words. Call on individuals to read the words in random order. Ask students to tell the meanings of the words.

3. Direct students to lines 2 and 3. Have them read the words. Then, call on individuals to read the words in a different order. Ask students to tell the meanings of the words.

▼ To Correct
For Multisyllabic Words: **What is the first word part? What is the next part? What is the word?** If students do not know the meaning of the word, review the word and/or word parts to determine the meaning of the word.

For Sounds in Words: Say the correct sound(s), then ask students to repeat the sound(s). Have them read the word again with the correct sound(s). If students do not know the meaning of the word, review the word and/or word parts to determine the meaning of the word.

> **1.** delinquents eliminate reputation sledgehammer
> **2.** expression constructive submissions vandalism
> **3.** destructive canvasses permission accomplishes

Sight Words

1. Direct students to line 1. Have them point to the first word. **This word is *menace*. Read the word.** (menace) **This is not a regular word. Let's read the word again.** (menace) **Let's spell the word.** (m-e-n-a-c-e) **What is the word?** (menace) Repeat with the remaining words. Then, have students read the words. Ask students to tell the meanings of the words.

2. Direct students to lines 2 and 3. **Let's read these words.** Remind students that the rows of words consist of regular and irregular words. Point to the first word. **What is the word?** (misguided) Repeat with the remaining words. Call on individuals to read the words in a different order. Ask students to tell the meanings of the words.

▼ To Correct
For Regular Words: Say the sound(s) in the word, then ask students to repeat the sound(s). Have them read the word again with the correct sound(s). If students do not know the meaning of the word, review the word and/or word part to determine the meaning of the word.

For Irregular Words: Immediately say the correct word. Then have students read the word, spell it, and read it again. If students do not know the meaning of the word, review the word.

> **1.** menace I graffiti I mural I hideousness I
> **2.** misguided I rhyme I young I mechanics I
> **3.** individuality I varied I artistic R mayor I

Anthology Selection

Graffiti Is a Crime!

To the Editor:

¹Things used to be different here in Pleasantville. When I was growing up back in the 1940s, people had respect. They had respect for other people. They had respect for the law and for teachers. But most of all, they had respect for property. Back in my day, we didn't have to have big, ugly billboards telling us to "Keep Pleasantville Pleasant." We knew better than to throw trash on the street or spray paint our names on someone else's building.

²Kids these days don't seem to have that kind of respect any more. Don't believe me? Think I **exaggerate** the problem? Then just take a walk down Main Street some day. Main Street used to be the sparkling pride of all Pleasantville citizens. But today the sidewalks and gutters are filled with filth, and it seems like every square inch of wall space is covered with ugly, spray-painted scrawls. Some people call this hideousness graffiti. I call it what it is—a crime. It's a crime against the **industrious** people who are trying to run businesses inside the buildings that these youngsters deface with their spray paint. It's a crime against the **prestige** of a town that used to be known across the state for its cleanliness and its public-minded citizens. And it's a crime against every citizen whose eyes get polluted by this awful vandalism.

³Some people say that graffiti is a form of art. They say that these vandals are just "expressing their innermost feelings" or "representing their culture for all to see." Horsefeathers! Poppycock! Graffiti is vandalism, pure and simple—nothing more, nothing less. Graffiti vandals are no more artists

282

than I am a flying horse. Real artists express themselves by painting on canvas, not on somebody else's building. Real artists don't have to commit crimes to represent their culture.

⁴That's why I fully support Mayor Fowler's plan to eliminate graffiti. Unlike other city leaders who throw their hands up and act helpless in the face of this menace, the mayor is trying to do something. Mayor Fowler wants to issue **instructions** to all city meter readers to wipe out graffiti in the course of their daily work. If the mayor has his way, meter readers will carry a can of paint and a paintbrush. Any time they spot graffiti, they will immediately cover it up with paint. No questions asked.

⁵The only problem with the mayor's idea is that it doesn't go far enough. We need to crack down on the juvenile delinquents who are damaging and defacing our buildings and our reputation as a city. Right now, these vandals are treated as if they have done nothing more serious than jaywalking. They get a ticket and have to pay a small fine. That's not going to stop these criminals. Rather than giving them a slap on the wrist, we should let graffiti vandals know we mean business. They should face the same punishment as someone who takes a sledgehammer and smashes a hole in a building. A little time in the city jail might make them think twice before they pull out a can of spray paint and deface someone else's property.

Sincerely,
Ernest J. Hassleblad

Is graffiti nothing more than vandalism, or is it a form of art?

283

Turn Vandals into Artists

To the Editor:

⁶I know a lot of Pleasantville citizens are angry about the graffiti that has been popping up around town lately. They say that graffiti makes our beautiful buildings ugly. They say that graffiti is no better than vandalism. In most cases, their **criticism** is valid. There is certainly a lot of ugly graffiti around town. But contrary to what some think, not all graffiti is ugly. In fact, some graffiti has a lot in common with fine art. Some graffiti, like fine art, is a personal expression that shows a great deal of thought and originality by the artist. Graffiti might not be the best way for artists to proclaim their individuality. But in some cases it's hard to miss the artistic ability of these misguided Michelangelos.

⁷I'm not saying I'm pro-graffiti. Like most citizens, I think it's wrong to paint things on walls and buildings without permission. All I'm saying is that I think there's a better solution to the problem of graffiti than Mayor Fowler's idea. Arming city workers with paintbrushes would just make a bad situation worse. Instead of city walls being covered with graffiti, they would be covered with big blotches of paint. How is that going to "Keep Pleasantville Pleasant"?

⁸My solution is to channel the creativity of graffiti artists into a project that will improve the city for us all. Most people would agree that graffiti has made the Pleasantville Public Library an eyesore. The front of the building is in good shape, but both sides and the back have been spray painted with thousands of names and symbols over the years.

⁹I propose that the city sponsor a contest. Invite graffiti artists from all three major areas of town to submit plans for painting a mural on each of the

284

Is graffiti nothing more than vandalism, or is it a form of art?

three messed-up sides of the library. The murals should reflect some aspect of life in Pleasantville—either our history or our current culture. Then the city council could narrow the submissions to three or four for each wall and let citizens vote on their favorites. Once the winners are picked, the city can appoint a supervisor for each of the walls to make sure everything goes smoothly. Then everyone who submitted an idea would be invited to help paint the winning entries on the library walls.

¹⁰My solution accomplishes two things. First, it covers up the graffiti on the library while improving the appearance of the building. Second, it provides graffiti artists with **acknowledgment** of their talents while giving them a constructive way to express themselves. Some of these artists are extremely talented. With a little guidance, they could turn their talents away from destructive graffiti and toward a career in the fine arts.

¹¹I'm positive that my solution will work. If you don't believe me, ask the citizens of Culver City, California. They had a similar graffiti problem five years ago. Then they invited graffiti artists to paint a mural on a run-down fire station. Not only did the program reduce graffiti, it also inspired the entire neighborhood to start sprucing up. It worked so well that the city now sponsors a mural contest every year. They raise money with bake sales and car washes to provide the winner with money for a college scholarship.

¹²Now doesn't that sound better than just throwing graffiti artists in jail?

Sincerely,
Wanda Mercurio

285

Comprehension and Vocabulary   *Before Reading*

1. Review the topic of identity by using the questions from Anthology page 271 and DVD 15.1 to generate prior knowledge. After showing DVD 15.1, call on individuals to read the questions. Have students discuss their responses using information from the DVD and the Lessons 1–4 texts.

2. **In this Expedition, we've been reading texts about identity—who we are and how we come to be this way.**

   • **In Lesson 1, we read an autobiographical essay. What story did it tell?** (the story of how the author learned English as a young immigrant to the U.S.) **What did the author learn along with English?** (She learned how to find herself and feel at home through language.)

   • **In Lesson 2, we read an autobiographical poem. What story did the poem tell?** (an anecdote about the author's introduction to English and baseball as a young immigrant to the U.S.) **How did the author feel about adjusting to his new home before and after the experience?** (Before, he felt awkward, unnatural, and self-conscious. After, he felt happy and hopeful about learning English, fitting in, and making friends.)

   • **In Lessons 3 and 4, we read poems that gave two different views of life in America. What view did Walt Whitman express in "I Hear America Singing"?** (Possible response: that Americans are happy with their work)

   • **What view was presented in "I, Too," by Langston Hughes?** (Possible response: that he and other African Americans were waiting for equal rights and representation among the workers that Whitman described)

3. **These texts show us how each of the authors sees himself or herself in American culture. In the readings for this and the next lesson, two authors share their views on the line between expressing identity and violating the rights of others.**

Introduce Vocabulary

Vocabulary

Review Words

exaggerate	*to make something seem larger or greater than it really is*
industrious	*hard-working; driven to get things done*
prestige	*respect or influence*
instruction	*an explanation of how to do something*
criticism	*finding fault or pointing out a weakness*
acknowledgment	*credit for achievement; recognition of someone's rights or authority*

Challenge Words

Word Building

vandalism	*vandal, vandalize, vandalistic*

Word Meaning

submission	*something put forward so that someone can consider it or make a decision about it* Your *submission* to the poetry contest has won first prize!

4. **This lesson's texts contain words with meanings we have already learned. We will review these words within the texts we are reading.**

5. Write each Review Word on the board. Then ask students to locate the word in the article. Instruct them to read aloud the sentence containing the word, as well as any other sentences that provide context.

   • **What can you tell me about the word?**

   • Ask other questions that allow students to explore the word's meaning. (For example: **How is *prestige* different from *acknowledgment*? What word means the opposite of *industrious*?**)

6. Ask students to respond to the following questions. Provide correction and feedback as necessary.

   - **What are some ways people *exaggerate* what they do in sports? Why might they do this?**
   - **Which are more *industrious*—ants or cats? Explain.**
   - **What is something that would give you more *prestige* in the eyes of your friends?**
   - **When you buy something with "some assembly required," do you find it difficult to follow the *instructions*? Why or why not?**
   - **Give an example of helpful *criticism* and an example of hurtful *criticism*.**
   - **What kind of *acknowledgment*, if any, do you expect when you give a gift?**

7. Work with students to write a definition for each word on the board.

8. Include the Challenge Words to meet the needs of students who are advancing. For the Word Building Challenge Word, have students identify the base word (vandal), then guide them in determining how the base word can help them figure out the meaning of the larger words.

Review Text Structure: Persuasion

9. **One kind of expository text we have studied is persuasive text. In a persuasive text, what does the author attempt to do?** (to convince the reader to do or believe something)

10. **Most persuasive texts contain four elements. What are those elements?** (opinion statement, supporting reasons and details, counterargument, and conclusion) Have students look at the title of the first letter. **Which element is reflected in the title of this letter?** (opinion statement)

11. **Why do authors include supporting reasons and details in a persuasive text?** (Reasons support the author's opinion, to tell *why* the reader should do or think something; details give extra information about each reason and help make reasons clearer to the reader.) **In this reading, the author uses the technique of comparison and contrast to present some of his reasons and details. Let's review the signal words that can help you recognize these comparisons and contrasts in the text.** Write *Signal Words* on the board. List and review comparison and contrast signal words including *like, both, also, too, unlike, different, but, similarly, contrary to, rather than, better, best, worse, worst, more,* and *most.*

12. **What is a counterargument?** (an argument against other opinions) **Why do authors use counterarguments?** (to anticipate ways the reader or other experts might object to the author's points; to drain other viewpoints of their power; to help convince the reader that the only sound opinion is the author's)

13. **What is a conclusion and why is it important in a persuasive text?** (It is the author's summary of his or her argument; it can make a strong and lasting impression on the reader.)

14. **As we read the article, let's try to identify all of these elements in the text. Also, pay attention to the effect these elements have on you as a reader.**

Reading for Understanding

Reading

Places and Names to Look For:
- Pleasantville
- Ernest J. Hassleblad
- Culver City, California
- Mayor Fowler
- Wanda Mercurio

1. **In the readings for this and the next lesson, you may come across some unfamiliar places and names.**

   - Write the words on the board.
   - Point to each word as you read the following:

   In these letters to the editor, two citizens express their views on the graffiti problem in their town of *Pleasantville*. The first, *Ernest J. Hassleblad*, supports *Mayor Fowler's* plan for painting over graffiti. The second, *Wanda Mercurio*, thinks Pleasantville should follow the example of *Culver City, California,* and showcase the work of graffiti artists.

   - Call on individuals to read the words.

2. **Fluency** Read the first paragraph aloud while students follow along in their books. Then have partners read the remainder of the first letter by switching readers after each paragraph. If necessary, review the following fluency correction procedure with students to ensure accuracy: **Offer help when your partner comes to an unfamiliar word or makes a reading error. Pause, then say, "That word is _____. Let's read it again."** As students read, monitor for reading rate, accuracy, and expression.

3. When students have finished their reading, check for literal comprehension by asking the following questions: **KNOWLEDGE**

   - *Paragraph 2:* **According to the writer, what is the cause of the graffiti problem in Pleasantville?** (Children have no respect.) **What does the writer say to do so they will know how bad the problem is?** (take a walk down Main Street)
   - *Paragraph 3:* **What does the writer say graffiti is not?** (art) **What does he say that it is instead?** (vandalism)
   - *Paragraph 4:* **What plan of the mayor's does the writer support?** (having meter readers wipe out the graffiti they encounter every day on their rounds)
   - *Paragraph 5:* **What additional measure does Hassleblad say the city needs to take?** (giving vandals stiffer penalties)

ELL Encourage English language learners to respond to texts by completing the following sentence starters and then sharing their responses with a partner.

- *The thing I liked best about today's reading is ____.*
- *I would change the title to ____.*
- *An important piece of information is ____ because ____.*
- *I would like to know more about ____.*
- *In my opinion, ____ is the most important vocabulary word in today's lesson because ____.*

For a complete model of this strategy, see Expedition 14, Lesson 1.

Checking for Comprehension *After Reading*

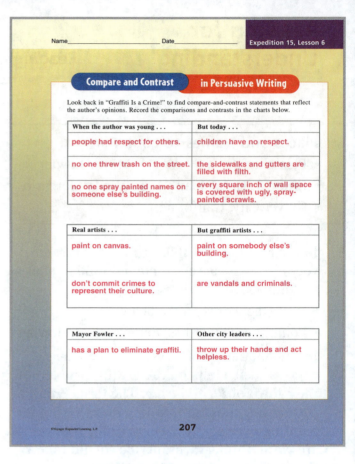

1. Have students apply what they understood from the text by asking the following questions:

   SKILL ✓

   • **What are some descriptive, concrete details Hassleblad includes in his letter?** ANALYSIS (Possible responses: Sidewalks and gutters are filled with filth; every square inch of wall space is covered with ugly, spray-painted scrawls.)

   • **Paraphrase the counterargument the author includes in his letter.** SYNTHESIS (Some say graffiti is art that expresses feelings and represents culture, but real artists don't commit crimes to represent their culture.)

   • **Hassleblad compares and contrasts graffiti artists to other people. Whom does he mention in *contrast* to graffiti vandals?** ("real" artists) **Whom does he mention in *comparison* to graffiti vandals?** SYNTHESIS (someone who smashes a hole in a building with a sledgehammer)

2. **Hassleblad used comparison and contrast to present some of his reasons and details. Let's look more closely at how he used that technique.** Have students turn to Student Book page 207. Read the instructions aloud, and then have students work with a partner to complete the activity. Review and discuss students' responses as a class.

Student Book page 207

Name_____ Date_____ Expedition 15, Lesson 6

Compare and Contrast **in Persuasive Writing**

Look back in "Graffiti Is a Crime!" to find compare-and-contrast statements that reflect the author's opinions. Record the comparisons and contrasts in the charts below.

When the author was young . . .	But today . . .
people had respect for others.	children have no respect.
no one threw trash on the street.	the sidewalks and gutters are filled with filth.
no one spray painted names on someone else's building.	every square inch of wall space is covered with ugly, spray-painted scrawls.

Real artists . . .	But graffiti artists . . .
paint on canvas.	paint on somebody else's building.
don't commit crimes to represent their culture.	are vandals and criminals.

Mayor Fowler . . .	Other city leaders . . .
has a plan to eliminate graffiti.	throw up their hands and act helpless.

©Voyager Expanded Learning, L.P.   207

Connect to Science

Use the following activity to help students compare the safety, effectiveness, and environmental effects of various graffiti-removal methods.

Materials: resource materials (library, classroom, or online) for four methods of graffiti removal (painting over graffiti, chemical removal, water blasting, sandblasting)

- On the board, write these methods of removing graffiti:
  - *painting over the graffiti*
  - *chemical removal*
  - *water blasting*
  - *sandblasting*
- Arrange students into five groups. Tell them that four of the groups will compete to be hired by the fifth group—a local company—to remove graffiti from the company's downtown building.
- Assign one of the four graffiti-removal methods to each of the four competing groups. Have students in each group conduct research to learn the basics about its method of paint removal: technique, material and equipment, effectiveness, and safety to living things and to the environment.
- When the four groups have completed their research, have a spokesperson from each group give a presentation to the fifth (company) group. Ask students in the fifth group to take notes on the presentations.
- After the presentations, have students in the fifth group decide on the group they will hire, giving reasons for their choice.

To increase difficulty: Have students prepare a chart of the pros and cons of each of the four graffiti-removal methods, using information from all the groups as well as from this Web site: http://www.las-cruces.org/pio/graffiti/remove.shtm.

Science

Lesson 7

Anthology Selection

Graffiti Is a Crime!

To the Editor:

¹Things used to be different here in Pleasantville. When I was growing up back in the 1940s, people had respect. They had respect for other people. They had respect for the law and for teachers. But most of all, they had respect for property. Back in my day, we didn't have to have big, ugly billboards telling us to "Keep Pleasantville Pleasant." We knew better than to throw trash on the street or spray paint our names on someone else's building.

²Kids these days don't seem to have that kind of respect any more. Don't believe me? Think I **exaggerate** the problem? Then just take a walk down Main Street some day. Main Street used to be the sparkling pride of all Pleasantville citizens. But today the sidewalks and gutters are filled with filth, and it seems like every square inch of wall space is covered with ugly, spray-painted scrawls. Some people call this hideousness graffiti. I call it what it is—a crime. It's a crime against the **industrious** people who are trying to run businesses inside the buildings that these youngsters deface with their spray paint. It's a crime against the **prestige** of a town that used to be known across the state for its cleanliness and its public-minded citizens. And it's a crime against every citizen whose eyes get polluted by this awful vandalism.

³Some people say that graffiti is a form of art. They say that these vandals are just "expressing their innermost feelings" or "representing their culture for all to see." Horsefeathers! Poppycock! Graffiti is vandalism, pure and simple—nothing more, nothing less. Graffiti vandals are no more artists

---

than I am a flying horse. Real artists express themselves by painting on canvas, not on somebody else's building. Real artists don't have to commit crimes to represent their culture.

⁴That's why I fully support Mayor Fowler's plan to eliminate graffiti. Unlike other city leaders who throw their hands up and act helpless in the face of this menace, the mayor is trying to do something. Mayor Fowler wants to issue **instructions** to all city meter readers to wipe out graffiti in the course of their daily work. If the mayor has his way, meter readers will carry a can of paint and a paintbrush. Any time they spot graffiti, they will immediately cover it up with paint. No questions asked.

⁵The only problem with the mayor's idea is that it doesn't go far enough. We need to crack down on the juvenile delinquents who are damaging and defacing our buildings and our reputation as a city. Right now, these vandals are treated as if they have done nothing more serious than jaywalking. They get a ticket and have to pay a small fine. That's not going to stop these criminals. Rather than giving them a slap on the wrist, we should let graffiti vandals know we mean business. They should face the same punishment as someone who takes a sledgehammer and smashes a hole in a building. A little time in the city jail might make them think twice before they pull out a can of spray paint and deface someone else's property.

Sincerely,
Ernest J. Hassleblad

Is graffiti nothing more than vandalism, or is it a form of art?

Turn Vandals into Artists

To the Editor:

⁶I know a lot of Pleasantville citizens are angry about the graffiti that has been popping up around town lately. They say that graffiti makes our beautiful buildings ugly. They say that graffiti is no better than vandalism. In most cases, their **criticism** is valid. There is certainly a lot of ugly graffiti around town. But contrary to what some think, not all graffiti is ugly. In fact, some graffiti has a lot in common with fine art. Some graffiti, like fine art, is a personal expression that shows a great deal of thought and originality by the artist. Graffiti might not be the best way for artists to proclaim their individuality. But in some cases it's hard to miss the artistic ability of these misguided Michelangelos.

⁷I'm not saying I'm pro-graffiti. Like most citizens, I think it's wrong to paint things on walls and buildings without permission. All I'm saying is that I think there's a better solution to the problem of graffiti than Mayor Fowler's idea. Arming city workers with paintbrushes would just make a bad situation worse. Instead of city walls being covered with graffiti, they would be covered with big blotches of paint. How is that going to "Keep Pleasantville Pleasant"?

⁸My solution is to channel the creativity of graffiti artists into a project that will improve the city for us all. Most people would agree that graffiti has made the Pleasantville Public Library an eyesore. The front of the building is in good shape, but both sides and the back have been spray painted with thousands of names and symbols over the years.

⁹I propose that the city sponsor a contest. Invite graffiti artists from all three major areas of town to submit plans for painting a mural on each of the

---

Is graffiti nothing more than vandalism, or is it a form of art?

three messed-up sides of the library. The murals should reflect some aspect of life in Pleasantville—either our history or our current culture. Then the city council could narrow the submissions to three or four for each wall and let citizens vote on their favorites. Once the winners are picked, the city can appoint a supervisor for each of the walls to make sure everything goes smoothly. Then everyone who submitted an idea would be invited to help paint the winning entries on the library walls.

¹⁰My solution accomplishes two things. First, it covers up the graffiti on the library while improving the appearance of the building. Second, it provides graffiti artists with **acknowledgment** of their talents while giving them a constructive way to express themselves. Some of these artists are extremely talented. With a little guidance, they could turn their talents away from destructive graffiti and toward a career in the fine arts.

¹¹I'm positive that my solution will work. If you don't believe me, ask the citizens of Culver City, California. They had a similar graffiti problem five years ago. Then they invited graffiti artists to paint a mural on a run-down fire station. Not only did the program reduce graffiti, it also inspired the entire neighborhood to start sprucing up. It worked so well that the city now sponsors a mural contest every year. They raise money with bake sales and car washes to provide the winner with money for a college scholarship.

¹²Now doesn't that sound better than just throwing graffiti artists in jail?

Sincerely,
Wanda Mercurio

Comprehension and Vocabulary *Before Reading*

1. **In Lesson 6, we read the first of two letters to the editor on the issue of graffiti.**

   • **In the opinion of the author of "Graffiti Is a Crime!" what two things should be done about the graffiti problem in Pleasantville?** (The town should adopt the mayor's solution; graffiti vandals should be given harsher punishments.)

   • **What elements of persuasion does the author use in his letter?** (supporting reasons and details, counterargument, emotional appeal)

2. **In addition to other elements of persuasion, the author of the first letter uses comparison and contrast in presenting his view. In this lesson, we're going to read the views of another citizen who takes a different approach to the same topic.**

Vocabulary Review

3. Arrange students with partners, and have them turn to Student Book page 208. Read the instructions aloud. Then call on individuals to read a word and to tell what it means.

4. To model the first item, read the first three sentences of the letter aloud. **Notice the underlined phrase. Let's scan the words in the box, looking for a word that might be related to this phrase.** *Exaggerate* **means "to make something seem larger or greater than it really is." That doesn't relate to a list of things applicants must do. And** *industrious* **means "hard-working or driven to get things done." That could possibly relate to a list of things that have to be done. I'll keep looking, just to make sure. The next word is** *instructions*. **This means "an explanation of how to do something." That relates directly to this phrase, because the list tells applicants how to apply for the program.** *Instructions* **must be the answer. Let's write it on the first line.**

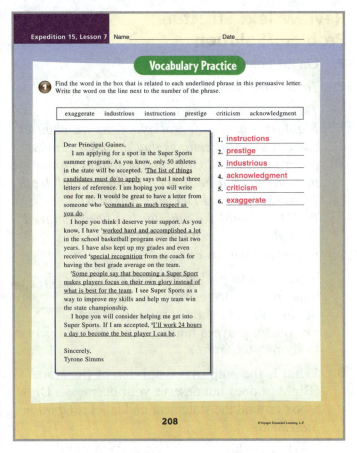

5. Have students complete the remaining items with partners. When all students are finished, call on students to report their responses and to explain their thinking.

6. **Challenge Words** Use the following activities to review the Challenge Words with students.

   • Have students write a sentence including the word *submission* that might appear at the very end of the letter on the Student Book page.

   • Next, write the following on the board: *From the word* vandal, *we can make other words such as _____.*

     – Call on students to complete the sentence, and write their responses on the board.

     – **What does** *vandal* **mean?** (Possible response: a person who destroys or damages someone else's property)

     – Ask students how knowing the base word helps them figure out the meaning of each word.

   ▶ Have students record these words and their possible meanings in the Vocabulary Log.

Review Text Structure: Problem/Solution

7. On the board, write:

To all BigMart customers,

This store does not deserve your business! BigMart is an unsafe workplace. Its warehouses contain asbestos ceilings that drop dangerous fibers into the air. Government studies prove that breathing asbestos causes illness and death. Please support us! DO NOT SHOP AT BIGMART until the asbestos has been removed from all of its warehouses. Doing our jobs should not cost us our health!

This is a sign posted in front of a store by employees who are on strike against the BigMart company. What are the employees hoping you will do? (Refuse to shop in the store.) [SKILL ✓]

8. **What is the employees' opinion of the store?** (BigMart does not deserve your business.) Draw a box around the statement and label it *Opinion Statement*.

- **What problem do the employees point out?** (BigMart warehouses expose workers to dangerous asbestos fibers.) Draw a box around the sentences that describe the problem and label it *Problem*. **What solution do they suggest?** (removing the asbestos from all BigMart warehouses) Draw a box around this statement and label it *Solution*.

- **What other elements do persuasive texts often include?** (counterarguments, supporting details, emotional appeals, quotations from experts, etc.) **Does this text include any of these elements?** (emotional appeal in the last sentence; reference to government studies is similar in effect to quotation from experts)

9. **In this lesson, we'll read a letter written by a woman who wants to persuade readers to accept her solution to the problem of graffiti. As we read "Turn Vandals into Artists," we'll look for the author's opinion statement and reasons. We'll identify her solution to the problem as well as benefits, or effects, that she promises. Last of all, we'll evaluate her** *credibility*. **Has she done her homework? Does she offer strong reasons to persuade us?**

Reading for Understanding
Reading

1. Read the first paragraph aloud while students follow along in their books. Then have students read the remaining paragraphs independently. Encourage students to monitor their own comprehension of the text by pausing occasionally to ask themselves *Am I understanding what I'm reading?* Tell students that when they do not understand what they are reading, they should reread that portion of the text.

2. When students have finished their reading, check for literal comprehension by asking the following questions: **KNOWLEDGE**

- *Paragraph 6:* **What is this writer's opinion about the graffiti in Pleasantville?** (She thinks that some of it is artful.)

- *Paragraph 7:* **Why is this writer opposed to the mayor's idea?** (She doesn't believe big blotches of paint are much of an improvement over the graffiti.)

- *Paragraph 9:* **What other solution does the writer propose?** (She believes the city should hold a mural contest for the sides and back of the public library.)

- *Paragraph 10:* **What two things does the writer say her contest will accomplish?** (It will make the library attractive, and it will give graffiti artists a constructive way to express themselves.)

Checking for Comprehension *After Reading*

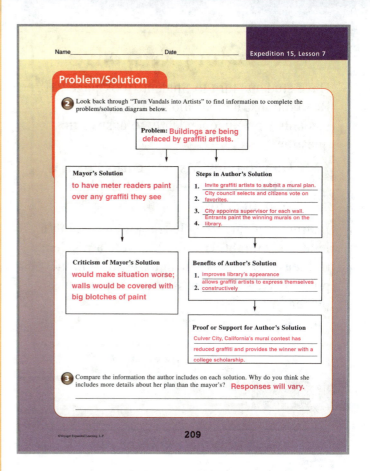

1. Have students apply what they understood from the text by asking the following questions:

   - **Why does the author begin her letter by agreeing in part with the opposing view?** ANALYSIS (Possible response: so readers who agree with Hassleblad won't feel attacked and will be more likely to consider her ideas)
   - **What signal words follow that introduce the author's contrasting view?** ANALYSIS ("*But* not all graffiti is ugly.")
   - **What is the author's purpose in writing paragraph 7?** ANALYSIS (to point out out weaknesses in the mayor's solution)
   - **Why does the author include information about a similar program in Culver City, California?** ANALYSIS (Possible responses: to add credibility to her own proposal; to give proof that her solution will work)

2. **Challenge Questions Reread the last sentence of the letter. How would you answer Mercurio's question? Why?** APPLICATION (Responses will vary.)

3. **In presenting her opinions, Mercurio criticizes the mayor's solution and suggests one of her own. Let's take a closer look at the problem/solution structure within her letter.** Have students turn to Student Book page 209. Read the instructions for sections 2 and 3 aloud, and then have students work with a partner to complete the activities. Review and discuss students' responses as a class. Provide correction and feedback as necessary.

Reading Response

Have students turn to Student Book page 210. Read the instructions aloud. Then have students work independently to answer this question:

 Do you think Ms. Mercurio's plan is better than the mayor's? Explain your thoughts.

Instruct students to include their answers in a letter they might write if they were a resident of Pleasantville. Ask them to write from the point of view of a graffiti artist or a business owner.

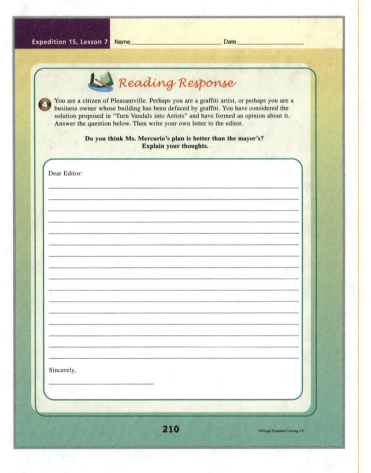

Extending Vocabulary

Affix Review

- Write *pro-* and *-less* on the board. Ask students to tell the meaning of each word part. Provide the meaning if necessary. (*pro-*: "in front of" or "forward"; *-less*: "lacking" or "without")

- Have students work in pairs to scan paragraphs 1 through 12 for words that contain the prefix *pro-* or the suffix *-less*.

- When students are finished, call on individuals to name the words they located. (*helpless* [paragraph 4], *proclaim* [paragraph 6], and *propose* [paragraph 9]) Write these on the board.

- Point to *helpless*. **What word part is in this word?** (the suffix *-less*) **How does this suffix help you figure out the meaning of the word?** (*-Less* means "without" or "lacking," so *helpless* must mean "without help.")

▶ Have students write this word and its meaning in the Vocabulary Log.

- Repeat the process with the remaining words. (*Pro-* means "in front of" or "forward"; *proclaim* means "to stand in front of others and declare or claim something to be true"; and *propose* means "to put forward a plan or idea.")

- Have students name other words they know containing the word parts *-less* and *pro-* and to use the meanings of the word parts to determine the meanings of the words.

▶ Have students record an additional word containing each word part in the Vocabulary Log.

Passport Reading Journeys Library

Building Fluency

1. Place students in pairs according to reading level to build fluency. When pairing students, be sure that one student is a stronger reader (Student A) than the other student (Student B). However, do not reveal that stronger readers are paired with weaker readers. See *Passport Reading Journeys* Library Teacher's Guide for grouping guidelines.

2. Have students quickly choose reading material from the *Passport Reading Journeys* Library or another approved selection that is at the reading level of Student B. If students have not finished the previously chosen selection, they may continue reading from that selection. See *Passport Reading Journeys* Library Teacher's Guide for material selection guidelines.

3. Tell students that Student A will read one paragraph, and Student B will reread that same paragraph.

4. Have students follow this routine until the end of class.

5. If necessary, review the following practices to enhance fluency:
   - Rate and accuracy of reading
   - Expression during reading
   - Correction procedures

Library Highlights

Reading Independently

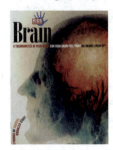

Level I

Students interested in how their brain works and what role good nutrition plays in staying healthy will enjoy *Kids Discover: Brain* or *Odyssey: Weighing In. Kids Discover: Brain* examines parts of the brain and what role those parts play in our daily lives.

Level II

Odyssey: Weighing In explores good nutrition and the role nutrition plays in a healthy lifestyle.

Advanced Word Study

Spelling

1. Direct students to Student Book page E15, Lesson 8. **We use the sounds we know and hear in a word to spell the word. Let's use what we know about syllables, prefixes, and suffixes to spell longer words. The first word is** *reduction.* **Say the word parts in the word** *reduction.* (re, duc, tion) **What is the prefix?** (re-) **What are the sounds in** *re-*? (/r/ /ē/) **Write those sounds. What is the next word part?** (duc) **What are the sounds in** *duc*? (/d/ /u/ /k/) **What is the suffix?** (-tion) **What are the sounds in** *-tion*? (/sh/ /u/ /n/) **Write those sounds.** Repeat with *atonement, thankfulness, irresistible, inactive,* and *unselfish.*

2. Write the words on the board as students check and correct their words. Have them read the list of words.

> **1.** reduction **4.** irresistible
> **2.** atonement **5.** inactive
> **3.** thankfulness **6.** unselfish

Sight Words

1. Direct students to line 1. Have them point to the first word. **This word is** *beauty.* **Read the word.** (beauty) **This is not a regular word. Let's read the word again.** (beauty) **Let's spell the word.** (b-e-a-u-t-y) **What is the word?** (beauty) Repeat with the remaining words. Then, have students read the words. Ask students to tell the meanings of the words.

2. Direct students to lines 2 and 3. **Let's read these words.** Remind students that the rows of words consist of regular and irregular words. Point to the first word. **What is the word?** (graffiti) Repeat with the remaining words. Call on individuals to read the words in a different order. Ask students to tell the meanings of the words.

▼ To Correct

For Regular Words: Say the sound(s) in the word, then ask students to repeat the sound(s). Have them read the word again with the correct sound(s). If students do not know the meaning of the word, review the word and/or word part to determine the meaning of the word.

For Irregular Words: Immediately say the correct word. Then have students read the word, spell it, and read it again. If students do not know the meaning of the word, review the word.

> **1.** beauty **I** ingredients **I** cylinder **I** waddling **I**
> **2.** graffiti **I** armadillo **R** created **I** stethoscope **R**
> **3.** menace **I** hideousness **I** mural **I** especially **I**

Building to Fluency

1. Direct students to the phrases in the Student Book. Have them read through each phrase for accuracy. Then, have students reread the phrases to increase their accuracy and fluency so that the phrases sound like natural speech.

2. Direct students to the Anthology article to locate the sentences containing the phrases. Have them read the sentences in the article accurately and fluently. Remind students to read in a way that sounds like natural speech.

▼ To Correct

Immediately say the correct word. Have students reread the word, then read the phrase or sentence again.

> **1.** . . . the very finest in makeup and skin products . . . *paragraph 8*
> **2.** . . . made with seaweed, green tea, and vitamins C and E! *paragraph 14*
> **3.** . . . top is open to reveal a tube of tinted foundation . . . *paragraph 19*

Anthology Selection

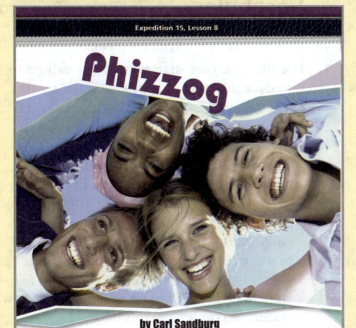

Phizzog

by Carl Sandburg

The title of this poem, "Phizzog," is pronounced FIZ-og. It is a shortened form of the word physiognomy (fizzy-AHG-nuh-me), which means "a person's facial features or expression." It also refers to the study of those features. Ancient philosophers believed that the study of a person's facial features could reveal their character. Aristotle, for example, believed that people with sharp noses were easily angered and people with thick noses didn't care about other people's feelings.

286

This face you got,
This here phizzog you carry around,
You never picked it out for yourself, at all, at all—did you?
This here phizzog—somebody handed it to you—am I right?
Somebody said, "Here's yours, now go see what you can do with it."
Somebody slipped it to you and it was like a package marked:
"No goods exchanged after being taken away—"
This face you got.

Connect to the Author

Carl Sandburg

"Trying to write briefly about Carl Sandburg," a friend of his once said, "is like trying to picture the Grand Canyon in one black-and-white snapshot." Sandburg did so much in his long life that just to list everything he wrote would take 400 pages. During his lifetime, Sandburg was famous as a historian, a poet, and a musician. He was devoted to America and the people in it. It was a love that showed in all his work, and one that he developed at an early age. Born in Galesburg, Illinois, in 1876, Sandburg was the son of poor immigrants. He quit school when he was 13 years old to work as a laborer. He held many jobs: delivery boy, fireman, housepainter, soldier, and newspaper reporter. He devoted 13 years to writing a biography of Abraham Lincoln. The biography was extremely well respected—and enormous. (The section about Lincoln's war years alone is longer than all of Shakespeare's works combined.)

Sandburg gave lectures to adoring crowds. He played guitar and sang. Above all, he wrote poems for the people, in a style that everyone could understand. When Sandburg died in North Carolina in 1967, at the age of 89, he had become one of America's best-known and best-loved poets.

287

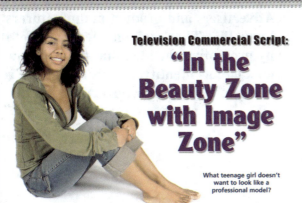

Television Commercial Script:

"In the Beauty Zone with Image Zone"

What teenage girl doesn't want to look like a professional model?

¹**C**amera focuses on a life-size cutout of a slim, beautiful, happy Latina girl, about 15 years old. Upbeat music plays in the background.

²ANNOUNCER [female teenage voice]: You want to look like this. But sometimes you feel like this . . .

³Camera pans down the cutout. It shows an armadillo waddling from behind the cutout across the floor and out of view.

⁴ANNOUNCER: That can be an **obstacle** to happiness. There's no need to feel down about the way you look, though.

⁵The girl shown in the cutout steps from behind the cutout. She speaks to the camera. Hers is the voice of the announcer.

288

⁶ANNOUNCER: IMAGE ZONE has a whole **arsenal** of products to improve your looks and bring out your natural beauty. Whether you're 12 or 20, it's never too soon to start doing what you can to look your best!

⁷Camera shows an African American female. She's 30-ish and wears a physician's white coat and has a stethoscope around her neck. She is examining the face of a teenage Caucasian female. The girl is seated in a chair in the doctor's examining room.

⁸ANNOUNCER: A well-known doctor has helped the scientists at IMAGE ZONE develop the very finest in makeup and skin products for girls just like you. We know that you want the very best in teen beauty products, and IMAGE ZONE delivers. That's why our products cost a little more than others.

⁹Camera shows a close-up of a young teenage girl's face. Her skin is clear and healthy looking.

¹⁰ANNOUNCER: You've heard that beauty is skin deep? Well, that's where the experts at IMAGE ZONE begin: with your skin. The **beneficial** ingredients in "Clean & Clear" wash away daily grease and grime. That includes the subsurface stuff that most soaps can't reach.

¹¹Camera shows a plastic bottle labeled "IMAGE ZONE Clean & Clear." The same teenage girl shown in the previous shot is washing her face with the product.

¹²ANNOUNCER: Use "Clean & Clear" every morning and every night. It gets your skin deep-down clean.

¹³Camera shows the same teenage girl. She's looking in a mirror at her face. Her expression is distressed.

¹⁴ANNOUNCER: Uh-oh! Even though you keep your face clean, you can still get a pesky pimple every now and then. Don't worry. IMAGE ZONE's "Spot Remover" attacks and dries up blemishes. It's made with seaweed, green tea, and vitamins C and E!

289

Expedition 15, Lesson 8

¹⁵Camera shows a tube of "IMAGE ZONE Spot Remover" on a bathroom counter near the sink. The teenage girl shown in previous shots picks up the tube, opens it, and applies a dot of it to a spot on her chin.

¹⁶ANNOUNCER: Apply "IMAGE ZONE Spot Remover" before going to bed. The next morning, you'll be amazed at the results! "Spot Remover" is effective and fast.

¹⁷Camera shows same teenage girl looking in the mirror at the spot on her chin. She looks amazed. Next shot is of the announcer in the same setting as in the first scene of the commercial.

¹⁸ANNOUNCER: Okay. Now let's get down to business. It's a fact of life that we all want to look like the models on TV and in magazines—right? Well, who says we can't? IMAGE ZONE is here to help, with their line of makeup created especially for teens.

¹⁹Camera shows a brightly colored box. The top is open to reveal a tube of tinted foundation, a cylinder of mascara, and a tube of lipstick. All have the name IMAGE ZONE on them.

²⁰ANNOUNCER: Looking like a fashion model is as easy as one, two, three! One—

²¹Camera shows a close-up of the tube of foundation. The name IMAGE ZONE and the numeral 1 are clearly shown on it.

²²ANNOUNCER: —smooth on IMAGE ZONE 1. Then notice how that oily look disappears. Your skin seems to glow with a silky, natural smoothness. Two—

²³Camera shows a close-up of the cylinder of mascara, with the name IMAGE ZONE and the numeral 2 clearly shown on it.

²⁴ANNOUNCER: —brush on IMAGE ZONE 2. Watch your eyelashes lengthen and darken. All eyes will be on you when you use IMAGE ZONE 2! And three—

290

Expedition 15, Lesson 8

²⁵Camera shows a close-up of a tube of lipstick with the name IMAGE ZONE and the numeral 3 on it.

²⁶ANNOUNCER: IMAGE ZONE 3 lip gloss comes in three great tints. Your lips will look fuller and softer—just like a model's. That's a **guarantee**.

²⁷Camera returns to a close-up shot of the announcer.

²⁸ANNOUNCER: So, becoming beautiful is as simple as one, two, three with IMAGE ZONE products. Oh, yeah—the folks at IMAGE ZONE wanted me to tell you something else. They think you should accept yourself for who you are. They believe that we're all beautiful in our own way. It's just that we can use a little help, sometimes. So there's no need to feel like this—

²⁹Camera shows the announcer reaching down, although it doesn't show what she's picking up—just a shot of her upper body. Then the shot reveals that she has picked up the armadillo, which she holds in both hands.

³⁰ANNOUNCER: —when you can look like this!

³¹The announcer walks over to her identical cutout. She stands next to it, tilting her head toward it with the word "this." Then she smiles at the camera. [time: 1:00 minute]

291

Comprehension and Vocabulary *Before Reading*

1. Use the following statements and questions to introduce the topic of appearance and identity.

   • **The other day, I heard some teachers talking about some possible new rules in the school district. They were saying that next year, female students might not be allowed to wear makeup until their senior year.** Allow several students to offer opinions.

   • **They're also talking about some other rules. Male students might not be allowed to wear earrings or clothes or hats with sports logos. They think the rules will help students stay focused on schoolwork.** Allow students to respond to this news.

   • **I didn't really overhear a conversation about new rules. By telling this little story, what do you think I was trying to illustrate about appearance and identity?** (Possible response: that we feel that our appearance expresses our identity—who we are, what we value, who we want to be, and what we want others to *think* we are)

   • **Advertisers and product manufacturers know this. They make money—a lot of it—by promoting the idea that the way you look equals identity. In this lesson, we're going to explore how advertisers do this.**

Introduce Vocabulary

Vocabulary

Review Words

obstacle	*something that gets in the way or stops progress*
arsenal	*a collection of things, often weapons, that will be used to accomplish a purpose*
beneficial	*of or related to benefits; helpful*
guarantee	*a promise that something will happen or be done*

Challenge Words

Multiple Meaning

devoted — *having great love or loyalty for someone or something*
My grandmother was *devoted* to her husband and seven children.
giving a lot of time or energy to something
The students *devoted* a month to their study of Picasso.

Word Building

stethoscope — *scope, telescope, microscope*

2. **This lesson's texts contain words with meanings we have already learned. We will review these words within the texts we are reading.**

3. Write each Review Word on the board. Then ask students to locate the word in the text. Instruct them to read aloud the sentence containing the word, as well as any other sentences that provide context.

   • **What can you tell me about the word?**

   • Ask other questions that allow students to explore the word's meaning. (For example: **What is a synonym for *obstacle*? What is the opposite of *beneficial*?**)

4. Ask students to respond to the following questions. Provide correction and feedback as necessary.

   • **What kind of *obstacles* might you find on an *obstacle* course?**

   • **Suppose you are caring for three high-energy toddlers who get into trouble if they are not entertained. What are some good things to have in your babysitting *arsenal*?**

   • **Which is more *beneficial* to the environment— riding a bicycle or a motorcycle? Why?**

   • **If you started a lawn-mowing service, would you offer a money-back *guarantee* to your customers? Why or why not?**

5. Work with students to write a definition for each word on the board.

6. Include the Challenge Words to meet the needs of students who are advancing. For the Word Building Challenge Word, have students identify the base word (scope), then guide them in determining how the base word can help them figure out the meaning of the larger words.

Extending Vocabulary

Affix Review

• Write *sub-*, *-tive*, and *-ive* on the board. Ask students to tell the meaning of each word part. Provide the meaning if necessary. (*sub-*: under, beneath, below; *-tive*, *-ive*: having the quality of or ability to)

• Have students work in pairs to scan paragraphs 10 and 16 for words that contain the prefix *sub-* or the suffix *-tive* or *-ive*.

• When students are finished, call on individuals to name the words they located. (*subsurface* [paragraph 10]; *effective* [paragraph 16]) Write these on the board.

• Point to *subsurface*. **What word part is in this word?** (the prefix *sub-*) **How does this prefix help you figure out the meaning of the word?** (*Sub-* means "under" or "beneath," so *subsurface* must mean "under the surface.")

▶ Have students write this word and its meaning in the Vocabulary Log.

• Repeat the previous step with *effective*. (*-Ive* means "having the quality of" or "having the ability to," so *effective* must mean "having the ability to cause an effect.")

• Have students name other words they know containing the word parts *sub-*, *-tive*, and *-ive* and use the meanings of the word parts to determine the meanings of the words.

▶ Have students record an additional word containing each word part in the Vocabulary Log.

Review Persuasion

7. Have students return to Anthology page 288 and preview the text by looking at the photo and reading the title.

- **What kind of text is this?** (a script for a TV commercial)

- **What is the purpose of a TV commercial?** (to persuade the viewer to purchase something)

- **Based on the image and the title, what do you think this commercial will try to persuade the viewer to buy?** (beauty products)

- Write *We think you should buy our beauty products.* on the board. **In a persuasive text, what do we call this kind of statement?** (the opinion statement) Write *Opinion Statement* under the sentence on the board. **Do you think this statement will actually appear in the TV script? Do you usually hear direct statements like this in commercials?** (no) **The message is usually *implied*, or not stated directly.**

8. **In most persuasive texts, what do writers offer to convince readers to think or do something?** (They provide reasons.) Write *Reasons* under *Opinion Statement* on the board. **Do they usually state these reasons directly?** (yes) **What about in TV commercials— are reasons stated directly or implied?** (usually implied, but sometimes both)

9. **Think of a commercial you like.** Call on a student to describe the commercial. **What makes you like this ad? What elements does it have that, say, a persuasive news article does not?** (Possible responses: music, images, humor, celebrities) Write *Music, Images, Humor,* and *Celebrities* on the board. **TV ads often use these additional elements to persuade their audiences. If their audiences are entertained, advertisers reason that they will be more likely to remember and buy their products.**

10. **As we read "In the Beauty Zone with Image Zone," we'll look for the *implied* opinion statement and reasons that are stated or implied. We'll also watch for other elements that make the ad persuasive—and entertaining.**

Reading for Understanding   *Reading*

Names to Look For:	
• Image Zone	• Clean & Clear
• Spot Remover	

1. **As you read this text, you may come across some unfamiliar names.**

- Write the words on the board.
- Point to each word as you read the following:

In the first text, we will read a poet's views on appearance. In the second, we will read the script for a commercial. The commercial features an attractive young announcer who introduces beauty products by *Image Zone*. She tells viewers how two skin products, *Clean & Clear* cleanser and *Spot Remover*, can give them amazing results. She also explains how Image Zone cosmetics can make them look great.

- Call on individuals to read the words.

2. Have students turn to Anthology page 286.

- **What kind of text is this?** (a poem) **We read three other poems in this Expedition. How did the poem "How I Learned English" relate to the topic of identity?** (It showed how coming to America made a young immigrant feel unsure of his identity until he connected with American boys, baseball, and English.)

- **What view of American identity did Whitman show in "I Hear America Singing"?** (American workers proudly expressing, or "singing," who they are through their work) **What was Langston Hughes's purpose in writing "I, Too"?** (to show a side of American life Whitman ignored; to express his own identity as an African American)

3. **The poem we will read is by Carl Sandburg, a poet who loved America and wrote his poems in language most Americans would understand.** Read the introductory paragraph aloud.

4. **Fluency As I read the poem "Phizzog," listen to find out what the poet thinks *physiognomy*, or a person's face, has to do with identity.** Read the entire poem aloud. Then have partners take turns reading the poem to each other. If necessary, review fluency goals with students and monitor for reading rate, accuracy, and expression.

5. When students have completed their reading, check for literal comprehension and have students apply what they understood by asking the following questions:

   SKILL ✓

   - **What is *phizzog* short for?** KNOWLEDGE (physiognomy)

   - **What does *physiognomy* mean?** KNOWLEDGE (a person's facial features, and the study of those features to see what they say about a person's character)

   - **How would you sum up the main idea of this poem?** EVALUATION (You don't choose your face, so you have to make the best of the one you were given.)

   - **Do you think Sandburg's casual style of writing makes his message more or less powerful? Why?** EVALUATION (Responses will vary.)

6. **Challenge Questions Did the poem succeed in giving you a different perspective about appearance? Why?** APPLICATION (Responses will vary.)

 Provide English language learners support in interpreting the figurative language they encounter when reading literature. As students read the selections with a partner, have them stop after specific paragraphs to do the following:

- Look for sentences containing the word *like*. For example:
  Somebody slipped it to you and it was like a package marked: "No goods exchanged after being taken away—" (lines 6–7)
- Decide whether the author is using the word to compare one thing to another.
- If so, identify the two things being compared.
- Discuss what the author may want to show by using this particular comparison.

If students are still confused by the comparisons, draw a literal picture of them, and have students decide if the pictures make sense in the context of the story.

For a complete model of this strategy, see Expedition 13, Lesson 2.

Connect to the Author

Read aloud the information about Carl Sandburg in the Connect to the Author feature on Anthology page 287. Then discuss the following questions with students:

- **How did Sandburg's love of America affect his identity?**

- **Is there something you love so much that it could help shape your identity in a similar way?**

- **What message about identity do you take from Sandburg's poem?**

7. Now let's look at a different kind of persuasive writing. Have students turn to Anthology page 288. Read the first paragraph aloud.

- **What do you notice about this paragraph?** (It is indented; the type does not look like the script.) **This is like a stage direction in a play. It gives a description of the camera shot and of what will be seen and heard in the commercial.**

- **When we've talked about description in the past, what did we say its purpose was?** (to bring a scene to life in the mind of the reader) **The stage directions in this script do that, too—they bring this scene to life in your mind as you read it. They also have another purpose. What do you think it is?** (to tell the TV producers how to make the commercial)

8. Look at the next paragraph. Read it aloud. **In the commercial, these words will be said by the announcer. Throughout the script, the words of the announcer or an actor will appear after that person's name, which is set in all capital letters.**

9. Assign the role of announcer to a stronger reader while you take the part of reading the stage directions. Have the rest of the class follow along in their books as you and the announcer read the first two pages of the script aloud. Then arrange students in pairs, assigning roles to each student, and have them finish reading the script.

10. When students have finished their reading, check for literal comprehension of the text by asking the following questions: KNOWLEDGE

- *Paragraph 6:* **What does the commercial claim that Image Zone products will do?** (improve your looks)

- *Paragraphs 13 and 14:* **Why does the girl in the commercial look distressed?** (because she has spotted a pimple on her face)

- *Paragraph 16:* **According to the commercial, how long will it take for Image Zone Spot Remover to remove or reduce the pimple?** (one night)

- *Paragraphs 20 through 26:* **What are the three steps of looking like a fashion model, according to the commercial?** (using Image Zone foundation, mascara, and lip gloss)

Checking for Comprehension *After Reading*

1. Have students turn to Student Book page 211. Read the instructions aloud. Then work together as a class to fill in the implied opinion statement, reasons, and other persuasive elements used in the commercial.

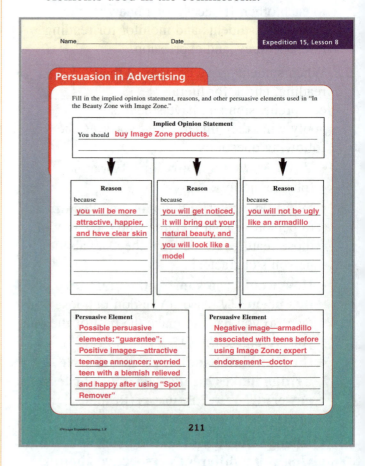

2. After you complete the Student Book activity, use the following questions to help students draw connections between the TV script and the topic of identity:

- **How does the ad tap into worries or insecurities viewers may have?** ANALYSIS (Possible responses: It shows a teenage girl upset about blemishes; it contrasts the beautiful girl with an armadillo, implying the viewer may be as unattractive as the armadillo.) Write these on the board.

- **How does the announcer imply that Image Zone products can help viewers?** ANALYSIS (It can remove obstacles to happiness; improve looks; bring out natural beauty; turn worry into happiness by clearing blemishes; make ordinary people look like models; make people notice you; make it easy to be beautiful.)

- **How does the ad try to persuade viewers they should pay more for Image Zone products?** ANALYSIS (By saying "we know you want the best," viewers will feel they *should* pay more so they will get products that can really guarantee miracles.)

- **Imagine you are seeing this commercial on TV. What do the makers of the ad want *you* to think to yourself?** APPLICATION (Possible response: Oh, gosh. I'm sort of like the creepy armadillo and I need to be like the pretty announcer. Look at her smiling! If I just looked like she does, I'd be as happy as she is.)

- **What would the ad make viewers think if the announcer was a famous celebrity?** EVALUATION (Possible responses: I admire and trust that famous person. The product must be good if she says so; maybe I should use this product she likes so I will be more like her.)

- **The ad mentions that you should accept yourself for who you are and that we're all beautiful in our own way. Is that the main message the ad gives you? Explain.** EVALUATION (No, the overall ad points out all the flaws viewers need to fix with beauty products. It gives me the message that unless I already look as good as the announcer and feel as happy as she does when she smiles into the camera, I need to use Image Zone beauty products.)

3. **Challenge Questions Who do commercials help? Who can they hurt? How?** SYNTHESIS Discuss what teenagers are trying to achieve by using products that promise to make them look "ideal." Ask students what they think an obsession with looks shows about the way a person sees himself or herself. Have them explain whether they believe identity comes from what we look like on the outside, or from what we believe on the inside and what we do.

Connect to Careers

Use the following activity to help students explore the work of cosmetic scientists.

- Bring to class and display various cosmetics, such as shampoo, mascara, nail polish, and lipstick. Alternatively, display magazine photographs of cosmetics. **What's the connection between these cosmetics and science?** (The cosmetics are made of chemicals.)

- Explain that the people who create cosmetics have to understand chemistry. **Cosmetic scientists are constantly working in the lab to make new products and improve existing ones. In addition to chemistry, these scientists have to understand aspects of the human body such as the structure, function, and metabolism of the outer layer of the skin.**

- Tell students that several universities in the U.S. offer degrees in cosmetic science. Point out that many jobs in this field are available, since the sale of cosmetics is a huge industry. **U.S. consumers spend about $30 billion a year on cosmetics.**

- Explain that cosmetic companies in the U.S. spend about $750 million each year on research and development. **Most companies can afford to have cosmetic laboratories that rival labs in the best universities.**

- On the board, write the ingredients of some or all of the cosmetics you brought to class. Have students use encyclopedias or other resources to learn more about these ingredients. Call on individuals to report on what they learned.

- If possible, have students view the brief video at http://pbskids.org/dragonflytv/show/makeup.html, in which two girls make batches of lip gloss and test them on consumers.

To increase difficulty: Have students visit the Web site of the Food and Drug Administration (FDA) to learn about its role in the regulation of the cosmetics industry.

Careers

791

Lesson 9

Anthology Selection

Social Studies

Wheatsville Daily News   SOUND OFF   March 23

Immigrants in America: Wheatsville Sounds Off

The Melting Pot Works

[1]If you're like me, you've noticed that migrant workers are changing the face of Wheatsville these days. Some of you are not too happy about the newcomers because they haven't yet learned our customs and language. But I think we should all make these new arrivals welcome. We should help them become true Americans. After all, immigrants are part of our heritage.

[2]Being a nation of immigrants is one thing that has made America great. Our founding fathers came here from England. Throughout our history, America has been a safe haven for people in trouble. Thousands came to escape starvation during Ireland's potato famine. When times got hard in the rest of Europe, people from all over the continent came to find jobs in America's cities. Chinese workers struggling to make a living crossed the ocean to join the Gold Rush in America. Jews fled from the Nazis and found safety here. These early groups came, worked hard, and embraced American life. I think that is what today's immigrants need to do too. Like those early groups, immigrants today come from countries with poor economies or unfair political systems. In this country, they can leave their difficult past behind and learn to live the American way.

[3]There is plenty of proof that immigrants can fit in and learn to be great Americans. Albert Einstein, a German immigrant, was perhaps the greatest scientist ever. Madeleine Albright, who came from the Czech Republic, became our Secretary of State. An immigrant from Chile, Isabel Allende, is a world famous writer. Fernando Valenzuela came from Mexico to become a great major league pitcher. And I'm sure many of you will agree that Arnold Schwarzenegger did us a favor by coming from Austria to star in American action movies! You can probably think of many more examples, too. That's because immigrants have made contributions in almost every field. Isn't that reason enough to

292

welcome them and help them adjust to American life?

[4]Instead of resenting immigrants, we should become their teachers. We should go out of our way to talk to them and help them learn the language. We should share our recipes, our music, and our celebrations. As they learn about these things, immigrants can slowly become true Americans, just as immigrants have been doing for more than 200 years.

[5]Farmers around here set a great example for how to help immigrants. I'm sure you know what I mean because you, too, see local farmers going the extra mile. They hire whole families of migrant workers and often help them find housing. They teach workers our way of farming and help them learn English on the job. The rest of us can follow their example by making immigrants welcome at community events, such as parades and the county fair. We can invite them to church services and potluck dinners. We can encourage them to sign up their children for scout groups and Little League. I believe that the more we help immigrants participate in our community, the faster they will blend in and feel a part of it. They can truly become our neighbors and friends.

[6]Immigrants need time, along with our help and understanding, to learn how to be Americans. That's what they have come here to do. If we welcome them and share our language and customs, I'm sure that migrant workers in our area will become good citizens of Wheatsville and true Americans.

Trade the Melting Pot for a Salad Bowl

[7]America should quit trying to be a melting pot. People only want to blend newcomers into one American culture so that everything "foreign" will disappear. When they say that we must become alike to be American, they really mean, "Everyone must become like me because my way is best." Rather than a melting pot, America should be a salad bowl filled with many textures and flavors. In a salad, separate ingredients are mixed together without losing their distinct colors and flavors. In that same way, we should "mix" immigrants into America while allowing them to preserve their heritage.

[8]While a melting pot melts away differences that cause conflict, it also melts away differences that make America better. In countries with a single culture, people think alike. They have fewer disputes over how to govern, what laws are fair, and what rights people should have. That is far more convenient than having many cultures and viewpoints. But putting up with the inconvenience of differing cultures yields a big payoff. That payoff is diversity. Diversity helps keep Americans open to new ideas. I believe it is that openness that makes America a leader in the arts, in invention, and in research. Tolerance of diversity also attracts great thinkers from other countries. They are eager to study and work in America, where they can dare to express new ideas. America can only keep that "think tank" appeal if it is a place that values the contributions of all kinds of people and cultures.

[9]Another problem with the "melting pot" is that it is disrespectful. Immigrants shouldn't have to give up their native culture in order to fit in. This kind of "blending" destroys people's self-respect along with valuable traditions. I know this from experience. My family came to America when I was very young. We were excited about living in a land that offered so much opportunity. But when I went to school, I found that my opportunities were limited. The only way I could understand the teacher was to ask for help from other students who spoke Spanish. When I did, my teacher made me stand up for a public scolding. She told me I would never learn English unless I quit speaking Spanish. I was humiliated for simply being who I was. After that, I sat silently, wasting time in a classroom where I could not use the beautiful language I knew. Like so many immigrants, I was denied access until I could learn English. I was made to feel irrelevant and invisible. The worst thing was that it made me ashamed that my culture and my family were different. If only that teacher had been able to respect my culture instead of expecting it to "melt" away, I could have asked questions and taken part while I learned English!

[10]It is time for Americans to do more than allow immigrants to "melt" into the culture. They must recognize that having many cultures is part of what makes America great. Immigrants like myself who have blended in and found a place here can still find a better life. That life is one in which we are free to be proud of our culture and proud to be ourselves. Give us this, America, and we will give you the best that we have to offer.

293   294

792

Expedition Review

1. On the board, write the following: *Julia Alvarez, Gregory Djanikian, workers in Whitman's poem, Langston Hughes, and other African Americans.* **In the texts, we've read in this Expedition, each of these people (or groups of people) had a part of their identity shaped by another person, an experience, or an idea.**

2. Arrange students in groups, and assign each group one of the people or groups of people listed on the board. Have students return to the text(s) about their subject to help them answer these questions:

   • **Who or what helped shape this person's (or group of people's) identity?**

   • **Do you think this change or influence was for the better, or for the worse? Why?**

3. Before students begin, have group members work together to select a leader and to specify the leader's duties. Then have students work together to write several sentences in response to the questions. Instruct students to use one or more of the following words in their sentences: *nurture, banished, mason, varied, exaggerate, industrious, prestige, instructions, acknowledgment, obstacle, beneficial.*

4. **Challenge Words** If students have learned the Challenge Words, instruct them to include at least one of those words in their sentences, as well.

5. When all groups are finished, have a representative from each read aloud the group's sentence(s). Call on other individuals to identify and give a meaning for the vocabulary word they heard.

Assessment

1. Have students turn to Student Book pages 212–216. Then have them turn to Anthology page 292. Explain to students that they will read both letters in "Immigrants in America: Wheatsville Sounds Off" before they answer the questions on the Student Book page.

2. Read aloud the Tips for Success and assessment instructions. Then have students complete the assessment independently.

Reteaching Guidelines

Comprehension

If students incorrectly answer more than 2 out of 11 questions on the Comprehension Assessment, refer to the Reteach lesson on page 796a. Using the Comprehension section, reteach the skills, guide students in completing the practice activity, and reassess comprehension.

Vocabulary

If more than 20 percent of the students miss certain vocabulary items, reteach and practice those words using the Vocabulary section of the Reteach lesson on page 796c.

EXPEDITION 15 • LESSON 9

Panel 1 (page 212)

Expedition 15, Lesson 9 Name_____ Date_____

Comprehension Assessment

Tips for Success! **Use Multiple Strategies:** Even if you have a favorite test-taking strategy, do not ignore the others. Some of the strategies you have practiced are Find Key Words, Eliminate Answers that Overgeneralize, Preview the Questions, Make Notes as You Read, Eliminate Obvious Answers, and Use Your Head.

Multiple Choice 3 points each

Read "The Melting Pot Works" and "Trade the Melting Pot for a Salad Bowl" to answer questions 1–5. Look back in the texts. Fill in the bubble next to the best answer.

1. According to "The Melting Pot Works," why do immigrants come to America?
   (A) to escape poor economies and unfair political systems
   (B) to become teachers, musicians, and cooks
   (C) to learn to speak and read English
   (D) to contribute ideas to the American "think tank"

2. What does the author of the second letter mean when he says America should be a "salad bowl"?
   (A) Americans should provide food for migrant workers.
   (B) Immigrants should leave their past behind to be part of the American mix.
   (C) Immigrants should live where they can work on vegetable farms.
   (D) Americans should mix while keeping their distinct cultures.

3. With which of the following opinions do BOTH authors agree?
   (A) Immigrants should speak only English.
   (B) Immigrants make America better.
   (C) The melting pot idea is disrespectful to immigrants.
   (D) Immigrants want to leave their past behind.

4. According to "Trade the Melting Pot for a Salad Bowl," what makes America a leader in invention and research?
   (A) industriousness
   (B) conflict
   (C) tolerance
   (D) diversity

5. Both "The Melting Pot Works" and "Trade the Melting Pot for a Salad Bowl" are examples of what kind of text?
   (A) fiction
   (B) description
   (C) persuasion
   (D) biography

212

Panel 2 (page 214)

Expedition 15, Lesson 9 Name_____ Date_____

Extended Response 20 points

Read "The Melting Pot Works" and "Trade the Melting Pot for a Salad Bowl" to plan your answer for question 11. Look back in the texts. Use the information you find to complete the chart.

11. The authors of these letters to the editor have very different opinions. Write them below. Then give the problem as each author sees it and the solution each author suggests. Next give an example of a persuasive element each author uses. Give an example of each element by listing the number of the paragraph in which it appears. Finally, tell which author you find more credible, or trustworthy, and why.

	Author of "The Melting Pot Works"	Author of "Trade the Melting Pot for a Salad Bowl"
Opinion: Problem as the author sees it	Immigrants haven't learned American customs and English so they can blend in as true Americans.	Americans shouldn't expect immigrants to lose their culture and language to blend in with other Americans.
Author's solution	Americans should go out of their way to speak to immigrants so they can learn English and to involve them in American customs and organizations.	America should become more like a salad bowl with the distinct flavors and textures of varied cultures. Immigrants should be allowed to preserve their culture and traditions.
One persuasive element author uses	supporting facts—paragraph 3; creating common ground with the reader—paragraphs 1 and 5	counterargument—paragraph 8; personal experience—paragraph 9

Which author is more credible? Why?
Responses will vary, but should be supported with logical reasons.

214

Panel 3 (page 213)

Name_____ Date_____ Expedition 15, Lesson 9

Short Response 4 points each

Read "The Melting Pot Works" and "Trade the Melting Pot for a Salad Bowl" to answer questions 6–10. Look back in the texts. Then write your answer on the line(s).

6. What does "American melting pot" mean?
   America is a place where immigrants "melt" or blend together to make one American culture.

7. Why does the author of "The Melting Pot Works" mention Albert Einstein?
   The author names him as an example of how immigrants can blend in and become great Americans.

8. What is a "true American" according to the author of "The Melting Pot Works"?
   someone who shares American customs, speaks English, and takes part in the community

9. The author of "Trade the Melting Pot for a Salad Bowl" states that the melting pot is disrespectful to immigrants. What proof does the author offer that this statement is true?
   The author relates a childhood experience in which he or she was humiliated for not knowing English and made to feel ashamed of his culture.

10. With whom do you mostly agree—the author of "The Melting Pot Works" or the author of "Trade the Melting Pot for a Salad Bowl"? Why? Give two reasons. **Responses will vary.**

I mostly agree with _____
because _____
and because _____.

213

Panel 4 (page 215)

Name_____ Date_____ Expedition 15, Lesson 9

Vocabulary Assessment 3 points each

For questions 12–26, read each sentence. Fill in the bubble next to the correct meaning for the underlined word.

12. The student was banished to the back of the room for speaking English. What does the word *banished* mean?
    (A) embarrassed
    (B) hidden away
    (C) tutored
    (D) sent away

13. The industrious immigrant had two jobs. What does the word *industrious* mean?
    (A) hard-working
    (B) confused
    (C) soft-spoken
    (D) penniless

14. I followed the instructions on the back of the face cream. What does the word *instructions* mean?
    (A) warning
    (B) ingredients
    (C) directions
    (D) diagram

15. We hired a mason to build a new chimney. What does the word *mason* mean?
    (A) a fire specialist
    (B) an architect
    (C) a stoneworker
    (D) a woodworker

16. When the beam rotted, the roof caved in. What does the word *beam* mean?
    (A) shingle
    (B) thick piece of lumber
    (C) heavy stone pillar
    (D) frame

17. The lunch hour was a pleasant intermission for the exhausted workers. What does the word *intermission* mean?
    (A) bonus
    (B) break
    (C) entertainment
    (D) surprise

18. The manufacturer claimed its cleanser was beneficial for every type of skin. What does the word *beneficial* mean?
    (A) helpful
    (B) irritating
    (C) enjoyable
    (D) safe

19. The teacher tried to nurture her students' love of learning. What does the word *nurture* mean?
    (A) develop
    (B) understand
    (C) explain
    (D) test

215

794

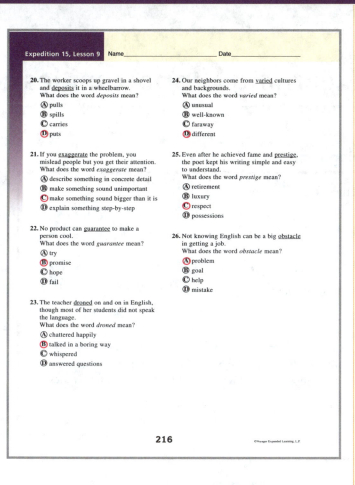

20. The worker scoops up gravel in a shovel and <u>deposits</u> it in a wheelbarrow.
What does the word *deposits* mean?
Ⓐ pulls
Ⓑ spills
Ⓒ carries
Ⓓ puts

21. If you <u>exaggerate</u> the problem, you mislead people but you get their attention.
What does the word *exaggerate* mean?
Ⓐ describe something in concrete detail
Ⓑ make something sound unimportant
Ⓒ make something sound bigger than it is
Ⓓ explain something step-by-step

22. No product can <u>guarantee</u> to make a person cool.
What does the word *guarantee* mean?
Ⓐ try
Ⓑ promise
Ⓒ hope
Ⓓ fail

23. The teacher <u>droned</u> on and on in English, though most of her students did not speak the language.
What does the word *droned* mean?
Ⓐ chattered happily
Ⓑ talked in a boring way
Ⓒ whispered
Ⓓ answered questions

24. Our neighbors come from <u>varied</u> cultures and backgrounds.
What does the word *varied* mean?
Ⓐ unusual
Ⓑ well-known
Ⓒ faraway
Ⓓ different

25. Even after he achieved fame and <u>prestige</u>, the poet kept his writing simple and easy to understand.
What does the word *prestige* mean?
Ⓐ retirement
Ⓑ luxury
Ⓒ respect
Ⓓ possessions

26. Not knowing English can be a big <u>obstacle</u> in getting a job.
What does the word *obstacle* mean?
Ⓐ problem
Ⓑ goal
Ⓒ help
Ⓓ mistake

216

©Voyager Expanded Learning, L.P.

Expedition Wrap-Up

1. After students have completed the assessment, bring them together to discuss the probing questions as a way to provide closure for Expedition 15. Briefly discuss each of the Expedition articles. Then watch DVD 15.2 together as a class. Have students turn to Anthology page 271. Ask students to summarize the response to each probing question that was given on the DVD.

2. Conclude the Expedition by having students name some of the forces that can shape identity. Then have students use poster board, paper and markers, cut-out magazine images, or written words to create a mask they think symbolizes or represents their identity. Call on students to present their masks to the class. Encourage students to identify in their presentation some of the forces that have helped to make them who they are today.

Strategic **O**nline **L**earning **O**pportunities®

Session 2 | http://solo.voyagerlearning.com

Students read a passage about types of music that together formed a new sound—jazz.

Content Connection

Fine Arts

Jazz Ingredients
by Heather Mitchell Amey

Lexile Levels
Passage B 900L
Passage C 1,000L

Assessment

- Metacognition
- Content
- Vocabulary
- Main Idea
- Summary

Based on their assessment scores, students automatically are assigned either the Skills Practice for reinforcement or the Independent Practice and Extension Opportunities.

SKILLS PRACTICE

Vocabulary Strategies
- Context
- Word Parts: Prefixes and Suffixes
- Word Parts: Compound Words

Dictionary Skills

Main Idea Strategy: W–I–N
- Identifying the Most Important *Who* or *What*
- Identifying the Most Important *Information*
- Stating the Main Idea in a Small *Number* of Words

Questioning

Writing
- Responding to Texts
- Writing a Summary Statement

INDEPENDENT PRACTICE

Vocabulary Strategies

Writing
- Writing a Summary Statement
- Responding to Texts

EXTENSION OPPORTUNITIES

- Online Books
- Book Cart
- Review of Previous Passages

■ Comprehension

> ## Reteach Skills
> ✔ **Expository and Narrative Texts**   Lesson 1
>
> ✔ **Expository Text Structures**   Lessons 3, 4, 6, 7, 8

Before Reading

Expository and Narrative Texts
Expository Text Structures

1. Write these titles on the board: *Stuart Gets Stuck* and *Exploring the Gulf of Mexico*. Ask students which text they think would be expository, which would be narrative, and why. (The first would be narrative; it would tell a story. The second would be expository; it would give information.)

2. **All expository texts give *information* to the reader. They often do something more. They might tell the reader how to do something. They might set forth solutions to a problem. They might try to convince the reader to do something or believe something.**

3. **We have learned that authors use different kinds of expository text structures, depending on their purpose for writing. Let's briefly review these different kinds of expository texts: *Sequential Order, Compare and Contrast, Cause and Effect, Problem/Solution*, and *Persuasion*.**

4. Ask students to tell what each kind of expository text does. When discussing sequential order, remind students that this kind of text might describe events as they happened in time, or it might give the steps in a process.

5. Point to *Exploring the Gulf of Mexico* on the board. **If this title were *Gulfs vs. Oceans*, what kind of text structure would the author probably have used?** (compare and contrast) Repeat with the title *How to Surf the Gulf's Tiny Waves* (sequential order/how-to) and *Gulf of Goo: It's Time to Clean up the Oily Mess!* (persuasion).

Then ask students to provide titles on the same topic for cause-and-effect and problem/solution.

6. If students have difficulty explaining or identifying one of the text structures, display Transparency 6 (compare and contrast), 8 (cause-and-effect or problem/solution), 9 (persuasion), or 15 (sequential order). Model how *the Gulf of Mexico* might be treated using each text structure.

Reading for Understanding

1. Have students turn to "Trade the Melting Pot for a Salad Bowl" on Anthology page 293. **As we read this text, let's think about the kind of text structure the author uses. Remember that elements of more than one text structure can appear in a single text.**

2. Read aloud the first paragraph of "Trade the Melting Pot for a Salad Bowl," then have students read the remainder of the text aloud with you.

After Reading

Expository Text Structures

1. Distribute copies of Reteach page 29 and read the instructions aloud. Review the contents of the checklist with students. Then guide them to answer each question and to place check marks where the answer is *yes*. Have students skim the text before answering each question.

2. Read aloud the instructions for section 2. Remind students that most texts include elements of different kinds of texts, but that the author usually has one main purpose in mind. Guide students to answer the three bulleted questions.

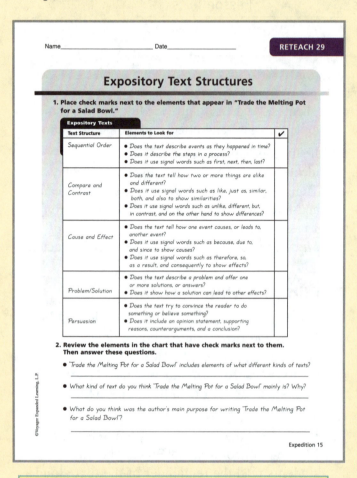

Checking for Comprehension

1. Distribute copies of Reteach page 30. Have students turn to "Trade the Melting Pot for a Salad Bowl" on page 293. Explain to students that they will read this text before answering the questions on Reteach page 30.

2. Read aloud the Keys to Comprehension section and the assessment instructions. Then have students complete the assessment independently.

3. Review the correct answers and discuss any questions that students answered incorrectly.

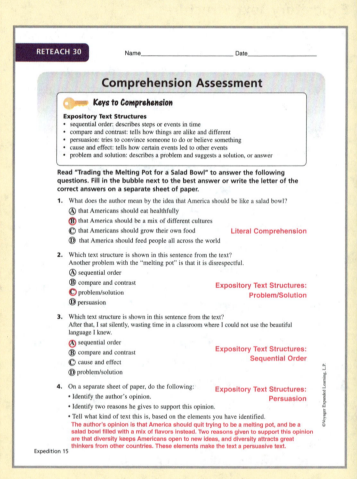

Extra Support

Expository Text Structures

If students need additional support, provide copies of news magazines, science magazines, health and fitness magazines, and nonfiction books. Challenge students to go on a scavenger hunt to find one example of each text structure listed in the checklist. Encourage students to use their previewing strategies as they look through the publications. Guide students as needed. Have students present their findings to the class.

■ Vocabulary

1. Write on the board the specific words that students have missed. Then have students use a Venn diagram to compare and contrast one of the words with another similar or related word that you provide. Guide students to identify similarities and differences by asking questions such as the following:

   - **When might you use *either* of these words?**
   - **When could you use *only* _____?**
   - **Which of these words would you use to describe or name _____?**
   - **Which word sounds more formal? more casual?**
   - **Which word is more specific? more general?**

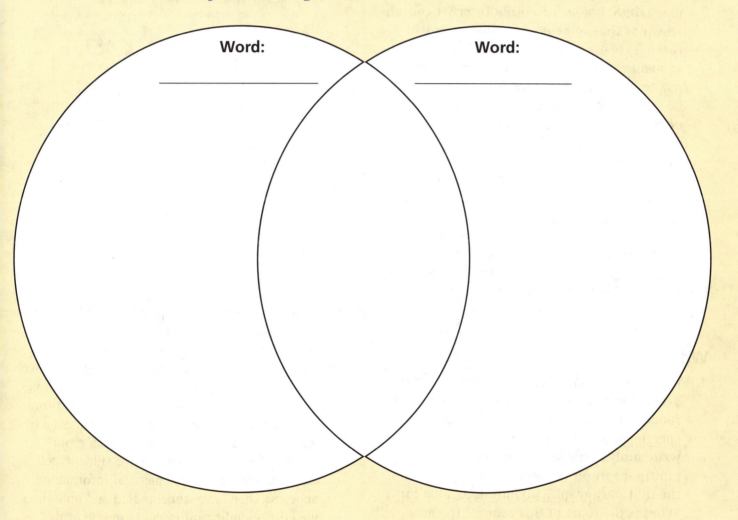

Word: _____   Word: _____

2. When students have completed the graphic organizer, check comprehension by having them write in their own words the meaning of each vocabulary word.

◼ Research Report

Teach and Model

1. Distribute students' papers from the Expedition 14 writing lesson. **In the last writing lesson, we learned how to research a topic. We located two credible sources and took notes about our topic. In this lesson, we are going to turn the information we found into a research report.**

2. **Almost all expository texts you read in magazines, books, or on the Internet contain research that someone has done. Some of these texts use research to try to persuade someone to think or do something. Others use research to show how a problem might be solved, or how one thing might be better or more valuable than another. A research report, on the other hand, has a single purpose: to give information on a subject in a clear, understandable way. In the process, a research report might convince someone that, for example, a new kind of food is worth trying. A good research report doesn't *have* to change the way someone thinks. What it *should* always do is expand the reader's knowledge about a topic.**

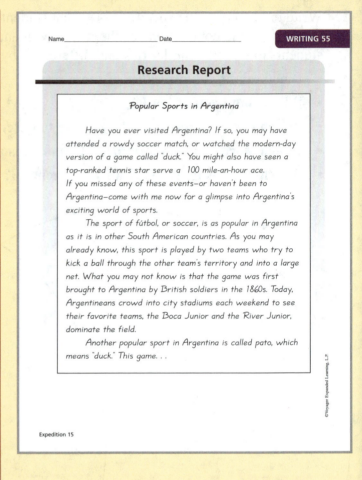

Name_____ Date_____

WRITING 55

Research Report

Popular Sports in Argentina

Have you ever visited Argentina? If so, you may have attended a rowdy soccer match, or watched the modern-day version of a game called "duck." You might also have seen a top-ranked tennis star serve a 100 mile-an-hour ace. If you missed any of these events—or haven't been to Argentina—come with me now for a glimpse into Argentina's exciting world of sports.

The sport of fútbol, or soccer, is as popular in Argentina as it is in other South American countries. As you may already know, this sport is played by two teams who try to kick a ball through the other team's territory and into a large net. What you may not know is that the game was first brought to Argentina by British soldiers in the 1860s. Today, Argentineans crowd into city stadiums each weekend to see their favorite teams, the Boca Junior and the River Junior, dominate the field.

Another popular sport in Argentina is called pato, which means "duck." This game. . .

©Voyager Expanded Learning, L.P.

Expedition 15

Writing Sample

1. Distribute Writing page 55 to students. **These are the opening paragraphs of a research report.** Have students read the first two paragraphs aloud. **We have already learned to write multiparagraph texts. In a multiparagraph text, what is the purpose of the first paragraph?** (to introduce a topic) **What is the topic of this report?** (popular sports in Argentina) **What different Argentinean sports does the introduction mention?** (fútbol, duck, and tennis) **If there are three body paragraphs in this report, what might each paragraph discuss?** (one of these three sports)

2. Read the second paragraph aloud while students follow along. **What is the topic of this paragraph?** (fútbol, or soccer) Have students return to the sample encyclopedia entry and web page on Writing pages 49 and 50, and the notes they took about Argentinean sports on Writing pages 53 and 54. Then reread each sentence of the second paragraph in the research report aloud. After each sentence, have students tell where in their notes this piece of information appears. Then have students find and underline the corresponding information in one of the sources.

Evaluating Writing

1. Distribute Writing page 56 to students. **This rubric focuses on research reports— expository texts whose purpose is to give the reader clear, relevant information.** Read the rubric aloud.

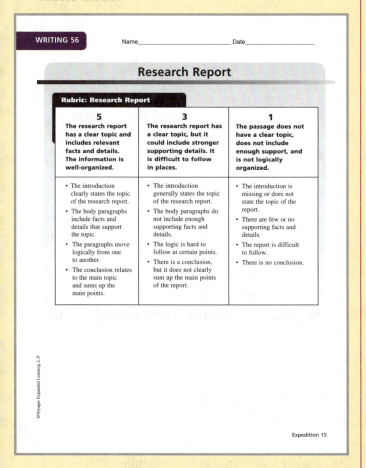

2. Call on an individual to reread the paragraphs on Writing page 55. Have students use the criteria on the rubric to evaluate the paragraphs, identifying the following:
- the introduction and main topic
- the topic of the first paragraph
- supporting facts and details

3. **Using the rubric, what score would you give these paragraphs?** (5) **Why?** (It clearly introduces the main topic; the body paragraph includes facts and details that support the main topic; and the first paragraph leads logically into the second.)

Guided Practice

1. Have students turn to the rubric on Writing page 56. Review the criteria for a research report that scores a 5 on the rubric. **Now we'll work together to begin writing our own research report. As we work, we will keep these criteria in mind.**

2. Distribute Writing pages 57 and 58 to students. Draw the first paragraph frame on the board. Read the instructions above the graphic organizer.

3. **For your introductory paragraph, you will use the notes you took on pages 53 and 54.** Verify that each student is using the notes he or she took during the Expedition 14 Writing lesson about the sports of their chosen country.

WRITING 58

Name_____ Date_____

Writing a Research Report

Paragraph 3   Second Sport

Another popular sport in _____

is _____,

This sport _____

_____

_____

Paragraph 4   Third Sport

_____

_____

_____

_____

_____

Paragraph 5   Conclusion

_____

_____

_____

_____

_____

_____

©Voyager Expanded Learning, L.P.

Expedition 15

---

4. Read the first partial sentence aloud, and have students write the name of their country in the blank. Then read the second partial sentence aloud. **In an introduction, it is a good idea to give an overview of the different sections of information you will cover in your report. In this case, each of your different sections, or paragraphs, will discuss a different sport. Look back at your notes. What sports are listed there? Choose the two for which you found the most information, and write them in the blanks in the second sentence.** After students do this, have them complete the third sentence with the third sport. Then read the last partial sentence aloud. **This sentence clearly states the main topic of the report. Complete it by writing the name of your country in the blank.**

5. Guide students to complete paragraphs 2 and 3 on Writing pages 57 and 58. Read each sentence starter aloud, and direct students back to the relevant sections of the outlines on Writing page 53 and 54 to locate the needed information. If students' information does not correspond exactly with the sentence starters provided, have them write their own paragraphs on a separate sheet of paper. As students compose paragraph 3, have them refer to the sentence starters in paragraph 2 for ideas. Encourage them to change words and phrases to make this paragraph unique, but remind them to include similar information on the history of that kind of music and the instruments used.

6. As they work, remind students to keep an eye on the additional information they recorded in the bottom box on pages 53 and 54. Explain that if this information relates to any of the three sports they are discussing, they could include it in that paragraph.

7. Be sure all students have completed the first three paragraphs before moving on.

Independent Practice

1. **Now you will finish writing your research report on your own.** Direct students' attention to the remaining two paragraphs. **These paragraph frames do not contain any sentence starters. You will have to write them on your own. You know from writing paragraphs 2 and 3 what kinds of information paragraph 4 should contain. What will paragraph 4 be about?** (the third sport you took notes about)

2. **Like an introduction, the conclusion of a research report usually gives an overview of the information that was covered. When you write your conclusion, you might mention each of the three sports you discussed again. You might also include a new piece of information from the Additional Information boxes on pages 53 and 54.**

SKILL ✓

3. Have students write the last two paragraphs of their research report independently. Remind them to indent the first line of each paragraph, and to use connecting words and phrases to link each idea to the next. Encourage them to refer to earlier paragraphs for ideas. Monitor students as they write, providing correction and feedback as needed. You may want to have students copy or use a word processing program to type the entire research report at this time.

4. After students have completed their reports, have them share their work with the class. Discuss which reports provide the most relevant facts and details; which flow most logically from one paragraph to the next; and which conclusions are written most effectively.

5. Arrange students in pairs for peer editing. Instruct them to exchange reports, then read each other's work aloud. Students should first tell one thing the writer did well. Then students should choose a score for the story based on the rubric on Writing page 56. Finally, students should offer one idea for improving the report. Remind students that they should treat each other with respect as they work together.

6. Have students return to their reports and strengthen their details or their organization, returning to their notes as needed. Remind students that this step is called revision, and explain that they should revise their reports just as they have revised their other texts. **When you *revise*, you go back over your writing and make changes to improve it.**

7. Distribute Writing page 59, and have students create a list of the sources they used. Have them write the source information as it appears on Writing pages 53 and 54, or have them use another standard style such as MLA.

8. Collect students' reports, organize them alphabetically according to the country, and collate them into a booklet. Have students work together to create a cover and title page for the book.

Writing and Technology

If students use a word processing program to create a draft of their research report, remind them to save the file so that they can return to it later to make revisions. Explain that after making revisions, students can save the document under a different name; for example, they might name the first draft *Research_Draft1.doc*, the second *Research_Draft2.doc*, and the final draft *Research_Final.doc*. Point out that as writers revise, they sometimes decide to reinsert an idea that was cut from an earlier draft, and that for this reason it is helpful to keep copies of each draft you produce. Suggest that students create a folder in which to place their multiple drafts.

Reteach
Blackline Masters

Compare and Contrast

1. Answer the question below. Then write details in the chart that show the text structure you have named.

The author of this expository text uses what text structure?

_____

The Birth of American Car Culture		
	Before World War II	After World War II
What transportation did most people use?		
Who owned cars?		
Were cars thought of as a luxury or a necessity?		
How affordable were cars?		

2. Write two sentences telling how "car culture" was different before and after World War II.

• _____

• _____

Comprehension Assessment

 Keys to Comprehension

Compare-and-Constrast Text	**Sequential Order Text**
• tells how one event leads to another	• describes events or steps as they happen in time

Read "Birth of the Car Culture" to answer the following questions. Fill in the bubble next to the best answer or write the letter of the correct answer on a separate sheet of paper.

1. How were cars after World War II different from cars before World War II?
   - Ⓐ They were faster.
   - Ⓑ They were cheaper.
   - Ⓒ They were slower.
   - Ⓓ They were more expensive.

2. Why did car companies stop making cars during the war?
   - Ⓐ People stopped buying cars.
   - Ⓑ Their factories were destroyed.
   - Ⓒ Roads needed to be repaired.
   - Ⓓ They made war supplies instead.

3. What happened in 1929?
   - Ⓐ The American city spread outward.
   - Ⓑ American car production topped 1 million.
   - Ⓒ The American economy collapsed.
   - Ⓓ America and its allies won the war.

4. On a separate sheet of paper, write two ways the American family was different after World War II than it was before World War II.

Elements of Description

Find concrete details and sensory details in "Invasion." Write concrete details in the boxes below. Write sensory details in the ovals.

Concrete Detail

Sensory Detail

Sensory Detail

Descriptive Details in "Invasion"

Concrete Detail

Concrete Detail

Sensory Detail

Name_____ Date_____

Comprehension Assessment

 Keys to Comprehension

Descriptive Text
• tells how something looks, moves, or feels

Concrete Text
• gives specific information about an object or person

Sensory Details
• appeals to the senses of seeing, hearing, feeling, or tasting

Read "Invasion" to answer the following questions. Fill in the bubble next to the best answer or write the letter of the correct answer on a separate sheet of paper.

1. What annoys Carlos about Luis?
   Ⓐ He sings golden oldies.
   Ⓑ He has a loud, goofy laugh.
   Ⓒ He follows Carlos around.
   Ⓓ He has a skateboard like Carlos's.

2. Which of the following is NOT a concrete detail?
   Ⓐ Luis, my new stepbrother
   Ⓑ his car
   Ⓒ new carburetor
   Ⓓ end-overs

3. Which detail appeals to the sense of hearing?
   Ⓐ blaring all afternoon
   Ⓑ cheesy little skateboard
   Ⓒ standing in the hallway
   Ⓓ burned into my memory

4. On a separate sheet of paper, write the following:

   • a concrete detail that describes a toy

   • a detail that appeals to the sense of seeing

Narrative Text Elements

1. Fill in the story map.

Story Title: _____

SETTING
Place: _____ Time: _____

CHARACTERS

PLOT		
Beginning (Problem)	Middle (Chain of Events)	End (Problem Solved?)

2. Answer these questions.

A. What was Nick's motivation for killing Catfish? _____

_____

B. Does this motive come from the inside, the outside, or both? _____

_____

Name_____ Date_____

Comprehension Assessment

🔑 **Keys to Comprehension**

Narrative Text Elements
- characters—the people or animals that take part in the story
- setting—where and when the story takes place smaller words
- plot—events that make up the story

Character Motivation
- the reasons a character has for doing something

Read "A Death in the Family" to answer the following questions. Fill in the bubble next to the best answer or write the letter of the correct answer on a separate sheet of paper.

1. To what family does the story's title refer?

Ⓐ Jacob, his parents, and his brothers and sisters

Ⓑ Catfish and his girlfriend

Ⓒ the group of men Jacob has joined

Ⓓ Nick and his girlfriend

2. Which sentence tells you this story is set in the past?

Ⓐ I figured Ma and Pa had their hands full.

Ⓑ We weren't welcome in most places.

Ⓒ Martino looked as shocked as I did.

Ⓓ That's when I remembered the locket.

3. What problem starts the story's chain of events?

Ⓐ Jacob leaves home.

Ⓑ Catfish gets killed.

Ⓒ Catfish's locket is missing.

Ⓓ Nick confesses to the murder.

4. Answer these questions on a separate sheet of paper:

• What is Nick's motivation for killing Catfish?

• Does this motivation come from the inside or the outside?

Direct Quotations

Find a quotation from the text that illustrates each detail below. Write the quotation in the chart.

Detail about Ralph Gilles's Life	Quotation
Gilles believes that an American car should make a statement.	
People responded strongly to the new Charger Gilles's team designed.	
Gilles loves his job.	
Gilles plans on staying put.	

Name_____ Date_____

Comprehension Assessment

 Keys to Comprehension

Biography
- tells the story of someone's life
- is written by someone other than the person it is about

Autobiography
- tells the story of the author's own life

First-Person Narrative
- is told from the writer's point of view
- uses, *I, me,* and *we*

Direct Quotations
- appear between quotation marks
- are the actual words of someone other than the author

Read "From Sitcom Junkie to King of Bling" feature to answer the following questions. Fill in the bubble next to the best answer or write the letter of the correct answer on a separate sheet of paper.

1. What kind of text is this?
   Ⓐ a biography
   Ⓑ an autobiography
   Ⓒ a first-person narrative
   Ⓓ a direct quotation

2. Which quotation tells one of Gilles's goals as a car designer?
   Ⓐ "It's bringing back what's good about American cars."
   Ⓑ "Wow, this car looks like it's angry!"
   Ⓒ "The first 10 years have been pretty, pretty cool."
   Ⓓ "I really have no desire at all to look elsewhere."

3. What was Gilles's first assignment at Chrysler?
   Ⓐ studying cars in TV shows
   Ⓑ creating 10 sketches of cars
   Ⓒ designing a speedometer needle
   Ⓓ designing the new Chrysler 300

4. On a separate sheet of paper, write a direct quotation from the text that shows how Gilles feels about American cars.

Expository Text Structures

1. Place check marks next to the elements that appear in "Trade the Melting Pot for a Salad Bowl."

Expository Texts

Text Structure	Elements to Look for	✔
Sequential Order	• Does the text describe events as they happened in time? • Does it describe the steps in a process? • Does it use signal words such as *first, next, then,* and *last*?	
Compare and Contrast	• Does the text tell how two or more things are alike and different? • Does it use signal words such as *like, just as, similar, both,* and *also* to show similarities? • Does it use signal words such as *unlike, different, but, in contrast,* and *on the other hand* to show differences?	
Cause and Effect	• Does the text tell how one event causes, or leads to, another event? • Does it use signal words such as *because, due to,* and *since* to show causes? • Does it use signal words such as *therefore, so, as a result,* and *consequently* to show effects?	
Problem/Solution	• Does the text describe a problem and offer one or more solutions, or answers? • Does it show how a solution can lead to other effects?	
Persuasion	• Does the text try to convince the reader to do something or believe something? • Does it include an opinion statement, supporting reasons, counterarguments, and a conclusion?	

2. Review the elements in the chart that have check marks next to them. Then answer these questions.

• "Trade the Melting Pot for a Salad Bowl" includes elements of what different kinds of texts?

_____

• What kind of text do you think "Trade the Melting Pot for a Salad Bowl" mainly is? Why?

_____

• What do you think was the author's main purpose for writing "Trade the Melting Pot for a Salad Bowl"?

_____

Name_____ Date_____

Comprehension Assessment

 Keys to Comprehension

Expository Text Structures
- sequential order: describes steps or events in time
- compare and contrast: tells how things are alike and different
- persuasion: tries to convince someone to do or believe something
- cause and effect: tells how certain events led to other events
- problem and solution: describes a problem and suggests a solution, or answer

Read "Trading the Melting Pot for a Salad Bowl" to answer the following questions. Fill in the bubble next to the best answer or write the letter of the correct answers on a separate sheet of paper.

1. What does the author mean by the idea that America should be like a salad bowl?

   (A) that Americans should eat healthfully

   (B) that America should be a mix of different cultures

   (C) that Americans should grow their own food

   (D) that America should feed people all across the world

2. Which text structure is shown in this sentence from the text?
   Another problem with the "melting pot" is that it is disrespectful.

   (A) sequential order

   (B) compare and contrast

   (C) problem/solution

   (D) persuasion

3. Which text structure is shown in this sentence from the text?
   After that, I sat silently, wasting time in a classroom where I could not use the beautiful language I knew.

   (A) sequential order

   (B) compare and contrast

   (C) cause and effect

   (D) problem/solution

4. On a separate sheet of paper, do the following:
   • Identify the author's opinion.
   • Identify two reasons he gives to support this opinion.
   • Tell what kind of text this is, based on the elements you have identified.

Writing
Blackline Masters

Multiparagraph Writing

Change the Driving Age to 14!

I believe that the driving age should be lowered to 14. I believe this for several reasons. First of all, kids are more mature these days than they used to be. They have more activities to go to than they did 30 years ago. Second, this would save grown-ups money, because parents spend a lot of extra money driving their kids around. Third, this would make the streets safer. Adults are in too much of a hurry. They're the ones having all the wrecks! In conclusion, I'd like to remind you that at age 14, kids are tall enough to reach the gas pedal. Nature is on our side. Lower the driving age to 14!

Multiparagraph Writing

Passage 2

Change the Driving Age to 14!

Adults and teenagers of the world: Listen up! I believe that the driving age should be lowered to 14. Some might think this idea is crazy, but I think it is totally sane. I believe this for several reasons.

First of all, kids are more mature these days. They have more activities than they did 30 years ago. Sometimes these activities are far away, and it can be hard for us to get rides. As a result, our social lives suffer. Also, adults always tell teens to get jobs babysitting, mowing lawns, and delivering papers. If we could drive, we would be much more likely to take this advice.

Second, lowering the driving age would save grown-ups money. Parents today spend a lot driving their kids around. For example, if I want to go to a movie, my mom has to drive me to the theater. Then she drives back home. Two hours later, she drives back to pick me up. She uses the gas I would use to get myself to the movie. Kids go to lots of movies. Think how much money we would save on gasoline as a nation!

Third, letting 14-year-olds drive would make the streets safer. Adults hurry too much. Their days are filled with jobs, lunch dates, errands, and evening events. Their over-scheduled lives cause them to have all the wrecks! Kids' lives are simpler. We are only responsible for ourselves. Therefore, we have fewer places to go, and would drive to those places slower.

Let me remind you that at age 14, kids are tall enough to reach the gas pedal. Nature is on our side. We were <u>meant</u> to drive at a younger age. So let's respect kid's lives, save grown-ups some money, and make the streets safer. Let's lower the driving age to 14!

Name_____ Date_____

Multiparagraph Writing

Read the prompt below. Write an opinion statement that responds to the prompt. Use the graphic organizer to start planning your writing. List three reasons that support your opinion statement. Add elaboration to support each reason.

Prompt: The student council is trying to decide how students can raise money for the school. They are considering a car wash or a bake sale. Write a persuasive letter to the school paper taking a side and giving your opinion on this issue.

Supporting Reason:

_____

_____

Elaboration:

- _____

- _____

Supporting Reason:

_____

_____

Elaboration:

- _____

- _____

Supporting Reason:

_____

_____

Elaboration:

- _____

- _____

Multiparagraph Writing

| **Paragraph 1** | **Introduction** |

We all know that the student council wants to _____

_____

_____. A couple of good ideas have been put

forth. Personally, I _____

_____.

| **Paragraph 2** | **First Reason** |

My first reason is that _____

_____. This is because _____

_____

_____

_____.

| **Paragraph 3** | **Second Reason** |

Another reason we should _____ is that

_____

_____. It is a very simple process. First, you _____

_____. Then, you _____

_____. Isn't

that easier than _____?

Multiparagraph Writing

Paragraph 4   **Third Reason**

Yet another reason for students to _____

is that _____.

Just think about it. _____

_____

_____.

Paragraph 5   **Conclusion**

I know that not all students agree, but I firmly believe _____

_____.

Such an event is _____, it _____.

_____, and it _____

So, _____!

Multiparagraph Writing

Writing Checklist

✔	Elements of Good Writing	Points to Look For
	Ideas and Elaboration	I have a focused idea and specific details to elaborate it.
	Word Choice	I use specific and colorful words to talk about my ideas.
	Sentence Fluency	My sentences create a pleasing rhythm as they flow smoothly from one to the next.
	Conventions	The names of people or places begin with a capital letter. I have written complete sentences.
	Organization	My paragraphs have a clear organization that is easy to follow.

Name_____ Date_____

Multiparagraph Writing

Rubric: Multiparagraph Persuasive Writing

5	3	1
The writing is persuasive and divided into clear paragraphs. The writer's opinion is clearly stated, and valid reasons are given. The counterargument and conclusion make a strong impression.	The writing states an opinion, but the reasons are not always clear or in separate paragraphs. The counterargument and conclusion are adequate.	The writing is not persuasive. The writer does not state an opinion or give clear reasons. The counterargument and conclusion are missing or weak.
• The first paragraph gives a strong opinion statement. • Paragraphs contain clear reasons, each elaborated with details and personal observations. • A convincing counterargument goes against the writer's opinion, then is convincingly rejected. • A strong conclusion paragraph summarizes the argument and restates the opinion statement. It makes an impact on the reader.	• The opinion statement is not clearly stated. • Paragraphs contain reasons that are mostly clear and somewhat elaborated. • A counterargument is presented, but it is not convincingly rejected. • The conclusion summarizes the argument and restates the opinion but makes little impact on the reader.	• There is no opinion statement or the opinion statement is confusing. • Reasons are missing or confusing. Details do not properly relate to reasons. • There is no counterargument. • The conclusion offers no summary of the argument. It makes no impact, and it does not restate the opinion statement.

Description

Love Letters?

I received a very unusual Valentine card this year. It is made of folded paper, like those open-and-close fortune telling games. The paper is crisp and pink. Under each flap is glued a soft, silky rose petal with a single letter written on it. When I lift a flap, I catch the mild, sweet scent of roses. In fact, holding the card in my hands is like holding a small bouquet. I haven't unscrambled the message yet, but in the meantime, I'm enjoying a beautiful mystery!

Name_____ Date_____

Description

©Voyager Expanded Learning, L.P.

Rubric: Description

5	3	1
The passage clearly describes something using concrete details. The writer uses sensory details and figurative language to paint a picture in the reader's mind.	**The passage describes something but the details could be more concrete. Some sensory details and figurative language are used but do not paint a very vivid picture.**	**The passage does not provide a description and does not include concrete details, sensory details, or figurative language.**
• The topic sentence clearly presents the main idea of the paragraph.	• The topic sentence generally states the main idea of the paragraph.	• The topic sentence is missing or does not present the main idea of the paragraph.
• The writer includes vivid concrete details and details that appeal to the senses.	• The writer does not include enough concrete details or details that appeal to the senses.	• There are no specific, concrete details or sensory details.
• The writer uses figurative language clearly to tell how something seems.	• The writer tries to use figurative language but some of the language is confusing.	• The writer uses no figurative language.
• The conclusion clearly sums up the description.	• There is a conclusion, but it does not clearly sum up the descriptions.	• There is no conclusion.

Description

1. **Read the writing prompt. Use the graphic organizer to brainstorm at least two concrete details, two sensory details, and two examples of figurative language.**

> There are many new residents in your community. They joined your community when a huge hurricane destroyed their homes. Your class is writing a guide to your community for these new neighbors. Descriptions of all parts of your community will be included in the guide.
>
> Write a descriptive paragraph in which you use details to describe a place in your community. You can write about a particular neighborhood, a building, a business or restaurant, or an outdoor location. Include at least one concrete detail, one sensory detail, and one example of figurative language in your paragraph.

Location you are writing about: _____

Descriptive Details	
Concrete Details	
Sensory Details	
Figurative Language	

2. **Write your descriptive paragraph on your own paper using the information in your graphic organizer. In addition to specific details, make sure you have a clear topic sentence and a conclusion that summarizes your ideas.**

Name_____ Date_____

Description

Writing Checklist		
✔	**Elements of Good Writing**	**Points to Look For**
	Ideas and Elaboration	I have a focused idea and specific details to elaborate it.
	Word Choice	I use specific and colorful words to talk about my ideas.
	Sentence Fluency	My sentences create a pleasing rhythm as they flow smoothly from one to the next.
	Conventions	I use apostrophes correctly to show possession, as in **Jimmy's book**. I use commas correctly, as in **I am hungry, so I will have a snack. I see red, green, and yellow apples.**
	Organization	My paragraphs have a clear organization that is easy to follow.

Narrative

A Big Flash

Morgan walked up to the soccer field at the park with her little dog, Flash, who was a whopping 12 inches tall. The morning sun sparkled through the leaves on the trees. The other contestants were already warming up their dogs—their big dogs. People sent disks sailing through the air. Their dogs ran, turned, and jumped, catching the disks in mid-flight. Morgan unpacked her gear and began gently tossing a disk to Flash. Jay and Patricia saw Morgan and burst into laughter. They realized that Morgan was there to compete with Flash in the contest. Jay and Patricia weren't even sure the rules allowed dogs as small as Flash to enter. Morgan was sure, though. She knew that Flash could compete and she knew he would win. She scooped up her disks, called her dog, and marched onto the field.

Name_____ Date_____

Narrative

Rubric: Narrative

5	3	1
The story is interesting. The characters and setting are clearly introduced. The plot makes the reader want to read more.	**The story is a bit dull. The characters and setting are introduced but are not especially interesting. The plot does not grab the reader's imagination.**	**The story is boring. The characters and setting are not introduced. The plot is vague or confusing.**
• Characters are interesting and described with some details. • The time of the story and the location where it takes place are clearly described. • The action of the story (the plot) is set in motion when a problem is revealed.	• Characters hold the reader's attention but need more description. • The time and location of the story are suggested but could be more clearly described. • The story does contain some action (a plot) but a problem is not clearly revealed.	• Characters are not introduced at all or are boring. • The time and location of the story are not made clear. • There is no clear plot action and no problem is revealed.

Narrative

1. Read the prompt. Use the story map to plan your story. Create at least one character and a setting that tells when and where the story takes place.

Two friends arrive at the park for the annual park clean-up. A neighbor who lives nearby leads the clean-up. Other kids and adults are there to help. As the cleanup begins, the workers face problems and make a surprising discovery.

Story Map

Story Title: _____

Characters	Setting

Name_____ Date_____

Narrative

2. **Continue planning your story by creating your plot. Tell what the problem is, what events happen to develop it, and how it is resolved.**

Plot Map

Beginning: What is the problem?

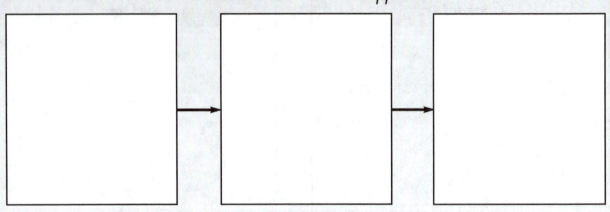

Middle: What events happen?

End: How is the problem solved?

3. **Write the first paragraph of your story on your own paper. Use the narrative elements you described above, and add as many descriptive details as you can.**

ARGENTINA

Argentina is the second-largest country of South America. It is located in the southern tip of the continent, stretching north to south alongside its neighbor, Chile. Argentina is made up of a wide variety of landforms, climates, and peoples.

GOVERNMENT

Argentina has a federal government consisting of three branches. The executive branch is made up of a president and a vice president, who are elected every four years. The legislative branch consists of the National Congress, which has two houses, the Chamber of Deputies and the Senate. Its judicial branch consists of a supreme court and a federal court system.

CULTURE

Argentineans enjoy a wide array of fine arts and leisure activities, including music, dance, and sports. It is also well-known for its delicious foods, many of which are grown or produced in the country. Argentina is home to many writers and artists, and has one of the strongest movie-making industries in Latin America.

Music. Argentinean music is closely tied to a variety of dances. The most well-known of these is the tango. Folk music such as chacacera, zamba, and milonga are also popular forms of Argentinean music. These forms combine Spanish music, inherited from early settlers from Spain, and native Indian music. The guitar is one of the most common instruments in Argentinean music.

Food. Argentinean cuisine is a mixture of European and native Indian flavors and dishes. Many Argentinean dishes contain beef or other meat, along with regionally grown vegetables and grains. Carbonada, a beef stew with rice, potatoes, corn, squash, apples, and pears, is a typical Argentinean dish. The empanada, a fried or baked dumpling filled with meats and vegetables, is another traditional Argentinean favorite.

Sports. The people of Argentina love sports, soccer or fútbol in particular. The Argentinean national soccer team has won two World Cups and has come in second place twice. Native Argentinean sports include a game called pato, which is played on horseback.

Expedition 14

Name_____ Date_____

Thomas Barwick/Getty Images

Fig.-3: Argentineans enjoy participating in team sports.

ARGENTINA *continued*

ECONOMY

Traditionally, Argentina's economy is based on agriculture, although in the years following World War II its government encouraged industrialization.

Agriculture. In spite of the growth of manufacturing in the late 1900s, agriculture remains a vital part of Argentina's economy. Corn, soybeans, and wheat are its major crops, and grapes and other fruits are grown in the foothills of the Andes mountains.

Manufacturing. Most of Argentina's manufacturing occurs in and around the cities of Buenos Aires, Córdoba, and Rosario. Major industries include

64

©Voyager Expanded Learning, L.P.

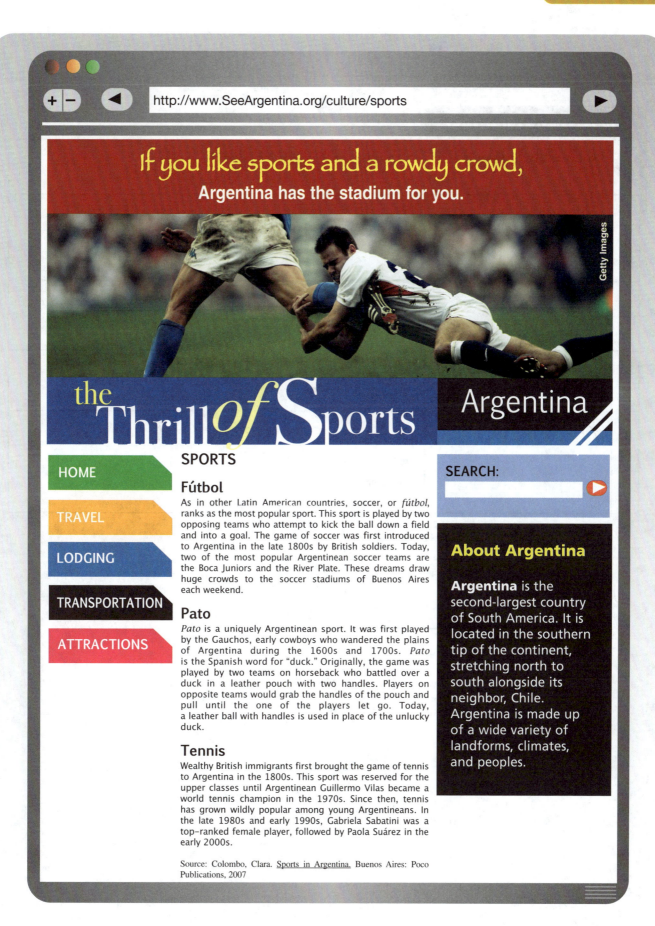

http://www.SeeArgentina.org/culture/sports

If you like sports and a rowdy crowd,
Argentina has the stadium for you.

Getty Images

the Thrill of Sports

Argentina

HOME

TRAVEL

LODGING

TRANSPORTATION

ATTRACTIONS

SPORTS

Fútbol

As in other Latin American countries, soccer, or *fútbol*, ranks as the most popular sport. This sport is played by two opposing teams who attempt to kick the ball down a field and into a goal. The game of soccer was first introduced to Argentina in the late 1800s by British soldiers. Today, two of the most popular Argentinean soccer teams are the Boca Juniors and the River Plate. These dreams draw huge crowds to the soccer stadiums of Buenos Aires each weekend.

Pato

Pato is a uniquely Argentinean sport. It was first played by the Gauchos, early cowboys who wandered the plains of Argentina during the 1600s and 1700s. *Pato* is the Spanish word for "duck." Originally, the game was played by two teams on horseback who battled over a duck in a leather pouch with two handles. Players on opposite teams would grab the handles of the pouch and pull until the one of the players let go. Today, a leather ball with handles is used in place of the unlucky duck.

Tennis

Wealthy British immigrants first brought the game of tennis to Argentina in the 1800s. This sport was reserved for the upper classes until Argentinean Guillermo Vilas became a world tennis champion in the 1970s. Since then, tennis has grown wildly popular among young Argentineans. In the late 1980s and early 1990s, Gabriela Sabatini was a top-ranked female player, followed by Paola Suárez in the early 2000s.

Source: Colombo, Clara. <u>Sports in Argentina.</u> Buenos Aires: Poco Publications, 2007

SEARCH:

About Argentina

Argentina is the second-largest country of South America. It is located in the southern tip of the continent, stretching north to south alongside its neighbor, Chile. Argentina is made up of a wide variety of landforms, climates, and peoples.

Name_____ Date_____

Research Process

Credibilty Checklist

✔	A Credible Source Is . . .	Questions to Ask Yourself
	Relevant	• Does this source relate to my general topic? • Does this source contain information about my specific topic?
	Objective	• Is the author's main purpose to inform? • Is the author's main purpose to make money?
	Current	• Was this source printed, posted, or updated within the last several years?
	Accurate	• Is the source well-known for its correct facts? • If not, does the source tell where its information came from?

Finding Sources and Taking Notes

**Use the graphic organizer to find sources and take notes on your topic.
Use an extra sheet of paper, if needed.**

TOPIC

My research topic is sports in the country of _____.

SOURCE 1

My first source is: _____.

What are some popular sports in this country?

I.   **First sport**: _____
      A. How is it played? _____
      _____
      B. How or where did it get started? _____
      _____
      C. Who are some famous players or teams? _____
      _____

II.   **Second sport**: _____
      A. How is it played? _____
      _____
      B. How or where did it get started? _____
      _____
      C. Who are some famous players or teams? _____
      _____

III. **Third sport**: _____
      A. How is it played? _____
      _____
      B. How or where did it get started? _____
      _____
      C. Who are some famous players or teams? _____
      _____

Additional Information

_____

Finding Sources and Taking Notes

SOURCE 2

My second source is: _____.

What are some popular sports in this country?

I. **First sport:** _____

   A. How is it played? _____

   _____

   B. How or where did it get started? _____

   _____

   C. Who are some famous players or teams? _____

   _____

II. **Second sport:** _____

   A. How is it played? _____

   _____

   B. How or where did it get started? _____

   _____

   C. Who are some famous players or teams? _____

   _____

III. **Third sport:** _____

   A. How is it played? _____

   _____

   B. How or where did it get started? _____

   _____

   C. Who are some famous players or teams? _____

   _____

Additional Information

_____

_____

Research Report

Popular Sports in Argentina

Have you ever visited Argentina? If so, you may have attended a rowdy soccer match, or watched the modern-day version of a game called "duck." You might also have seen a top-ranked tennis star serve a 100 mile-an-hour ace. If you missed any of these events—or haven't been to Argentina—come with me now for a glimpse into Argentina's exciting world of sports.

The sport of fútbol, or soccer, is as popular in Argentina as it is in other South American countries. As you may already know, this sport is played by two teams who try to kick a ball through the other team's territory and into a large net. What you may not know is that the game was first brought to Argentina by British soldiers in the 1860s. Today, Argentineans crowd into city stadiums each weekend to see their favorite teams, the Boca Junior and the River Junior, dominate the field.

Another popular sport in Argentina is called pato, which means "duck." This game . . .

Name_____ Date_____

Research Report

Rubric: Research Report

5	3	1
The research report has a clear topic and includes relevant facts and details. The information is well-organized.	The research report has a clear topic, but it could include stronger supporting details. It is difficult to follow in places.	The passage does not have a clear topic, does not include enough support, and is not logically organized.
• The introduction clearly states the topic of the research report. • The body paragraphs include facts and details that support the topic. • The paragraphs move logically from one to another. • The conclusion relates to the main topic and sums up the main points.	• The introduction generally states the topic of the research report. • The body paragraphs do not include enough supporting facts and details. • The logic is hard to follow at certain points. • There is a conclusion, but it does not clearly sum up the main points of the report.	• The introduction is missing or does not state the topic of the report. • There are few or no supporting facts and details. • The report is difficult to follow. • There is no conclusion.

Writing a Research Report

Use the notes you took on pages 53 and 54 to write a research report. Use the paragraph frames on this page and the next one.

Paragraph 1 **Introduction**

Have you ever visited the country of _____?

If so, you may have seen _____

or _____. You might have

_____. Let's take a closer look at

the exciting sports of _____.

Paragraph 2 **First Sport**

One of the most popular sports in _____

is _____. This game is played by

_____.

It first came to _____

_____.

Some famous _____

_____.

Name_____ Date_____

Writing a Research Report

Paragraph 3 **Second Sport**

Another popular sport in _____

is _____.

This sport _____

_____

_____.

Paragraph 4 **Third Sport**

_____

_____

_____

_____

_____

Paragraph 5 **Conclusion**

_____

_____

_____

_____

_____

_____

Writing a Research Report

List of Sources

1. _____

   _____

2. _____

   _____

3. _____

   _____

Additional Resources

Vocabulary List
Expeditions 1–15

A absolutely

access

accumulate

accurate

achieve

acknowledgment

actual

affect

affirm

aggressively

agree

alliance

analyze

ancestor

annual

anticipate

apparel

application

array

arsenal

artificial

associate

assurance

astronaut

attached

audio

authentic

authorize

available

B balmy

banish

barren

basis

beam

beneficial

biofuel

bloat

bombard

boredom

boycott

brilliant

budget

bulky

C calculate

calorie

cancer

capacity

casualty

celebrate

challenge

choice

claim

classify

clog

clot

confidence

confidential

consequence

conspicuous

consumer

contradict

correspondence

criticism

D daze

debate

decade

decay

decline

decompress

demonstrate

dense

deposit

deprive

deserted

desolate

destination

detect

devise

difficult

digest

digital

disagreeable

discipline

disorder

displace

distinct

document

doubtful

download

drone

E ease

economy

elevate

eligible

encourage

endeavor

endow

enforce

enlist

entire

entitle

epidemic

equipment

estimate

eternity

eventually

evidence

exaggerate

expand

extract

extreme

extremely

F fabric

facility

factor

falter

fiery

fitness

fossil

fragile

fragrant

G gadget

geoscientist

goal

guarantee

H hemisphere

historical

humid

I identity

illegally

image

impact

impatient

implement

import

impossible

inconvenience

industrious

infinite

influential

inhabited

inherit

institution

instruction

interminably

intermission

international

interview

invisible

irresistible

isolate

K kidnap

L landscape

layer

liable

M magnitude

mason

meager

melodious

mentor

method

microsurgery

migrant

miniature

minimum

miserable

misery

misuse

N network

nonresident

nurture

O objective

obstacle

occur

opportunity

orbit

P paltry

particle

patent

pave

penalty

penetrate

permit

persist

persistent

phonetically

plank

policy

popular

portable

portion

portray

possess

postpone

potent

potential

precaution

precision

prefer

premises

prescribe

preserve

pressure

prestige

priority

procedure

production

program

prohibit

prominent

prompt

prone

proportion

protrude

R range

recent

reception

recycle

reliable

remnant

renew

repetition

resist

responsibility

restraint

revenue

ritual

rocky

S sanitize

scorched

select

sensor

site

skeleton

slander

slavery

sliver

somber

source

sparse

specific

speculate

sterilize

strand

structure

subscription

subtle

symmetrical

T technology

tedious

tendency

texture

theory

thinness

throughout

tolerant

transfix

transform

trek

tremendous

trend

typical

U unanimous

unbearable

underneath

unleashed

V valuable

varied

variety

various

vast

vehicle

vitamin

W welfare

windpipe

Content-Area Reading Selections

Expedition 1: *Connections: How We Fit Together*

Reading Selection	Science	Social Studies	Math	Fine Art
Anything But Burgers!		✔		
What's Really American?		✔		
A Juneteenth to Remember		✔		
Coming to America		✔		
The Rock 'n' Roll Band		✔		
American Music		✔		

Expedition 2: *Forensics: Digging into the Past*

Reading Selection	Science	Social Studies	Math	Fine Art
The Case of the Rich Man's Will	✔	✔		
A History Mystery: The Athlete and the President	✔	✔		
How Can a City Disappear?	✔	✔		
How Did the Bog Man Die?	✔	✔		
What Really Happened at Jamestown?	✔	✔		

Expedition 3: *Space: Traveling into the Unknown*

Reading Selection	Science	Social Studies	Math	Fine Art
The Space Race		✔		
The International Space Station	✔	✔		
What's Next in Space?		✔		
Spinoffs from Space	✔			
Working on the Space Station	✔	✔		

Expedition 4: *Your Health: Fit Minds, Fit Bodies*

Reading Selection	Science	Social Studies	Math	Fine Art
Fueling the Fire: Energy, Food, and Nutrition	✔	✔		
Y Workout				
Getting Stronger, Getting Fit	✔	✔		
Pushing Past Normal: Forcing Body Changes	✔			
What's in a Good Night's Sleep?	✔			

Expedition 5: *Shockwaves: Eathquakes, Volcanoes, Tsunamis*				
Reading Selection	Science	Social Studies	Math	Fine Art
Lessons from Earthquakes	✓	✓	✓	
Volcano Camp	✓			
Krakatoa!	✓	✓		
Earth's Moving Continents	✓	✓		
To the Rescue!	✓	✓		

Expedition 6: *The Internet: A Wired World*				
Reading Selection	Science	Social Studies	Math	Fine Art
Online and In Touch		✓	✓	
Computer Crime: Identity Theft	✓			
Looking for a Job Online				
CopyRIGHT or CopyWRONG?		✓		
A Store the Size of Earth		✓		

Expedition 7: *Money Matters*				
Reading Selection	Science	Social Studies	Math	Fine Art
It's Your Money!			✓	
Charge It!			✓	
Is It Real or Counterfeit?	✓	✓		
JEANology		✓	✓	
Rich and Famous		✓		✓

Expedition 8: *The Environment: Keep It Green*				
Reading Selection	Science	Social Studies	Math	Fine Art
Fill Up, Then Pay Up	✓			
All-Terrain Vehicles: All Too Common				
Good News About Recycling: It's Working	✓			
Paper or Plastic? It Doesn't Really Matter	✓			
Power Failure	✓			
The Wrong Picture of Nuclear Energy	✓			
Pedal Power				

Expedition 9: *Diseases: Tiny Killers*

Reading Selection	Science	Social Studies	Math	Fine Art
Bloodthirsty and Bold	✔			
Attack of the Body Invaders	✔			
Creepy Medicine		✔		
A Day at the CDC	✔	✔		
When Your Body Attacks	✔			

Expedition 10: *Technology: Keeping in Touch*

Reading Selection	Science	Social Studies	Math	Fine Art
The Printing Press		✔		
Communicating to Win	✔	✔		
Rocking the Microphone	✔			✔
Letters at the Speed of Light	✔			
Telephones to Go	✔	✔	✔	

Expedition 11: *Car Culture*

Reading Selection	Science	Social Studies	Math	Fine Art
A Fast Argument		✔		
Service to Go		✔		
You Need This Car				
How to Sweeten Your Ride				✔
Birth of the Car Culture		✔		

Expedition 12: *Changes*

Reading Selection	Science	Social Studies	Math	Fine Art
Long Distance Love				
Game Day				
Blown Away		✔		
The Loss of Love				
Invasion				

Expedition 13: *Literature and Life*				
Reading Selection	Science	Social Studies	Math	Fine Art
from Holes				
from The Joy Luck Club				
Kipling and I				
If—				
adapted from The Call of the Wild				
A Death in the Family				

Expedition 14: *Imagine the Possibilities*				
Reading Selection	Science	Social Studies	Math	Fine Art
Dolores Huerta: Striking for Justice		✓		
from A Migrant Family		✓		✓
from Gig: Americans Talk About Their Jobs		✓		
from Keeping the Moon				
The Fast Track		✓		
Making History at Indianapolis		✓		
Out of Many, One		✓		
From Sitcom Junkie to King of Bling		✓		✓

Expedition 15: *Who Are We?*				
Reading Selection	Science	Social Studies	Math	Fine Art
from Learning English: My New Found Land		✓		
How I Learned English		✓		
I Hear America Singing		✓		
I, Too		✓		
Graffiti Is a Crime!				✓
Turn Vandals into Artists				✓
Phizzog				
In the Beauty Zone with Image Zone				✓
Immigrants in America: Wheatsville Sounds Off		✓		

Index